EVOLUTION AND THE COMMON LAW

This book offers a radical challenge to all existing accounts of the common law's development. Contrary to received jurisprudential wisdom, it maintains that there is no grand theory that will satisfactorily explain the dynamic interactions of change and stability in the common law's history. Offering fresh and original readings of Charles Darwin's and Hans-Georg Gadamer's works, the book shows that law is a rhetorical activity that can only be properly appreciated in its historical and political context; tradition and transformation are locked in a mutually reinforcing but thoroughly contingent embrace. In contrast to the dewy-eyed offerings of much contemporary work, it demonstrates that, like life, law is an organic process (i.e., events are the products of functional and localized causes) rather than a miraculous one (i.e., events are the result of some grand plan or intervention). In short, common law is a perpetual work-in-progress – evanescent, dynamic, messy, productive, tantalizing, and bottom up.

Allan C. Hutchinson is professor and associate dean at Osgoode Hall Law School at York University in Toronto. He has published on a variety of subjects, including civil litigation, constitutional law, torts, jurisprudence, the legal profession, and legal ethics. In 2004, he was elected a Fellow of the Royal Society of Canada and awarded Osgoode Hall's inaugural Excellence in Teaching Award.

Evolution and the Common Law

ALLAN C. HUTCHINSON
Osgoode Hall Law School
York University

CAMBRIDGE
UNIVERSITY PRESS

CAMBRIDGE UNIVERSITY PRESS
Cambridge, New York, Melbourne, Madrid, Cape Town,
Singapore, São Paulo, Delhi, Mexico City

Cambridge University Press
The Edinburgh Building, Cambridge CB2 8RU, UK

Published in the United States of America by Cambridge University Press, New York

www.cambridge.org
Information on this title: www.cambridge.org/9780521614917

First published 2005

A catalogue record for this publication is available from the British Library

Library of Congress Cataloguing in Publication Data
Hutchinson, Allan C., 1951–
Evolution and the common law / Allan C. Hutchinson.
p.   cm.
Includes bibliographical references and index.
ISBN 0-521-84968-3 (casebound) – ISBN 0-521-61491-0 (pbk.)
1. Common law – Methodology.   2. Common law – Study and teaching.
3. Evolution – Philosophy.   4. Darwin, Charles, 1809–1882.
5. Gadamer, Hans Georg, 1900–   I. Title
K588.H88   2005
340.5′7 – dc22   2004023976

ISBN 978-0-521-84968-5 Hardback
ISBN 978-0-521-61491- 7 Paperback

This Book is Dedicated to

my Pilot of the Purple Twilight

Our fate, for better or worse, is political. It is therefore not a happy fate, even if it has an heroic sound, but there is no escape from it, and the only possibility of enduring it is to force into our definition of politics every human activity and every subtlety of human activity. There are manifest dangers in doing this, but greater dangers in not doing it.

LIONEL TRILLING

Contents

Preface

This preface can be short and sweet. This project began, like most of my academic undertakings, more by chance than design. After writing a couple of papers, I realized that a certain pattern was taking shape and a unifying theme was emerging. In a manner of speaking, a book was beginning to evolve. This is the final product of that trial-and-error process; there have been the usual mutations, couplings, and mistakes along the way. Some of the work saw the light of day in earlier essays in *Legal Studies, Chicago-Kent Law Review, Current Legal Problems,* and *Irish Law Teachers.* Nevertheless, the contents of the book are almost entirely original in source and style, if nothing else.

As usual, many people have played important parts in helping me to complete this book. A variety of students have put in time as research assistants and have tried to keep me on the straight and narrow – Simon Lee, Nigel Marshman, Rishi Bandhu, Archana Mathew, Jim Smith, Abbas Sabur, Merel Veldius, Daved Muttart, and Luke Woodford. I have also benefited from a host of critics and colleagues, mostly friendly, who have shared their time and insights – Harry Arthurs, Derek Morgan, Richard Lucy, Tsachi Keren-Paz, Neil Duxbury, Celia Wells, Joanne Conaghan, Michael Freeman, Toni Williams, Francis Jay Mootz III, and John McCamus. In particular, I am especially grateful to Simon Archer, whose erudition, good humor, and sheer talent got this project off on the right foot; to Charles Lynch, who, catching the spirit of the project, saw me through to the end, and to Casia Czajkowski, who completed the index and tidied up the final manuscript. I was the grateful beneficiary of a generous grant from the Social Sciences and Research Council of Canada.

Most of all, this book is for Beverly. We met a couple of days after I made my first serious foray into the world of Darwinian scholarship through a lecture at University College, London in November 2000 – almost 141 years to the day on which *The Origin of Species* was first published. The intervening time has been a great ride so far, and an exciting road stretches ahead. She has shown me all that is best in love and life, giving me my joy and forgiving me my crotchetiness. This book is, I hope, the best blah-blah-blah that I can presently muster.

October, 2004

Table of Cases

Evolution and the Common Law:
An Introduction

The law must be stable, but it cannot stand still.[1]

ROSCOE POUND

B Y ITS NATURE, OF COURSE, GENIUS DEFIES EASY UNDERSTANDING OR
simple elucidation. This is particularly so with the common law; its reputed genius is much vaunted but little explained. However, the common
law's peculiar forte is seen to lie in its capacity to allow for change and innovation in an overall process that emphasizes the importance of continuity and
stability. Indeed, the legal community insists that a large part of adjudicative
activity involves reliance on the legal past, whether by way of substantive
results or argumentative consistency, to resolve present problems and to
influence future results. This way of proceeding is adopted and defended,
at least in part, as a means to keep judges in check and to preserve the legitimacy of an unelected bureaucracy in a system of governance that claims
to set great store on the importance and priority of democratic processes
and values. Nevertheless, although operating within an official culture of
institutional conservatism, all judges and jurists not only acknowledge that
the law does indeed respond and change to new circumstances and fresh
challenges, but they also celebrate and champion the law's capacity to do
so. If not for its rather continental flavor, the motto of the common law
might be a slight twist on the old adage that *plus c'est la même chose, plus ça
change*. This, of course, leads to an obvious dilemma that continues to haunt
and energize jurisprudential inquiry: How do we explain change in an institution whose controlling motif is still that judges largely apply law rather
than create it? Or, in a way that better captures the deeper tensions of the

---

[1] Roscoe Pound, *Interpretations of Legal History* 1 (1967).

1

common law, how do we balance the restraining push of tradition and the liberating pull of transformation?

It is my objective in this book to offer a convincing response to this central and persisting conundrum. However, in so doing, I maintain that my first task is to dispense with almost all the past and present efforts to provide a theory of common law adjudication and development. Contrary to received jurisprudential wisdom, there is no grand theory that will satisfactorily explain the dynamic interactions of change and stability in common law's history. Indeed, it is this continuing commitment to the belief that there is some grand theory that will both explain the workings of the common law and, by that achievement, also command our political allegiance that discredits the traditional jurisprudential project. Accordingly, in order to provide a satisfactory response to the perplexing conundrum of balancing continuity and variation, I find it necessary to reframe the underlying issues and rephrase the questions to be answered. Once this is done, I find it possible to offer a more convincing and fruitful account of the common law's workings. In order to achieve this, my critical focus is less about how to explain change in an institution that claims to ground itself on its stability. Instead, I concentrate more on how it might be possible to account for stability in a process that is marked by its dynamism and organic quality. Once it is grasped that transformative change is at the heart of the common law process, it will be for jurists to determine whether the common law can or should be used to advance particular political initiatives or interventions. In facilitating such an appreciation, jurisprudence might regain something of its practical usefulness and subversive potential.

The Common Law Tradition

Nineteenth-century positivists' savage assessment of the common law is as good a place as any to start. As unabashed enthusiasts for legislation and codification, they were no friends of the common law. Bentham and Austin's extended and uncompromising analysis led them to the firm conclusion that "as a system of rules, the common law is a thing merely imaginary" and that it is a "childish fiction employed by our judges that . . . common law is not made by them, but is a miraculous something made by nobody, existing . . . from eternity, and merely declared from time to time by the judges."[2] They were

---

[2] J. Bentham, *A Comment on the Commentaries* 125 (J. Everett ed. 1925) and J. Austin, *Lectures on Jurisprudence II*, 634 (5th ed. 1885). It should be clear that I use the term *common law* to denote those whole systems of law that derive from medieval English practice

particularly concerned with the fact that the rules of law were nowhere available in any accessible or agreed-on manner. For them, any effort to enumerate such rules or to pin down their content was doomed to failure. Moreover, any attempt to apply those putative rules in an objective manner to different fact-situations was a hopeless undertaking. Nevertheless, Bentham and Austin's critique shares more with the objects of their wrath than it pretends. At bottom, they lament the law's failure to live up to the quixotic standards that are claimed for it. In this way, they naively believed that law could be clear, but that its common law format was unable to attain this desirable ideal: It was necessary to effect wholesale statutory codification.[3] Accordingly, they were disappointed romantics, not the hard-headed realists that they often pretended to be and that they are still occasionally portrayed to be. Indeed, although a perverse few might want to take exception to their charge, almost every modern jurist would be prepared to concede the general force of Bentham's and Austin's point about the common law's elusiveness. However, their strategy is one of confession and avoidance – they acknowledge that the common law cannot be adequately represented as "a system of rules" whose precise structure and practical application is uncontroversial, but they insist that the common law does exist and can be operated in a sufficiently objective manner. Moreover, they take Bentham's point not as a criticism, but as a compliment: The common law is not a static body of norms but is a flexible and evolving entity; its nuanced and organic quality is the common law's strength, not its weakness.

Within the jurisprudential community, it has become almost trite to acknowledge that law is neither only about rules (i.e., it also comprises principles, policies, and values) nor, even if it is about rules, a system (i.e., it is far from being complete, organized, and certain). Indeed, while debate is intense and hostile over the nature of the common law as a source of institutional norms, most jurists do not think about the common law as only an entity, systematic or otherwise. There is considerable agreement that the common law tradition is as much a process as anything else. Some observers go so far as to insist that common law "is something we do, not something we

---

and can be contrasted to European civil law jurisdictions. In this way, it encompasses those rules and principles that are statutory, equitable, or constitutional in origin and operation.

3 See J. Bentham, Supplement to Papers Relative to Codification and Public Instruction, 29 *Edinburgh Rev.* 105–08 (1817) and M. Romilly, Review of Bentham's Papers Relative to Codification, 29 *Edinburgh Rev.* 217 at 223 (1817) ("the judges, though called only expounders of law, are in reality legislators"). Indeed, some reformers expected codification to make the law clear to laymen as well as to lawyers. Bentham touted codification as a means of making "every man his own lawyer." Bentham, id. at 115.

have as a consequence of something we do."[4] Although this assessment will be too strong for many commentators, it does capture the crucial idea that common law adjudication is a dynamic and engaged activity in which how judges deal with rules is considered as vital to the political legitimacy of the legal performance as the resulting content of the rules and actual decisions made. Consequently, the common law is largely characterized by the craft-skills that judges bring to their task. This is not to reduce common lawyering or judging to a purely technical proficiency, because the best craftspeople are those that bring vision and imagination as well as technique and rigor to the fulfillment of their discipline. Accordingly, when it is viewed in this way, the activity of being a common lawyer involves not only the deft utilization of particular analytic tools but also an accompanying perspective or frame of mind that offers the intellectual component of the practical activity and that pervades all that lawyers do.[5]

Understood as much as an intellectual mind-set to lawmaking as a tech-nical practice, the common law approach tends to transform a natural ten-dency to utilize past performance as a guide to future conduct into an institutional imperative. It is in this sense that the common law is a tradi-tion. However, if law was only thought of as a repository of rules, principles, and methods that can be accessed by its practiced adepts, law would be no different than many other traditional practices. What distinguishes the common law is that it is not only a tradition but also a traditional practice that embraces the idea of traditionality – the common law accepts that its past has a present authority and significance for its participants in resolving present disputes and negotiating future meaning. By way of the doctrine of *stare decisis et non quieta movere* (let the decision stand and do not disturb settled things), the common law method insists that past decisions are not only to be considered by future decision makers but also to be followed as being binding. Judges accept the responsibility to curb their own norma-tive instincts and to respect the limits of extant decisions: "The principle of stare decisis does not apply only to good decisions: if it did, it would have neither value nor meaning."[6] This means that lawyers and judges assume an

---

[4] P. Bobbitt, *Constitutional Interpretation* 24 (1991). For other accounts of the common law as an exaltation of method over substance, see V. Curran, Romantic Common Law, Enlightened Civil Law: Legal Uniformity and the Homogenization of the European Union, 7 *Colum. J. Eur. L.* 63 (2001) and A. Scalia, *A Matter of Interpretation: Federal Courts and the Law* 25 (1997).

[5] See D. Sugarman, Legal Theory, the Common Law Mind and The Making of the Textbook Tradition, in *Legal Theory and Common Law* 26–61 (1986).

[6] *Jones v. DPP*, [1962] AC 635 at 711 per Lord Devlin. See also J. Newman, Between Legal Realism and Neutral Principles: The Legitimacy of Institutional Values, 72 *Cal. L. Rev.* 200 at 204 (1984) ("The ordinary business of judges is to apply the law as they understand it

institutional obligation to justify their present actions and arguments by reference to those results and arguments that are recorded in the official documents and materials of the law. In this way, judging is a very traditional practice that gives central importance to the normative force of traditionality; "the past of law . . . is an authoritative significant part of its presence."[7]

This commitment to the so-called traditionality of the common law tradition is often premised on the unstated notion that there is something normatively compelling or worthy about what has come before; the past is not followed simply because it precedes but because it is superior to present understandings. Having withstood the test of time, tradition binds not simply because it has not been replaced or altered; it binds because it has its own normative force. For common lawyers, therefore, the legal past is not simply a store of information and materials but an obligatory source of value and guidance. In this strong version of traditionality, past decisions possess a moral prestige and accumulated wisdom that are entitled to be given normative preference over present understandings and uninhibited ratiocination; the past is what makes society into what it is today, and the decision to respect it is what gives meaning to the lives of future generations. Thus, the common law is traditional in the conservative Burkean sense that "we are bound, within whatever limits, to honour the past for its own sake, to respect it just because it is the past we happen to have."[8] When this quality is added to the fact that judges have independent institutional justifications for steering clear of open-ended and creative decision making, the claims of tradition and traditionality are very strong in defining the appropriate approach and limits to common law adjudication. By viewing themselves as custodians rather than creators of tradition, judges can fulfill their controversial roles with seriousness and safety. However, while this strong defense of the common law's strictly backward-looking nature receives considerable

---

to reach results with which they do not necessarily agree") and generally R. L. Brown, Tradition and Insight, 103 *Yale L. J.* 177 (1993).

[7] M. Krygier, Law As Tradition, 5 *Law & Phil.* 237 at 245 (1986). See also *The Invention of Tradition* (E. Hobsbawm and T. Ranger eds. 1983) and R. Williams, *Keywords* 320 (1981). For a good example of the difference between tradition and traditionality, see *Rutan v. Republican Party of Illinois*, 497 US 62 (1990). Whereas Scalia J looks to the actual practices alone, Stevens J seeks to incorporate a critical normative element to those practices.

[8] A. Kronman, Precedent and Tradition, 99 *Yale L. J.* 1029 at 1037 (1990). Burke talks about "the great primeval contract of eternal society" in which "the partnership . . . between those who are living and those who are dead, and those who are to be born." E. Burke, *Reflections on the Revolution in France* 85 (J. Pocock ed. 1987) and, also, F. Hayek, *Law, Legislation and Liberty: The Political Order of Free People* 153–76 (1979). For more jurisprudential work in this vein, see also C. Fried, The Artificial Reason of the Law; or What Lawyers Know, 60 *Texas L. Rev.* 35 (1981); A. Watson, *The Evolution of Law* (1985); and C. Fried, Constitutional Doctrine, 107 *Harv. L. Rev.* 1140 (1994).

lip service in the law reports and academic literature, it cannot claim to provide a viable descriptive account of the common law. Indeed, it offers an entirely implausible explanation of the common law's actual development – the law does change and often in ways that mark a sharp discontinuity with the past.

What is most important is that, although it is framed in the language of tradition, such a strong traditionalist view misunderstands the whole idea and purpose of traditionality. When treated as a tradition of traditionality, the common law must be distinguished from both history and custom. Whereas tradition has a normative and prescriptive dimension, history and custom tend to be only descriptive (or, more accurately, aspire to be as detached and impartial as is possible under the contentious circumstances under which all history has to be written). Because tradition has a critical and judgmental character, it is less than the sum total of accumulated decisions and more than the extant practices of the legal system. As well as being an attitude to those precedents and how to utilize them in the present process of decision making, the common law tradition comprises a whole repertoire of techniques for the selection, maintenance, transmission, and change of its substantive holdings: It involves an evaluative assessment of what does and does not work and what should and should not persist. As Lord Diplock put it, "the common law subsumes a power in judges to adapt its rules to the changing needs of contemporary society – to discard those which have outlived their usefulness, to develop new rules to meet new situations."[9] However, lawyers need not apologize to historians for their poor historical method; they are not trying to be historians, but lawyers. Whereas the historian is interested in trying to understanding the past on its own terms, the lawyer is interested in utilizing the past for present purposes. Accordingly, the common law is a tradition that treats its own traditions seriously. By demanding a normative commitment to select and transmit aspects of past practice, the common law decides among and between the different (and often competing) substantive traditions to which the mass of decisions have given rise.

When understood in this way, the common law is more realistically grasped as a tradition-respecting process rather than a past-revering obsession; it is critical tradition that is not averse to change for its own sake, but only change that ignores the past as a matter of course. Moreover, such a posture allows

---

[9] *Cassell & Co. Ltd. v. Bloom*, [1972] AC 1027 at 1127 per Diplock LJ. See also *De Lasala v. De Lasala*, [1980] AC 546 at 557. For a jurisprudential rendition of this, see F. Schauer, Precedent, 39 *Stan L. Rev.* 571 (1987) and generally E. Shils, *Tradition* (1981).

for a more honest and suggestive response to the most pressing challenge that confronts the courts. In a rapidly changing world, the judges must be able to operate the system of precedent so that the need for stability is balanced off against the demand for change: They must not allow formal certainty to eclipse substantive justice. The success of such an undertaking cannot be judged in technical terms alone; it calls upon the substantive discourses of ideals and ideology. In an important sense, the common law is to be found in the unfolding struggle between the openings of decisional freedom and the closings of precedential constraint. Consequently, in order to ensure that the common law does not grind to a halt and begin to slide into irrelevance and injustice under the weight of its own backward-looking mind-set, the courts have developed a whole series of techniques that allow them to avoid or loosen the binding force of precedent. In a manner of speaking, institutional necessity has been the parent of judicial invention. There are several important and acknowledged devices that courts use to circumvent inconvenient or undesirable precedents – the court that rendered the earlier decision was not a superior court; the precedent was given *per incuriam*; the precedent has been subsequently overruled or doubted in other cases; the precedent was based on a faulty interpretation of earlier cases; the scope of the precedent is unclear; the precedent can be distinguished; social conditions have changed; and the precedent has been criticized by academic commentators (although this may be just wishful thinking by academics).[10]

Nevertheless, the availability of such tradition-cutting techniques threatens to undermine the whole legitimacy of the common law tradition. So powerful are these tools that they are capable of destroying the very tradition that they are designed to protect and enhance. If used without any respect for the legal tradition within which they are supposed to function, they will jeopardize the continued existence of the common law as a tradition of traditionality. Not only will cases and precedents be merely informational rather than influential, but judges will be left to do whatever they think is best in cases before them. Accordingly, the courts and commentators have cultivated an attitude and approach to their usage that is decidedly traditional in orientation and operation. While acknowledging the occurrence

---

[10] See, for example, R. Cross and J. W. Harris, *Precedent in English Law* (4th ed. 1991); J. Stone, *Legal System and Lawyer's Reasoning* (1964); R. W. M. Dias, *Jurisprudence* (5th ed. 1985); M. D. A. Freeman, *Lloyd's Introduction to Jurisprudence* (7th ed. 2001); W. Huhn, *The Five Types of Legal Argument* (2002); S. J. Burton, *An Introduction to Law and Legal Reasoning* (1995); R. Case, *Understanding Judicial Reasoning* (1997); M. Golding, *Legal Reasoning* (1984); A. Halpin, *Reasoning with Law* (2001); and L. H. Carter and T. F. Burke, *Reason in Law* (6th ed. 2002).

and need for change in the substantive law, the pervasive spirit of the common law is that such change will be occasional and exceptional. The law reports and secondary literature are full of admonitions and sentiments to the effect that "the system is based on precedent, and centres on individual decisions and building up principles by a gradual accretion from case to case."[11] Indeed, in the great bulk of situations and for the greatest part of the time, judges do claim to follow past decisions with little or no reflection on the common law's deeper rationale(s) or its broader structure of fundamental rules; common law decision making is very much about the apparent routine application of rules and precedents and the belief that this will result in substantive justice in the individual case.

While this is credible as far as it goes, the problem is that it does not go anywhere near far enough; any claims to credibility are fatally undermined. Most deferences to tradition are more properly characterized as veiled approvals of the substantive content of a tradition because it chimes with the present political commitments of the judge. It is entirely unclear what it means to respect the past for its own sake. There is no compelling reason why a decision to follow the past is any less political than a decision to ignore the past. Both strategies depend on a much thicker theory about the worth of the past as a substantively attractive vision of present and future arrangements for social living than the traditionalists offer. Moreover, the past is not the monolithic entity that defenders of a tradition-based approach to common law adjudication insist or pretend it is. It is not realistic to imagine accepting or rejecting the past holus-bolus. Like the social past on which it draws, the law's traditions are rich, multiple, and competing; they are notoriously difficult to pin down with any specificity or precision. Like anything and everything else, traditions do not speak for themselves but must be spoken for. It is hard to see how they control or require certain decisions when they themselves must first be interpreted. As has been constantly reiterated, "regard to what history teaches are the traditions from which [the United States] developed as well as the traditions from which it broke."[12] This is true not only for the American constitutional tradition but also for any society or jurisdiction that has an advanced legal system. The only real choice for tradition-committed judges is not whether to follow the past but to determine which aspects of that past they intend to emphasize or treat as

---

[11] J. Beatson, Has the Common Law a Future?, 56 *Camb. L. J.* 291 at 295 (1997). See also Lord Goff, The Search For Principle, 50 *Proc. Brit. Acad.* 169 (1983).

[12] *Poe v. Ullman*, 367 US 497 at 542 per Harlan J (1961). For a punishing application of this insight, see J. Balkin, Tradition, Betrayal, and the Politics of Deconstruction, 11 *Cardozo L. Rev.* 1612 (1990).

dominant in their interpretations. In other words, there is no way that judges can simply follow the past in a mechanical or legal way without taking some critical and political stance about the particular past they intend to follow, its present meaning, and its implications for future activity. Therefore, the stark resort to tradition is an avowedly political stance rather than a hedge against politics. Of course, contemporary jurists have sought to resist this result with all the theoretical might and means at their disposal.

An Evolutionary Method

It is not so much that contemporary accounts of common law adjudication have abandoned their commitment to the doctrine of precedent, but more that they have relaxed and reworked the nature of law's backward-looking stance. Jurists have recognized that the traditional virtues of precedential authority (i.e., it produces certainty, allows reliance, curbs arbitrariness, effects equality, and encourages efficiency) are not to be underestimated. They understand that any explanation of what common law judges do or should do in a democratic system of governance must involve a strong attachment to such formal qualities. Nevertheless, it is largely recognized that, while the legal past must and should play a central role in the law's present and future development, resort to the legal past need not be restricted to particular decisions made or a mechanical application of them. Incorporating but not restricting itself to such decisions, the modern perception of common law development emphasizes that the most appropriate use of the legal past is less about a formal and technical enforcement of precedential authorities and more a dynamic and expansive meditation on their underlying rationales and structure. It is accepted that the past matters, but there is considerable disagreement over why and how it matters. Taking as their slogan Holmes' statement that "it is revolting to have no better reason for a rule of law than that it was laid down in the time of Henry IV,"[13] modern jurists look as much to the substantive values that animate and integrate the law as to the formal attributes of stare decisis.

Accordingly, common law adjudication is viewed as an exercise in principled justification in which the body of previous legal decisions is treated as an authoritative resource of available arguments, analogies, and axioms. Judges are considered to judge best when they distill the principled spirit of

---

[13] O. W. Holmes, Jr., *The Common Law* 5 (1881). For discussions about the cherished virtues of precedential constraint, see R. Wasserstrom, *The Judicial Decision: Toward a Theory of Legal Justification* 56–83 (1961); P. Atiyah and R. Summers, *Form and Substance in Anglo-American Law* 116–20 (1987); and F. Schauer, supra, note 9 at 595–602.

the past and rely on it to develop the law in response to future demands. As Lord Scarman put it, "whatever the court decides to do, it starts from a baseline of existing principle and seeks a solution consistent with or analogous to a principle or principles already recognized."[14] From a more theoretical standpoint, the prevailing idea is that it is the task of legal theory and also the responsibility of adjudication to understand the accumulation of legal decisions as fragments of an intelligible, if latent or implicit, plan of social life and to extend law in accordance with the plan so that it becomes less fragmentary and more intelligible. In a dangerously close to bootstrapping argument, the claim is that, although there are recalcitrant areas, the common law is best understood as being the practical expression of connected and abstract principles. The task of the judge is to elucidate those deeper ideals and to extend that structure so as to better render the common law more practical and coherent. Although there are many advantages to this more sophisticated way of proceeding over an old-style practice of stare decisis, the pressing challenge remains the same: How is it possible to balance stability and continuity against flexibility and change such that it results in a state of affairs that is neither only a case of stunted development nor a case of 'anything goes'?

The traditional set of answers to this balancing conundrum is that, by and large,the law evolves according to its own methodology. Indeed, the evolutionary methodology of the common law is defended and celebrated by almost all traditional jurists and lawyers. Eschewing notions of revolution or stasis, most judges and jurists insist that law evolves incrementally rather than leaps convulsively or stagnates idly. Glossing over its apparent messy, episodic, and haphazard workings, they would choose to treat and defend the common law as a polished, integrated, and teleological process that gives rise to a resourceful, flexible, and just product. Although there is much disagreement among traditional scholars about the precise dynamics and thrusts of this process, there remains the unifying commitment to demonstrating that not only can the common law balance the competing demands of stability and change, but that it can do so in a legitimate way that respects the important distinction between law and politics. In doing this, jurists strive to move beyond a discredited formalism to a more sophisticated account of adjudication as a creative and disciplined practice without turning it into an open-ended ideological exercise. Accordingly, although the

---

[14] *McLoughlin v. O'Brian*, [1983] AC 410 at 430 per Lord Scarman. In Holmes' famous phrase, the common law develops "from molar to molecular motions." *Southern Pacific Co. v. Jensen*, 244 US 205 at 221 (1917).

extent of their confidence waxes and wanes, traditional jurists and judges maintain that it is possible to provide compelling answers to the questions about how to balance tradition and transformation, about how to justify creativity in a supposedly stable system, and about how to distinguish the common law from its informing political and social context.

This kind of account of the workings and development of the common law underpins most legal literature and is endemic in jurisprudential writings. For example, in an otherwise unexceptional judgment on personal injury damages, the Chief Justice of Canada gave expression to the common understanding about how the law evolves. So typical is her account and so uncontroversial is it in most legal circles that it deserves stating in full:

> Generally speaking, the judiciary is bound to apply the rules of law found in the legislation and the precedents. Over time, the law in any given area may change; but the process of change is a slow and incremental one based on the mechanism of extending an existing principle to new circumstances. While it may be that some judges are more activist than others, the courts have generally declined to introduce major and far-reaching changes in the rules hitherto accepted as governing the situation before them.
>
> There are sound reasons supporting this judicial reluctance to dramatically recast established rules of law. The court may not be in the best position to assess the deficiencies of the existing law, much less problems which may be associated with the changes it might make. The court has before it a single case; major changes in the law should be predicated on a wider view of how the rule will operate in the broad generality of cases. Moreover, the court may not be in a position to appreciate fully the economic and policy issues underlying the choice it is asked to make. Major changes to the law often involve devising subsidiary rules and procedures relevant to their implementation, a task which is better accomplished through consultation between courts and practitioners than by judicial decree. Finally, and perhaps most importantly, there is the long-established principle that in a constitutional democracy it is the legislature, as the elected branch of government, which should assume the major responsibility for law reform.
>
> Considerations such as these suggest that major revisions of the law are best left to the legislature. Where the matter is one of a small extension of existing rules to meet the exigencies of a new case and the consequences of the change are readily assessable, judges can and should vary existing principles. But where the revision is major and its ramifications complex, the courts must proceed with great caution.[15]

---

[15] *Watkins v. Olafson*, [1989] 2 SCR 750 at 760–61 per McLachlin J (as she then was).

In its relatively short span, Justice McLachlin's judgment encapsulates and highlights all the motifs of the traditional understanding of how the common law does and should work both as a general process and as a particular undertaking for individual judges – slow growth, principled extension, institutional deference, professional competence, political neutrality, cautious revision, and, what is most important, progressive development. It is entirely clear that, while she is attuned to the competing demands of tradition and transformation, she also is convinced that some satisfactory, principled and long-term trade-off is possible and recommended. In this view, the common law is a firmly grounded, finely balanced, ethically defensible, institutionally justified, politically legitimate, and self-improving enterprise.

In championing an evolutionary methodology, common lawyers trade off the established theories of biological development and benefit from its scientific pedigree. It has been a constant worry of many common law judges and jurists that their discipline is treated as unscientific and, therefore, is considered second-rate or substandard by other scholars.[16] By drawing striking parallels between nature's operation and common law development, legal theorists have been able to reduce that insecurity. In one fell swoop, they can both explain the common law's development and legitimate it as an objective and natural process. This is a powerfully seductive possibility for judges and jurists. Of course, the idea of evolution is almost as old as society itself. It can be traced to the Greeks, of whom Aristotle offered the most compelling ideas about the continuity and developing nature of all living things. In the many centuries before Darwin's mid-nineteenth-century seminal contribution, so-called evolution appeared in many different incarnations. However, the common thread to most offerings was that there was some notion of progress at work in which the world was not simply on the move but heading toward some sophisticated end point, be it theological in plan and purpose or not. The etymological roots of evolution are in the Latin word *evolvere*, which means "to unroll" or "to unfold"; it was generally used as a synonym for "predictable progress." Perhaps because of its own insecurities, jurisprudence jumped on the Darwinian bandwagon of the nineteenth century more quickly and more zealously than most other disciplines. Indeed, from the pioneering work of Maine, Holmes, Wigmore,

---

[16] It remains a constant jurisprudential refrain that the study of law can and should become more "scientific" if it is to be accorded sufficient scholarly respect. See, for example, T. S. Ulen, A Nobel Prize in Legal Science: Theory, Empirical Work, and The Scientific Method in the Study of Law, [2002] *U. Ill. L. Rev.* 875 at 877 ("the move toward a more scientific study of law will have greater benefits than costs"). As this book asserts, this is a vain and unnecessary aspiration.

and Corbin through to more recent technical efforts, the evolutionary motif has always loomed large over jurisprudential efforts to explicate the nature of the common law. While the resort to an evolutionary methodology is well-nigh universal, it is deployed across the full range of uses from metaphorical through analogical and homological to even literal.[17] Contributing to a general tendency in the humanities at large, jurists have utilized evolution not only to explain the past of the common law and its present dynamic but also to predict and propose its future direction. Consequently, whether used in a casual or causal way, evolution is a ubiquitous and persisting concept in jurisprudential discourse about the common law.

The depth and extent of this continuing commitment to such an evolutionary method is evidenced by two pertinent illustrations: One is from the ostensibly practical English world of judging and the other is from the more ethereal reaches of Anglo-American jurisprudence. For example, in a lecture delivered a few years ago, the Master of the Rolls (England's highest-ranking civil judge) offered an audacious testimony to the power of the traditional legal credo of the common law's evolutionary development. In an effort to explain why the introduction of the European Convention of Human Rights into English law would not be as revolutionary as some feared or expected, Lord Woolf observed that "although we were not previously aware of it, all along these principles [of the European Convention] have been part of the common law! They were, so to speak, not foreign intruders but English princesses sleeping peacefully, waiting for the kiss of a judicial prince to bring them in turn to life when deciding a case."[18] With considerable ingenuity and without any apparent irony, he seemed to be suggesting not only that the common law was so compendious and so prescient that it contained the resources for revolution within its own evolutionary existence, but also that it could effect such a revolution on its own. In a manner of speaking, progress was already hardwired into the common law's own methodology. While most lawyers might be a tad embarrassed by such boldness, they would largely subscribe to Lord Woolf's implicit vision of the common law – that it was a dynamic and indigenous process whose natural progress, if left to its own restrained devices and regardless of judicial guardians' shortcomings, could be relied on to meet future challenges in a thoroughly satisfactory

---

[17] For a brief history of this historical division and other suggestions, see H. Hovenkamp, Evolutionary Models in Jurisprudence, 64 *Texas L. Rev.* 645 (1984); E. D. Elliot, The Evolutionary Tradition in Jurisprudence, 85 *Columbia L. Rev.* 38 (1985); and A. Watson, *The Evolution of Law* (1985).

[18] Lord Woolf, Bringing Home the European Convention on Human Rights, [1997] *Denning L. J.* 1.

and eminently just way. Although it may appear the stuff of fairy tale, the common law has a life of its own in that there is benign Godlike force or figure at work in its unfolding and growth.

The most exuberant jurisprudential example of this sanguine approach to law and life is Ronald Dworkin's work. In a constant stream of sophisticated writings, he combines a daring proposal to read law's doctrinal history "in the best light" with a sustaining belief that the law is "working itself pure." Although he insists that judges must treat the legal past "as important for its own sake" because "law as integrity supposes that people are entitled to a coherent and principled extension of past political decisions," Dworkin's Herculean judicial alter ego is lauded much less for his ability to wreak changes in the law's order than for his godly capacity to capture the whole tradition of the law in its fullest and most illuminating sense. As the very model of the exemplary common law judge, his political obligation is to apply the law dutifully, deferentially, and reliably to present cases. In short, Dworkin advances an understanding of adjudication as a political practice that works the space between law's institutional past and its future possibilities. For Dworkin, therefore, any interpretation of the legal materials must be able to demonstrate some plausible connection to society's legal history and, in that important sense, be continuous with that past: "law's attitude . . . aims, in the interpretive spirit, to lay principle over practice to show the best route to a better future, keeping the right faith with the past."[19] This prescription is a potent cocktail that contains a volatile brew of ethical optimism, evolutionary inevitability, and methodological discipline. Not surprisingly, this has intoxicated many common lawyers and judges. Drinking deep at this particular intellectual well, they are reassured that what they are doing is both politically attractive, ethically defensible, and impersonally driven. However, Dworkin's Panglossian approach is merely the most profligate illustration of a wider jurisprudential trend. Jurists of much more modest and less grandiose ambitions rely on such evolutionary and methodological tropes to underwrite the legitimacy of their engagement in common law adjudication and scholarship.

One obvious problem with these neoformalist attempts to balance tradition and transformation in a principled and disciplining structure is that jurists (and judges) might be imposing their own personal normative commitments on the law in the name of professional analysis. Indeed, it is telling that the result of applying such a disciplinary method is almost always exactly

---

[19] R. Dworkin, *Law's Empire* 132, 134, 219, 239, and 413 (1986).

the same as what the judge or jurist would have done if left to their own legally untutored political devices. Even when there is some distance maintained between what the law is and what a judge might like it to become, it is so narrow that its practical relevance is negligible.[20] However, for my purposes, there is another and even more pertinent problem. In adopting such an explanation of the common law's facility for adaptation, what begins its jurisprudential life as a reassuring promise of justifying incremental development runs the risk of quickly and easily turning into a subversive threat of permitting wholesale transformation. In their fragile search for developmental equilibrium between stability and change, defenders of the common law tradition are obliged to tread a precariously thin line between a legitimate practice of unfolding reform and an illegitimate exercise in episodic revolution. Therefore, in accordance with its self-imposed task, mainstream jurisprudence must be able to persuade us that incremental adaptation is not simply a cover for radical realignment. As importantly, it must also show that the balance between stability and change is neither ad hoc nor unpredictable; the balance must itself be explained by something other than ideological or personal preference. As I will demonstrate, this is an impossibly tall order for any legal theory.

Work-in-Progress

It is my central ambition in this book to reorient the study and practice of the common law. In particular, I want to resist the traditional characterization of the common law as a mythical or mystical enterprise that largely has an existence of its own, that is propelled forward in large part by dint of its own intellectual and moral integrity, and that is always fashioning itself into a better and more just system. In this way, the common law's development cannot be presented as an evolutionary stairway to juridical heaven in which the acolytes' task is to adopt an appropriate frame of mind, locate the first step, and then follow it to wherever it leads. Instead, the common law is better understood as a rutted and rough road that has innumerable twists and turns and no particular destination; any particular route taken has been chosen from among the countless and constantly proliferating possibilities for change. Efforts to provide maps or timetables for future development are simply wishful thinking and only have later impact by that fact alone.

---

[20] See, for instance, R. Dworkin, *Freedom's Law* 35–38 (1996). Of course, the fact that there is often no difference between what the law is and what a judge might like it to become ought not to surprise as, over an extended period, there is likely to be a reducing gap between the two. See D. Kennedy, *Adjudication Fin de Siècle* (1997).

This, of course, is no bad thing and ought to offer some hope to the radical or progressive critic. Moreover, any comfort that traditionalists draw from the idea of evolution is cold and, therefore, misleading: There is no idea of progress that is inevitable or ingrained in the common law. Such a belief only leads to an arrogant attitude that masks a shallow and ultimately oppressive account of human development that subjugates ingenuity and compassion to conformity and acquiescence. Grand theories do not work, whether they are generated from a moral–religious perspective or from a biological–scientific standpoint; there is no grand design or *deus ex machina* that helps in predicting what will or must happen next.

In contrast to traditional accounts, I want to provide an account of the common law that is thoroughly profane and that cleanses the "strong flavour of secularised theology," "noble alchemy," and "occult science"[21] that still lingers in traditional renderings of the common law's performance and development. While I still want to emphasize the dynamic quality of the common law as a historical process, the claim that the common law is or ever was a rational body of organized rules enforced by the doctrinal dictates of stare decisis is entirely belied by the historical data, the sociological record, and philosophical analysis. Resorting to precedent and its binding procedural force is often a convenient tool to preserve the status quo for other more substantive reasons. When it is viewed from a more robustly pragmatic stance, a better understanding of the common law's operation is found in an account that emphasizes how its development is contingent upon social and historical circumstances and that insists that any understanding of law must be deeply political if it is to go beyond a static and, therefore, useless account. However, while it is important to isolate and explain the dynamic that is at the heart of law, it is equally crucial not to use that dynamic as a prescriptive device to ground any proposals as to what to do next. As an antidote to this "naturalistic" malaise, I will offer a critique of the present situation as well as suggest an alternative way of proceeding. In effect, I want to recommend a shift from philosophy to politics so that legal academics will be less obsessed with abstraction and formalism and more concerned with relevance and practicality. Or, more jurisprudentially, I want to engender a mode of legal theory and scholarship that takes its lights less from analytical philosophy and more from democratic politics. In contrast to the hubristic and occasionally mystical aspirations of mainstream scholars, I will present

---

[21] O. Kahn-Freund, <u>Reflections of Legal Education</u> in *Selected Writings* 364 (1978); W. Blackstone, *Commentaries on the Laws of England IV*, 371 (1768); and *The Collected Papers of Frederic William Maitland* vol. II, 483 (H. A. L. Fisher ed. 1911).

a more humble depiction of the worth and efficacy of the jurisprudential and scholarly project in which usefulness is given pride of place. As Richard Rorty recommends, there must be "a moratorium on theory," and those committed to reform, whether on the political right or left, "should try to kick the philosophy habit" and "not let the abstractly decided best be the enemy of the better."[22]

In order to achieve this critical ambition, I will draw on the work of two giants of the human sciences – Charles Darwin and Hans-Georg Gadamer. Although they are engaged in very different endeavors and might make for an odd couple, their writings share a very similar energizing dynamic and overall thrust. Both are committed to rejecting absolutist, essentialist, and foundational accounts that attempt to understand the path of human progress by establishing some fixed form, core function, or overarching goal to which social life is supposed to conform. Instead, they embrace a thoroughly historicized and contingent view of life and human activity in which form, function, and goal are never given but shift and vary with context and over time. While Darwin and Gadamer are both scrupulously rigorous in their work, they challenge the whole idea of what counts as scientific method in both its biological and hermeneutical guises. In a rather ironic fashion, both challenge traditional science in the name of a more transformative understanding of science that is less detached from its historical milieu and more informed by its enabling environment. Neither Darwin nor Gadamer believes that scientific method in its biological or hermeneutical manifestation can provide much help in determining what should be done next. Both Darwin and Gadamer offer no panaceas but simply purgatives against all dogmas about the inevitability of progress. They combine in the insistence that a historical account is the only viable account of human endeavor and that such an accounts holds no moral or political import in and of itself. Indeed, Darwin and Gadamer's ideas make it possible to admit that "humans have to dream up the point of human life and cannot appeal to a non-human standard to determine whether they have chosen wisely . . . [and that] the meaning of one human life may have little to do with the meaning of any other human life, while being none the worse for that."[23]

In this book, therefore, I want to illuminate the study of the common law and jurisprudence by reference to Darwin's evolutionary insights and Gadamer's hermeneutical critique. I explore what it means to treat law seriously as a living rhetorical tradition or work-in-progress. Of course, the

---

[22] R. Rorty, *Achieving Our Country: Leftist Thought in Twentieth Century America* 91 and 105 (1998).
[23] R. Rorty, *Philosophy and Social Hope* 266 (1999).

idea of understanding law as a social practice or tradition is not new and the appreciation that law is always changing is hardly novel. Nevertheless, the received wisdom remains that, while law and adjudication are squarely situated in the historical flow of social life, they march largely to the uniform beat of a different drummer than society's competing and cacophonous percussionists; that drummer and that beat are contended to be distinctly legal rather than insistently ideological. In contrast, my critical response is that, because law is a social practice and society is in a constant state of agitated movement, law is always a work-in-progress that not only is never complete or finished but also is always situated inside and among, not outside and beyond, the ideological forces at work in society. Insofar as adjudication is a bounded tradition, it is one in which those bounds are part and parcel of the political contestation from which they are intended to insulate the law. There are no solid and secure footings for law and legal theory that are not themselves inside the very political and situated debate that they are intended to ground and underwrite; there is no escape from the messy and contingent facts of social living. Insofar as it is possible to think critically about law, it cannot be done by escaping the concrete and ideological circumstances of law and legal theorizing: Law is a political enterprise, and theory is a specialized form of politics.

In order to address these difficult and hotly debated issues, I intend to come at them through a particular reading of Darwin's and Gadamer's ideas. I say *through* rather than *with* because I want to suggest the indeterminacy and dynamism of interpretive work, whether in legal practice in particular or scholarly endeavor in general. As I will explain, my approach to the conundrum of explaining change and continuity in the law is influenced by my reading of Darwin and Gadamer. It is neither determined by my reading of Darwin and Gadamer nor does it claim to be the definitive reading of Darwin and Gadamer because, like the common law itself, the genius of Darwin and Gadamer defies easy understanding or simple elucidation. Throughout, I want to insist that Darwin and Gadamer's ideas as well as the tradition of common law adjudication are best understood as works in progress whose meaning is never fixed or determined but is constantly and continually open to appropriation and transformation. This is not to say that 'anything goes' or that the perceived postmodern nightmare has become a waking reality. It is intended as an acknowledgment that there is no master narrative that can explain or do away with the need or responsibility for choice: What counts as meaning is always unstable and cannot be a foundation for anything, let alone the legitimacy of common law adjudication as a mode of objective and nonideological decision making. Moreover, my own views on what is and is not a cogent or useful account of law and adjudication is also a work-in-progress, in that this book acts as a series of glosses and shifts on the basic themes that my work has addressed over the years; it develops and elaborates on earlier ideas as it interrogates and alters them.[24]

Ironically, in writing about both Darwin and Gadamer, I will take a line that not only diverges from most conventional accounts of what these two scholars' writings are said to be about but that also challenges both Darwin and Gadamer's own understandings of what it is that their writings are about. I will push through on the revolution that both Darwin and Gadamer began but did not follow through and that most adherents have been unwilling or unable to embrace. Indeed, a considerable part of my task is to discredit and dismiss much of the literature and work that has been done in the name of these two thinkers. This is especially so in law. There is a rich and extensive literature that seeks to put Darwin and Gadamer to work in the service of a traditional jurisprudential project – to demonstrate that, while the common law is a historical process and practice, it can be and should be understood as something separate from the political forces that permeate such a process. In short, Darwin and Gadamer have been enlisted in the continuing struggle to preserve the legitimacy of common law adjudication as a bounded, methodical, and self-improving performance. In contrast, I trace the more general repercussions of my insistence that the historicization of law and adjudication must also entail its politicization. Throughout the book, I rely on the notion of "work-in-progress" as a productive optic through which to view and appreciate the dynamic and unfinishable quality of law, interpretation, and criticism. I want to recommend an understanding of the common law adjudicative tradition that will abandon once and for all the misguided effort to treat it as if it were a significantly bounded and largely neutral tradition of argument that is something other than one more site for the encounter, albeit stylized and staged, between contesting ideological forces.

The common law is an organic and messy practice that is always moving and, like the society in which it moves and is moved, is incapable of being subsumed under any one theory that can transcend or finesse ideological contestation. Darwin and Gadamer's insights combine to suggest a useful way to think about this thoroughly historical and inescapably political process. Indeed, Darwin and Gadamer's great contribution was to show that

---

[24] The most recent and most sustained account of my ideas on law, politics, and adjudication can be found in A. Hutchinson, *It's All in the Game: A Nonfoundationalist Account of Law and Adjudication* (2000). Consistent with the claims made here, this is simply one more phase in a continuing life's work-in-progress.

the order and truth of nature was not to be found in the mind of God or in some quasi-divine method. Instead, it is revealed in the dirty details of a historical process that does not lend itself to a triumphal or Whiggish rendition that contrives "to emphasise certain principles of progress in the past and to produce a story which is the ratification, if not glorification of the present."[25] Explanations of origin and development are far removed from inquiries into worth and progress. In the same way that Darwin and Gadamer made the study of biology and hermeneutics into a historical discipline, so it is important to make jurisprudence into a truly historical practice. However, in so doing, it is also vital to ensure that such a historical study is itself thoroughly politicized. Once such a historical and political analysis is performed, this need not be the deathblow for common law and adjudication that many believe it to be. It is possible for us to understand law and adjudication as thoroughly political without recommending its complete abandonment. Indeed, when looked at in this way, the common law *might* lend itself well to local, episodic, contextualized, focused, and work-in-progress kinds of political interventions. I emphasize *might* because it is folly, as the overall tenor of this book insists, to propose that the common law has any necessary substantive qualities or overall organizing dynamic at all. However, as a process that operates as an incremental and localized response to present conditions, the common law is not inimitable to its appropriation as possible complement to certain modes of political engagement. However, this is not to suggest that, when it is viewed in this way, it will produce particular or defensible outcomes. Insofar as there might be a continuing resort to the common law, it should be on the basis that it might be one political process, among many, through which to advance a variety of political initiatives. Any inclination to utilize the common law will, of course, be a political and contingent gamble, not a naturalistic or evolutionary imperative.

Any attempt to utilize Darwin's (and, to a lesser extent, Gadamer's) work is fraught with danger and controversy. Consequently, I want to introduce an early and important caveat to my reliance on such ideas. As much as I admire Darwin's writings, I resist all Darwinisms – *I am most definitely not trying to offer a Darwinian theory of the common law.* Nor do I claim that there actually is a Darwinian dynamic at work in the common law's development in the same way that there is in the natural world. Although efforts to so use Darwin's ideas to analogize legal and natural development are patently misguided, it has not prevented scores of scholars from undertaking such projects. However, it is

---

[25] H. Butterfield, *The Whig Interpretation of History* v (1931).

a major goal of this book to deny the possibility or feasibility of any effort to put Darwin to prescriptive or moral effect. Any account of human behavior that attempts to ground itself on so-called natural predispositions is fatally flawed. My project is very different. Armed with a Darwinian disposition, I intend to push through on an antiessentialist and nonmiraculous critique of the traditional and absolutist ambitions of jurisprudence. Law is about values, and that fact cannot be ignored or played down. However, there is no requirement to move from that trite claim to one that insists that the common law has a self-sustaining ethical core that lawyers must identify and to which they must adhere. Darwin's radical insight was to propose a causal theory of natural development that had no truck with notions of inevitable progress, natural harmony, or universal *telos*. While there might well be local purposes or local progress in the sense of a better adaptation to prevailing conditions, I reject the assertion that these interventions can accumulate into or are driven by an overarching purpose. As so many have tried to resist and finesse, Darwin's account completely sabotaged the possibility that there is any necessary connection between the biological course of people's lives and their ethical value: Knowing what nature has been or that it will change has nothing to tell us about what is morally right and wrong or what social change should be encouraged or discouraged. In short, evolution is an empirical phenomenon of successive alteration that has no necessary link to normative claims of value. Adaptation to changing conditions is the only standard of success – and this is only temporary and local in character. Contingency is the order of the day.

Making a Start

The particular questions and answers that I want to explore are, of course, those that concern the defense of common law adjudication as an institutional tradition of bounded and neutral decision making. The so-called hermeneutical turn in jurisprudence – the acknowledgment that, insofar as law concerns texts, adjudication is an interpretive exercise – has obliged theorists and lawyers to take seriously (again) the idea that law is a rhetorical tradition of specialized arguments. While this greater hermeneutical awareness has strengthened the jurisprudential project and rendered the resulting theories more plausible and cogent, it has also revitalized and strengthened the subversive force of the critical claim that law is not the bounded and objective process that the mainstream project of jurisprudential theorizing demands that it be. Once it is conceded that law is a more vital and less closed affair than was traditionally supposed, the fear resurfaces that the law will collapse into politics and that there will be no way to distinguish adjudication from more open-ended processes for the resolution of moral and political disputes. Moreover, jurisprudential accounts will themselves run the risk of being treated as simply an exercise in political rather than philosophical analysis in which truth and reason are not so much constraints on debate but constructs of it. It is this effort to take on board the hermeneutical insight in order to salvage the jurisprudential project without also fatally undermining its traditional ambitions that is at the heart of this book. At its most general, my critical claim is that, once history is included in the task of understanding and justifying the adjudicative process (as the hermeneutical insight insists that it must be), there is no effective way to keep the larger forces of ideological contestation out of the jurisprudential frame. Despite jurists' best efforts to the contrary, it is my contention that this effort to historicize law and adjudication in the name of rhetorical knowledge cannot be done without also politicizing them; the performance of legal adjudication will be revealed as a thoroughly and unavoidably ideological exercise.

In developing the idea that the common law is a work-in-progress, I begin in Chapter 2 by introducing the revolutionary work of Charles Darwin and tracing the different uses to which it has been put in the natural sciences and the humanities. Chapters 3 and 4 draw parallels with biology in the way in which evolutionary ideas have been put to jurisprudential work in attempting to explain the operation and development of the common law. Situating those theoretical debates in the historical practice of the common law, Chapter 5 demonstrates how its routine and the revolutionary dimensions are displayed in the careers of so-called great cases of the judicial tradition. Chapter 6 supplements the evolutionary critique with some critical insights drawn from a particular reading of Hans-Georg Gadamer's hermeneutical writings; Chapter 7 reveals how such a resulting pragmatic account of law illuminates constitutional adjudication in a common law system. Ranging broadly across the natural and legal landscape, Chapter 8 explores the contested notions of progress that animate both biological and jurisprudential accounts of development and change. Finally, Chapter 9 pulls together the different threads of the argument and offers a different way of thinking about the common law; recent constitutional developments around gay rights are used as a case in point. With such an ambition in mind, I find that the truly iconoclastic work of Charles Darwin is as good a place to start as any.

⤸ 2 ⤷

Darwin's Excellent Adventure:
Evolution and Law

> The attraction of biological analogies on social scientists, in par-
> ticular, seems to be so great that even the best minds are led
> astray.[1]
>
> JON ELSTER

FEW VOYAGES COULD HAVE HAD SUCH A PROFOUND EFFECT AS DARWIN'S
five-year stint on the *H.M.S. Beagle.* A novice naturalist on his departure
in 1831, he returned a mature scientist with the set of basic ideas that were to
prove truly revolutionary not only in biology but also in human affairs generally. If Galileo had shown that humankind was not at the center of the universe, Darwin was to demonstrate that humans were not the be-all and end-all
of creation. Yet, as great oaks from small acorns grow, so Darwin's monumen-
tal ideas developed from his localized studies. For instance, while on his travels along the coast of South America with the *H.M.S. Beagle,* Darwin witnessed
a volcano erupt and was literally shaken by an earthquake. He recorded
in eloquent detail the physical effects of such natural upheavals and their
geological implications. However, he reserved his most telling description
for the effect that these events had on his philosophical state of mind – "a
bad earthquake at once destroys our oldest associations: the earth, the very
emblem of solidity, has moved beneath our feet like a thin crust over a fluid;
one second of time has created in the mind a strange idea of insecurity which
hours of reflection would not have produced."[2] Darwin found himself not
only obliged to reflect on the physical causes of his earthly security but also
moved to challenge old theses and to question conventional accounts. In
an attitude that was to mark his entire intellectual life, Darwin resolved

---

[1] J. Elster, *Ulysses and the Sirens* 4 (1979).
[2] C. Darwin, *The Voyage of the Beagle* 270 (1839; S. Jones ed. 2001).

to take nothing for granted and to put all propositions to rigorous and uncompromising scrutiny. The result was itself truly seismic. Two decades later, on November 24, 1859, this inspired, if wealthy, amateur published his *The Origin of Species* and ignited "perhaps the greatest intellectual revolution experienced by mankind."[3]

Not surprisingly, this revolution sent shock waves through even the sheltered confines of the jurisprudential world. Ebbing and flowing with larger intellectual tides, the efforts to apply evolutionary ideas to law and legal development have continued during the intervening 150 years. However, it is not my intention to offer one more account of how the common law's development somehow manages to conform to a Darwinian dynamic. On the contrary, it is my objective is to show that any jurisprudential effort to mine the fields of biological research or trade off its prestige is fraught with perils. There is no reason at all to suppose (and many reasons not to suppose) that evolutionary science can be of any assistance in understanding the common law's historical operation or in grounding future initiatives in common law reform. However, there is much in the Darwinian canon that can be helpful in illuminating more clearly the failed efforts of modern jurisprudence to appreciate the workings of the common law. In particular, the debates around Darwin's great ideas provide a useful analogy to the debates and interventions that presently characterize jurisprudence. In talking about evolutionary biologists generally, the waggish Steve Jones might be speaking about their juristic counterparts when he notes that "evolution is a political sofa that molds itself to the buttocks of the last to sit upon it."[4] In this regard, common lawyers have put notions of Darwinian evolution to tendentious use. They have not only pummeled the political sofa, but, as is their wont, they have also insisted that there is something essential that is morally and politically attractive about the evolutionary process. They have been at pains to demonstrate that the shape into which the sofa has been molded is independent of their buttocks or anyone else's. The sofa of the common law has a shape and contour that, while molded by legal craftspersons and sat on by legal sojourners over the centuries, conforms to an overarching design and structure.

My foray into the evolution debate seeks to demonstrate law's pragmatic character while at the same time confirming adjudication's political quality. This chapter is divided into five parts. In the first part, I sketch the initial

[3] E. Mayr, *What Evolution Is* 9 (2001). For a more modest assessment of Darwin's influence, see J. Barzun, *Darwin, Marx, Wagner* 25 (1958).
[4] S. Jones, *Darwin's Ghost: The Origin of the Species Updated* 329 (1999).

terms of engagement over Darwin in the scientific community; the emphasis is on mapping the territory, not on mining it. In the second section I explore the central tenets of Darwin's seminal contribution to science and identifies the hallmarks of a Darwinian approach as contrasted with other pseudo-Darwinian or Darwinistic approaches. In the next section, I take stock of recent efforts to extend the Darwinian explanatory dynamic beyond organic development to patterns of behavior: The implications for studying law, as one of the important arenas of human behavior, are both obvious and troubling. In the fourth section I examine the different ways in which the evolutionary insight has found its way into legal studies and by which it claims to enhance an appreciation of law's historical development. In the final section, I point up the serious obstacles in the way of grounding an account of legal development in a parallel process to organic evolution: Law moves and 'evolves' in a more reflective and less serendipitous way than the human beings that establish and fashion it. Throughout the chapter, I hint at a less imperialistic and more modest approach to evolutionary theory's relevance to appreciating the operation of the common law. The jurisprudential challenge ought to be more about explaining stability than explaining change, about accepting that no change is good or bad in itself, and about appreciating that local context is the measure of law's worth. By way of conclusion, I recognize that, when it comes to law and adjudication, evolution is as much a political responsibility as it is a natural necessity.

The Oxford Debate

The venue – the annual meeting of the British Association for the Advancement of Science in Oxford's newly built Museum of Natural History – and the occasion – a lecture on European social development by a relatively unknown American scholar – were fairly unremarkable. However, the impromptu debate that followed, although much anticipated by the unprecedented and eminent 700 persons in attendance, has become the fabled stuff of historical moment. Occurring on Saturday, June 30, 1860, only six months after the publication of Charles Darwin's *The Origin of Species*, the face-off over the controversial theory of evolution by natural selection was between the conservative and sceptical Bishop of Oxford, "Soapy Sam" Wilberforce, and the uncompromising scientist and leading public intellectual of the day, the thirty-four-year-old Thomas Henry "Bulldog" Huxley. Darwin himself was not present because, as well as having a natural aversion to such appearances, he was suffering from a severe bout of an undiagnosed illness that was to plague him throughout his life and for which he was availing himself of the services of Dr. Lane's Hydropathic Clinic. The Oxford session was to be chaired by Reverend Robert Stevens Henslow, Darwin's old mentor from Cambridge. While the topic was supposed to be the subtle scientific implications of Darwin's evolutionary account, the agenda was much broader and more polarized. It pitted the established church order against an emerging scientific new wave: Who was to speak for Nature, the clerics, or the scientists? In so doing, this Victorian debate set the tone and terms for intellectual debate about evolution and much more over the next century and a half. Ironically, in a building that was known as Oxford's new cathedral of science and whose construction had been made possible by biblical funds, intellectual enlightenment seemed too readily sacrificed to personal vanity.

There was no actual session on Darwin's *Origin* scheduled on the meeting's program. However, the publication of the book and the heated reviews it had received were a central topic of conversation. With all the major players present (and Darwin himself absent), all was in place for a major and public set-to. On that Thursday, there was a preliminary skirmish when Charles Daubeny, Oxford's professor of botany, gave a lecture on "The Final Causes of the Sexuality of Plants, with Particular Reference to Mr. Darwin's Work." A mild supporter of Darwin's views, Daubeny offered a lecture that was marked more by its efforts to avoid partisanship than by its intellectual stimulation. This did not deter Robert Owen, a paleontologist and one of Darwin's staunchest scientific critics, from using the occasion to ignite fierce debate by venting his criticisms of Darwin's ideas. He argued that all the anatomical evidence was against Darwin's theory: The human brain was entirely distinct from that of gorillas and, therefore, humans were not related to or descended from apes. Unable to contain himself, Huxley jumped to his feet and disparaged Owen's anatomical claims. He promised to refute Owen at length at a later date and in a more suitable forum. However, Huxley could not end without making some intemperate remarks about the clergy and suggested that churchmen should not worry "even if it should be shown that apes were their ancestors." If Owen had lit the spark, Huxley had fanned the flames; the debate was ablaze and further fireworks were sure to follow.

News spread among the attendees that the expected showdown between the warring factions was likely to take place on Saturday afternoon. The pretext was a lecture on "The Intellectual Development of Europe Considered with Reference to the Views of Mr. Darwin" by Dr. William Draper of New York. Even though the Museum was finished, all its furnishings had not been fully installed, so the lecture was to be held in the empty Radcliffe's Library on the upper West Gallery. So small were these rooms and so large was the audience that the reputed 700 persons in attendance spilled out onto the gallery itself and some adjoining rooms. Dr. Draper's lecture was rather boring, even though he promoted the controversial view that cultural progress was dependent on enlightened science's being able to loosen the grip of stultifying theology. Needing no other encouragement, a righteous Bishop Wilberforce took the floor. Briefed by Owen, the fifty-four-year-old Wilberforce, while still an intellect to be reckoned with, had begun to rely more on bluster than brains. He was not known as Soapy Sam for nothing. As expected, he gave a powerful if overwrought renuncia-tion of Darwin's theory, lambasting the evolutionary initiative and restating the Creationist case. Echoing the words of his yet-to-be-published review of *The Origin*, Wilberforce made sport with Darwin and his earnest defend-ers. After noting Darwin's apparent observations about "our unsuspected cousinship with mushrooms," he asked, "is it credible that, even if transmu-tations were rapidly occurring, all favourable varieties of turnips are tending to become men?"[5] At the end of his rather bombastic harangue and with the meeting already running to two hours, Wilberforce turned to Huxley, who was sitting close by him, and said, "I should like to ask Professor Huxley who is about to tear me to pieces when I sit down, as to his belief in be-ing descended from an ape. Is it on his grandfather's or his grandmother's side that the ape ancestry comes in?" Wilberforce sat down to thunderous applause.

As Huxley stood up to speak, the tension was high. However, the normally snappy and high-strung Huxley managed to muzzle his bulldog tendencies. Turning to his neighbor, Sir Benjamin Brodie, the Queen's surgeon, he whispered that "the Lord hath delivered him into my hands." Huxley was by no means entirely persuaded by the full import of all Darwin's ideas about natural selection. Indeed, he shared some of Wilberforce's more substantive and less rhetorical misgivings about the new evolutionary science. However, Huxley was prepared to suppress his reservations and to come to the de-fense of science against the religious establishment; even a flawed scientific

---

5   There is no contemporaneous or verbatim record of the encounter. My account is pieced together from Huxley, Hooker, and Darwin's recollections as well as from other journalistic anecdotes. See R. Clark, *The Survival of Charles Darwin: A Biography of a Man and an Idea* 137–47 (1984); M. White and J. Gribbin, *Darwin: A Life in Science* 219–25 (1995); C. Aydon, *Charles Darwin: The Naturalist Who Started a Scientific Revolution* 216–23 (2002); J. Browne, *Charles Darwin: The Power of Place* 113–28 (2002); and http://oum.ox.ac.uk/debate.htm. Some portray the Oxford event more as a traveling road show than a site for profes-sional exchange; see D. Knight, *Ordering the World: A History of Classifying Man* 167–71 (1981). Others view the debate in much less (melo)dramatic terms; see J. Lucas, Wilberforce and Huxley: A Legendary Encounter, 22 *Historical Journal* 313 (1979); J. V. Jensen, Return to the Wilberforce-Huxley Debate, 21 *Brit. J. for Hist. Sci.* 161 (1988); and C. Gauld, The Huxley-Wilberforce Debate, 22 *Res. in Sci. Educ.* 149–56 (1992).

theory was much preferred to stifling theocratic dogmatics. Lacking the oratorical skills of Wilberforce, he began his retort by ably defending the basic structure of Darwin's arguments. Then, in a deft stroke of gamesmanship, Huxley replied to Wilberforce's provocation by righteously stating that "I should feel it no shame to have risen from such an origin, but I should feel it a shame to have sprung from one who prostituted the gifts of culture and eloquence to the service of prejudice and falsehood – I unhesitatingly affirm my preference for the ape." At the time, this was very strong stuff; a pregnant member of the audience, Lady Jane Brewster, fainted at hearing a Bishop so publicly denounced (and in such a hot and crammed room). Huxley's performance was met with equally raucous approval to Wilberforce's, suggesting that the audience was impressed as much by the theatrics of the performances as their substance.

But the debate was not finished. Several noted members of the audience rose to speak, including a Bible-brandishing Robert Fitzroy, Darwin's former friend and captain of the *H.M.S. Beagle* on which Darwin had made his fateful trip some thirty years before. An increasingly unstable Fitzroy, later to commit suicide, denounced Darwin as a heretic and apostate. Expressing regret at the fact that he had given Darwin the opportunity to formulate his theory on his world travels, he asserted that he could not "find anything ennobling in the thought of being the descendant of even the most ancient ape." Less impassioned contributions were made by Robert Henslow and John Lubbock, a noted mathematician and astronomer, in defense of Darwin. The final speaker was Joseph Hooker, the Director of the Royal Botanical Gardens at Kew, who had his own political as well as scientific reasons for championing the Darwinian cause. In contrast to the fevered interventions that preceded his, Hooker wisely made a less emotional and more learned riposte to Wilberforce's assault. Although not as memorable as Huxley's verbal fireworks, his hard-hitting arguments against Wilberforce probably did more for the longer-term benefit of the Darwinian cause: "Facts in this science which before were inexplicable to me became one by one explained by [Darwin's] theory, and conviction has been thus gradually forced upon an unwilling convert." After Hooker's point-by-point refutation of Wilberforce's remarks, the Bishop declined an invitation to respond and the meeting was closed after almost four hours. It had been a historic occasion that left its mark on both science and religion for decades to come.

Opinion was divided on which side came out best. Whereas a rampant Huxley and the scientific academy claimed to have routed a chagrined clerical establishment, a smug Wilberforce felt that he had won the day over the parvenu scientists. The fact that the debate took place at all was at least as important as its immediate outcome: The terms had been set for a contest between science and religion that still rages today. Darwin himself was kept fully informed of events by his legion of correspondents. Not surprisingly, the temper of these reports was largely positive. Although Hooker claimed to have been "as dull as ditchwater," Darwin was grateful for his support (and Huxley's support) and ranked his affection as more important than "talk of fame, honour, pleasure, wealth" – "I would like to have heard your triumphing over the bishop. . . . I fully believe that our cause will in the long run prevail." In a letter to Darwin, Hugh Falconer gave his own firsthand recollections and reported that "the saponaceous Bishop got basted and larded by Huxley. Owen also came in for such a put down by Huxley as I have never witnessed within my experience of scientific discussion. Your interests . . . were most tenderly watched over by your devoted eleves." In light of these heartening comments, Darwin was further galvanized and, although he wrote to Asa Gray that *Origin* had "stirred up the mud with a vengeance," he stuck to his selectionist guns.[6] Over the remaining twenty years of his life, Darwin spent his time with his large family at his beloved Down House, working productively on a prolific series of monographs and books. While he eschewed the public spotlight and struggled with his poor health, his stature grew. On his death in 1882, he had left an intellectual and social legacy that continues to dominate society's scientific and social agenda. Ironically, he was buried in Westminister Abbey, the epicenter of the English Christian establishment.

Whatever the immediate aftermath of the Oxford debate, evolution remains one of the hottest of hot-button issues: The battle between religion and science continues apace. As the intervening decades have powerfully revealed, while science has gone from strength to strength, organized religion is not so easily vanquished. Being based on faith, it is not as susceptible to reasoned argument and scientific refutation as some would like to believe. The persistence of the Creationist cause, especially in the United States, is a powerful reminder of the profound challenge that Darwin's ideas offer to traditional understandings. Moreover, the scientific cause has not always been helped by the fact that many of those who claim to be inspired by Darwin's work have pursued their own supposedly secular theories with an orthodox zeal and evangelical spirit that would embarrass all except the most devoted religious fanatic. In the hands of such evolutionary fundamentalists,

---

[6] See letters of Joseph Hooker to Darwin on July 2, 1860; Darwin to Hooker on July 2, 1860; Hugh Falconer to Darwin on July 9, 1860; and Darwin to Asa Gray on July 3, 1860. All of these can be found in the Darwin Archive in the Library of Cambridge University.

Darwinism becomes "a world view that encompasses the hierarchically related concepts of change, order, direction, progress, and perfectability."[7] Bishop Wilberforce might well disagree with its content, but he would likely sympathize with its antiselectionist sentiments. Indeed, fired by a deep antipathy toward all forms of established privilege, Huxley's own later work on social evolution was as much driven by his political desire to professionalize science and to effect a meritocracy as by any simple scientific impulse. In general, it can be reported that, in the ensuing 150 years since *Origin* was published, the understandable temptation to put Darwin to moral, political, or even religious effect has proved irresistible in many quarters.

However, as the Oxford quarrel plainly suggests, there is much more at stake in discussing Darwin than the details of a recherché biological theorem. Whatever else it is, science is never only science and the difference between science and other pursuits is much less stark than is generally conceded: "The negotiations [between working scientists] as to what counts as a proof or what constitutes a good assay are no more or less orderly than any argument between lawyers and politicians."[8] In the case of Darwin, the stakes are so high because it seems to promise a possible solution to the most pressing questions of human existence – Where did it all begin? How did we get here from there? What can we do about the future? – and to do so with the authority of science. Along with Isaac Newton and Albert Einstein, Darwin is considered one of the greatest scientists ever. His work has not only changed the way that scientists go about their work but has also affected the way people think about the world and their place in it. In this way, *Darwin* has come to represent something apart from the historical person and published words of the actual Charles Darwin. Indeed, what Darwin himself did and did not mean is much less important than what can be said about evolution in light of reading Darwin against and within a context of twenty-first-century science and sensibilities. Nevertheless, as is the double-edged fate of all great ideas, Darwin's account of evolution through "natural selection" is the subject of heated debates about its meaning, import, and implications. Many have been unable to withstand the dangerous tendency to utilize his factual explanations as evaluative guidelines and to convert what is into what should be. At its worst, this has resulted in the situation in which many faux Darwinians embrace the Promethean impulse to put

---

[7] R. Levins and R. Lewontin, *The Dialectical Biologist* 9 (1985).

[8] B. La Tour and S. Woolgar, *Laboratory Life: The Social Construction of Scientific Facts* 237 (1979). See also T. Kuhn, *The Structure of Scientific Revolutions* (3rd ed. 1996). This is not suggest that science and politics are the same, only that they are not as separable or independent as is often thought.

evolutionary theory and therefore nature in the service of a preferred social or ideological vision. In an ironic twist, by insisting that a Darwinian world has Darwinian purposes, evolutionary science has become the new theology, with Darwin himself as its reluctant messiah figure.

Nonetheless, insofar as there is something that has come to be called a Darwinian account of evolution, it deserves to be distinguished and rescued from the spectrum of derivative theoretical offerings that are more Darwinistic than Darwinian. It is tantamount to ideological sophistry or religious fundamentalism to claim that something is true simply because Darwin did or did not say something. It is much better to view Darwin's theory as a launching pad for various ideas about the phenomenon of change and development in the natural world. Indeed, it is a common rap against Darwin himself that his theory is simply a reflection of and justification for prevailing social conditions and values in that it relied on the whole nineteenth-century capitalist laissez faire mentality of competition, struggle, violence, self-interest, and so on.[9] While he did place some of these values at the heart of his work, Darwin's ideas amount to so much more than an abject apology for the status quo. Of course, Darwin was affected by his own cultural and social milieu, but no more (or less) than any other scholar. The response to such a charge is not to dismiss the ideas or else there will be no ideas left to consider; all ideas are generated somewhere by someone. The challenge is to read the impugned writings with knowledge of their creative context. So instructed, one can acknowledge Darwin's ideas as being part of their milieu but not as being entirely confined by it. In particular, one can note that, unlike many of his intellectual friends and foes, Darwin resisted the naturalistic fallacy of turning his descriptive ideas to prescriptive effect: His was a tale about what happened, not what should happen. Indeed, Darwin resisted all efforts to discover any ethical imperatives in his biological analysis. Unfortunately, this cannot be said of many who claimed to be writing under his tutelage or influence.

Darwin's Evolution

In the early nineteenth century, the prevailing view of evolution was that there was a hierarchical arrangement to nature that placed humans at its apex; change and variation had come to a natural end with humanity's ascendancy. Further, when Darwin took his fateful trip on *H.M.S. Beagle* to the

[9] See G. Himmelfarb, *Darwin and the Darwinian Revolution* (1959) and J. Rifkin, *The Biotech Century: Harnessing the Gene and Remaking the World* 197–226 (1998).

Galapagos Archipelago in the 1830s, the prevailing wisdom among biologists was the Lamarckian notion that individuals adapt to their environment and those altered characteristics are inherited by the individuals' progeny. Darwin took this attractive suggestion and turned it on its head. He got the basic idea in 1838 that, "in the struggle for existence, . . . favourable variations would tend to be preserved and unfavourable ones to be destroyed."[10] After over twenty years of further experiments and reflection, Darwin published his revolutionary *The Origin of Species* in 1859. He had actually produced a first draft by 1844, but his natural caution persuaded him to hold off publishing until he had more evidence and was more confident of the veracity of its central thesis. It was only in 1858, when he learned that Alfred Russel Wallace, a younger naturalist, was about to steal his thunder with a similar account of evolution, that Darwin finally resolved to pull together and complete his ideas on natural selection. He had the finished manuscript in his publisher's hands in less than a year. In his elegant and technical tome (translated into ten European languages in his lifetime alone), Darwin's revolutionary contribution was manifold – he explained how that process worked, how all species are related, how evolution was not planned or inevitable, and how *Homo sapiens* was not only related to more primitive life-forms but also was not the necessary outcome of the evolutionary process. Accordingly, Darwin did not so much introduce the idea of evolution as develop a particular version of evolution and highlight the particular mechanism by which evolution occurs. Conceding that nature had the appearance of being designed by some grand and benevolent hand, he asserted that the apparent design was the relentless result of blind chance; a designing deity is displaced by the impression of one who might not actually exist. *Origin* was to begin a revolution in human thought that would at least parallel, if not actually surpass, any before it.

Although Darwin's fabled book is densely packed with his amassed evidence and supporting argumentation, the central thesis of *Origin* is as simple as it is seismic. Organisms create more offspring than can survive. In the procreation of these offspring, mutations occur randomly, naturally, and are as likely to be detrimental as beneficial to the organism. These mutations do not occur, as Lamarck had insisted, as a designed function of willed

---

[10] C. Darwin, *The Autobiography of Charles Darwin 1809–1882* (N. Barlow ed. 1958). Darwin did not use the word *evolution* until the fifth edition of *Origin* in 1869 and only referred to his process of natural selection as *evolution* in *The Descent of Man* (1871). In many ways, Lamarck's contribution has been treated unfairly. He opened up a vital space for Darwin, taking the brunt of the theological assault. In so doing, he established the principle of evolution, even if he got the mechanism entirely wrong.

adaptation. Those mutated offspring that are more able to adapt to the local environment will survive and thrive – "mutation proposes; selection disposes."[11] Over time and across populations, these successful variations will accumulate slowly and steadily so that small local changes will have massive enduring effects; new species will develop and even more species will disappear. Darwin called this process "natural selection," and it was offered as the destructive as well as the creative force of evolution. In what became his most controversial claim, Darwin insisted that there is no predetermined path or design to evolutionary development because there is a contingent mix of chance (i.e., organisms mutate unpredictably) and necessity (i.e., selection favors the most adaptive or the least maladaptive). In the biological sciences, '*evolution*' is simply a synonym for change. Unlike in the social sciences (including law), there is no common supposition of improvement or advancement in any universally appealing sense. In short, evolution is an empirical phenomenon of successive alteration that has no necessary link to normative claims of value. Adaptation to changing conditions is the only standard of success, and this is only temporary and local in character; once conditions change, an adapted feature can become maladapted to its circumstances. Contingency is the order of the day. The dynamism in nature is brought about by the fact that organisms selected by past conditions exist in present conditions, such that any change in conditions will result in different challenges for those organisms and, therefore, different organisms will begin to thrive: "[Natural selection] is a game of tag in which the past never catches up . . . [and] the naturally selected become the selected unnatural; the fittest survive and become unfit and do not survive."[12]

Darwin's work makes it clear that he had no tolerance for the view that evolution was a purifying Platonic process (i.e., variant forms are eliminated so that a species' "true being" can assert itself) or Panglossian process (i.e., everything happens for the best). Although quantitative change will ultimately result in qualitative difference, evolution is basically the long and gradual process through which natural selection works on genetic variations so that organisms adapt to their surrounding environment. Because that environment is constantly changing and interacting with these adapted mutating

---

[11] G. Dover, *Dear Mr. Darwin: Letters on the Evolution of Life and Human Nature* 90 (2000). It was left to later biologists, especially through the posthumously published work of the Bohemian monk Gregor Mendel, to explain the precise genetic process by which variation and mutation occurred. See R. Henig, *The Monk in the Garden* (2000). Darwin could only report that "our ignorance of the laws of variation is profound." See C. Darwin, *The Origin of the Species by Natural Selection* (1859).

[12] E. Harrison, *The Masks of the Universe* 115 (1985).

organisms, there is no guarantee that progress in any normative sense will occur: Evolution is about historical change, not normative advancement. Indeed, evolution can be instructively viewed as being about failure and elimination. Some organisms simply do not have the luck to get the right genes at the right time and so are not better able to adapt to prevailing conditions. It simply is not the case that nature is continually building the so-called better organism and moving toward some perfected form. There are no fixed or real types, only continuous variations; type is an abstraction and variation is real. While a workable level of prediction is possible in local circumstances and over short periods of time, the sheer complexity and richness of contingent life ensure that more ambitious predictions about nature's unfolding determinacy are futile. The lesson of Darwin is that, like all other organisms, humans breed for reproduction and survival, not for finding deep truths about the universe. This does not mean that humans cannot search for philosophical truths, but it is not their purpose or raison d'etre. Thus, evolutionary biology can only help fix where we have been, not where we are going: Humanity "does not evolve *toward* anything, but only *away* from something."[13] Evolution is about the been-and-gone and the here-and-now; it does not plan for or cater to the future. To maintain otherwise is to mistake entirely the central thrust of an evolutionary process.

To say more than this about Darwin's basic evolutionary thesis is to court controversy. Even the truncated account that I have given will probably arouse suspicion and dissent in some quarters. This is because, in a sardonic twist of historical appreciation, Darwin's work has come to be treated as having political, ethical, and even religious significance. Sometimes, Darwin is treated as a messianic figure, like Jesus or Mohammed; other times, he is considered to have midwifed, like Karl Marx and Adam Smith, the birth of a secular ideology. Cast in such extravagant terms, the struggle to claim the soul of Darwinian evolutionary theory for a particular political, ethical, or religious campaign has gone on largely unabated. As well as join issue over the basic merit of Darwin's central thesis, scholars and commentators divide into different camps over its reach and provenance. Given a little bit of time to acclimatize and update, Bulldog Huxley and Soapy Sam Wilberforce would soon be at home in contemporary debates over the meaning, significance, and reach of evolution. Indeed, the Creationist and Social Darwinian projects still have a considerable hold over contemporary

---

[13] J. Horgan, *The End of Science: Facing the Limits of Knowledge in the Twilight of the Scientific Age* (1997). See also Mayr, supra, note 3 at 116–19 and 150 ("adaptation is a by-product of the process of elimination").

imaginations. Ironically, it is Darwin who might be more disturbed at the turn that events have taken. As things have turned out, Darwin has as much to fear from some of his evolutionary chums as his Creationist enemies. Too many have failed to remember that the strength of a good idea is in its conceptual limits as much as in its central insights. Whatever else it is, Darwin's account of evolution is not the elusive philosopher's stone. Nevertheless, this has not prevented scores of scholars from treating it as an alchemical device to answer all the mysteries of the biological world and human affairs, including law. In the next section, I pursue and contrast one particular and popular take on Darwin, the so-called ultra-Darwinian approach, with a more traditional continuation of the Darwinian initiative. This will serve as an introduction to efforts to apply an evolutionary perspective to the problems of jurisprudence and law.[14]

Designing Genes?

There is still a significant group that holds to a fairly traditional understanding of Darwin's ideas. While there are some differences between them, these Darwinians adopt a view of evolution that Darwin might himself recognize and find palatable. This Darwinian stance is entirely different from the popularized Spencerian concept of a natural world at war with itself and in which a nature-red-in-tooth-and-claw ethic drives the struggle over "the survival of the fittest," a infamous phrase that is Spencer's, not Darwin's.[15] Darwin talked much more about organisms that, seeking to find an equilibrium with their environment and neighbors, were constantly responding and adapting to change. Nor did Darwin believe that there was any pattern to this endless proliferation of mutated organisms and new species. For him, evolution was a haphazard process with no ex ante trend, but only ex post tendencies; evolution only revealed itself in hindsight and then only to the practiced eye. Evolution has no foresight and, therefore, is unable to anticipate or accommodate future effects. Because change is small, mutation unpredictable, and the interaction between organism and environment so increasingly and bafflingly complex, it is futile to search for or speculate on a grand plan: Evolution is a blind, contingent, haphazard,

---

[14] I deal extensively with the Creationist legacy of Soapy Sam and the Social Darwinianism of Bulldog Huxley in Chapters 3 and 4, respectively, where I look at their deployment and fate in jurisprudential literature.

[15] H. Spencer, *The Principles of Biology*, vol. 1, 444 (1882). It has been suggested that the standard for survival is usually more like "satisficing" or good enough. See H. Simon, *The Sciences of the Artificial* 48 (3rd ed. 1996).

and entirely opportunistic affair. In particular, Darwin's refusal to concede that humankind's existence was necessary, inevitable, or preordained and that it, like all other species, is the continuing product of contingent circumstance is what got Darwin into such metaphysical hot water. Adherence to this critical insight is what has kept his scientific heirs there. While Darwin concluded *Origin* by stating that "there is a grandeur in this view of life ... [and] from so simple a beginning endless forms most beautiful and most wonderful have been and are being evolved," he expressly resisted the temptation to reach a more heroic or hubristic resolution.[16] While Darwin had offered a theoretical explanation that was intended to account for all living development, that theory was entirely descriptive and made no claim to prescribe or predict such development along moral lines.

Nevertheless, even within this Darwinian (as opposed to the faux Darwinian or Darwinistic) camp, there are divergences and differences of opinion. These disputes are the stuff of scientific development. Many of the debates concern issues and gaps left open by Darwin; much turns on differing emphases in competing explanations rather than on fundamental divergences in assumptions. For instance, considerable energy is expended over the disputed pace of evolution. Darwinian evolutionists divide over whether evolution proceeds at a steady and gradual rate or by stages of punctuated equilibrium in which change happens in geologically brief speciation events separated by long periods of stasis.[17] While resolution of this issue is important (and its continued irresolution is utilized by the Creationists in their antievolution critique), it does not go to the heart of the Darwinian account or demand a radical reformulation of its central components. However, in some cases, what begins as an in-house dispute turns into something larger and results in a breakaway approach. An important instance of this is the disagreement over the level at which speciation and evolution occurs. Whereas some insist that the struggle for survival is best understood from the perspective of genes rather than individuals, others prefer to emphasize the operation of evolution at many levels, not simply the genetic, and the historical importance of environmental factors on the evolutionary process.[18] Behind this apparently technical clash is a much

---

[16] *Origin*, supra, note 11 at 429.

[17] See A. Somit and S. Petersen, *The Dynamics of Evolution* (1992) and S. J. Gould, *Ontogeny and Phylogeny* (1977). For an accessible introduction to this technical debate, see S. J. Gould, *Wonderful Life: The Burgess Shale and the Nature of History* (1989).

[18] See, for example, R. Dawkins, *The Extended Phenotype: The Long Reach of the Gene* (1999) and R. Lewontin, S. Rose, and L. Kamin, *Not in Our Genes: Biology, Ideology and Human Nature* (1984).

more fundamental quarrel about the basic dynamic of evolution. Is natural selection the exclusive or primary explanation of all organic behavior and change, or are there other important factors at work? Do Darwin's basic insights apply to cultural–psychological development as well as biological–genetic evolution? From a jurisprudential perspective, can legal development be satisfactorily explained in terms of principles analogous to natural selection? Answers to these questions tend to determine whether particular scholars make the shift away from traditional and pluralistic Darwinian ideas to a more radical and monistic neo-Darwinianism.

It is not so much that these so-called ultra-Darwinians disagree over the basic Darwinian thesis or that they see any grand design at work; it is that they wish to extend Darwin's notion of natural selection to absolutely everything. Indeed, there is much about the ultra-Darwinians that is entirely compatible with a traditional Darwinian view and that advances many of its basic commitments. For instance, Richard Dawkins's conclusions that "there is nothing inherently progressive about evolution" and that, over a long enough time and under particular conditions, it is possible "to derive anything from anything else" contribute greatly to the Darwinian canon.[19] Nevertheless, it is the extent to which Dawkins and others have been prepared to push these claims that has proved so controversial. Not content to explain the evolution of all biological organisms in line with a Darwinian evolutionary dynamic, they have made the audacious claim that the behavior of such organisms, including and especially humans, is entirely explicable in the same terms. Whether scavenging for food or going shopping for watches and whether scrambling for sexual supremacy or reflecting on sexual mores, humans and other organisms are seen to be striving to adapt to their environment and ensure the survival of the fittest. Accordingly, the central claim of ultra-Darwinians is that a relentless process of natural selection resulted in brains equipped with particular information-processing predispositions that consequently yield nonrandom and hence evolutionarily driven behaviors. In the same way, therefore, that flora and fauna thrive or die as a result of their genes' ability to survive and prosper, so human behavior is said to be coordinated and controlled by a similar dynamic.

Picking up on these themes, Daniel Dennett argues that absolutely everything, including culture, religion, language, psychology, and morality, is subject to and conditioned by natural selection. Chastising others for their fearful failure to accept the full ramifications of Darwin's "dangerous idea,"

---

[19] R. Dawkins, *The Blind Watchmaker* 180 and 318 (1986). See also R. Dawkins, *The Selfish Gene* (1976).

he offers an understanding of natural selection as an uncompromising denial of all biological essentialism and as a neutral, algorithmic process, applicable to an extremely wide range of phenomena and capable of achieving immense feats by slow accumulation over large extents of time and space. Though there are obvious differences between those things produced by human design and those produced by evolution, biology is considered to be engineering at some fundamental level. While he rejects Leibnizian Panglossianism, Dennett sees adaptionism as a fertile source of explanations for natural development. However, in offering such explanations, he insists that there is no place at all for "skyhooks" (i.e., entirely mysterious, preexisting devices that enable some problem to be solved entirely independently of ordinary processes of design) and that the only bad reductionism is a greedy reductionism that tries to do without "cranes" (i.e., tricks that allow design to proceed faster but that build on existing foundations). He predicates his application of Darwinian evolution to culture on the concept of *memes*. These are to concepts or ideas what genes are to biology: They are propagated from person to person, they compete with one another, and they allow humans to transcend their genetics. While Dennett doubts that an equally powerful science of memetics is possible, he concludes that genetics and memetics work on the same principles of design-by-unthinking-processes-of-selection.[20]

Traditional Darwinians reject these ultra-Darwinian claims. Not only do they take exception to the contention that the gene is the basic unit of evolution and that individuals are disposable vehicles for the survival of genes, but they also resist the imperialistic assertion that all mental and cultural life is completely explainable by a fundamental Darwinian process of natural selection in which human genes and memes struggle for survival. Traditional Darwinians take a much more pluralistic stance and insist that it is mistaken to bracket Darwin's neglected rider that "I am convinced that natural selection has been the main but not the exclusive means of modification."[21] However, theirs is much more than a fundamentalist argument over what Darwin did or did not say. As evidence that it is a profound error to credit

---

[20] D. Dennett, *Darwin's Dangerous Idea: Evolution and the Meanings of Life* (1995). While Dennett deplores the excesses of some sociobiologists (so-called greedy reductionists), he sees no grounds for rejecting an evolutionary origin for morality. In a brief final chapter, he explains how Darwin's dangerous idea has influenced his own political and ethical beliefs. He sees it as a basis for assigning value to diversity, whether artistic, cultural, or biological. However, this seems to be exactly the kind of normative so-called skyhooking that Dennett's basic thesis is at pains to reject.

[21] *Origin*, supra, note 11 at 4. It was in the 1872 edition of *Origin* that Darwin added this rider to his original thesis. He went on to state that "this has been to no avail. Great is the steady power of misrepresentation."

natural selection with being the exclusive or primary cause of all organic behavior, they point to the crucial role that statistical accidents, environmental
devastation, structural limits to organisms, long-term drift, and blind chance
play in the history of evolutionary development on function and form. In
this way, the traditional Darwinian stance cautions against any theoretical
offering that attempts to shoehorn everything into one closed and therefore static and mechanistic explanation; human will struggles within and
against a particular environment and affects as it is affected by that environment in its efforts to do what is best. Offering science on a grand scale,
the ultra-Darwinians' work seems to be premised on the belief that it might
be possible to understand all there is to know about everything, including
problems not yet known or even understood, by resort to one simple evolutionary formula. This is indeed a dangerous idea and a reductionist one
that stands in stark contrast to both the exposition of evolutionary theory
and the actual practice of evolution itself. While Occam's razor can often
be a useful intellectual tool, it can cleave deeply as well as shave closely.

For the more traditional Darwinians, it is silly to assume that all aspects of
physiology and behavior are optimally adapted responses to environmental
challenges; there are constraints on short-term gains that may become long-
term losses. It is accepted that "natural selection remains the only theory
that explains how *adaptive* complexity, not just any old complexity, can arise,
because it is the only nonmiraculous, forward-direction theory in which *how
well something works* plays a causal role in *how it came to be.*"[22] Nonetheless, Darwinians refuse to assume that an organism's current utility has any necessary
connection to its evolutionary origin or that no other formative forces are
in play. Psychological traits can be inherited through learning and cultural
adaptation. Moreover, the recognition of nonadaptive features does not imply an arbitrary or nonintelligible process of change and even less a rejection
of a Darwinian perspective. It is simply not enough to tell a plausible story
that is consistent with natural selection to prove that its processes are the inevitable causal origin of particular innovative features. There are many plausible explanatory possibilities and there is a much heavier burden on those
who wish to claim that natural selection is the only dynamic at work. Moreover, Darwinians maintain that it is a false contest to pit selection against
constraint; the former is a function of the constraining context as much as a

---

[22] S. Pinker, *How the Mind Works* 162 (1997). Those who can be reasonably included in the
vanguard of the Darwinian group are S. J. Gould, *The Structure of Evolutionary Theory* (2002); S.
Rose, *Lifelines: Biology, Freedom, Determinism* (1997); and M. Rose, *Darwin's Spectre: Evolutionary
Biology in the Modern World* (1998).

separate process. Without context and constraint, there would be no natural selection in the sense of a recognizable process. Consequently, it is simply wrong to explain everything in terms of adaptive necessity. Organisms are the result of manifold compromises between variability and stability; *fittest* is an entirely contingent, relative and descriptive label and may signify nothing more compelling than being the immediately best, although globally not very good, of a bad bunch. In this way, evolution is a strange mix of universal predictability (i.e., natural selection is a dominant process in biological development) and local unpredictability (i.e., the actual outcome of that general process in any given local and historical instance cannot be predicted). The environment is subject to various stochastic processes that, by definition, lead to unpredictable and contingent results in any specific situation.

As regards human development, the major challenge for the ultra-Darwinians is to demonstrate that a particular behavior is genetically driven rather than socially conditioned. This will require the designation of a particular genotype or allele pairing for each particular behavior and, on the basis of existing scientific predictions, will be well-nigh impossible to do. Also, while traditional Darwinians can concede that there may well be a contingent mix of the natural and the nurtured, the ultra-Darwinians are obliged to defend the extravagant claim that behavior is almost all genetically driven. While the mind itself may be a product of natural selection, it does not follow that any particular patterns of behavior are also similarly produced. Conversely, although evolution is an amoral and nonteleological process, it does not mean that it cannot produce moral and purpose-driven entities. However, it is an unwarranted leap to assume that such morality and purposefulness is reducible to a single and simple formula. As one commentator has neatly put it, "even if you can build a bottle from which the desired genie emerges, you can't reduce the genie to the bottle once it's out."[23] While it is decked out in the trappings of empirical science, the ultra-Darwinians are offering a very idealistic and metaphysical proposal. At bottom, I think that it is neither possible nor desirable to reduce inquiries into human culture to an entirely empirical enterprise that obviates the need for ethical reflection and contextual appreciation. Within such a mind-set, there is a grave danger that people will be reduced only to their genes and that natural inclination (e.g., violent behavior) will trump social imperative (e.g., individual responsibility). This cautionary insight has particular

[23] A. Brown, *The Darwin Wars: The Scientific Battle for the Soul of Man* 154 (1999). For a devastating critique of the memetic theory, see M. Midgley, Why Memes? in *Alas Poor Darwin: Arguments Against Evolutionary Psychology* 67–84 (H. Rose and S. Rose eds. 2001).

salience for understanding the relevance of Darwinian evolutionary theory to law and adjudication.

At its most essential, therefore, the basic bone of contention between Darwinians and ultra-Darwinians is over the application of Darwin's ideas to human behavior. There is general agreement that, because humans are a biological species, their creation and development are readily explicable by the simple logic of Darwinian evolution. This means neither that the existence of humans was inevitable or planned nor that continued existence is guaranteed. Like dinosaurs and dodos, humans are vulnerable to the extreme deprivations of their natural environment. However, unlike all other organisms (to date), humans have a greater and more sophisticated capacity for conscious planning and impacting the environment in which they live; they manage to affect and shape their environment as they are affected and shaped by it. Consequently, human development is not entirely reactive or adaptive; people are able to exert a powerful influence on the very factors that Darwinian evolution considers to be the motive force of biological progress. This means that any attempt to reduce the study of human activity to the same familiar evolutionary dynamic that works for fish and fowl is unconvincing. As the leading Darwinian (and unabashed critic of ultra-Darwinianism), the late Stephen Jay Gould, puts it, "we are glorious accidents of an unpredictable process with no drive to complexity, not the expected results of evolutionary principles that yearn to produce a creature capable of understanding the mode of its necessary construction."[24] A key question, therefore, for Darwinian adherents is how to account for those human behaviors that are the result of conscious planning and intellectual design. Can they be brought within the explanatory provenance of a modified Darwinian dynamic, or are they outside its descriptive ambit and, therefore, a challenge to its whole scientific status?

Law is one of those human processes. At bottom, law is a collective human endeavour to cope with and control the world around them. Indeed, law is an artifact that, like morality and psychology, seeks to check as much as adapt to the environmental forces and natural tendencies that comprise its nurturing context. Accordingly, at the nexus of the intersection between evolution and law are the problematic claims for the nature of human progress and the progress of human nature. In addressing these claims, the ultra-Darwinians' ideas amount to a bold and unsettling contribution that has considerable relevance to the debate about the development and operation of the common law. Of course, the power of a good idea is to be found in its limits

[24] S. J. Gould, *Full House: The Spread of Excellence From Plato to Darwin* 216 (1996).

and caveats as well as its depth and force. In this, the application of ultra-Darwinian ideas to legal evolution is no exception. It is to a consideration of the efforts by lawyers and legal theorists to utilize Darwinian evolutionary ideas in the jurisprudential project of understanding the common law that I now turn.

Jurisprudence and Evolution

Since its first expression almost 150 years ago, Darwin's controversial thesis about biological development has been cannibalized or poached by most other disciplines. Law is no exception to this trend. Indeed, the evolutionary metaphor has always loomed over jurisprudential efforts to explicate the nature of the common law. At times, its invocation has been modest, oblique, and implicit; at other times, its usage has been much more sweeping, bold, and explicit. The most potent use of the evolutionary narrative in law has been distinctly non-Darwinian (and, not infrequently, anti-Darwinian) in thrust and ambition. *Evolution* has most often been used as a catchall term for general development and change. Insofar as this usage is entirely casual, those jurists who talk about law evolving do not analogize or seek identification with evolutionary theory in any strictly Darwinian or scientific sense. Not averse to trading off the hard currency of scientific explanation, such theorists intend to connote some aspect of systematic and directed development in their accounts of the common law.[25] However, there has also been a more Darwinian tendency in the jurisprudential literature. In taking this general approach, contemporary jurists participate in the much more expansive project of the humanities that attempts to explain the idea and history of progress through a recourse to the prestigious discourse of scientific authority. In these modernist efforts, evolutionary theory has proved to be a useful and authoritative device; its advocates claim to resolve the complex mysteries of human progress by reference to one simple formula. This is an ambitious and, if successful, truly momentous achievement in the history of jurisprudential thought.[26]

[25] See K. Stern, The Genesis and Evolution of European-American Constitutionalism: Some Comments on Fundamental Aspects, 18 *Comp. and Int. L. J. of S. A.* 187 (1985); S. M. Mead, Evolution of the "Species of Tort Liability" Created by 42 U.S.C. § 1983: Can Constitutional Tort Be Saved from Extinction?, 55 *Fordham L. Rev.* 1 (1986); and E. E. Sward, Values, Ideology, and the Evolution of the Adversary System, 64 *Indiana L. J.* 301 (1989). A particular favorite is L. J. Dhooge, From Scopes to Edwards: The 60 Year Evolution of Creationism in the Public School Classroom, 22 *U. Rich. L. Rev.* 187 (1988).

[26] For a brief history of this historical division and other suggestions, see H. Hovenkamp, Evolutionary Models in Jurisprudence, 64 *Texas L. Rev.* 645 (1984); E. D. Elliot, The Evolutionary Tradition in Jurisprudence, 85 *Columbia L. Rev.* 38 (1985); and A. Watson, *The Evolution of Law* (1985).

Like individuals in many other disciplines, legal theorists were initially captivated by the seductive appeal of a Darwinian approach. Indeed, some of the American titans of the jurisprudential pantheon – Arthur Corbin, John Wigmore, and Oliver Wendell Holmes, Jr. – looked to Darwin's ideas to explain the gradual development of the common law over time. For instance, Holmes talked about how law evolves in line with the "felt necessities of the time" in much the same way as evolution adapts existing biological structures to different uses in different time periods. Drawing on the work of Savigny and Maine, he saw that the rudimentary ideas of primitive legal systems were transformed over time into the complex features of modern legal systems by a process in which the "struggle for life among competing ideas" led to "an ultimate victory and survival of the strongest":

> It is like the niggardly uninventiveness of nature in its other manifestations, with its few smells or colours or types, its short list of elements, working along in the same slow way from compound to compound until the dramatic impressiveness of the most intricate compositions, which we call organic life, makes them seem different in kind from the elements out of which they are made, when set opposite to them in direct contrast.[27]

The most interesting feature of these late-nineteenth-century ideas is the location of *agency* in this evolutionary analogy. Attempting to marry change and development with some unitary coherence and unchanging quality, the tendency was, if only rhetorically, to use descriptive terms that slip too easily between the passive and the active or even between descriptive and prescriptive. Indeed, some contemporary scholars have continued this unfortunate tradition by effecting such a merging of perspectives.

After a considerable fallow period in which evolutionary accounts fell out of intellectual fashion, there has been a revival of efforts in the past few decades to utilize evolutionary theory to illuminate legal and jurisprudential problems. These modern efforts have been much bolder, more explicit, and more sophisticated. Contributing to a tendency in the humanities generally, modern jurists have now begun to extend this scientific theory not only to explain the past of the common law but also to analyze its present dynamic and predict future direction. Inspired by the evolutionary insight, jurists, through such jurisprudential efforts, have taken their self-defined responsibility to be the sustained attempt to delve a little deeper and offer

[27] O. W. Holmes, Law in Science and Science in Law, 12 *Harv. L. Rev.* 443 at 449 and 446–47 (1899). See also J. Wigmore, Planetary Theory of the Law's Evolution in 3 *Evolution of Law: Selected Readings on the Origin and Development of Legal Institutions* 163 at 531 (A. Kocourek and J. H. Wigmore eds. 1915–18).

a more compelling and defensible account of how this common law process actually works. Their basic task has been divided into three components – to offer a narrative that explains the basic legal material being described, to identify a direction or purpose to that narrative, and to elucidate a mechanism by which changes or developments in the narrative occur. While some accounts only focus on a couple of these components, a few seek to provide an integrated theory that claims to tie all three together by way of a simple logic or algorithm. This reliance on evolutionary narratives ranges from extended analogies to full-blown homologies. Viewed collectively as a series of complex narratives describing the development of law, morality, social systems, and biological explanations of behavior, they seek to fuse the prestigious cache of scientific explanation with the normative framework, imputed or asserted, of legal systems. There are three main tendencies:

> The first suggests that law develops through gradual and slow incremental change in much the same way that organisms change in the natural world. The historical development of particular legal doctrines are explicated in such a way as to reveal the striking analogy with organisms' experience in grappling with the demands of their environmental situation. No explicit claim is made that there is an actual as opposed to metaphorical connection between law and evolutionary theory.[28]

> The second uses so-called complexity theory to emphasize the "sustainability" of legal ideas or rules in given contexts. Emphasizing that law and context are mutually determinative, it claims to explain legal development through mathematical modeling, not as compared with it. While it offers a more nuanced account of systemic adaption and fitness, it draws directly on the work of the ultra-Darwinians. Thus, it stands somewhere between analogy and homology.[29]

> The third offers an autopoeitic theory of law as an organism-like entity that adapts, transforms and stabilises itself from its own resources in response to changes in its broader environment. Pointing up the

---

[28] See R. Clark, The Interdisciplinary Study of Legal Evolution, 90 *Yale L. J.* 1238 (1981); M. B. W. Sinclair, The Use of Evolutionary Theory in Law, 64 *U. Detroit L. Rev.* 451 (1987); and W. H. Rodgers, Where Environmental Law and Biology Meet: Of Panda's Thumbs, Statutory Sleepers, and Effective Law, 65 *U. Colo. L. Rev.* 25 (1994).

[29] See C. Fried, The Evolution of Legal Concepts: The Mimetic Perspective, 39 *Jurimetrics* 291 at 304–07 (1999); J. B. Ruhl, Fitness of Law: Using Complexity Theory to Describe the Evolution of Law and Society and Its Practical Meaning for Democracy, 49 *Vand. L. Rev.* 1408 at 1419–37 (1996); and J. Balkin, *Cultural Software: A Theory of Ideology* (1998).

complex dynamics of legal systems, it attempts to explain legal development as a self-validating process of reflexivity.[30]

There is an increasing sophistication in the analogies or indeed the modeling used in these evolutionary paradigms. This includes attempts to purge from these models any sort of purpose or directedness and to reframe that characterization in terms of stochastic models, including scientific terms such as *exogenous* and *endogenous factors, equilibria, variability, dynamics,* and the like. Nevertheless, whereas some go on to claim some nature to law and others merely assert that such analogies are good heuristic devices by which we might understand change and development in law, they all claim to rely on some notion of Darwinian evolution. However, each theorist cannot seem to avoid falling into the same trap that Darwin was assiduous to avoid – turning the descriptive power of the evolutionary insight into a platform for prescriptive efforts at reform or redirection. For example, in an otherwise enlightening and rigorous account of corporate law, Robert Clark is not content to identify contingent patterns in the law but seems compelled to attribute them to law's universal nature; his drift from descriptive analysis to prescriptive proposal is almost seamless.[31] Moreover, these legal Darwinians seem unable to keep the notions of evolution and progress separate; they not only see change everywhere but also treat progress as something that is almost inevitable. Indeed, although many of these scholars warn against the pitfalls of a Panglossian mentality in which it is considered that 'this is the best of all possible worlds' and 'everything that happens in it is for the best', they still manage to put a wonderfully positive and normative gloss on law's development. In so doing, they begin to desert the one commitment that seems to divide the Creationist Soapy Sams from the Darwinian bulldogs – that there is no redemptive or miraculous force that is orchestrating or driving the world forward in some particular direction and to some pre-assigned destination. Looked at from a traditional Darwinian standpoint, the Legal Creationists and the neo-Darwinians are simply flip sides of the same coin: They both trade in the same moral currency and barter in the same marketplace, albeit with different styles and ambitions.

These are big and sweeping claims, and they have to be substantiated. Consequently, instead of ranging broadly and loosely over the whole of the

---

[30] See N. Luhmann, *A Sociological Theory of Law* (2nd ed. 1985); G. Teubner, *Law as Autopoietic System* (1993); and A. Jacobson, Autopoietic Law: The New Science of Niklas Luhmann, 87 *Mich L. Rev.* 1647 (1989).

[31] See R. Clark, supra, note 28. For a decisive critique, see D. Kennedy, Cost-Reduction Theory as Legitimation, 90 *Yale L. J.* 1275 (1981).

evolutionary terrain, I concentrate in this chapter on one particular and fundamental argument. Putting aside the more overtly Creationist and Social Darwinian themes of much contemporary jurisprudence until later, I analyze the extent to which these neo-Darwinian perspectives on law do or can satisfy the basic requirements of any account that claims to be Darwinian as opposed to Darwinistic in form and content. Fortunately or unfortunately, their project cannot be sustained. Despite its obvious academic allure and apparent intellectual pedigree, evolutionary theory has little to offer traditional efforts to understand the development and direction of the common law. *If* (and even this must remain a moot point) Darwin's basic insights – contingent development, indeterminate content, nonessentialist analysis, local predictability, and universal indifference – have anything to tell lawyers and jurists, it is that evolutionary development is a corrosive idea that does more to undercut the grand explanatory ambitions of mainstream jurisprudence than to ground or achieve them. Darwin's central message was to warn against any inclination toward explanations that turn scientific method into moral or political philosophy. He was diligent in his efforts not only to avoid crude reductionism but also to resist turning evolution to evangelical effect; "the wonder indeed is, on the theory of natural selection, that more cases of the want of absolute perfection have not been detected."[32] If this has been a hard lesson for biologists and scientists, it has been a near impossible one for lawyers and jurists to learn and accept.

After Darwin

It has often been observed that it is a dangerous maneuver to attempt the crossing of a canyon in two leaps. As sage and obvious as this advice is, it has been ignored by most jurists who seek to offer a evolutionary account of legal development. Indeed, full of scientific bravado, they have actually sought to cross the gaping chasm of jurisprudential exposition in three distinct leaps; audacity is no substitute for common sense. In mounting a convincing case for *why* and *how* the common law develops and changes in line with an evolutionary dynamic, jurists must overcome the same hurdles

[32] *Origin*, supra, note 11 at 236. See S. J. Gould, *The Panda's Thumb: More Reflections in Natural History* (1980), and S. J. Gould, *Hens' Teeth and Horses' Toes: Further Reflections in Natural History* (1983). Although he reaches some formalistic conclusions about law, Lawrence Tribe's cautions are worth noting on the benefits and pitfalls of utilizing science to understand law. See L. Tribe, The Curvature of Constitutional Space: What Lawyers Can Learn from Modern Physics, 103 *Harv. L. Rev.* 1 (1989) and Seven Deadly Sins of Straining the Constitution Through a Pseudo-Scientific Sieve, 36 *Hastings L. J.* 155 (1984).

as their biological counterparts – they must be able to provide theories of variation (i.e., the mechanism by which slightly different and potentially new organisms are created), selection (i.e., the process by which a choice is made as to which of the different candidates so generated are favored and which are discarded), and transmission (i.e., the method by which the relevant characteristics of the successful organisms are passed on to succeeding generations). In the physical sciences, there is substantial agreement on the variation and transmission theories. However, as I have tried to demonstrate, there is considerable disagreement over the selection process, at least as it applies to human behavior. Some simply insist that natural selection is tantamount to being the exclusive process for both organic and behavioral changes. Others maintain that, while it is a dominant process, it is by no means the exclusive one because natural selection is also affected by statistical accidents, environmental devastation, structural limits to organisms, long-term drift, and blind chance. However, notwithstanding these disagreements, there exists a core set of shared beliefs about the basic operation of the evolutionary dynamic. Before showing how this plays out in the legal world of human behavior, I want to present a simple and stylized example of evolution in the natural world.

A black-furred animal lives in a fairly temperate climate in a geographical area with abundant shelter and sustenance. Although it does have certain predators, it has become reasonably well suited to its environmental circumstances; it flourishes. However, over time, the climate begins to change; the weather becomes colder, shelter and sustenance are reduced, and there is a vastly increased amount of snowfall, which remains for most of the year. Less camouflaged and more exposed to its predators, the animal is no longer so well suited to its environment, and reproductive success is diminished. It would clearly be of assistance to the animal if it became better adapted to its changed environment. In particular, a lighter shade of fur would be beneficial so that it would be less conspicuous in the snowy conditions. However, the animal cannot plan or will such a beneficial change; it is simply not possible for an animal to change its own organic structure as best suits its present environmental situation. Nevertheless, all is not lost; animals do change over time, but in an entirely unplanned and unpredictable way. Because no animal reproduces in perfectly clonelike fashion, different mutations of the black-furred animal will be constantly produced. Some might well be lighter furred than others. Those that are will likely be favored in the reproductive cycle and those that are not will likely perish; the light-fur genes will pass on to offspring in greater numbers than darker-fur ones. None of this is predictable as there may be no mutations that produce lighter fur and so, all other things being equal, the brown-furred animal might become extinct, like almost 99 percent of all species that have ever existed. Mutation is a chance process that has no sense of the needs of an organism's situation and no ear for its adaptive demands: "adaptations are shaped by selection, not by mutation."[33]

Assuming that the animal evolves into a white-furred species, it might become well suited to its environment and begin to flourish again. However, imagine that over time the climate begins to change and, instead of remaining cold and snowy, reverts to a more temperate climate. The white-furred animal might now be ill suited to its environmental conditions and will face different challenges to its thriving or even survival. Again, unable to make any planned or desired changes to its genetic composition, its fate will be left to the hazards of mutation and selection. It might well be that some changes (e.g., keener nose to detect food under the snow) that had occurred as adaptations to different past conditions prove to be particularly useful in dealing with the newly changed climatic conditions. Or it might be that some past changes (e.g., extra layers of fat) prove to be doubly prohibitive in adapting to the new temperate conditions. Either way, the lot of the animal will be in the unreliable hands of the evolutionary dynamic. In particular, mindful of how the Darwinian process works, it will be seen to be fatuous to talk of the black- or white-furred animal's becoming a better or worse version of some ideal or essential form of itself; the best form an animal can be is the one that best suits it to the local environment. As that environment changes, so will the animal's optimal form. Moreover, while the animal may have some impact on its surrounding environment, it will be the environment that drives the evolutionary process and determines what is and what is not a successful mutation or improvement in any particular organism. Accordingly, from a Darwinian perspective, nature is based on nothing grander than individual organisms struggling against local conditions to maximize their own reproductive success; there is no standing accorded to claims about natural harmony or progressive refinement. Evolution is a hit-and-miss affair in which survival goes to the situationally lucky rather than the intrinsically worthy.

Leaving aside the thorny problem of human behavior for a moment, this account of evolutionary change should be largely uncontroversial. However, its recounting should set off the alarm bells for any jurist who inquires into whether such a dynamic is at work in the legal world. To begin with, reproductive success is not the be-all and end-all of legal development and

---

[33] G. Dover, supra, note 11 at 90.

mutations are not the stuff of pure chance. It is insufficient to simply show that law changes in response to environmental conditions or that there are, as in the natural world, some presently useless patches that were once useful structures (e.g., the postal rules in contracts) and some very useful patches that arose as incidental or unintended effects of an earlier adaptive change (e.g., the use of "passing off" tort to regulate Internet domain squatting). Such demonstrations are consistent with an evolutionary dynamic, but they are also equally consistent with a whole range of competing causal and non-Darwinian explanations, especially a Creationist version of adaptation by design. Moreover, while it is true that law responds to changes in its environmental conditions, it sometimes does not change at all; it can ignore environmental pressures or make a positive decision to hold fast in the hope that the present changes are temporary and exceptional. Furthermore, if law does decide to change, the direction in which it changes and the options available to it are often determined by forces that are internal to the law. Whereas biological transformation is by necessity a step-by-step process in which certain structural constraints channel certain changes over time, legal change can be rapid and revolutionary; legal bears can become legal lambs almost overnight. Whatever else law can or cannot do, it is not entirely at the hands of its environmental fate. The participants in the legal system can both reflect on their predicament and make changes intended to improve the situation; there is some crude Lamarckian dynamic at work in law in that it is labile and directional. It is possible to plan for change in different ways and to anticipate different conditions; "a biological system is limited to 'local maximizing,' decision making on the basis of immediately adjacent data only..., [whereas], by contrast, humans can base decisions on data distant in time and space, real or projected; in the jargon, this is 'global maximizing.'"[34] Not that this means that law is entirely orchestrated by such internal pressures and reflective actions, but it does signify that any account of common law development that does not hold a place for conscious and planned action is severely wanting.

In light of these debilitating flaws in efforts to defend an evolutionary account of the common law, it hardly seems necessary to add that human elements of will, design, and purpose (which, of course, some ultra-Darwinians use evolutionary theories to support) are neither knowable entirely through experiment nor evident from the explanatory sense of the Darwinian narrative. Since Darwin's day and the first wave of social Darwinianism, this

---

[34] Sinclair, Evolution in Law: Second Thoughts, 71 *U. Det. Mercy L. Rev.* 31 at 46 (1993). For a fuller discussion of the Lamarckian element in legal change, see infra chap. 8.

unknowable component has been challenged or resisted in different ways by the claims of sociobiology, law and biology, and so on. In terms of the actual cause of change in individuals and species, the prevailing doctrine in evolutionary biology is clearly committed to the view that random change or chance errors in replication at the genetic level actually cause variation in individuals. This concept of change is at odds with most uses of the evolutionary metaphor in law and works quite against the traditional directed idea of an evolutionary narrative. As such, it would seem that the exact correspondence of law and biology is very difficult to support. Law does not have species, nor does change occur independently of human endeavor. It is surely the case that human behavior is not *directly* subject to the theory of evolution or its explanatory power, no matter at what level evolution operates. The only plausible comparison between law and biology is in terms of relative analogy. Because humans are perhaps the only beings that have been able to transform their own environment so radically, it is not easy to claim that such behavior is selected in the classical narrative sense so that there is a sense of directed change. Such behavioral patterns are better seen as integral parts of a more complex interplay between humanity and its environment. If law is a social construct and human behavior is transformative of its context, there is a very different dynamic at work from that suggested by the traditional evolutionary metaphor. Moreover, as well as its troublesome naturalistic tendencies (i.e., explanatory power converts to predictive authority) and deterministic tendencies (i.e., genetic or behavioral traits are predetermined), the evolutionary narrative also works equally badly when viewed from inside as opposed to outside law – it reduces law's ethical dimension to a bald and barren description. This is simply another way of attempting to further the illusion that law is separate from politics and to deny the force of the critical claim that 'law is politics'.

Efforts to overcome some of these debilitating problems have concentrated on developing a parallel and complementary process to Darwinian accounts of biological change that can explain cultural development. For instance, Jack Balkin has sought to provide an ultra-Darwinian account of how shared understandings in law grow and spread from one generation to another. Drawing on the work of Dawkins and Dennett, he picks up on an understanding of natural selection as a neutral, algorithmic process, applicable to an extremely wide range of phenomena and capable of achieving immense feats by slow accumulation over large extents of time and space. Balkin contends that, while basic physiological information is contained in genes and is passed down through reproduction to new generations, there are also so-called memes that play a similar function to genes in facilitating the transmission of abstract ideas through cultural exchange over time. He argues that all mental and cultural life, including law, is adequately explainable by a mechanical Darwinian process of natural selection in which genes and memes struggle for survival. Seeking to fuse concepts of function in biology and meaning in philosophy, the theory utilizes adaptionism as a fertile source of both biological and social explanations. Rejecting the notion of any Panglossian tendency at work, Balkin asserts that this evolutionary process is less Darwinian than Lamarckian in that adaptation and variation occur in direct response to the environment rather than as part of a contest between random variations to fit better the environment.[35] In short, he offers a less assertive form of autopoeitic development using mimetic units. However, in attempting to provide a scientific basis for cultural evolution, Balkin only manages to offer a process that is unrealistically clinical and sterile in its political content. His theory of ideology is all so neutral and comforting in presenting the interaction between people and their social environment as relatively benign and harmless. Moreover, the alleged analytical strength of this kind of ultra-Darwinian theorizing runs out at the very point at which it might be thought to be most needed; the Panglossian tendency cannot be so easily cabined or contained.

Like all the other homological approaches, this ultra-Darwinian one bases much of its analysis on large numbers of instances occurring either in large numbers over short periods of time or in sequenced instances observed over longer periods of time. There are a couple of methodological objections to these explanations of change and development when they are applied to law. The first is a limitation of analogy. In open systems, it is impossible to recall or draw all instances of a hypothesis into its proof; there must be some selectivity, and this entails criteria or principles that are external to the system. However, if the model seeks to explain all elements by this hypothesis, it must make claims to be inclusive of all instances, which is where, in an open system, the narrative technique of so-called deselection operates.[36] Consequently, whether selecting or deselecting material, the need for some external referent is operationally required but is conceptually illegitimate.

A second difficulty is with the homologies of law and biology that involve statistical analysis. Any debate about accounts of transformation or change

---

[35] J. Balkin, supra, note 29. For a similar account of legal evolution in Lamarckian as opposed to Darwinian terms, see M. Roe, Chaos and Evolution in Law and Economics, 109 *Harv. L. Rev.* 641 at 665 (1996) ("Genes are Darwinian, but civilization is Lamarckian"). On Dawkins and Dennett, see supra, pp. 36–42.

[36] For an account of the replacement of determinism with probability, see L. Kruger, *The Probabilistic Revolution* (1987).

implied by the law of large numbers soon implicates the old chestnut of freedom and necessity. At their most seductive and reductive, systems theories in both the human and natural sciences manage to elide the central questions of freedom, agency, and will: Statistical generalizations eclipse and overwhelm human initiative. In terms of law, jurists must also ask themselves when a statistical "fact" becomes reliable enough to become an unexamined assumption and to take explanatory precedence over individual acts. However, the tendency to draw a distinction between behavior (which follows statistical laws and is thereby predictable) and deeds (which are posited as anomalies to those statistical laws and are therefore unpredictable) does not withstand critical inspection. These deeds are not just meaningless anomalies but actually comprise the important site of changes or events that are the main determinants of historical development. As Hannah Arendt put it, "the application of the law of large numbers and long periods to politics or history signifies nothing less than the wilful obliteration of their very subject matter, and it is a hopeless enterprise to search for meaning or significance in history when everything that is not everyday behaviour or automatic trends has been ruled out as immaterial."[37] In short, systems approaches prove both too much and too little for their own critical good.

Even if law is understood as an adaptive process through which people mediate the always contingent, usually contested, and often contradictory demands of human living, there is no reason to think that it will have any great success. Indeed, the very criteria for assessing success will be as contingent and contested as the process itself. Whereas ultra-Darwinians are intent on demonstrating that almost all human behavior can be explained as having its roots and explanation in the biological adaptation to environmental conditions, traditional Darwinians insist that much human behavior is maladapted and as likely to be the unanticipated result of something that did have an adaptive function. In short, the world is too contingent and complex to submit to such reductionist accounts. Often, the answer to the ubiquitous question of "what is the purpose of X?" is "nothing" or "it depends"; X might have developed as a by-product of some other adaptive change and therefore might or might not turn out to be more useful and lasting than the initial adaptive change itself, depending on the particular environmental context. Similar to the biological world, the legal world has its share of maladaptation in that the good and the bad, the adaptive and the maladaptive, can be packaged in a single unit (the good–bad) that must be taken as a whole. Law is much closer to the biological scenario

[37] H. Arendt, *The Human Condition* 43–44 (1989).

of gerry-built morphology, second-best physiology, and makeshift behavior than many jurists are prepared to recognize: "The useless, the odd, the peculiar, the incongruous" are the "signs of history" that are as much part of the evolutionary narrative as any other and, if excluded or marginalized, will entirely invalidate any account.[38]

One consequence of this ought to be some recognition that there is no one or even optimal strategy for dealing with the biological or legal world that can guarantee success. In addition, the adaptionist argument is banal and verging on the Panglossian in that, if adaption explains all developments, then it explains everything and, therefore, nothing. Because everything that does happen must happen, it has no critical edge or interesting force. Furthermore, some allowance has to be made for the fact that this process of adaption does not take place on a one-way street – there is two-way traffic. While law offers solutions to environmental problems, it also has an impact on that environment, thereby altering to it create a fresh set of problems to be resolved. This process is never ending. In the Darwinian vocabulary, adaptation is a process of becoming rather than a state of being because any reliance on the notion of perfect optimality would undercut the constant dynamism at work in nature and pave the way for the resurgence of Creationist thinking.

However, a commitment to resist the ambitious claims of the ultra-Darwinian theorists does not mean that a Darwinian explanation has no role to play in explaining and understanding legal development. To challenge cultural determinism is not to align oneself with the genetic determinists, and to reject the claims of sociobiologists is not to subscribe to a Creationist creed. Too often, what begin as correctives to the excesses of existing theories become full-blown and equally excessive alternative theories. It is surely right to insist, as Dworkin has, that "moral reflection . . . is as much a part of human nature as anything else."[39] However, to deny the universalistic and deterministic claims of a pseudoscientific approach to law and adjudication is not equivalent to taking the position that moral reflection, with its emphasis on philosophical analysis and justification, is determinative or comprehensive in its description of law. Even if judges did all engage in such exclusively heady pursuits, there is no reason to think that the resulting collective abstraction would be congruent or coherent. Nor would such a

---

[38] S. J. Gould, *Panda's Thumb*, supra, note 32 at 128 and 29 (1980). See also *Alas, Poor Darwin: Arguments Against Evolutionary Psychology* (H. Rose and S. Rose eds. 2000). For a powerful critique of efforts to justify existing legal arrangements as natural, even inevitable, products of evolution, see R. Gordon, Critical Legal Histories, 36 *Stan. L. Rev.* 57 (1984).

[39] R. Dworkin, Darwin's New Bulldog, 111 *Harv. L. Rev.* 1718 at 1737, footnote 76 (1999).

circumstance obviate the need for some further inquiry into the character-istics of that moral reflection and its relation to the environmental context. Indeed, the assertion that there is some presence or generation of pur-pose(s) from within the legal system itself is very problematic. Even if one assumes that law can be described as something organically distinct from other practices of political human behavior, the phenomena described (i.e., laws, doctrines, cases, etc.) are actually characterized as passive or automated entities. However, as soon as the analysis shifts to self-movement, learning, and self-reflexivity, the entity is assumed to have some form of *active* life. In theoretical terms, there has been a slippage from scene to agent and from description to purpose in which the system itself is imbued with a definite normative content. From that point on, it is all too quickly and easily presumed that uniform behavior gets treated as evidence of a unity or harmony of interests. This has manifested itself as an invisible hand in classical economics, as class interests in Marxian economics, and as norma-tive coherence in liberal jurisprudence. But, of course, ascribing a so-called harmony of interests does not do the work of explaining transformation in law without importing an operating principle of agency from outside. In fact, these systemic narratives of evolution attempt to have it both ways in their insistence that agency and context combine to produce change. The organism of law becomes depicted as something more than a passive body of conjoined phenomena, but one that is not sufficiently active or political to be an integrated part of the larger political world.

None of this need be taken as an indication that a Darwinian approach has no role to play in the jurisprudential enterprise. Darwinians are neither fatalist nor Panglossian, although some of them give a good impression of being that. At the heart of all Darwinian accounts is the notion of struggle; there is no one future determined by the past's present, but there are several possible futures that people struggle to bring about through their individ-ual and collective efforts at doing the best they can in accordance with what they think is the best. This, of course, is likely to be a haphazard, uncoordi-nated, and uneven process in which the collective effort might amount to much less than the sum of the individual parts. Moreover, evolution shows that knowledge of the principles by which evolution occurs does not mean that we are any more likely to know or calculate what will happen next by predicting future development or direction. Contrary to the expectations of many scholars in law and the humanities in general, and despite the hubristic claims of some scientists, science is more accurately thought about as being in the game of local prediction, not cosmic understanding. Rather than grope vainly toward a theory of everything for everywhere at every time, it is better to think of trying to construct a workable, but imprecise, travel schedule for getting from one place to another. Not only will we never know the exact nature of the traffic and why other travelers are going wherever they are going, but we also will expect delays and deviations because of changing and unpredictable local conditions and personal circumstances. From the users' standpoint, it is all about getting to the desired destination and working out a useful timetable, not finding something as big or as universal as the Absolute Truth about traffic, traveling, schedules or whatever.

Accordingly, the challenge for those who insist on the pertinence of Darwinian evolutionary insights for law is to include and explain the role that such moral reflection plays in human behavior and social development generally. What people do is affected by what people think they are doing. Unlike with other creatures in the rest of the natural world, humans are a species that has self-consciousness and, therefore, can reflect on the nature of its own doing. In this, lawyers are no different from other social actors. To different extents and with varying awareness, what lawyers do is affected by what it is that they think they are doing and what it is that they think they ought to be doing. Without some incorporation of that crucial element in any explanatory equation, the effort to understand judicial practice and legal development will be found wanting. However, while quantitative change will ultimately result in qualitative difference, there is no ultimate end or vision toward which change is directed; there is no perfect or ideal manifestation of humanity, society, or law. Whereas Darwin is about variation and contingency, too much contemporary jurisprudence is about convergence and purification. Insofar as the constraints on evolution are historical and environmental, behaviors only change to the extent that the local context allows or requires. As one biologist neatly captures the operation of the evolutionary dynamic, "the archaic features of life merely reveal its tortuous history, like the archaic features of human language or common law."[40] Any effort to obscure or sidestep that history will fail to capture an important dynamic in law's development. Rather than being on a preordained route to some exalted or transcendental state, the common law is simply a continuing work-in-progress that is always moving and that is always on the road to somewhere, but never getting anywhere in particular.

Conclusion

In this chapter, I have introduced the basic workings of Darwinian evolution and challenged its literal and strict application to law and legal development.

---

[40] M. Rose, *Darwin's Spectre: Evolutionary Biology in the Modern World* 81 (1998).

Any effort to respond to those strictures obliges jurists to amend their accounts of legal development. However, in so doing, it is likely that they will fall into the welcoming but suffocating embrace of either the Creationists or the Social Darwinians. Nevertheless, I have not sought to reject entirely the possible usefulness of such evolutionary work for jurisprudential study: It can be a helpful, if limited, metaphor to think about legal development. In so suggesting, I should *not* be taken to be making any claim that the common law is one thing or another. In particular, I should *not* be read as contending that the common law does or does not function and develop in line with an attenuated evolutionary logic. The most that can be said is that, insofar as evolutionary theory has anything to say about law (and it is entirely likely that it has very little to say), it undermines mainstream accounts of the common law. By that, I mean to say that treating law as if it were susceptible to an evolutionary explanation does not advance the jurisprudential cause of those who insist on claiming a certain autonomy, simplicity, systemization, and directionality to law's development. If anything, viewing law through the lens of evolutionary theory suggests that 'law is politics' and that the nature of that connection is unpredictable and contingent: Law's operation and practice simply will not conform to a reductionist and predictive algorithm. The salutary lesson of the evolution debate is that the best story is the one that weaves together lots of different threads into a quilt that is as complex and as complementary as circumstances allow; there is no one set of simple rules that can capture or explain the complexity and contingency of life. Sadly, this lesson has been ignored. Although neither offers a convincing or useful account of the common law, the Soapy Sams and the Bulldogs of the jurisprudential world have tended to dominate. It is to these distracting and confining influences that I now turn.

ᦋ 3 ᦋ

The Creationists' Persistence:
Jurisprudence and God

> We would like to think ourselves necessary, inevitable, ordained
> from all eternity. All religions, nearly all philosophies, and even
> part of science testify to the unwearying, heroic effort of mankind
> desperately denying its own contingency.[1]
>
> JACQUES MONOD

YEARS BEFORE NIETZSCHE'S APOCALYPTIC ANNOUNCEMENT THAT "GOD is dead," James Mill had confided to his more famous son that "there is no God, but this is a family secret." Nevertheless, over 100 years later (and much like Mark Twain's obituary), the announcement that *God is dead* remains as premature and as controversial today as it was then. As well as being a direct onslaught on Christianity, Nietzsche's broadside was targeted at all claims to some Absolute Truth or Authority. He maintained that the effort to fix some eternal set of values or to discover an immutable essence to mankind was not only futile but also dangerous. While the effects of that chilling obituary are felt everywhere and in every way across academe, there is still massive resistance to its challenge. This is particularly true in the world of jurists and jurisprudence. Indeed, a reader of much contemporary legal scholarship and jurisprudence could be forgiven for thinking that there is still a conspiracy of silence within the Law and Legal Theory family. Insofar as the announcement was intended to disabuse belief in a standard of instruction or guidance in regulation of human conduct that could be drawn from outside humanity, it remains a rather dirty family secret. While lawyers and jurists profess an entirely secular undertaking and concede that law is essentially a human artifact, there is still a deep-seated reliance on the idea that it might be possible to discern some superhuman or suprahuman force,

---

[1] Jacques Monod, *Chance and Necessity* 44 (1971).

however flawed or incomplete, at work in law's doings and development. Indeed, dreams of hubris still fire the jurisprudential imagination in the hope that lawyerliness might actually become next to or on par with godliness. Despite protestations to the contrary, contemporary lawyers and legal theorists have fulfilled Nietzsche's subsequent prediction that "given the way of men, there may still be caves for thousands of years in which [God's] shadow will be shown."[2] Jurisprudence is one of those enclaves where such spectral deities still roam and where its practitioners still aspire to mediate divine intimations of God's design. Rather than treat God's death as an opportunity to seize the democratic initiative, some philosophers and jurists have taken it as an invitation to turn themselves into gods.

Whether legal academics accept or appreciate it, legal scholarship is still in thrall to a daunting series of spectral influences that hold great sway over both the ambition and achievement of its most celebrated practitioners. In an important sense, jurisprudence – put simply, those efforts to step back from the actual practice and operation of law in order to make some general sense of it all – is where such ghostly tendencies are most frequently sighted, often invoked, and occasionally exorcised. Jurists strive to reduce law's sprawling and contingent complexities to a simple and singular sense of order and coherence. If it is far too gauche for jurists to contend that God has a visible hand in this process, they are unable to resist the quasi-divinistic urge, as Holmes put it, to "catch an echo of the infinite, a glimpse of its unfathomable process, a hint of the universal law."[3] There is something persistently mystical and almost cabalistic about jurists' continuing belief that there is some deep, subtle, and organizing force at work in the common law's development. Within this philosophical account, law always manages to be more than the historical heap of its human-made parts; it has a qualitative force that transcends its quantitative mass. Judges and jurists are portrayed as being involved in the almost theological task of illuminating the transcendent wonders of human-made law with the intellectual lightning of jurisprudential insight. This influence is as strong and baneful today as it ever was. Although the jurists phrase their analysis in evolutionary terms, the link to Soapy Sam and his Creationist acolytes should be obvious: Many jurists are Creationist wolves in Evolutionist sheep's clothing. Like their religious cousins, contemporary jurists do not rely on some legal equivalent of the Genesis story to explain the common law. Instead, they see a force at work that is more detached and distant. Its presence is no

---

[2] F. Nietzsche, *The Gay Science* sec. 108 (W. Kaufmann trans. 1974).

[3] O. W. Holmes, *The Collected Papers* 202 (1920).

less profound and irreducible for that. Jurisprudence remains caught in the hold of this precious mentality from the most doctrinal of legal scholarship through to the most abstruse of legal theorizing. Nevertheless, there is likely no Coherent Truth or Objective Integrity that inheres and endures in the heavens, humanity's essential nature, or the general legal scheme of things. Furthermore, if there is, it most certainly cannot be divined from the erstwhile musings of jurists and judges across space and time. As a thoroughly human and thus flawed artifact, law is a hodgepodge of the good and the bad, the useful and the useless, the enduring and the ephemeral. If lawyers and jurists are to help society make good on itself, they must surely resist the temptation to pay homage to the dubious deities of Truth and Objectivity.

Of course, these fundamental charges are not applicable to all legal scholars. However, as rich and as vibrant as it is, the critical literature remains marginal and underlines the prevalence of the traditional model. Accordingly, in this chapter, I first outline the different forms that Creationism has taken and place Bishop Wilberforce's contribution in a more contemporary context. In the second section I examine the black-letter tradition in law and reveal its deeper theological resonances. In the third section, I concentrate on the influential writings of the leading legal Wilberforcian, Ronald Dworkin, and display their continuing attachment to the dubious virtues of abstraction and scholasticism. In the fourth section, I take something of a philosophical detour and unearth some of the problematic philosophical foundations that underlie the Creationist project in law. Finally, I canvass the politics of essentialist theories of the common law and suggest a limited way in which rational design might retain a semblance of jurisprudential legitimacy. Like some biologists, legal theorists have not been able to give up the supernatural claim that there is some force beyond nature and themselves that is orchestrating the parochial efforts of the legal community. In conclusion, I substantiate the charge that, if you scratch many evolutionary jurists, they so often bleed a theology of miraculous design.

All Things Bright and Beautiful

Charles Darwin went to Christ's College at Cambridge University in 1827. He stayed in the same rooms that the former student and fellow, William Paley, had fifty years before. Although there is no reason to think that this was more than a matter of curious coincidence, the lives of the two men share a certain perverse synchronicity. In completing his degree, the young Darwin was obliged to study Paley's extensive writings. A theological scholar of some repute, Paley had been an eloquent proponent of the so-called argument-by-design rejection of evolution. Paley's central contention was that the sheer complexity of biological organisms, especially humans, defied explanation as being the result of chance evolution rather than deliberate design. He asked his readers to suppose that, in crossing a heath, they had come across a stone. If asked how the stone came to be there, a reasonable answer might be that it had been there forever. However, if the reader had come across a watch, a similar answer would be unlikely and unconvincing. Paley contended that, in the same way that the watch's integrated complexity and perfected functionality was the result of its creation by a highly intelligent designer, so the even more complex and functional properties of natural organisms must also have been created by an even higher intelligence. As it was too fantastical to imagine that such universal order and beauty could have occurred almost serendipitously across time, Paley was drawn to the seemingly inevitable conclusion that "the marks of design are too strong to be got over. Design must have a designer. That designer must have been a person. That person is God."[4] The elegant force of this simple claim attracted much support at the time and still manages to capture many antievolutionists' attention. Indeed, so taken was Darwin by Paley's work that he spent much of his life demonstrating why Paley's claims were false and that even the most complex of biological creatures or designs required no designing hand or orchestrating intent. Nevertheless, Paley's design thesis remains attractive to today's Creationists and others. In the continuing evolutionary quarrel, the guises may have changed and the arguments might be more scientifically sophisticated, but the antievolutionists' and Creationists' essential moves remain much the same as in Soapy Sam's days.

There is a strong and vocal minority of protagonists who offer a tantalizing blend of science and cryptotheology. Explicitly relying on the Victorian notion of providential design, they contend that the Earth's unique fitness for carbon-based life generally and human beings particularly is not the result of contingent or coincidental circumstances; it is the designed and inevitable outcome of a cosmic plan. It is accepted that all the cosmic activity over the billions of years from primeval swamps to postmodern conurbations is specifically directed and designed to produce the kind of intelligent life that presently exists, namely *Homo sapiens*. In maintaining that life's being is also part of a design for life's becoming, it is a bold and clever thesis that emphasizes the seamless, harmonious, and teleological basis of all phenomena's development and sophistication in line with a series of natural laws; "science

---

[4] W. Paley, *Natural Theology* 473 (1970); this is a reprint of W. Paley, *Natural Theology: Or, Evidences of the Existence and Attributes of the Deity, Collected from the Appearances of Nature* (1802).

has revealed a universe stamped in every corner, riven in every detail, with an overwhelmingly and all-pervasive biocentric and anthropocentric design."[5] However, these offerings put forward little scientific support for such radical conclusion; their accounts are based as much on awe as argument and tend to rely on faith as much as analysis. Indeed, this modern reworking of old ideas makes some colossal and unsubstantiated leaps from "is" to "ought" and from appearance to reality. While masquerading as cutting-edge scientists, these latter-days Paleys and Wilberforces are committed to transforming evolutionary biology from a purely historical study to a logic-based system and, in the process, to defending the inevitable and moral force of the status quo – it is more akin to political ideology than scientific inquiry. Evolutionary biology can only help fix where life has been, not where it is going: Humanity "does not evolve *toward* anything, but only *away* from something."[6]

In contrast, the Creationists flip-flop between a scientific gambit and a religious strategy as best fits their present needs or predicament; they challenge the scientific basis of Darwinian evolution or claim that it is no less a religion than a fundamentalist Protestantism. They argue that Darwinianism is unsubstantiated on the facts, ill conceived as scientific method, and mischievously biased. Moreover, mindful that available evidence of events over billions of years is limited and impressionistic, they insist that their own approach is as plausible as any other and that ultimately Darwinians fall back on intellectual faith as much as demonstrable proof. Concentrated mainly in the Unites States, there is still a huge number of people who believe in a Genesis-inspired account of nature's origins – "And the Lord God formed man of the dust of the ground, and breathed into his nostrils the breath of life, and man became a living soul" – in which the earth and its current life forms were created by God at some time much more recent (usually Archbishop of Armagh James Ussher's computation of October 23, 4004 BC) than the 4.5 billion years claimed by scientists.[7] At their most

5 M. Denton, *Nature's Destiny: How the Laws of Biology Reveal Purpose in the Universe* 380 (1998). See also M. Behe, *Darwin's Black Box: The Biochemical Challenge to Evolution* (1996); P. Davies, *The Cosmic Blueprint* 203 (1987) ("The impression of design is overwhelming"); S. Kauffman, *At Home in the Universe* 112 (1995) ("ultimately, in our creation myth, we are expected after all"); and B. Goodwin, *How the Leopard Changed Its Spots* 168 (1995).

6 J. Horgan, *The End of Science: Facing the Limits of Knowledge in the Twilight of the Scientific Age* 44 (1997).

7 The public face of Creationism is seen in the battle over the educational curriculum in legislative and constitutional arenas; see E. Larson, *Evolution: The Remarkable History of a Scientific Theory* 199–218 and 245–63 (2004). For critical accounts of the history of the Creationist stance, see R. T. Pennock, *Tower of Babel: The Evidence Against the New Creationism*

confident, they propose that there is an abstract permanence to all Creation and that species were made for a preordained purpose, with humans standing at the head of a divine chain of being; there may have been some minor variations through microevolution but no Darwinian-style macroevolution. At their more conciliatory, the Creationists adopt a less revelatory and more analytical demeanor. Exploiting gaps and uncertainties in the fossil record, they suggest that God is to be found in the details of so-called intelligent design that characterize evolution and whose purpose and direction are divine but unknowable. When presented in such a modest form, the Creationist argument tends to hover at the very edge of theology and, with God taking on a decidedly human guise, to merge with the more ambitious efforts of secular scientists who talk only of design, not deities.

The polarized framing of the debate leaves little room for those who wish to accept evolution entirely and still hold onto a religious faith. Indeed, Darwin himself can be understood in such terms. While his work might imply a thoroughgoing rejection of any form of divine presence or godly involvement, he avoided taking any definitive stance. Along with his Victorian values, Darwin's love of his devout wife, Emma, prevented him from vigorously pursuing the idea that there was no God.[8] While he had lost his own faith on the death of his young daughter, he constantly tried to reconcile faith and science or, at least, not to render the two entirely incompatible. Of course, some would say that this effort to combine evolution and God was not religion at all; it is as much a part of the problem as anything else. Indeed, this is exactly what Phillip Johnson (who is incidentally a law professor) asserts: "The acceptance of naturalistic assumptions in science by Christian and secular intellectuals alike has moved God steadily into some remote never-never land ('before the Big Bang') or even out of reality altogether."[9] While most of his antievolutionist defense of Creationism is fairly standard

---

(1999); E. Larson, *Summer for the Gods: The Scopes Trial and America's Continuing Debate Over Science and Religion* (1997); and N. Eldredge, *The Triumph of Evolution: And the Failure of Creationism* (2000). To believe in God is not necessarily to believe in Creationism; most organized religions do not. See Pope John Paul II, *Address to the Pontifical Academy of Sciences* (1996).

[8] See generally N. Gillespie, *Charles Darwin and the Problem of Creation* (1979) and M. Ruse, *Mystery of Mysteries: Is Evolution a Social Construction?* (1999). In typically humble fashion, Darwin wanted to be buried in the modest surrounds of the local Down churchyard. However, after a hasty campaign by supporters and politicians after his death in April 1882 and with Emma's approval, it was agreed that Darwin should be buried in Westminster Abbey next to Isaac Newton. This is surely an ironic tribute to the supposed scourge of the Anglican establishment. Did Soapy Sam turn in his grave?

[9] See P. Johnson, *Reason in the Balance* 111 (1995). See also *Darwin on Trial* (1991). Another high-profile lawyer who takes an explicitly antievolutionary stance is R. Bork, *Slouching Toward Gomorrah: Modern Liberalism and American Decline* 294–95 (1997).

fare and makes the predictable critical moves about speciation, fossil gaps, and bewildering complexity, he does add a more subtle but no less flawed argument to the Creationist canon. A devout Christian and as much against Paleyian design theory as any Darwinian devotee, Johnson maintains that, as there is an all-knowing and all-caring God who is involved in all the personal details of daily living, science should be interested in that fact if it claims to be concerned with providing a complete account of the physical world, including its basic properties and their causal relations. In a relatively sophisticated account, he contends that science is premised on a "philosophical naturalism" that only allows for natural explanations and, therefore, is fundamentally atheistic. This is said to be antithetical to science's claim that it is agnostic on such matters as the existence of God and the nature of good and evil. Because his is an argument based on faith, particularly the unquestioned authority of the biblical text and the indisputable existence of God, Johnson and other like-minded Creationists are unlikely to be vanquished by rational argument or scientific proof. Theirs is a belief based on religious faith, which, by definition, is not susceptible to logical debunking; it assumes exactly that which is contested and to be proved – the existence of a supreme or supervising God.

In so many ways, the good Bishop would still have felt relatively at home in the contemporary debate. Samuel Wilberforce was a man in and a child of the Victorian Age. Born in 1805 to the renowned and influential antislavery politician, William Wilberforce, he was a precocious talent. Having earned a first class in mathematics and a second class in classics at Oxford, he entered the clergy and was ordained as a Church of England vicar in 1829. By the time of the Oxford debate in 1870, he had matured into a leading religious and intellectual figure of the day, having been Bishop of Oxford for twenty-five years. During his tenure, Wilberforce made it his professional and personal mission to unify the fracturing church and head off the increasing threat of the Catholic Church. Gifted with a rare intellectual eloquence and an enviable popular charm, Wilberforce managed to sermonize the laity into improved observance and to become the very model of the hard-working churchman. However, his achievements were not simply those of the consummate leader and charismatic organizer; he possessed a genuine religious devotion and believed to the end of his life in 1873 that, despite desertions by his family to Catholicism, God had not forsaken him in his true Anglican faith. His involvement in the Oxford debate was typical. In his lifelong struggle to secure the Church of England's place and values in the burgeoning British world, he saw the exchange with the diligent Huxley as simply one more battle to be won in a many-sided war. For Wilberforce, the significance of Darwin's thesis itself was relatively marginal.

Indeed, while the Oxford debate piqued Wilberforce's intellectual curiosity, it is hardly mentioned in the various biographies of him. For instance, Standish Meacham framed Wilberforce's contribution to the debate in terms of the broader tension between the established church and contemporary science:

> It would be wrong, he insisted to argue the truth or falsehood of the theory on religious grounds. But this does not make it the less important to point out on scientific grounds scientific errors, when those errors tend to limit God's glory in creation, or to gainsay the revealed relations of that creation to Himself. . . . Far more distressing, [Darwin] had suggested that man himself was only a part of this long evolutionary chain, thereby reducing him to the level of a beast. Free will, reason, redemption, the Eternal Spirit, all these attributes a Christian must attach to man's nature if he is to believe and to partake in God's glorious plan for his salvation – all are equally and utterly irreconcilable with the degrading notion of a brute origin of him who was created in the image of God and redeemed by the eternal Son, assuring to Himself His nature. Evolution and natural selection took from God his omnipotence and from man those divine attributes God had willed him. Far from reflecting God's design, nature moved at the behest of chance; random accident denied divine purpose.[10]

In taking such a stance, Wilberforce was by no means out on a limb. He was taking a stand that had not only a proven heritage in religious circles but also considerable support in the scientific community. He had no sympathy for a literalist account of Genesis in which creation is seen as a swift and complete six-day task by an all-doing Creator. Echoing the powerful ideas of William Paley, the Bishop defends the "the previous existence of an intelligent Designer" who, being "wise . . . and all-powerful," put into effect "the highest conceivable rule of regularity and order," which resulted in "regular progression from the less to the more highly organised."[11] In this respect, Wilberforce's views were more sophisticated and informed than much of the so-called Creationist lobby today. He recognized the cogent force of much

---

[10] S. Meacham, *Lord Bishop: The Life of Samuel Wilberforce, 1805–1873* 213–14 (1970).

[11] S. Wilberforce, *Sermons Preached on Various Occasions* 184, 188, and 189 (1877). There is a strong jurisprudential tradition that insists that the common law is rooted in Christian theism. See J. Wu, *Fountain of Justice* 64–65 (1955), and P. Miller, *The Life of the Mind in America* 123–24 (1966). While this claim has some obvious historical plausibility, there is no necessary or persisting philosophical force to it.

scientific work in establishing the evolution of the existing world over deep geological time, but he refused to believe that this had occurred without God's intention and to his greater glory. Indeed, although Wilberforce's views are often caricatured as quaintly Victorian in their style and provenance, their general force is still a very powerful current in contemporary debate almost 150 years later. If Wilberforce were to be reincarnated, he would likely be surprised (and slightly pleased) by the fact that the scientific wave has not submerged all beneath it. The Creationist gambit remains a strong and popular one, particularly in the United States. Indeed, as I demonstrate next, it is the intellectual heirs to Paley and Wilberforce that still manage to dominate contemporary jurisprudence. Such jurists tend to be weak Creationists, in that they do not posit a divine purpose but instead identify purposes in the nature of legal things themselves – law becomes more than an accumulation of individual human actions and its coordination and coherence over time is sustained by some supernatural or superhuman force.

Paint It Black

Much legal scholarship continues to operate within the cramping and pervasive spirit of a 'black-letter' mentality. By this, I mean the tendency of lawyers to focus almost exclusively on formal material in a way that rarely gets beyond a taxonomic stock taking. Originally a typographical term, 'black-letter law' was used to refer to rudimentary principles that were printed in boldface type in traditional law texts.[12] However, it has come to designate an approach to law that claims to concentrate on narrow statements of what the law is and eschews resort to any extradoctrinal considerations of policy or context: The textual formulation of the law is regnant and is treated as a world unto itself. In scholarly terms, the limited aim of black-letterism is to identify, analyze, organize, and synthesize extant rules into a coherent and integrated whole; there is much talk of As and Bs in illustrative exegesis with almost no reference to political context or social identity. Fostering jurisprudence as an inward-looking and self-contained discipline, law is treated as a world of its own that is separate from the society within which it operates and purports to serve. Criticism is largely confined to highlighting formal inconsistencies and rooting out logical error. This organizational function is seen as an end in itself, with the corollary that any study of the social or

---

[12] *A Dictionary of Modern Usage* 109–10 (B. Garner 2nd ed. 1995).

political context in which those rules arise or have effect is considered, at best, to be someone else's jurisdiction, like the social scientist's or political theorist's. It is not that such work is unimportant, but that it is not a necessary part of the lawyer's learning or expertise. In a manner of speaking, the ghosts of Blackstone and Coke not only prowl the corridors of academe but are welcome souls in its offices and classrooms. Although mainstream scholars feign a modesty and subservience to law, their work smacks of a hubris that is no less acceptable for its more humble presentation.

In undertaking such a black-letter task, the ambition of the scholar is to collate the available cases and materials and then whip recalcitrant areas into conceptual shape. At its most sophisticated, there is an insistence that the common law is much more than the sum of its precedential parts; the precedents are not the law, only evidence and illustrations of it. The informing assumption is that what the courts are doing is largely right: Jurisprudence is the "rational science of general and extensive principles" and the common law is "fraught with the accumulated wisdom of the ages."[13] In short, it is taken for granted that legal doctrine is underpinned by an intelligible and just plan of social life such that the task of the legal scholar is to extend law in accordance with the plan so that it becomes less fragmentary and more intelligible. This tradition of black-letterism runs from Coke, Hale, and Blackstone through Dicey, Pollock, and Anson to Smith, Treitel, and Beatson; it remains as alive and kicking today as it ever has been. A cursory glance at the leading English textbooks strongly supports such an assessment: Smith and Hogan's *Criminal Law*, Cheshire and Furmston's *Contract*, and Winfield's *Tort* all speak to the narrow and precious approach to legal scholarship that dominates legal study. The ambition is to provide a comprehensive and systemic account of the law; any criticism is about discrete errors and particular mistakes rather than any systematic shortcomings. Almost without exception, these authors tend to be male. For instance, Smith and Hogan offer a large tome that is purely about conceptual analysis whose main task is a descriptive account of the law and in which principled consistency within judgments, areas, and between areas is the organizing device. There is no contextual setting offered about crime or its informing forces, with readers being asked to "judge for himself how far

---

[13] *Blackstone's Commentaries* I, 2 and II, 425 and IV, 435. See also *Fisher v. Prince* (1762), 3 Burr. 1363 per Lord Mansfield ("the reason and spirit of cases make law, not the letter of particular precedents"); *Jones v. Randall* (1774), Cowp. 37 per Lord Mansfield ("precedents serve to illustrate principles and to give them fixed certainty"); M. Hale, *History of the Common Law* 67 (4th ed. 1739) ("Though such decisions are less than a law, yet they are greater evidence thereof"); and C. K. Allen, *Law in the Making* 213 (6th ed. 1958).

these [the stated purposes of criminal law] are fulfilled by English criminal law."[14]

This black-letter literature is not without its jurisprudential champions. Although black-letter law resists larger theoretical concerns and infiltrations, it has been defended in theoretical terms. In a wide-ranging essay, Peter Birks argues that traditional legal literature has played a massive role in the modern development of the common law and is the perfect theoretical complement to the common law's more casuistic practice. Defending the canon of legal literature, he acknowledges "great academics" as much as great judges, lawyers, and cases as the fixed points in the common law. Birks is very clear that what is "great" is to be assessed by the extent to which a work contributes to "the search for principle," rationally organizes the case law, and is able to advance "the magic of the common law" in its "capacity to achieve sensitive pragmatic change without sacrificing structured rationality and predictability."[15] Accordingly, black-letter law is not simply the product of academic practitioners who are unable or cannot be bothered to engage in a broader and different intellectual exercise; it results from the noble efforts of those who undertake such a task as a matter of principle and pride. These scholars do not so much reject the Blackstonian influence as embrace it in a less grandiose and more focused incarnation. Nevertheless, modesty is no excuse and humility is no escape from the shortcomings of its full-blown exercise. It is such a full-blown exercise that contemporary jurisprudence has become.

Herbert Hart served the legal community of black-letter scholars well. His enlightened brand of legal positivism in *The Concept of Law*, with its analytical emphasis on rules, regularity, and reasonableness, provided a jurisprudential support that enabled black-letter writers to continue with their academic

---

[14] J. Smith and B. Hogan, *Criminal Law* (8th ed. 1996). This is especially so on so-called unnatural offenses (492–97), although they note that this term may be "offensive, but it is in the heading of the Act." See 492, footnote 20. See also E. H. Burn, *Cheshire and Burn's Modern Law of Real Property* (15th ed. 1994) (no account of what is idea of property or homelessness, but lots on estates and titles); G. Treitel, *Law of Contract* (9th ed. 1995); J. Beatson, *Anson's Law of Contract* (27th ed. 1998) (account of contract as a single body of general principles); and M. Brazier and J. Murphy, *Street on Torts* (10th ed. 1999). There are a number of texts that offer a more contextual approach, but this is usually token and used to explain deviations as though the general principles simply just *are*. See P. Atiyah, *An Introduction to the Law of Contract* (5th ed. 1995); J. Furmston, *Cheshire, Fifoot and Furmston on Law of Contract* (13th ed. 1996); and E. Dias and B. Markesinis, *Tort Law* (2nd ed. 1995).

[15] P. Birks, Adjudication and Interpretation in the Common Law: A Century of Change, 1 *Legal Studies* 156 at 168 and 176 (1994). In a similar vein, see Lord Goff, In Search of Principle, 69 *Procs. of Brit Acad.* 169 (1983) and J. Beatson, Has the Common Law a Future?, 56 *Camb. L. J.* 291 (1998).

craft without too many qualms about the legitimacy or efficacy of their work. This is not surprising, as Hart's avowed aim was to provide an essay in descriptive sociology in that he sought to make sense of lawyers' daily practices. He offered a commentary rather than critique.[16] While this garnered obvious support among the adherents to a black-letter approach, it did little to convince sceptics or critics. Many jurists began to suggest that Hart's ideas ran out of steam at the very point that they were most needed; they had little to say about the resolution of hard cases, where rules are unclear or clashed, other than that judges had a discretion and responsibility to do the best they could. While this gave comfort to the critics (who tried to use this opening as a way to establish and further the claim that 'law is politics'), others were convinced that, while law is a system of rules, it is not only that – law is about values as much as it is about rules. These naturalist jurists were dismissive of black-letter scholarship; it was considered to be too limited, unduly isolated, and even woefully inadequate. Accordingly, a new generation of jurists began to develop a theory of law that took account of law as a thoroughly political enterprise. Perhaps as a way to balance this excursion into the realm of values and morals, there was a felt need to become ever more abstract and formal in the hope that this would insulate the resulting theories from charges of partisanship. In this effort, the traditional impulse to abstract organization and formal coherence proved irresistible. However, this explicitly theoretical strain of legal scholarship criticizes the textbook tradition from within the same disciplinary mind-set. Whatever its claims to the contrary, mainstream jurisprudence implicitly alleges that the ambition of black-letter scholarship is correct, but that its focus and execution are severely at fault. Thus, jurists have dislodged black-letter law only to replace it with black-letter theory: Blackstonian commitments have come out of the closet and become a celebrated ideal, not an embarrassing corollary of legal scholarship.

As traditionally understood, jurisprudence applies to all those efforts to step back from the actual practice and operation of law in order to make some general sense of it all. As Karl Llewellyn phrased it, "jurisprudence is as big as law – and bigger."[17] This venture can be carried out from all manner of perspectives and indeed has been. Economists, sociologists, literary critics, anthropologists, political scientists, psychologists, and many others have

---

[16] H. L. A. Hart, *The Concept of Law* (2nd ed. 1994). I say "too many qualms" because Hart's work can be read as being much more subversive and unsettling than many jurists allow. See A. C. Hutchinson, *It's All in the Game: A Nonfoundationalist Account of Law and Adjudication* 54–85 (2000).

[17] K. Llewellyn, *Jurisprudence* 372 (1962).

sought to place the world of law under closer critical scrutiny. However, in recent years, jurisprudence has been hijacked by philosophers. Apart from their usual imperialist claims about philosophy being the intellectual discipline that is assumed and incorporated by all others, legal philosophers claim to be first among jurisprudential equals. They insist that, while there is much of value to be learned about law when viewed from the outside as a social or political activity, the effort to understand law in its own terms and as a viable internal operation is entitled to theoretical priority. It is not so much that they dismiss other types of study, but that they claim that they are of a secondary and derivative importance to lawyers. While such jurists concede that not all problems and issues in law are philosophical, they do contend that all those problems and issues are capable of becoming philosophical ones and that they are premised on some inescapable philosophical assumptions.

Construed in this way, jurisprudence soon found itself on the familiar terrain of many traditional philosophical conundrums and, in the process, has become dominated by philosophical preoccupations. Mindful of law's blackletter tradition and the challenge of maintaining democratic legitimacy for courts in a society in which important social questions are routinely left to judicial resolution, jurists have considered a central part of the jurisprudential project to develop an epistemology of law: How is it possible to have knowledge about law or to know what counts as knowledge of or about law? What counts as good and bad knowledge about law? Jurisprudence has adopted a traditional and philosophical stance in developing a series of truth claims about the legal enterprise. All the problems of legal philosophy or jurisprudence have tended to begin and, in some cases, to end with this inquiry: "Most of the important arguments in legal thought are epistemological in nature."[18] What begins as a preliminary condition for any jurisprudential progress or enlightenment to be made soon becomes, once achieved, a way to underwrite the particular intervention as universally valid and, therefore, superior to all other offerings. Ironically, the jurisprudential attention to values has resulted in a turn away from the world rather than a return to it. Legal theorists have come to subscribe to a greater or lesser degree to the Blackstonian cause in which rigor, sweep, form, consistency, and integrity

---

[18] J. Boyle, The Politics of Reason: Critical Legal Theory and Local Social Thought, 133 U. Pa. L. Rev. 685 at 779 (1985). See, generally, R. Tur, Jurisprudence and Practice, 14 J. S. P. T. L. 38 (1976) and What is Jurisprudence?, 28 Phil. Q. 149 (1978). This tendency toward arid conceptualism and abstract coherence is particularly marked in traditional jurisprudence textbooks and courses. See R. Barnett, The Province of Jurisprudence Determined – Again!, 15 Legal Studies 88 (1995).

are the watchwords. Matters of material or substantive justice are treated as distinctly secondary.

Although this way of presenting the ambition and agenda of jurisprudence seems to speak in the mystical tones of bygone days, it remains the implicit mission and mind-set of modern jurisprudence. Mainstream jurists seem united in their belief that *Law* is more than the sum total of extant laws and decisions: It is felt to be both the expression and repository of a political insight that transcends the bounds of its temporary articulation. In this way, it is generally agreed that popular lawmaking cannot be left entirely to its own promptings but must be judged by its willingness to conform to the dictates of a loftier discipline. Consequently, legal theorists strive to explain and justify the delicate (and elusive) relation between law's immanence – the idea of law as the rational embodiment of an indwelling harmony – and law's instrumentality – the practice of using law as an institutional tool for social problems. In searching for that balance, the cool detachment of philosophical reflection is considered more conducive to democratic advancement than the heated contestability of popular debate over localized justice. Despite the regular incantation of the Holmesian wisdom that 'the life of the law has not been logic, but experience', what counts as 'experience' is limited to law's own workings and lawyers' own wiles. Moreover, the jurisprudential examination of that experience is abstract and logical. In an important sense, modern jurists are still held captive to one of the most enduring tropes in common law history – Lord Mansfield's stricture that the law is constantly working on and through itself to satisfy better its own self-transforming ambitions. In a relatively unimportant Chancery case about testimonial competence, he concluded that "a statute very seldom can take in all cases, therefore the common law, *that works itself pure* by rules drawn from the fountain of justice, is for that reason superior to an act of parliament."[19] Always traveling, but never arriving, the common law is portrayed as continuing process that fulfills and refreshes itself from its own self-generated resources. If lawyerliness is not next to godliness, it is at least a quasi-divine enterprise of Purity and Great Design.

Law's Destiny

The leading so-called purist among the elite of modern jurisprudence is Ronald Dworkin. He has placed the notion that *the law works itself pure* at the

---

[19] *Omychund v. Barker* (1744), 26 ER 15 at 23 (emphasis added). At the time, Lord Mansfield was still Mr. Murray, a young solicitor-general.

dynamic core of his legal theory. Over three decades, Dworkin has developed a constructivist theory of law and adjudication at the heart of which is the naturalist insistence that "law . . . is deeply and thoroughly political."[20] The general sweep of Dworkin's jurisprudence is too familiar to warrant another full or detailed rehearsal. Accordingly, my introduction to his ideas and claims concentrates on the basic philosophical commitments that inform and animate his jurisprudential offerings. Although there have been several twists and turns over the past couple of decades, the central themes and ambitions of Dworkin's writings remain remarkably clear and consistent – law is a moral practice; intellectual coherence is a primary value; and there are right answers to legal controversies. Bloodied, but unbowed, Dworkin remains as defiant and as unapologetic as ever in defending these basic philosophical commitments. From a Darwinian perspective, he is a distant cousin to Soapy Sam, the juristic heir apparent to the Creationist tradition of evolutionary thinking.

Conflict is at the heart of the law; it is its animating force as well as its operating focus. In dealing with the conflicts represented by litigation, lawyers and judges are conflicted over not only what is the correct resolution of any particular conflict, but also what is the correct method by which to arrive at the correct resolution. For Dworkin, it is this underlying conflict about legal reasoning that forms the raison d'etre of jurisprudence. He is interested in the theoretical disagreement over the grounds of law – namely, under what circumstances should "particular propositions of law . . . be taken to be sound or true." While jurists may disagree over what those propositions are and how one identifies them, there is widespread agreement about the fact that there are some standards that determine what propositions of law are true and sound. Accordingly, Dworkin wants to provide a theory of law that will tell judges what it is that they are supposed to be doing when resolving competing accounts about what decision to make in any particular case. To do this, Dworkin argues that, while the disagreement appears to be about what the law is, it is really a disagreement about what the law should be. For Dworkin, therefore, jurisprudence concerns "arguments over whether and why propositions of law can be controversial." What is most important is that this challenge is concentrated on the internal viewpoint of participants; jurisprudence "tries to grasp the argumentative character of

---

[20] R. Dworkin, *A Matter of Principle* 146 (1985). Another purist is Ernest Weinrib, who seeks to show that contemporary law is a deserving philosophical object of democratic allegiance precisely because the essence of law is its capacity to "work itself pure." See E. Weinrib, *The Idea of Private Law* 3 and 13 (1995).

our legal practice by joining that practice and struggling with the issues of soundness and truth participants face." It is not that other external inquiries are invalid or useless, only that they do not amount to jurisprudence proper. Consequently, Dworkin concludes that "propositions of law are true if they figure in or follow from the principles of justice, fairness and procedural due process that provide the best constructive interpretation of the community's legal practice."[21]

Under Dworkin's approach, therefore, any true and sound account of law is also a political account of the best moral practice that law can be. He denies that a valid jurisprudential account is simply a matter of providing an accurate historical description of what the courts have done in the past (as this leaves judges with no legal basis to evaluate past practice and no legal guidance when the past is silent on the controversy in hand). He further rejects it as making an accurate prediction of what the courts will do in the future (as this fails to tale legal reasoning seriously and offers no moral purchase on the course that the law should take). Rather, Dworkin offers an account of law and adjudication that is as much about moral principles as it is about legal tradition. Nevertheless, although he is treats law and justice as intimately connected, he insists that it is incumbent upon judges to treat the legal past "as important for its own sake" because "law as integrity supposes that people are entitled to a coherent and principled extension of past political decisions even when judges profoundly disagree about what this means." Therefore, the common law judge is required to apply the law dutifully, deferentially, and reliably to present cases. In this way, Dworkin advances an understanding of adjudication as a political practice that works the space between law's institutional past and its future possibilities. While the better interpretation is not necessarily one that accounts for the most decisions, the settled body of legal norms and justifications is claimed to be the motor force of principled adjudication: "Law's attitude . . . aims, in the interpretive spirit, to lay principle over practice to show the best route to a better future, keeping the right faith with the past."[22] In short, Dworkin maintains that the judges should treat the law as if it were a seamless web, providing complete and determinate guidance on all legal disputes. There is no need or justification to leave the law behind and engage in unconstrained ideological choice. Instead, judges are charged with treating the accumulation of legal decisions as fragments of an intelligible, if latent or implicit, plan of social life and, having elucidated those deeper ideals, to

---

[21] R. Dworkin, *Law's Empire* 110, 113, 114, and 225 (1986).
[22] Id. at 132, 134, and 413.

extend law in principled manner so that it becomes less fragmentary and more integrated. Insisting that it is not only sensible but necessary to talk about the truth-claims of law, Dworkin maintains that there are true and false legal answers to particular disputes and that such answers can only be arrived at by the judicial application of a suitably philosophical method. For Dworkin, there is a legal truth to the matter.

While Dworkin is uncompromising in his claim that adjudication is an inevitable exercise in moral judgment, he is equally forceful that this does not mean that legal decisions are nothing more than the judges' moral views writ legal or that legal justice is coterminous with judges' ideas of justice. Although judges' moral views will influence the common law's development and judges are encouraged "to be wide-ranging and imaginative in [their] search for coherence with fundamental principle," there are limits to how much and how far judges can rely on their own sense of justice. There is a definite and genuine difference between law as a public institution and morality as a personal commitment. Because judges' "central obligation is that of general fidelity to law" and "the brute facts of legal history . . . limit the role any judge's personal convictions of justice can play in his decisions," Dworkin's Hercules or any judge is duty bound to uphold the wisdom of the past, albeit in imaginative and innovative ways: "Anyone who accepts law as integrity must accept that the actual political history of his community will sometimes check his other political convictions in his overall interpretive judgment."[23] Moreover, these same restraints ensure that jurists, including Dworkin himself, do not get away with offering a moral reading of the law that is only a thinly veiled version of their own preferred moral stance. While Dworkin is unrelenting in his assertion that "telling it how it is means, up to a point, telling it how it should be," it is the "up to a point" that establishes the crucial space between valid legal interpretation and invalid personal moralizing.[24] Although judges and jurists will disagree over where that point is exactly, they are obliged to recognize its necessary existence and limiting force.

In the Dworkinian scheme of things, therefore, judges attain institutional success, professional esteem, and intellectual satisfaction by engaging in this demanding theoretical effort rather than by bringing it to some preordained conclusion. That judges do not agree on what the right answer is in any particular case is not a problem as long as they can agree that there is, at least theoretically, a right answer out there. How far judges travel on their so-called justificatory ascent before they are satisfied that they have achieved

---

[23] Id. at 208, 220, and 255.
[24] R. Dworkin, *Freedom's Law* 38 (1996).

a workable account of the law as a principled moral practice or until their theoretical resources no longer function adequately will be for each judge to determine. Notwithstanding the different capabilities of individual judges, it is the objective pursuit of truth through reason that is the hallmark of valid adjudication. It is only by adopting such an approach that judges will stand any chance of playing their designated part in societies, which are deeply divided in their politics and morality: "We cannot pursue that indispensable ambition [of living together as equals] unless we undertake, when necessary, to ascend high enough in our collective deliberations, including our adjudicative deliberations, to test our progress in [ensuring that the principles under which we are governed treat us as equals]."[25] This amounts to a Blackstonian imperative with a political conscience and a democratic mandate. As such, it is a tempting and tantalizing prospect. Nevertheless, in his classical efforts to continue through renovation the Blackstonian tradition, Dworkin has not managed to overcome its debilitating difficulties and drawbacks. Moreover, in presenting a more sophisticated theoretical project than his predecessors, he seems to have added a few more problems of his own. All in all, Dworkin's jurisprudence has condemned common law judges and lawyers to a practical task that is more Sisyphean than Herculean – they are doomed to pursue an ambition that becomes ever more out of reach as jurists appear to move ever closer to its grasping.

In his more recent work, Dworkin has not only held firm to these basic convictions but has confirmed them in the most unequivocal terms. In determining the correct legal answer to particular discrete legal problems, he still maintains that it is incumbent upon judges to have reflected on the whole system of moral and legal principles that comprise a particular area of law and to grasp them in their most coherent and appealing presentation. Consequently, Dworkinian judges are obliged to take a "theory-drenched" approach, even though they might well disagree over what that theory is and how it applies to the dispute at hand. As Dworkin expresses it,

> A claim of law ... is tantamount to the claim, then, that one principle or another provides a better justification of some part of legal practice. Better in what way? Better interpretively – better, that is, because it fits the legal practice better, and puts it in a better light. In that case, any legal argument is vulnerable to what we might call justificatory ascent. When we raise our eyes a bit from the particular cases that seem most on point immediately, and look at neighbouring areas of the law, or maybe even raise our eyes quite a bit and look in general, say, to

---

[25] R. Dworkin, In Praise of Theory, 29 *Ariz. St. L. J.* 353 at 359 and 376 (1997).

accident law more generally, or to constitutional law more generally, or to our assumptions about judicial competence or responsibility more generally, we may find a serious threat to our claim that the principle we were about to endorse allows us to see our legal practices in their best light.[26]

For Dworkin, therefore, adjudication is less a technical craft and more a philosophical adventure of the grandest kind in which formal integrity and abstract coherence are both its tools and their goal. Nevertheless, Dworkin concedes that not every judge has the necessary Herculean philosophical wherewithal to undertake such an ambitious challenge. Whereas a mythical Herculean judge might be able to master the arcane equipment of philosophical sophistication, synthesize all the available historical material, construct a perfectly attuned and all-embracing structure, and apply it consistently to detailed legal problems, this is far beyond the competence of merely earthly beings. Instead, what is important is that judges should do the best that they can by being prepared to enter the 'justificatory ascent' that might draw them into a more theoretical argument than they originally anticipated or wanted. Dworkin does not expect judges to make that 'justificatory ascent' as a matter of course, but he does remind judges and jurists that "the ladder of theoretical ascent is always there, on the cards, even when no one is tempted to take even the first step up it."[27] Dworkin maintains that reflective height is the guarantor of moral depth. At the very least, within the Dworkinian scheme of things, formal consistency with the law's own overarching principles is as important as substantive or local justice on any particular issue.

A Philosophical Excursus

Of course, this grand style of legal philosophy has not gone unchallenged. It has come in for stern rebuke. Critics condemn such scholarly efforts in which jurists not only seem to believe that law has a supernatural or suprahistorical life, but that it can be known and understood. The idea that law is an immanent whole that transcends the accumulated sum of its immediate parts and that there is a simple metaphysical formula that explains all law or that legal practice can be rendered philosophically pure is increasingly untenable in a world in which lawyers and society at large are increasingly diverse in composition, interests, and objectives. The value-claim that the

---

[26] Id. at 356–57.
[27] Id. at 359.

best way to provide solid and secure footings for law and legal theory is by becoming more and more removed and abstracted from its day-to-day operation is deeply mistaken. There are no solid and secure footings for law and legal theory that are not themselves part of the very political and situated debate that they are intended to ground and underwrite: There is no escape from the messy and contingent facts of social living. Despite the wishes of contemporary jurists, there is no difference in character or authority that distinguishes philosophical or jurisprudential debate from any other kind of debate; the standards used for judging the merits of particular arguments are part of that debate, not apart from it. While the standards will vary from one arena of debate to another (i.e., the standards for aesthetic appreciation will not be the same as those for moral judgment) and while there will be a constant hankering after more compelling or objective standards, there are none. There is no difference between what we honestly believe to be right or the case and what actually is right or the case. The belief that there is such a difference is simply one more belief. It is to a further elaboration of those broad critical claims that I now turn, especially as they apply to the debate over the evolutionary character of legal development and the creation-by-design approach.

Instead of reveling in the full amplitude and unbuttoned possibilities of human existence, jurists bring to it a narrow and smothering perspective. Wanting to reduce everything down to a dry and bloodless endeavor, they resemble taxidermists rather than naturalists; they want to capture and display legal wildlife in museums rather than marvel at its living color and glorious vitality. Under this tutelage, jurisprudence is less about awe and splendor and more about rigor and scrupulousness. Although they present their work in grand and confident terms, contemporary jurists are fearful and desperate – they are fearful that, if the activities of law and lawyers are not held in check, they will decline into a chaotic arbitrariness; they are desperate because their efforts to establish such a checking device are increasingly less convincing. Rather than celebrate society's diversity and energy, they wish to leash and corral them. Accordingly in its efforts to rescue law and lawyers from themselves, jurisprudence craves greater theoretical authority not only to bolster individual contributions but also to salvage its own waning prestige. This characteristic mix of conceit and timidity is held together by a commitment to the idea that there are certain moral and legal facts of the matter that transcend and discipline the beliefs of its participants about what the legal enterprise is and is not about. Maintaining that there are right methods that will produce right results, these jurists claim to speak with the authoritative accent of truth and objectivity. On closer inspection, though, these methodological claims are less the imprimaturs of a formalized justice and more the earnest ways of simply getting by. This is no bad thing. Stripped of their philosophical paraphernalia, these jurisprudential accounts might still have something to offer law in its task of being substantively just in a constantly shifting and changing world.

But this paraphernalia must go. The insistence that the theoretical effort to distinguish between 'what the world seems like to us' and 'what the world really is' will pay practical dividends must be abandoned. There is no worthwhile or sustainable distinction between what is thought to be the case about the world and what is the case about the world, and about what seems to be right and what is right. Despite philosophers' and jurists' best efforts, it is impossible to demonstrate that there is some critical distance between the world and our thoughts about it such that the world cannot only be what people think it is. To say something true and objective about the world is to do no more than report on what people presently believe or accept to be true and objective about the world. This is not deny that there is a reality or to fall into some absurdly solipsistic understanding of the world; it is simply to accept that there is no way of stepping outside our perceptions about the world in order to determine whether those perceptions correspond with what is really the case. The critical idea that a theory of truth is a theory of meaning and no more is offered as "an explanation of what people *do*, rather than of a non-causal, representing relation in which they stand to non-human entities."[28] There is no truth about what is really "there" over and above what are treated as the best prevailing beliefs about what is really there. What is best is whatever has managed to get itself accepted in the relevant community of inquiry.

Of course, many contemporary jurists do not insist that there are facts of the matter, such that what is the case or right is entirely independent of what is thought to be the case or right; so-called realists are few and far between. Instead, these "constructivists" deny the existence of any moral facts as something independent of beliefs; they recognize that truths are as much chosen as they are perceived. Opting for an account that treats what people would think of as right under ideal conditions to determine what is in fact right, they have traded in notions of fundamental objectivity for more modest notions of constrained objectivity; what they lose in universality, they hope to gain in relevance and credibility. To achieve this more restrained fulfillment of the philosophical project, the most popular strategy has been to keep the

---

[28] R. Rorty, Representation, Social Practice, and Truth in *Philosophical Papers*, vol. I, 154 (1991). See also R. Rorty, *Contingency, Irony, Solidarity* 5–13 (1989).

truth question separate from the reality question by providing an account of truth and objectivity that does not depend on there being a correspondence between what is thought to be the case about the world and what is the case about the world. Denying the realists' insistence on moral facts of the matter (or, at least, their accessibility to human demonstrations), they recognize that truth is caught within the social web of language. However, they go beyond the simplistic and uninteresting claims of correspondence theorists who deliver only empty tautologies about practice and objectivity.[29] Instead, they offer a so-called coherence account of truth and objectivity in which it is maintained that the most convincing account is the one that shows how a complex structure of relationships can best cohere. This means that the truth of any particular moral judgement is dependent on its coherence with all other moral intuitions and claims. In contrast to axiomatic or linear theories that establish first principles and then argue deductively from them to more detailed and particularized moral judgments, coherence accounts engage in a continual process of adjustment and revision between general moral principles and particular moral judgments until the most balanced and harmonized account is constructed.[30]

Nevertheless, despite their constructivist claims, most philosophers still manage to utilize realist heirlooms as part of modern theorizing rather than shelve them as historical curiosities. Although they accept that what is thought to be the case is related to what is the case or that moral beliefs are relevant to moral facts of the matter, they do not concede that there are no moral facts of the matter; it is more a question of accessibility than actuality. The motivating fear is that, if the attempt to demand what is true and denounce what is false is abandoned, efforts to distinguish right and wrong will also be hopeless and all moral claims will be relativized. Thus, each opinion, no matter how quirky or perverse, will merit equal attention. In such circumstances, it is dreaded that morality will be reduced to a crude triumph of might over right or, at best, the tyranny of the majority. Accordingly, modern philosophers do not insist that it must be possible to

[29] F. Fernandez-Armesto, *Truth: A History and a Guide for the Perplexed* 216–20 (1997). For a good introduction to these philosophical difficulties in jurisprudence, see B. Leiter, Objectivity and the Problems of Jurisprudence, 72 *Tex. L. Rev.* 187 (1993) and J. Coleman and B. Leiter, Determinacy, Objectivity and Authority, 142 U. *Pa. L. Rev.* 549 at 600 (1993).

[30] For a general account of coherence theories in moral and legal reasoning, see M. P. Hanen, Justification as Coherence, in *Law, Morality and Rights* 67 (M. A. Stewart ed. 1983); J. Stick, Can Nihilism Be Pragmatic?, 100 *Harv. L. Rev.* 332 (1986); R. Walker, *The Coherence Theory of Truth* (1990); C. Wright, *Truth and Objectivity* (1992); and K. Kress, Coherence in *A Companion to Philosophy of Law and Legal Theory* 533–52 (D. Patterson ed. 1996).

demonstrate that a statement is true, only that it can be true or would be true under ideal conditions; the truth of a statement is not entirely reducible to or completely settled by reference to extant practice or the accumulation of prevailing beliefs. The tendency, therefore, is to offer largely constructivist accounts, but to insist that there are limits on that enterprise and to bound it by some strong and realist-grounded claims about morality. It is a tacit acknowledgment that coherence alone will not guarantee justice or fairness. Coherence only works as a guarantor of truth and objectivity when the general orientation of a set of practices is basically just. Whether Apartheid or Nazism were wrong will not be determined by their greater or lesser compliance with the demands of coherence, but by their basic commitments and substantive consequences. Accordingly, the constructivist project rests on a foundational platform of realist assumptions. When coherence push comes to relativistic shove, most philosophers reassert their realist commitments by concluding that truth is something that can transcend what is believed to be the case – there is more to truth than belief because, in important and critical circumstances, truth acts to discipline an incorrect belief, even though truth is never entirely independent of belief.

It ought not to be surprising that jurisprudence has followed a similar course and reached a similar point in its development as philosophy generally. Cast as a particular corner of the philosophical action, jurists' efforts to understand law and adjudication have followed those of their more generalist colleagues. While there are still some dyed-in-the-wool philosophical realists around and there is a flourishing, if contained, revival of axiomatic theories,[31] the predominant approach to legal theory is constructivist. The task of providing a credible and workable account of legal truth and objectivity is achieved by developing the most coherent and compelling account of past legal practice. The most well-known and successful proponent of such an approach is, of course, Ronald Dworkin; the influence of his work has been enormous in academe and, if less so, in the courts. This is not surprising as he presents his jurisprudential theory as an account of what judges really do as much as what they should do. Moreover, Dworkin's

---

[31] For a defense of the view that truth is explained by resort to something that is beyond a particular practice and that there are moral facts that can be accessed in similar ways to other facts, see M. Moore, The Interpretive Turn in Modern Theory: A Turn for the Worse, 41 Stan. L. Rev. 871 (1989); A Natural Law Theory of Interpretation, 58 S. Cal. L. Rev. 277 (1985); and Moral Reality Revisited, 90 Mich. L. Rev. 2424 (1992). See also D. O. Brink, Legal Theory, Legal Interpretation and Judicial Review, 17 Phil. & Pub. Affs. 105 (1988). For an example of a more axiomatic account, see E. Weinrib, supra, note 20.

account is explicitly philosophical in orientation and elaboration. Although he offers an account that gives prominence to prevailing views and existing opinions, he insists that there are definite limits on the moral authority of such beliefs. For Dworkin, there are right answers to legal controversies, even if we disagree about what they are, and integrity's writ only runs as far as certain realist moral truths allow:

> The adjudicative principle of integrity [is not] absolutely sovereign over what judges must do at the end of the day ... [because], if a judge's own sense of justice condemned [a particular course of action], he would have to consider whether he should actually enforce it ... or whether he should lie and say that it was not law after all, or whether he should resign.[32]

For Dworkin, therefore, law is an epistemological undertaking of the most demanding and traditional kind; objectivity and truth are its watchwords and credentials.

This minimally scaled-down project retains all the elements of a Blackstonian understanding of scholarly propriety and success. Jurists cannot seem to accept that justification is not about the abstract or special relation between ideas, but is a social practice that has or requires an external authority to its own contextual development: Truth is no different from what passes as true. To insist that there is no distinction between 'what the world seems like to us' and 'what the world really is' is not itself offered as a metaphysical truth but as a statement about the current state of play in the social enterprise of understanding the world. Any standards of assessment and validity are not external to and thereby controlling of debate; they are internal to the debate in that they inform it as much as they are changed by it. Epistemology fails in the sense that there is no privileged ground on which knowledge or meaning can claim to stand. From an alternative pragmatic perspective, objectivity is about social agreement, whether imposed or assumed: It is not an approximation to some natural, neutral, or noncontextualized standard of verification. As Richard Rorty deftly puts it, "explanatory power is where

---

[32] See R. Dworkin, supra, note 21 at 218–19 and generally 213–28. Dworkin explicitly resists categorization as a pragmatist if that means sharing views with Rorty and other "new pragmatists" whose views he describes as comprising "a dog's dinner." See Pragmatism, Rights Answers and True Banality in *Pragmatism in Law and Society* 359 at 360 and generally 366–69 (M. Brint and W. Weaver eds. 1991). Dworkin has never abandoned the one-right-answer thesis, although he has modified it. As he states, "for better or for worse, I have not [changed my mind about the character and importance of the one-right-answer thesis]." Id. at 382, footnote 1. See also R. Dworkin, *Taking Rights Seriously* chaps. 4 and 13 (1978); R. Dworkin, supra, note 20 at chap. 5; and Dworkin, supra, note 21 at chap. 7.

we find it."[33] Accordingly, theoretical inquiry ought to concern itself less with the truth and objectivity of certain beliefs and more with the moral and practical implications of such beliefs. Again, as Darwin's work showcases, there are no normative consequences that flow from an evolutionary perspective and no particular values are embedded in nature's struggle.

Impure Thoughts

The whole idea of law 'working itself pure' is anathema to any kind of evolutionary account of law. Even under the most modest and nonsystemic account, evolution is most certainly not a purifying process in which deviant forms are eliminated so that a species' true being can assert itself. To suggest that there could be a perfect or essential form of law relies on a misleading understanding of legal development as an entirely intellectual and internal process that is affected by environmental factors in the only the most incidental and uninfluential way. No legal doctrine is or can be ideal and pure. The best that can be hoped for is that doctrines might develop that are successful in the sense that they serve particular purposes, that they adapt to local conditions, and that they have a certain flexibility to remain relevant in a changed environment. However, whether particular rules are good or bad or useful or useless is a local assessment; it is not a once-and-for-all judgment about the rule's universal desirability. Moreover, complexity is not an indicia of something's designed nature. The fact that the common law is a highly complex entity does not mean that it is, therefore, designed. It is not shaped like clay by an invisible hand that is guided by some economic animus or ethical mind-set. Furthermore, such a jurisprudential account runs up against the problem that, if law became perfectly adapted to its social and philosophical role, any change in the environment would immediately ensure that law was unsuited and unresponsive to challenges that occurred. Thus, if the idea of law 'working itself pure' is to have any validity or bite, it must rest on a particular theory of social development – that society will also reach a point of political equilibrium in which social tensions are in both philosophical and practical harmony – that is both fantastical and reactionary. Such assumptions place such crypto-Creationists in the dubious camp of end-of-history prognosticators like Francis Fukuyama

---

[33] R. Rorty, *Philosophy and the Mirror of Nature* 209 (1979). For more on this pragmatic approach, see infra chap. 4. See also R. Rorty, Texts and Lumps in *Rorty, Philosophical Papers*, vol. I, 81 (1991); R. Rorty, *Objectivity, Realism and Truth* 22–24 (1991); H. Putnam, *Representation and Reality* 115 (1988); And W. Quine, Two Dogmas of Empiricism in *From a Logical Point of View* 20–46 (1953).

who maintain that "there is a fundamental process at work that dictates a common evolutionary patent for *all* human societies – in short, something like a universal History of mankind in the direction of liberal democracy."[34]

Contemporary jurisprudence remains in the scholastic shadow of a formalistic need for scientific rigor and abstract detachment as if this were the key to unlock the normative secrets of the universe. The fact is that there are no normative secrets to the universe to be unlocked that are not the projections of our own ideals and desires. Contemporary jurists continue to waste valuable energies in this hapless pursuit; they have a lingering theological ambition in that they wish to ascend to some superhuman vantage point – what else is Hercules but a mythic and superhuman alter ego of Dworkin himself? For instance, Dworkin wants us to make a justificatory ascent to some abstract Promethean remove from which we can catch an echo of the infinitely true and carry it back to society for people's edification and enlightenment – the more recalcitrant the problem, the higher the ascent; the more entrenched the controversy, the more transcendent the escape; the more convoluted the possibilities, the purer the ambition. However, contrary to the Creationist instinct for escape, progress is not about becoming more objective and true, about achieving justificatory height in order to attain moral depth, or advancing toward some higher, more removed, and abstract plane on which rationality holds sway outside of the disabling influences of interests, commitments, fuzziness, history, culture, and ideology. Despite traditional theorists' wishes and work to the contrary, there is no way to escape the politics of human finitude and transmigrate to an infinite realm of pure reason that secures people against the need to make difficult and always-contestable choices. Elegance, coherence, and simplicity are valued attributes of any theory, but they are hollow and unattractive as ends in themselves. Accordingly, rather than commune with Mansfield's ghost and his juristic imitators about the common law *working itself pure*, it is more instructive to think about judges as engaged, through their own efforts and imagination, in the process of law simply "working itself" against and within local conditions.

There is much to admire in Dworkin's and other like-minded jurists' work. They are excellent at parsing moral issues, highlighting ethical quandaries, and, at their best, proposing creative solutions to normative dilemmas. However, this counts for little if it remains in the debilitating shadow of a Creationist and Blackstonian mentality that celebrates the ahistorical, abstract, and schematic. It is necessary to abandon the conceit that it is only possible

---

[34] F. Fukuyama, *The End of History and the Last Man* 48 (1992).

to be "theoretical" if one escapes the bounds of "cultural and social" context and seeks to transcend "traditions and genres".[35] Instead of being true to an emphasis on situated standards and engaged persuasion, Dworkinian-inspired jurists (and there are many, even if they remain in the naturalist closet) have once again entered on a justificatory ascent toward some superhuman realm where truth, objectivity, and, therefore, authority are the reward of those who best ape the gods. Indeed, the Chair of Jurisprudence at Oxford University shares much with the Bishopric of Oxford. Through Dworkin and Wilberforce, law and religion combine over the years and across the disciplines to share a common ambition. In the Dworkinian Empire, although the noble judges are princes of the legal realm and bear the brunt of applying and transforming the extant law in line with its own purer ambitions, they must leave it to philosophical "seers and prophets . . . to work out law's ambitions for itself, the purer form of law within and beyond the law we have." While such work and inspiration may elude rank-and-file lawyers, they are not left to their own devices, for their "god is the adjudicative principle of integrity," which is a "more dynamic and radical standard than it first seemed, because it encourages a judge to be wide-ranging and imaginative in his search for coherence with fundamental principle."[36] This divinistic rhetoric is not a million miles away from the uplifting Creationist waxings of Soapy Sam:

> Redeemed man may soar upon the wings of devotion, and rise through the middle sky of simple intellectualism to the purer atmosphere and clearer light of religious service. For instead of resting satisfied with simple intellectual triumphs, he may in each one of these see more of the Creator's glory as he studies His works, and fill his soul with clearer visions of power, and wisdom, and goodness, and love of Him who has breathed forth from His own eternal being all the wonders of the created universe.[37]

The dubious achievement of such Creationist scholarship is that, while Dworkin has obliged most legal scholars to concede that law is about values as

[35] R. Dworkin, Objectivity and Truth: You'd Better Believe It, 25 *Phil. & Pub. Affs.* 87 at 133–34.

[36] R. Dworkin, supra, note 21 at 407, 220, and 400. This kind of hubris is not uncommon in law or other fields. For instance, in his best-selling (but worst-read) book, Stephen Hawking states that his goal is "nothing less than a complete description of the universe we live in." See S. Hawking, *A Brief History of Time* 13 (1989). He concludes the book with the opinion that the discovery of why the universe exists will be equivalent to knowing "the mind of God." Id. at 175.

[37] S. Wilberforce, supra, note 11 at 191.

much as rules, he has done so in a way that does not disturb the informing black-letter commitment that underpins the mainstream academic enterprise. By presenting the resort to politics as being exclusively armchair philosophizing rather than getting one's hands dirty in the messy world of real-life circumstances, Dworkin has managed to chastize the black-letter tradition of legal scholarship at the same time that he has taken it to more abstract heights. Most dauntingly, this tendency to abstract theorizing is offered as a way to remain a spectator rather than a player in life's theatre of action. However, this is a canard as such an approach is really about being an active player while masquerading as a passive bystander. Once stripped of their philosophical paraphernalia, recherché juristic theories are revealed as simply another political and partisan intervention. The claim that all that is done in the name of black-letterism, whether doctrinal or theoretical, is done in a technical and nonideological way is no more convincing today than it ever has been. Under cover of this apparently modest and apolitical intellectualized approach, there is a very real set of substantive biases in play; what is claimed to pass for philosophical rigor in the name of coherence and intelligibility is really a barely disguised effort to maintain and defend a spruced-up status quo. In the same way that the immediate popularity and lasting appeal of Blackstone's *Commentaries* owed as much to the ideological leanings of its author as to its intellectual excellence, so the contributions of today's leading scholars to synthesize the law into a comprehensive and systematic body of rules and principles are neither neutral, objective, nor detached.[38] It is not that there is a vast and overt conspiracy in play, but that the naive craft commitments of the mainstream academic community are much less benign than many members recognize. However, the complacent assumption that the law is, by its nature as law, good and that this goodness will be enhanced in proportion to its increasing internal coherence and formal intelligibility wears extremely thin in light of much evidence to the contrary: The camel is no animal for legal academics to emulate and sand is a poor building material for law schools. As Pierre Schlag concisely puts it, "the progressive fallacy is the belief that the aspects of a practice . . . that are 'good' are constitutive or essential to the practice, while those aspects of the practice that are 'bad' are merely by-products of or contingent to the practice."[39]

---

[38] See W. Twining, *Blackstone's Tower: The English Law School* 130–32 (1994) and generally D. Kennedy, The Structure of Blackstone's Commentaries, 28 *Buff. L. Rev.* 205 (1979).

[39] P. Schlag, *The Enchantment of Reason* 99 (1998).

In short, black-letterism works as a convenient mode of denial. It enables legal academics and lawyers to engage in what is a highly political and contested arena of social life – namely, law – and to pretend that they are doing so in a largely nonideological way. The main advantage of this is that they can go about their daily routines without assuming any political or personal responsibility for what happens in the legal process. However, the insistence that lawyering is a neutral exercise that does not implicate lawyers in any political process or demand from scholars a commitment to any particular ideology is as weak as it is deceptive. Such a Wilberforce-like image is a profoundly conservative and crude understanding of what it is to engage in the business of courts, legislatures, and the like; it accepts and works within the bounds of the status quo. Lawyers tend to confuse legal justice with social fairness. Indeed, the power and prestige of lawyers flow from their professional allegiance to the state's official laws and existing institutions. In spite of the efforts of many individual lawyers, lawyers as a group are the enlisted custodians of the status quo. By pretending otherwise and renouncing responsibility for the system that their actions hold in place, lawyers and academics are able to maintain their so-called independence and apolitical authority. The black-letter tradition of legal scholarship is in the business of producing political tracts as much as the politician and polemicist; the fact that they are presented and styled in the opaque jargon of professional disinterest and technical expertise serves to compound the disingenuity. As such, black-letterism is an ideology in the profoundest sense of the word in that it presents a particular and partial view of the world as neutral and natural.

Notwithstanding all this, it is clear that there is some level of design in law that is lacking in biology. People do tend to make plans and act on them. After all, law is a reasoned activity in that people reflect on what is best to do and how that might be achieved; law is not a game of chance, and, one would hope, judges do not play dice. In contrast, biological adaptation is not a conscious or reasoned response to environmental situations. The main force of Darwin's great idea is that organisms adapt as a matter of necessity: Evolution is not planned or premeditated. Or, to put it more sharply, Lamarck has a role in legal development that is not present in biological evolution. However, that role is limited and attenuated; local intended initiatives take place, but this does not make law an entirely rational process. In the common law, individual judicial initiatives are overwhelmed by a more general unplanned and aggregating dynamic that is response to external conditions. The whole does not discipline the parts in the way that jurists believe, but tends to direct the parts in a way that is externally explicable, even if not internally rational. While doctrinal patterns and pathways arise, they do not respond to any overarching logic. As in the biological world, accidents and drift play a huge part in legal evolution; it is not all about rational adaptation and designed development. Jurisprudence is and never will be an exact science that determines what can and cannot happen or what should and should not happen – in law, sometimes $1 + 1 = 2$, but sometimes $1 + 1 = 3$. The common law is a work-in-progress in the most comprehensive and unmitigated sense. There are no unvarying essentials or eternal designs. There are most certainly no moral lessons that can be read mechanically from the bare historical facts of legal evolution. In human affairs, logic and rationality are as much the result of evolution as its generator. Because it is not possible to predict the future, lawyers and jurists are particularly susceptible to seeing the present as an inevitable consequence of the past and then projecting this concept on the move from the present to the future. After all, they say that "today is only tomorrow's yesterday."

Accordingly, while the common law and its adjudicative performance can be characterized with some credibility as comprising a self-reflective process of reasoned thinking, it is far from reducible to an activity that is governed by a strict philosophical discipline that is entirely internal to legal practice. All the talk about grand purposes or guiding minds is pitched at such a high level of generality that what they might or might not recommend in any particular situation is almost impossible to predict. Or, to turn that around, the solution to any particular problem can be interpreted in accordance with a variety of very different, often competing, and occasionally contradictory ideals that can plausibly claim a purchase on the extant legal materials. Consequently, while law is undeniably a teleological enterprise in that judges act with a purpose, the system as a whole cannot be said to have a directing mind such that it moves forward in one direction as if pulled along toward a given goal. In law, there are many theoretical possibilities, but the actual decision made is as much about external circumstances as anything else. Principles prosper or perish not only by dint of their intellectual merit but also by their capacity to adapt to material conditions. Although Holmes' claims for the relevance of evolutionary theory were misplaced, his warning remains pertinent and ought not to be ignored by those jurists who want to follow in his intellectual footsteps: "We have evolution in this sphere of conscious thought and action no less than in lower organic stages, but an evolution which must be studied in its own field."[40]

---

[40] O. W. Holmes, Law in Science and Science in Law, 12 *Harv. L. Rev.* 443 at 447 (1899).

Conclusion

In this chapter, I have sought to show that a major implication of the Darwinian idea is that people breed for reproduction and survival, not for finding deep truths about the universe and themselves. This does not mean that the search for philosophical truths is pointless, only that it is not our purpose or raison d'etre. After all, "God is dead." The whole idea of purification (or "perfectability," as biologists prefer to call it) is entirely incompatible with any vaguely Darwinian evolutionary account. It smacks of Creationism because it suggests both direction and goal as well as predetermined ends that include the continuing enhancement of what it is to be human. In this way, the limits of any jurisprudential theory might be as much about humanity's limits as reality's recalcitrance: "Created half to rise, and half to fall,/ Great Lord of all things, yet a prey to all;/ Sole judge of Truth, in endless error hurl'd;/ The glory, jest and riddle of the world."[41] Any study that takes the idea and practice of evolution seriously must be prepared to make the shift from philosophy to history. However, such a historical approach must itself resist the allure of an abstract approach and be prepared to get its hands dirty in the soil of politics. It is counterproductive to depict law as evolutionary and not treat it seriously as a phenomenon that only has meaning in its ever-changing historical shape and substance. Once contingency is accepted, its punishing force corrodes any static conception of law, society, jurisprudence, history, and even politics. In both the science and the humanities, the will to know is frequently accompanied by the will to power. At a minimum, it behooves biological and juristic pundits, like the Creationists, to come clean and at least admit that what they are offering is a faith-based doctrine, not a neutral science. To be a wolf is one thing, but to be a wolf in sheep's clothing only compounds the offense.

While it might be true that law and legal scholarship, like all stories, "are haunted by the ghosts of the stories they might have been,"[42] law remains thoroughly spooked by the jurisprudential phantoms of what it could and should never be. A more appropriate response to such jurisprudential fantasizing is not awe-induced toleration but a defiant and decisive act of ghost busting. The hold of Creationism rests on the fear that evolution undercuts all traditional values and suggests that everything is up for grabs. It is somehow assumed that, without values to ground them, people will be lost and adrift. Yet, without fealty to God or other lesser deities, there need be

---

[41] Alexander Pope, *An Essay on Man II*, ll.15–18 (F. Brady ed. 1988).
[42] S. Rushdie, *Shame* 116 (1995).

neither chaos nor tyranny. On the contrary, exorcising the ghost of Bishop Wilberforce and his latter-day juristic followers can encourage people to move beyond trepidation and subservience by providing an opportunity for transformation and renewal. An abandonment of the Creationist project will not render all knowledge illusory, turn all truths into falsehoods, throw all order into chaos, and reveal all objectivity as sham. This is a ghastly projection of the Creationists' imagination and ought to have no more hold on our intellects than Soapy Sam himself. When all is said and done, there are simply people, with all the frailties and possibilities that this entails, trying to make sense of themselves, the contingency of their situation, and the responsibility to make and remake their own lives in the best way that they see fit. But there is no bargain, Faustian or otherwise, that can get us out of the continuing present to some redemptive future or forgiving past. Despite what some hope and maintain, evolutionary theory is not the source of salvation to replace the Creationist tradition because no normative consequences at all flow from evolution's acceptance. It is to those misguided efforts to salvage some ethical guidance from the Darwinian insight and turn Darwin into an avenging moral prophet that I now turn.

❧ 4 ❧

Taming the Bulldog:
The Natural and the Pragmatic

"It's... well, it's a long story," he said, "but the Question I would like to know is the Ultimate question of Life, the Universe and Everything. All we know about it is that the answer is Forty-two, which is a little aggravating."[1]

DOUGLAS ADAMS

SCIENCE HAS ACHIEVED MUCH AND WILL NO DOUBT CONTINUE TO DO much more. As a prestigious discipline, the achievements of its greatest students – Copernican astronomy, Newtonian physics, Einsteinian mechanics – are deservedly included in the exalted feats of human history. Indeed, the evolutionary work of Charles Darwin is fully entitled to be mentioned in the same breath as these iconic endeavors. However, such accomplishments are often treated as if they have solved or hinted at some answers to enduring questions of humankind: How should we live? What is good and true? What is the meaning of life? While the pioneers of these scientific achievements usually appreciate the importance of their work, they also often recognize its limits. Conceding that such discoveries tend to prompt as many new questions as provide new answers, they accept that there is no necessary or proportionate relation between intellectual originality and technological utility; what we now know is an entirely different matter from what we will now do with such knowledge. Unfortunately, despite the wisdom of many great scientists, other lesser lights are not so perspicacious. Some seek to suppress and subvert new ideas, afraid that they will undermine all that is held sacred and thereby wreak social havoc; the response to Galileo's ideas is one such familiar example. Others attempt to turn scientific success into normative guidance. With an eye to the main chance,

---

[1] D. Adams, *The Hitchhiker's Guide to the Galaxy: The Trilogy of Four* 587 (2002).

such prognosticators and hangers-on want to see moral truth in scientific accomplishment. Darwin's work has been paid the dubious compliment of both responses. Both are mistaken. As much as the Soapy Sams have wanted to trash and discredit his ideas, the Bulldogs have striven to base a whole political manifesto on them.

Since its conceptual mapping by David Hume in 1739, the chasm between facts and value has remained wide and unbridgeable; its abysmal floor is strewn with the mangled theories of those foolish enough to countenance such an ill-advised crossing.[2] Quite simply, ethical mandates cannot be found in or gleaned from the biological facts of nature. Nevertheless, this has not deterred many commentators from turning Darwinian science into a kind of metaphysical ethics by synthesizing strict biological propositions with broader social behaviors; they cannot imagine a Darwinian world that does not have Darwinian purposes. The unifying goal of these so-called Social Darwinians is to offer a prescriptive dimension for future human progress – the struggle between individuals and between individuals and their environment becomes both the engine and engineer of good social organization. With friends like this, Darwin has little need of enemies. Indeed, even though the stalwart Bulldog Huxley defended Darwin against attacks from religion, even he later put Darwin to some very un-Darwinian uses. While it is wrongheaded to imagine that natured or inherited characteristics have no impact on people's lives, it seems equally untenable to avow that it is the dominant consideration, as many latter-day Huxleyians believe. Although they often couch them in technical language, their arguments are tantamount to elucidating some miraculous and, therefore, non-Darwinian designing hand at work. While there is nothing philosophically invalid in suggesting that the survival of the fittest is a worthy goal, this cannot be done under cover of evolutionary theory. In law as elsewhere, it simply has to be defended like any other moral or political theory. As a normative initiative, it cannot simply be posited as a fact of nature or as an uncontroversial extrapolation from such facts, because this assumes what is the major bone of contention in such an ethical and political inquiry; what counts as "facts" and "nature" are contested categories. In short, the road to ethical enlightenment cannot pass by way of Hume's chasm.

In this chapter, I want to implore jurists to resist the Promethean impulse to put evolutionary theory and therefore nature in the service of a preferred

---

[2] D. Hume, *A Treatise on Human Nature* bk. 3, pt. 1, sec. 1 (1739). For a timely reminder of this Humean wisdom, see A. Rosenberg, The Biological Justification of Ethics: A Best-Case Scenario, in *Darwinism in Philosophy, Social Science and Policy* 118–36 (2000).

social or ideological vision. In the first section I introduce the Huxleyian tendency to galvanize a political outlook with biological imperatives: The recent work of law-and-economics and law-and-biology scholars is introduced. In the second section, I utilize the bitter exchange between Ronald Dworkin and Richard Posner to highlight the failings of a pseudoscientific approach to jurisprudence. Next, I canvass the different pragmatic perspectives on law and adjudication; the emphasis is on defending a more radical and thoroughgoing version of this popular turn to pragmatism. In the fourth section I anticipate and answer some likely objections to my mode of pragmatism. In the final section, I make some tentative suggestions about how the common law might be used to deal with the pressing problem of homelessness. Throughout, I insist that, contrary to what many common law jurists maintain (and regardless of what they say that they maintain), the category of the natural is as contingent and contextual in law as it is in life and science generally. There is nothing less natural about the rapist or burglar than the lover or philanthropist: What is natural is humanly constructed and then imbued with normative and occasionally transcendent qualities that give it its place and purchase in the intellectual world. Nature holds no necessary or final answers to life's pressing challenges. In short, what is and is not useful is a local and pragmatic matter.

Of Darwin and Dogs

Although, like Wilberforce, Thomas Henry Huxley was a thoroughly nineteenth-century man, his life followed a different Victorian trajectory. Born in 1825 to a large and relatively poor family, he lived to achieve great success and widespread popularity until his death in 1895. Despite his lack of formal education, he managed to become proficient in a range of subjects – science, history, philosophy, and German – and, with the help of his brother-in-law, secured a medical apprenticeship. With a scholarship to Charing Cross Hospital, he set out on a career that was take him both across various disciplines and up through the hierarchy of nineteenth-century science. Having graduated in 1846 from London University with a gold medal for anatomy and physiology, Huxley entered the Royal Navy and worked as an assistant surgeon on the *H.M.S. Rattlesnake*. In a parallel move to Darwin's own life path, his four-year voyage took him through the South Seas, where he examined and collected an abundance of marine life (although, unfortunately, the ship's crew tossed many of his samples and equipment overboard). On the basis of this fieldwork, Huxley published a series of highly respected papers on plant and animal morphology that established him as a special up-and-comer in the elite world of science. However, his personal situation remained precarious and, unlike the wealthy Wilberforce and Darwin, he struggled to make ends meet. He eventually secured a position at the School of Mines in London, which enabled him to continue his scientific endeavors and to bring his fiancée over from Sydney, Australia. By the time of the Oxford debate in 1860, Huxley was getting by and had acquired an excellent reputation as a careful, thorough, and sharp scientist, albeit one who was not afraid to rock the establishment boat. He was committed not only to highlighting the importance of scientific method as a moral and intellectual discipline, but also to urging "the working classes to understand that science and her ways are great facts for them – that physical virtue is the base of all other, and that they are to be clean and temperate and all the rest – not because fellows in black with white ties tell them so, but because these are plain and patent laws of nature, which they must obey under penalties."[3]

As a result of his part in the infamous Oxford debate and his vigorous defense of Darwin's *The Origin of Species* generally, Huxley earned the sobriquet of "Darwin's Bulldog." Although he retained his doubts about a number of aspects of Darwin's evolutionary theory, he espoused the general scientific cause against all comers. His commitment to the ideal of a meritocracy was combined within an almost pathological antipathy to aristocracy and privilege. Ironically, Huxley's professional pursuit of science was almost a religious crusade. In particular, Huxley was implacable in his rejection of any incipient creation-by-design argument. He believed the world to be a rational place and held that, by doubting everything until conclusively proved, one could gain complete insight into all aspects of the natural world. Any argument from design was treated as a theological claim that neglected the scientific duty to question and thus had to be rejected. For Huxley, the Cartesian method was an inviolable imperative for all scientists. Indeed, it was this sceptical rigor that obliged Huxley to query even the ideas of Darwin. Noting the lack of any genuine empirical evidence (ironically, much as Wilberforce had done), Huxley was unconvinced that Darwinian gradualism and natural selection were the last word on evolution because he thought that they smacked of a lingering Creationist and Progressionist mentality that should be resisted at all costs. He maintained, much to

---

3   *Dict. Nat. Bio* 897, from letter written in 1855. See T. H. Huxley, *On the Educational Value of the Natural History Sciences* (1854) and *On the Cause of the Phenomena of Organic Nature* (1863). Huxley never managed to achieve financial stability, but he did achieve considerable status. He began a family dynasty of scientists and intellectuals. By that fact alone, he made a strong case for the evolutionary thesis!

Darwin's chagrin, that there were persistent species that did not necessarily change by descent. Nevertheless, while he resisted the details of Darwin's account longer than the evidence warranted and never did fully accept that evolution was gradual rather than advancing by leaps or saltations, he did finally come to embrace Darwin's theory.[4] Huxley did so with a vengeance that was entirely characteristic. By the end of his life, the younger Huxley had turned Darwin's distinctly biological thesis into a moral theory.

Huxley was in the vanguard of a movement to put Darwin's ideas to normative effect in the maelstrom of Victorian politics. At first, Huxley toyed with idea of a kind of biocommunism as was fashionable in the Europe of the 1880s. He soon moved on to more disturbing extrapolations. He saw that the facts of historical process did not constitute validity for moral conduct. Maintaining that inevitable struggle undermined any possibility of socialist cooperation, Huxley contended that society grows as so-called antisocial animal instincts are curbed and advances through the selection of individuals who are ethically the best, rather than physically the fittest. He envisaged a definite evolutionary hierarchy with humans at its head and having the capacity, if not always the inclination, to rise above and judge all else. With more bitter bombast than astute analysis, Huxley overplayed his Darwinian hand and, in a classic move typical of almost all Social Darwinians, passed off personal preference as universal truth. Not content to lecture about moral decay and deliverance, Huxley inserted his views into political debate by recommending a nationalist agenda that made workforce training obligatory if England was to win the economic "battle" against the competing industrial powers of Europe.[5] In short, Huxley could not resist the temptation to try and convert his scientific prestige into a harder political currency. The resulting Social Darwinism turned science against socialism and instilled a dubious patriotism. As with many others, Huxley's efforts failed as both science and politics. Moreover, in the process, he had become more vicious Rottweiler than loyal Bulldog.

Sadly, Huxley began a mode of Darwinian scholarship that has persisted to this day – the effort to underpin a particularized ethical or political outlook with biological imperatives and thereby render it somehow more legitimate and compelling. While the major thrust of this Social Darwinian tendency has been to promote a Christian laissez-faire mentality and capitalist mode

---

4 D. Lyons, Thomas Huxley: Fossils, Persistence and the Argument from Design, 26 *Journal of the History of Biology* 545 (1993).

5 T. H. Huxley, *The Struggle for Existence in Human Society* (1887) and *Ethics and Evolution* (1893). For an engaging biography of this Victorian renaissance figure, see A. Desmond, *Huxley; From Devil's Disciple to Evolution's High Priest* (1997).

of organization, there have been other attempts to utilize Darwinian ideas in more socialistic endeavors. Indeed, it has been Darwin's blessing and blight that his work has been put to work in the service of such a wide range of normative projects. The price of popular acceptance has been the cost of ideological perversion.[6] The fact is that there is both too little and too much in Darwinian evolution to warrant any reliance on it in ethical or political debate. It offers too little in that it was never intended to provide more than a descriptive account of organic development: It provides no assistance to those who want to predict what *will* happen next, let alone what *should* happen next. However, when it is imported into ethical or political study, it suggests too much in that almost all behavior can be seen to have a tenuous connection to some biological feature. Even if there are genetically favored behavioral traits, they are not only insufficiently specific to be of much predictive or practical use but also as likely to result in different behaviors in different contexts. Nevertheless, neither this conceptual barrier nor the tortured history to get over it has prevented a whole host of faux-Darwinians from turning evolutionary science into its own religion or ideology. While Huxley's own offering might be considered to be ill-advised and wrongheaded, the appeal of his overall project is as enticing today as it ever was. This is no better evidenced than in the arcane world of jurisprudential scholarship, where *predictability* and *explicability* continue to be erroneously treated as synonymous. The ghost of Huxley still does battle with Wilberforce's phantom for the soul of the contemporary jurist.

As part of the continuing effort in law to give scholarship and policy making prescriptive clout, some commentators have turned to evolutionary science for guidance and support. While they continue a long empirical tradition that began with Holmes and others, these contemporary theorists claim to be more sophisticated and modest in their ambitions.[7] However, although they are more polished and professional in their presentations,

---

[6] See H. Spencer, *Social Statics* (1851); P. Kropotkin, *Mutual Aid* (1902); E. O. Wilson, *Consilience* (1998); and L. Arnhart, *Darwinian Natural Right: The Biological Ethics of Human Nature* (1998). For an account of Darwin's social influence, see R. Hofstadter, *Social Darwinism in American Thought* (1955); G. Himmelfarb, *Darwin and the Darwinian Revolution* (1959); and J. Rifkin, *The Biotech Century: Harnessing the Gene and Remaking the World* 197–226 (1998). At their crudest and darkest, the Social Darwinians persist in claims about the genetic relationship between race, gender, and intelligence. See, for example, C. Murray and R. J. Herrnstein, *The Bell Curve: Intelligence and Class Structure in American Life* (1994).

[7] See supra, chap. 2. For instance, influenced by Herbert Spencer, William Graham Sumner advanced the notion of "rights as rules of the game of social competition" and described the jurists' role as being "to develop a legal theory of the state that would permit natural selection to run its course." See W. G. Sumner, Rights, in *Essays of William Graham Sumner* vol. 1, 362 (1934). See N. Duxbury, *Patterns of American Jurisprudence* 25–32 (1995).

they are no less ambitious and no more successful in their pursuits than the original Bulldog in striving to derive an *ought* from an *is*. Although it comes in many versions and operates on many different fronts, the law-and-economics field has appropriated the evolutionary theme in its attempts to explain the development of the common law. This reliance on Darwinian themes is subtle and indirect, but no less significant and acknowledged for that. Borrowing from systems theory and relying on econometric modeling, it is contended that most legal behavior can be explained in terms of the evolutionary drive toward efficient outcomes. In particular, these scholars argue that the common law evolves toward efficient rules for a variety of reasons, including judges' propensity to favor efficient rules, the greater likelihood that inefficient rules will be litigated, and the greater frequency of court settlement in cases in which the legal rules relevant to the dispute are inefficient. For them, past decisions, whether intended, contingent, or accidental, not only *do* affect or constrain present judicial making, but also *should* do so; there is a gamble (or more a "fix") that what has been done has a redeeming moral or political worth. Insofar as these modern law-and-economic efforts seek to identify a defining normative thread to law's historical development and then discipline present efforts in line with it, they are actually doing much the same as the reviled Creationists. The only difference is that the one does this at a disguised scientific step removed from the miraculous design thesis of the other.[8]

A more overt incorporation of Darwinian evolutionary themes occurs in the growing body of work by the so-called law-and-biology scholars. The modern phase retreats from an explicit directedness to legal development. Stressing the evolutionary nature of complex social behaviors such as morality or altruism, it seeks to incorporate evolutionary understandings of biology into a model of the development of law. Since law itself is a mode of social behavior acted out by and on human animals, it is maintained that biological insight should provide better tools to understand and regulate that behavior. There are at least three ways in which evolutionary biology can illuminate sociolegal analysis – predicting patterns of behavior; clarifying the contours of sociolegal values; and suggesting possible means toward achieving identified social goals. The basic argument is that evolution has not only developed people's brains but also biased them in certain behavior-influencing ways so that people do not act in random or unpredictable ways. Over time,

---

[8] See supra, chap. 3. Exponents of this view include G. Priest, The Common Law Process and the Selection of Efficient Rules, 6 *J. Legal Stud.* 65 (1977); P. H. Rubin, Why Is the Common Law Efficient?, 6 *J. Legal Stud.* 51 (1977); and M. Roe, Chaos and Evolution in Law and Economics, 109 *Harv. L. Rev.* 641 (1999).

environmental challenges have been met by a variety of human responses, and it is those genetically disposed forms of behaviors that have permitted or advanced genetic survival that have now become dominant. While evolution favors reproductively helpful traits, it does not create them; it simply picks the best possible among the available choices. In such an account, evolution is about strategic fitness, not theoretical perfection: Problems do generate solutions, even if they are often imperfect. Armed with this knowledge about the interaction of genes and environment, law-and-biology scholars claim that the effort to design laws will be improved and become more efficacious when such biological insights are understood. As one enthusiast has boldly put it, "behavioural biology, like economics, helps [lawyers] with both the 'is' and 'ought' dimensions of an issue."[9] Consequently, these scholars hope that, by grounding law in an evolutionary account that emphasizes that there are certain shared genetic functions and capacities that predispose humans to certain behavior in particular contexts, many of the philosophical and practical problems that paralyze much mainstream jurisprudence can be sidestepped.

These evolutionary accounts make several significant and erroneous assumptions in seeking to convert biological insights into a normative jurisprudence – that minute changes in biological causes bring about minute changes in behavioral effects; that simple patterns of behavior ground predictable outcomes; that complex systems can be understood by breaking them down into simple and separate components; and that exceptional behavior proves the systemic applicability of general rules. However, the fact is that systems combine and interact in such a complex and dynamic way that small variations on any one side of these social equations can result in large changes on the other side of the equation (e.g., small changes in biological causes can wreak large changes in behavioral effects; the behavioral whole can be very different from the sum of the individual behaviors; and small variations in social context can produce very different behavioral responses). While the mind itself may be a product of natural selection, it does not follow that particular patterns of behavior are: It is simply not possible

---

[9] J. E. Stake, Can Evolutionary Science Contribute to Discussions of Law?, 41 *Jurimetrics* 379 (2001). Other adherents to this approach include J. Beckstrom, *Sociobiology and the Law: The Biology of Altruism in the Courtroom of the Future* (1985); W. H. Rodgers, Where Environmental Law and Biology Meet: of Pandas' Thumbs, Statutory Sleepers, and Effective Law, 65 *U. Colo. L. Rev.* 25 (1993); J. B. Ruhl, The Fitness of Law: Using Complexity Theory to Describe the Evolution Of Law and Society and Its Practical Meaning for Democracy, 49 *Vand. L. Rev.* 1407 (1996); E. D. Elliot, Law and Biology: The New Synthesis?, 41 *St. Louis U. L. J.* 595 (1997); and O. D. Jones, DNA: Lessons from The Past – Problems for the Future, 67 *Brooklyn L. Rev.* 207 (2001).

to isolate satisfactorily whether particular behavioral traits are the product of natural or nurtured tendencies and at what point any so-called natural tendency is renurtured.[10] However, rather than pursue these criticisms generally, I will situate them in a focused and continuing debate that goes to the heart of modern jurisprudence – the battle royal between Ronald Dworkin and Richard Posner. The comparisons between this exchange and that between Wilberforce and Huxley almost 150 years ago are striking, not least because Dworkin and Posner not only resemble their historical antecedents but also think that they are more fundamentally dissimilar than they are. Some of the lessons to be learned from this bitter contemporary exchange are that bulldogs are sometimes only Soapy Sams in canine clothing, and that bulldogs sometimes bite the hand that feeds them.

When Ronnie Met Dick

Although the venue has been suitably ubiquitous in this technological age, the occasion for much of the furious and dyspeptic exchanges between Dworkin and Posner was the antics of President Clinton and the validity of (unsuccessful) efforts to impeach him. However, like the Oxford debate between Wilberforce and Huxley, the agenda is much broader and more polarized; it pits the established legal order, with its metaphysics, against a social scientific paradigm:

Ronald Dworkin: [Pragmatism] is philosophically a dog's dinner.
Richard Posner: I take it [Dworkin] does not much like dogs.
Ronald Dworkin: As it happens, I like dogs very much.
Richard Posner: As a cat person, I am disappointed. I hope I will be forgiven for having thought him distinctly feline.[11]

Beneath (or perhaps above) the personal invective and collateral point scoring, there is a very significant dispute over the nature and legitimacy of common law adjudication. In opposition to "Soapy Sam" Dworkin's frankly theological rendering of the jurisprudential project, "Bulldog" Posner offers a more pragmatic and scientific challenge that eschews all attempts to relate

---

[10] See J. L. Casti, *Complexification* (1994) and S. Pinker, *How the Mind Works* (1997).

[11] See R. Dworkin, Pragmatism, Rights Answers and True Banality in *Pragmatism in Law and Society* 359 at 360 (M. Brint and W. Weaver eds. 1991); R. Posner, *The Problematics of Moral and Legal Theory* 240 (1999); R. Dworkin, Posner's Charges: What I Actually Said, <http://www.nyu.edu/gsas/dept/philo/faculty/dworkin/papers/posner>; and R. Posner, Dworkin, Polemics, and the Clinton Impeachment Controversy, 94 *Nw. U. L. Rev.* 1023 at 1046 (2000).

the worth of grand theory to the practical operation of the adjudicative task: The law is less a theological pilgrimage of legal faith and more a technical craft of bureaucratic policy making. While there is something to admire in each of these positions, there is much more to reject. Whereas Posner is a typical lawyer who cannot resist turning the powerful descriptive thrust of Darwinian evolution to illegitimate prescriptive effect, Dworkin rejects entirely the critical force of evolutionary theory and reveals that he is more the Creationist than he might otherwise think or wish to be.

It will be remembered that, for Dworkin, adjudication is a philosophical adventure of the grandest kind in which formal integrity and abstract coherence are both the tools and goal of intrepid jurists. Combining ethical optimism and evolutionary inevitability, Dworkin glosses the messy, episodic, and self-correcting workings of the common law as a polished, integrated, and teleological process. Many lawyers and jurists reject such scholarly spiritualism and its claims that law has a miraculous suprahistorical life. Even if such an approach were once viable, it is increasingly untenable in a contemporary world in which lawyers and society at large are increasingly diverse in composition, interests, and objectives. In contrast, pragmatic critics argue that common law adjudication is much more earthly, less preposterous, and thoroughly practical in aspiration and execution. They maintain that Dworkin's plea for a 'justificatory ascent' to some abstract remove from which it might be possible to catch an echo of the infinitely true and carry it back to society for people's edification and enlightenment is exactly the wrong trip to take. For them, not only is there no escape from the messy and contingent facts of social living in history, but there also ought to be no fear or disappointment on realizing that fact. The most prominent of these pragmatic critics is, of course, Richard Posner. Once a firm believer himself in the truths of objectivity and integrity, he has now put his prodigious energy at the service of a more pragmatic creed. He has become, like Huxley, a Darwinian Rottweiler who can only be ignored at all lawyers' and jurists' peril.

Posner argues that moral theory not only has little to offer law but that it is positively dangerous to its actual operation. For him, a Dworkinian pilgrimage takes judges and jurists off into the kind of ideological and indeterminate speculation that is inimical to legitimate lawyering. Drawing explicitly on the writings of several neo-Darwinians and in the evolutionary wake of his intellectual hero, Oliver Wendell Holmes, Jr., Posner recommends "an adaptationist conception of morality, in which morality is judged – non-morally, in the way that a hammer might be judged well or poorly adapted to its function of hammering nails – by its contribution to the survival, or other goals, of a society."[12] In this way, Posner maintains that judges can act as evolutionary midwives by facilitating rather than steering society's moral development and progress. For Posner, this does not mean that law must be unprincipled or technocratic, only that it is wrong to equate "moral principle to principle, and morality to normativity." Instead, he concludes that what is required is that judges develop "a disposition to ground policy judgments on facts and consequences than on conceptualisms and generalities."[13] In short, judges and lawyers must eschew moral philosophy for social science. In fulfilling this bureaucratic role, judges and jurists, Posner recommends, should avail themselves of the economists' empirical tools and work to craft useful solutions to pressing and practical controversies.

While there is much to appreciate in Posner's pragmatic critique of Dworkinian-style theorizing, this audacious proposal – that the empirical tools of economists are morally neutral and ought to be adopted by judges – is no less troubling. Indeed, like the earlier Bulldog, Posner manages to subvert Darwinian ideas in the process of championing them; he turns a valid descriptive analysis into an illegitimate prescriptive theory. At the end of the day, by replacing moral philosophy with social science, he is in the same theological game as Dworkin. It is not simply that he tells society what it should do if it wants to be a better society (which is a fine and noble enterprise), but that he does so in the name of science. While it is true that judges and jurists would do well to take greater heed of the sociopolitical context in which they work and of the actual consequences of their decisions and suggestions, it is absurd to imagine that this can be done without some resort to social values or political commitments. As an empirical matter, it is simply not the case that there is "a fair degree of value consensus among the judges," such that they can "seek the best results unhampered by philosophical doubts."[14] What theory cannot do, whether in an ethical or scientific guise, is provide

---

[12] R. Posner, The Problematics of Moral and Legal Theory, 111 *Harv. L. Rev.* 1637 at 1641 (1998). Posner is partial to the work of Dawkins and other ultra-Darwinians; see supra, chap. 2. Holmes was influenced by biological studies and compared the transformations of legal doctrine to organisms' adaption to environmental conditions. See The Path of the Law, 10 *Harv. L. Rev.* 457 (1897) and Law in Science and Science in Law, 12 *Harv. L. Rev.* 48 (1899).

[13] R. Posner, Problematics, supra, note 11 at 133 and 227 (1999). See also C. Sunstein, *One Case at a Time: Judicial Minimalism on the Supreme Court* (1999) and E. D. Elliott, supra, note 9.

[14] R. Posner, id. at 262. This stands in stark contrast to Posner's earlier arguments that the legal and judicial profession has an increasing racial, gender, and class diversity and that this produces an increase in the diversity of political and moral views endorsed by lawyers and judges: "the nation's legal heterogeneity mirrors its moral heterogeneity." See R. Posner, *The Problems of Jurisprudence* 129 (1990).

a method that will relieve people from the responsibility and challenge of constantly arguing and rearguing what should and should not be done in particular contexts at particular times. Indeed, like many others before him, Posner fails to grasp that there are no secure footings for law and legal theory that are not themselves part of the very political and situated debate that they are intended to ground. Dworkin is surely right when he argues that Posner's claims about the political process are not descriptive or technical; they are moral in the sense that they are not only judgments about how best to achieve stipulated goals but also highly controversial claims about the distribution and exercise of government powers and the limits imposed by respect for individual moral rights. "[Posner] calls for the death of moral theory, but, like all of philosophy's would-be undertakers, he only means the triumph of his own theory."[15]

While it is perfectly appropriate to chastise Posner for drawing on values, it does not mean that this commits such a critic to the theological kind of grand theorizing in which Soapy Sams specialize. Espousing the merits of survival of the fittest or a related pseudobiological standard is less of a problem than the attempt to defend it as an evolutionary imperative. Debate over such proposals is a distinctly moral and, therefore, endlessly controversial engagement rather than an exercise in scientific demonstration. A sound defense of any moral theory need not entail the kind of abstract and pure speculation that Dworkin urges. For example, he seems to be insisting that there is no choice other than objective truth – "a matter of how things really are" – or subjective opinion – "in our own breasts."[16] Anything that does not live up to the objective standards of truth is mere conviction, mere convention, mere ideology, and so on. This kind of either–or, all-or-nothing thinking misrepresents the possibilities. To be against objective truth does not mean that one is left with only subjective opinion; to be against only subjective opinion does not imply that one is defending the existence of objective truth. Although the traditional search for objectivity is a lost cause, there are not only subjective opinions and relativized truths. Instead, one truth is not as good as another, if one understands by truth nothing more than that it meets the familiar procedures of justification that hold sway. It is not about striving to reach a promised land of truth that will make further justification unnecessary. Instead, jurisprudence must become more useful

---

[15] R. Dworkin, Darwin's New Bulldog, 111 *Harv. L. Rev.* 1718 at 1738–39 (1998).

[16] R. Dworkin, Objectivity and Truth: You'd Better Believe It, 25 *Phil & Pub. Affs.* 87 at 92. See also D. Farber and S. Sherry, *Beyond all Reason: The Radical Assault on Truth in American Law* 7, 22, 73, 119, and 133 (1997).

such that success is not vouchsafed by reliance on a particular epistemic method, but by the usefulness of the results arrived at and their effect on meeting certain objectives that are taken to be morally or politically significant. Moral choice is "always a matter of compromise between competing goods rather than a choice between the absolutely right and the absolutely wrong."[17]

Accordingly, instead of reflecting with the Soapy Sams upon universality to justify particular principles (which will turn out anyway as little more than a cover for the theorists' own political or moral agenda), there should be talk along with Posner about the concrete and relative advantages of choosing one over another. However, such talk must be openly moral and political, since there is no scientific or factual way to finesse that responsibility and opportunity. Sadly, Posner is pragmatic in the most unpragmatic of ways. Because he accepts much of the contextual situation as given, he restricts himself to tinkering with present arrangements and remains profoundly abstruse and rationalistic in his analysis: Abstract universality is ditched, only to be replaced with abstract particularity. There is little appreciation that legal reasoning operates in the real world of historical struggle or of how law does (and does not) change.[18] When the idea of social practices is given a more political than ethical spin, the operation of power is brought into the center of debate. Consensus (and, therefore, standards of persuasion and justification) can be treated as imposed as much as chosen. In moving from truth to usefulness, a thoroughly pragmatic jurisprudence does not set out to know things as they really are a la the Soapy Sams or to isolate a scientific criterion of usefulness a la the Bulldogs. In responding to the compelling question of what to do next, both a Soapy Sam Dworkin and a Bulldog Posner answer with far too much certainty or confidence than is good for them or anyone else; knowledge and usefulness are not the stable or secure footings on which the houses of law can be safely constructed. A Darwinian-informed pragmatism is much less modest and much more experimental. In Darwinian terms, law is only one more set of tools through which human beings are struggling to cope with the contingent circumstances of their environment and with the realization that these efforts, like the best laid plans of Robbie Burns' mice and men, often come to nought.

It was Justice Brandeis' prediction that little progress in society will made until the lawyers' obsession with "the logic of words" has been healed by their

---

[17] R. Rorty, *Philosophy and Social Hope* xxxii and xxix (1999).
[18] See D. Kennedy, *A Critique of Adjudication Fin De Siècle* (1998) and A. C. Hutchinson, Casaubon's Ghosts: The Haunting of Legal Scholarship, 21 *Legal Studies* 65 (2001).

attachment to the "logic of realities."[19] However, in emphasizing that law's development is better explained as a contingent responsiveness to historical circumstances than as the unfolding of law's inner logic, I ought not to be taken to be making the very different claim that law develops in line with some external deep logic of social reality – it is logic as much as the words or the realities that is the problem. There is no one account of the organic relation between law and social relations that is valid for all time, all societies, and all legal developments. The connections between legal doctrine and material interests are often as casual as they are causal and as contingent as they are necessary. It is not that legal doctrine is without any rhyme or reason at all, but that any efforts to go beyond either the most general or the most detailed account are confounded by the doctrinal and social facts. The explanations become either so abstract as to lack any practical predictive force or so elaborate as to capture only a particular historical moment in time. There are always too many plausible and competing rationales to satisfy the formalistic need for explanatory primacy or closure. In the same way that E. P. Thompson announced that "the greatest of all fictions is that the law evolves, from case to case, by its own impartial logic, true only to its own integrity, unswayed by expedient considerations,"[20] the reverse can be proclaimed with equal force – law does not evolve, from case to case, by the partial logic of class struggle, true only to established interests, unswayed by logical considerations. By different measures at different times, the development of law is a mix of the *logical* – in the sense of attempted compliance with law's own generated (and indeterminate) rationality – and the *expedient* – in the sense of responsiveness to society's own political (and indeterminate) demands. Both logic and expediency infiltrate and affect the operation of each other; lawyers and judges are neither only the lackey of established (or any other) interests nor always the intellectual captives of a professional tradition. Whereas Dworkin's naturalism emphasizes the *logical* at the expense of the *expedient*, Posner's pragmatism passes off the *expedient* as the *logical*.

This all having been said, it is not my intention to condemn theory *tout court*. It should be clear that I am not against theory per se but only its continued and exclusive black-letter self-image: A sophisticated antitheory is not same as a vulgar antitheoreticism or a crude practicalism. I am against grand theory and theoreticism, not theory or philosophy. If intellectuals are to be of use to societies that claim or aspire to democratic ideals, then they must abandon the belief that their task must be to lay down authoritative

---

[19] See *DiSanto v. Pennsylvania*, 273 US 34 at 43 per Brandeis J dissenting (1927).
[20] E. P. Thompson, *Whigs and Hunters: The Origins of the Black Act* 250 (1976).

blueprints for legal and political action in the name of some universal truth about the human condition or law. It is not only possible but also more effective to talk about politics and morality without a commitment to a theory of objective truths; an emancipatory or transformative project does not depend on or require a grand theory to back it up. In the same way that there is no sharp break between theory and practice, so too is there no gap between law and politics or between jurisprudence and practical lawyering. It is not that each collapses into the other and has no relevant differences, but that there is no bright line dividing one from the other that is not itself hostage to the context in which it arises and is sustained. In an important sense, it is more theory that is needed, not less. I agree with Dworkin that "we have no choice but to ask [judges and lawyers] to confront issues that, from time to time, are philosophical." However, I also maintain that such philosophical work need not and must not be of the abstract variety that he recommends; Dworkin's jurisprudence does not so much abandon "all the familiar legal phlogistons," as he claims, but in its attachment to integrity, truth, and objectivity adds to that alchemical collection.[21] Instead, what is required is a more useful jurisprudence. In the end, there must be talk about substance without the distracting diversion of talk about theory – not, however, as Posner and his dog-loving friends insist, as an exercise without values (or, more accurately, as values presented as facts) and not, as Dworkin and his Soapy colleagues insist, as a matter of grand theorizing. It is to a more useful and emancipatory account of legal theory that I now turn.

Toward a Useful Jurisprudence

As will be obvious to anyone vaguely familiar with the contemporary jurisprudential scene, pragmatism has become very much the de rigeur intellectual fashion of the day. While it is not quite accurate to report that every jurists announces that "we are all pragmatists now," there is a definite desire on the part of many jurists to be identified with the pragmatic turn in legal theory. In many ways, this is an encouraging trend. However, on closer inspection, it becomes clear that these conversions are more superficial than real, more a simple change of clothes than a substantial transformation of life-style. Many of those who call themselves pragmatists have done little more than incorporate pragmatic phrasings and vocabulary into their jurisprudential writings. Like Posner, they still subscribe to the same traditional understanding of the

---

[21] R. Dworkin, <u>In Praise of Theory</u>, 29 *Ariz. L. Rev.* 353 at 375–76 (1997).

jurisprudential project and what would count as its successful completion. In short, they practice pragmatism in the most unpragmatic of ways and deploy pragmatic means for distinctly unpragmatic ends. Accordingly, it is fitting to chart the different forms of jurisprudential pragmatism in terms of their willingness to pursue the full implications of a pragmatic sensibility. There seem to be three possible groupings – conservative, liberal, and radical.[22]

Whereas the first two hedge on the implications of a pragmatic critique, the third carries through that critique in the most uncompromising way. However, while I support a radical pragmatism, I do not do so because it is the best or only form of pragmatic jurisprudence – that would smack too much of a theological standard, and I would run the risk of the buying into the so-called naturalistic fallacy. Instead, I do so simply because it *presently* seems to offer the most useful and effective possibility for improving the lot of those most disadvantaged and disenfranchised in contemporary industrialized society. It is a pragmatically open and distinctly political claim. The three kinds of pragmatism can be summarized as follows.

'Conservative pragmatism' is conservative because, as the name implies, it accepts much of the contextual situation as given; there is no willingness to disturb present arrangements. In jurisprudence, conservative pragmatists propose a pragmatic mode of legal reasoning that rejects the theoretical pretensions of the grand theorists and treasures the virtues of technical craft and particularized judgement. While its practitioners make all the right noises,[23] their accounts remain profoundly abstruse and rationalistic in the sense that they are unsituated in the material circumstances of history and inured to their political dynamics. There is little appreciation that legal reasoning operates in a real world of historical struggle or of how law does change. The only experience and context that matters is the legal one: The experience of the law is the life of its own logic.

'Liberal pragmatism' is much less insulated and contained than conservative pragmatism. The whole idea and force of contingency is given much greater recognition. Stepping outside the hermetic world of legal experience, scholars look to legal reasoning as a much more constructed and contextualized practice. Under this view, law and jurisprudence are a language game that people play with greater or lesser facility; it is as much a

---

[22] I borrow the idea for this taxonomy from Roithmayr, although I organize it in a slightly different way. See D. Roithmayr, Guerrillas in Our Midst: The Assault on Radicals in American Law, 96 *Mich. L. Rev.* 1658 (1998).

[23] See C. Sunstein, *Legal Reasoning and Political Conflict* (1996) and R. Posner, *Problems*, supra, note 14 and *Overcoming Law* (1995).

matter of coping as it is of getting it right. Although many follow the conventional script, some struggle to escape from inherited descriptions and to offer fresh discursive options. Truth and objectivity are ethical practices that are not about "the accurate representation of something non-human," but "a matter of intersubjective consensus among human beings."[24] As ethical ideals, transformation and emancipation are treated as more a personal undertaking than a social project; the emphasis is on private salvation rather than public reconstruction.

Last, but not least, there is 'radical pragmatism'. In contrast to both conservative and liberal pragmatism, it does not hedge on the subversive implications of the antiessentialist insight. In a manner of speaking, radical pragmatism is radical because it accepts that it is pragmatism all the way down: There is no artificial distinction between what is and is not up for grabs. Because everything has been constructed, everything can be deconstructed and reconstructed. If conservative pragmatism ignores both history and politics, liberal pragmatism has succeeded in placing present arrangements in a historical context, only to fail to politicize that history; liberal pragmatism tends to apprehend more benign and accidental forces at work in social life than is the case. In law, this means that legal reasoning is as much about political oppression as it is about ethical consensus.[25] The liberal pragmatists' failure to appreciate adequately the grubby, materialistic, and public conditions under which private efforts at self-realization take place makes their notion of political struggle too clinical, too intellectual, and too individualistic.

Accordingly, by refusing to duck the corrosive consequences of a thoroughgoing pragmatism, the radical version ensures that what amounts to a useful politics or jurisprudence is opened up to the widest range of possible options and, what is most important, to the widest range of participants. By giving the idea of social practices a more political than ethical spin, it brings the operation of power into the center of debate; consensus (and, therefore, standards of persuasion and justification) can as easily be treated as imposed as much as chosen. Careful not to slip back into a discredited version of ideological suffocation, such a radical pragmatism can thereby work toward ensuring that those voices presently left out of democracy's sustaining conversation are included and able to articulate for themselves

---

[24] R. Rorty, *Achieving Our Country: Leftist Thought in Twentieth Century America* 35 (1998) and generally C. Anderson, *Pragmatic Liberalism* (1990). For a representative jurisprudential rendition of liberal pragmatism, see D. Farber and S. Sherry, <u>supra</u>, note 16.

[25] See D. Kennedy, <u>supra</u>, note 18.

what is and is not useful for them. I say "for themselves" because it is the lingering influence of a foundationalist hubris that mistakenly suggests that the educated and wise can speak best for the dispossessed. Instead, public and local efforts at transformation must be undertaken to permit the disenfranchised to speak in their own voices, with their own vocabulary, and through their own visions about usefulness. However, the voices of the presently excluded should not be valorized or given authority simply by virtue of their excludedness; democracy demands neither the demonization nor the romanticization of the oppressed. Moreover, as well as broadening and substantiating the popular franchise, there must be equally vigorous efforts to multiply and transform the institutions in which debate and struggle occur. A radical society is not one that has a fixed idea of usefulness or a set inventory of institutional opportunities for its elaboration; it is one in which the idea and institutions of usefulness are themselves being constantly revisited and revised. There is nothing about this plea for such a robustly democratic society that depends on any philosophical claim that such a society is more natural, more rational, more coherent, more pure, or more anything else than any other society. On the contrary, it is simply a substantive argument that such a society is best suited to ensure the emancipation of people from suffering and deprivation. As a political and topical proposal, it is defended and espoused in the name of usefulness, not truth.

In this radical view of pragmatism, the democratic ideal of a "free and open encounter" about values and commitments is to be encouraged, but that freedom and openness cannot be understood outside some context of power and politics.[26] While there is no truth or reason to set over against power or politics, it does not follow that one simply collapses into the other. Those critics who argue that reason is only power are as mistaken as those who argue that reason and power can be totally insulated from each other. Although truth and reason are always located within a context of power and politics, the possibility of maintaining standards of justification and persuasion is not thereby sabotaged entirely. Rather than attempt the impossible by seeking to establish standards that are pure and undistorted by power,

---

[26] R. Rorty, *Contingency, Irony, Solidarity* 60 (1989). As for Rorty himself, there was something of a shift in his thinking. He used to argue that consensus about conflicting vocabularies was generated through a "free and open encounter" undistorted by power. However, in his more recent work, while he still occasionally talks about "inter-subjective consensus" as a purely ethical ideal, he seems more willing to follow the more radical intimations of his pragmatic critique. For instance, he talks lately much more about public measures required to achieve "a classless and casteless society": The exclusive concern with private efforts at transformation has been replaced with a much more encompassing account of political action as a public responsibility. See R. Rorty, supra, note 24 and 42.

efforts should be taken to make standards more shared and to include the widest possible diversity of voices in their social construction. The claim to establish neutral or objective standards is fated to reflect the ideas, no matter how well intentioned, of a select few. Indeed, because "judgments of merit are inevitably culturally and ideologically contingent,"[27] an unbiased standard is simply one that does not favor one group over other; it is not one that is supposedly based on no values at all. Indeed, the problem is not the intervention of power in the halls of reason, but the traditional belief that power can be somehow excluded and that there exists some noncultural and nonsocial standard of merit. The democratic ambition is not to ensure that reason is detached from value or power, but that the values and interests that help constitute reason represent and are conducive to a truly democratic society. The debate must be about what counts as reason and merit and what standards are most useful to a democratic society. Accordingly, a meritocratic ideal is not antidemocratic, provided that what is understood as meritorious is a situated and substantive assessment, not a formal and far-fetched one.

In a similar vein, a radical brand of pragmatism insists that, although any accommodation to the status quo is not required, its root-and-branch rejection is not demanded. Being opportunistic rather than doctrinaire, those committed to significant transformation should be prepared to use whatever resources are available to them. On the basis that no strategy has any necessary or inevitable consequences, but will depend on the particular context in which it is utilized, radicals should be prepared to draw on the conservative and liberal repertoire to advance the cause of democratic empowerment. Because the present is the only place to begin the making of a better future, it is appropriate to utilize existing institutional arrangements at the same time that one works to effect their transformation in line with a more progressive and emancipatory ideal. To allow the ideal future to be the enemy of the flawed present is a recipe for resignation and complicity, not action and change. Ideological purity is no more attractive or useful than its philosophical relative. In short, because everything is constructed, it does not mean that everything has to be deconstructed or reconstructed all at once: The fact that everything is up for grabs does not demand that everything be up or grabbed at the same time.

One way to advance that useful agenda might be to treat the courts and common law as venues for the resolution of concrete disputes rather than

---

[27] D. Kennedy, A Cultural Pluralist Case for Affirmative Action in Legal Academia, 39 *Duke L. J.* 705 at 733 (1990).

as the site for the philosophical elaboration of doctrinal integrity or conceptual purity. While the courts have been a privileged site for defending the status quo and the history of the common law is more reactionary than revolutionary, radical pragmatists should countenance litigation as a possible tool for social change if or when the local conditions are propitious. This may demand a shift in jurisprudential emphasis from the law-making focus of judges to their problem-solving capacity. Indeed, despite their protestations to the contrary, Dworkin and his Soapy colleagues do not take law seriously. By asking judges to be open to 'justificatory ascent' and thereby turning them into grand-theorists, they neglect the pragmatic strengths of the common law and reduce politics to an abstract pursuit. The potential strength of the common law is its practicality and situatedness: The courts must concentrate more on practical solutions to practical problems than on philosophical responses to philosophical problems. It is not so much that a pragmatic account of the common law facilitates or frustrates particular political interventions, but that it neither forecloses nor guarantees their success. Again, in proposing this juristic realignment, I ought not to be taken as suggesting that the common law has been or necessarily can be the preferred complement to this kind of useful approach to jurisprudence. However, I do maintain that, when viewed from such a pragmatic perspective, the common law might be used as an institutional site for experimental, contextualized, and practical interventions to advance certain political initiatives. While the history of the common law ought not to impress the critics' sensibilities, resort to the courts need not be a hopeless or counterproductive diversion.

Within such a revisioning of the common law, jurists and legal scholars can play a number of roles. Foremost among them is that no study of law or ethics should be done, as black-letterism proposes, without recognizing the political context and conditions of that undertaking: The resilient black-letter practice of decontextualization must be strenuously combated. Instead, there has to be a greater recognition that law and politics are intimately and inseparably related; it is futile and well-nigh fraudulent to study one without the other. However, the study of politics and its relationship to law is not enough in itself. That study must be done in such a way that avoids the pitfalls and problems of black-letterism. There is little point in examining law's political context and determinants if it is done within the capacious reach but narrowing influence of a formalistic mind-set. To demand anything less is to allow the lingering spirit of black-letterism to intoxicate people into believing that clear directions and speedy routes can be mapped onto the messy and changing terrain of ethical and political inquiry, especially in mapping and exploring the relation of law and politics. Although the useful kind of legal scholarship recommended is scarce, it is not entirely absent; there is exciting work being done by – and this should come as no surprise – women and people of color. For instance, in the English context, for every Smith and Hogan, there is a Lacey and Wells; for every Treitel and Beatson, there is a Wheeler and Shaw; and for every Salmond and Street, there is a Conaghan and Mansell. In particular, in contrast to Smith and Hogan's scholarship, the feminist-inspired work of Nicola Lacey and Celia Wells is a breath of fresh air: They are truly interdisciplinary, making explicit their operative assumptions, moving socially relevant issues from margin to center, and focusing on the theoretical in the best practical sense.[28]

As a complement (and a compliment) to the work of such legal scholars, jurists can also play an explicitly and suitably theoretical role. Apart from tackling the lingering influence and fundamentalist practice of mainstream theory, they can bring fresh insights and appreciations to jurisprudence. In particular, jurists can develop alternative modes of discourse, so that philosophy will become more a discourse of dissent than a monologue of reverence. Rather than draft grand schema for political or legal action under the authority of some alleged universal truth, philosophers can seek out new possibilities and alternative openings. By cultivating "the ability to redescribe the familiar in unfamiliar terms,"[29] such useful theorists can help dislodge the deep-seated belief that present sociohistorical arrangements are inevitable and frozen in place. They can reassure people that, once epistemology has lost authority, mob rule will not fill the theoretical void. But empowered citizens might and, in doing so, can begin to claim authority over their own lives and participate more effectively in the civic elaboration of situated truths. By being activist in imagination and commitment, pragmatists may come to recognize that their philosophical task is to be as much inspired poets as robust political operatives. Or, to put it another way, jurists will recognize that the best way to do legal philosophy is to do it pragmatically, usefully, and poetically. The persistent belief that "law is the calling of thinkers," whether in the form of metaphysicians or economists, and "not

---

[28] See J. C. Smith and B. Hogan, *Criminal Law* (9th ed. 1999); N. Lacey and C. Wells, *Reconstructing Criminal Law: Critical Perspectives on Crime and the Criminal Process* (2nd ed. 1998); J. Beatson and M. H. Matthews, *Administrative Law: Cases and Materials* (1983); *Anson's Law of Contract* (J. Beatson 28th ed. 2002); G. Treitel, *The Law of Contract* (10th ed. 1999); S. Wheeler and J. Shaw, *Contract Law: Cases, Materials and Commentary* (1994); J. Salmond, *Essays in Jurisprudence and Legal History* (1987); J. Conaghan and A. Bottomley, *Feminist Theory and Legal Strategy* (1993); and W. Mansell, B. Meteyard, and A. Thomson, *A Critical Introduction to Law* (2nd ed. 1999).

[29] R. Rorty, supra, note 17 at 87.

the place for the artist or the poet" is to be discarded once and for all.[30] Like similar formalistic distinctions, the difference between art and science or literature and philosophy is one of emphasis and practice, not essence and theory. In becoming more artistic and poetic, jurists and legal scholars can also become better legal thinkers and political policy makers.

Radical Charges

An important charge against 'useful jurisprudence' and my radical version of it is likely to be that, although I urge a more useful performance of the jurisprudential craft, I am engaged in exactly the same kind of indulgent word-mongering that is typical of the traditional philosophical mind-set. Withdrawn from the real world, I am long on words and short on action – How many more people will be off the streets and in better accommodation as a result of this book? It might be suggested that, if I am true to my own critique, I must entirely abandon a commitment to legal philosophy and simply dedicate myself to political action. Otherwise, I run the risk of hypocrisy and possible complicity in the very project that I condemn. There are several responses to this. First, while there is much wisdom in this criticism, its force is more cautionary than condemnatory. I cannot disagree that it would be better if there were more political activists and fewer legal theorists. However, this does not mean that legal theorists have no role to play at all, only that it should be a more humble and limited one that receives far less kudos than it presently does. Second, as a legal theorist, I hope to be doing something useful in that I am challenging the way that jurists and legal scholars tend to turn all practical problems into philosophical ones, thereby unhelpfully re-presenting them as abstract puzzles rather than substantive problems. In contrast, I urge those involved in legal study to abjure such flights of fancy and to keep their feet firmly on the social ground, even as that ground shifts and changes with time and circumstance. It is situation sense that is best cultivated, not conceptual sophistication. However, the obvious riposte to this defense is that being a legal theorist, of whatever color or commitment, is the real problem. Even if the talk is about usefulness, it remains only talk and ignores the main lesson of a radical pragmatic critique – that it is better to live a life of beneficent activity than talk about

---

[30] O. W. Holmes, Jr., The Profession of the Law (Conclusion of a Lecture Delivered to Undergraduates of Harvard University, February 17, 1886), in *The Essential Holmes: Selection from Letters, Speeches, Judicial Opinions, and Other Writing of Oliver Wendell Holmes, Jr.* 218 (Richard A. Posner ed. 1992).

living one. Good intentions do little in themselves to alleviate suffering and cruelty. This is a stiff challenge and must be confronted directly.[31]

My third and more fundamental response, therefore, is to return to the basic thrust of a radical pragmatism and, in particular, its opposition to more traditional philosophical jurisprudence. The insistence on a hard-and-fast distinction between talk and actions is not as real or as compelling as some might think. Moreover, it is made no less palatable because it is deployed in the service of a more so-called progressive agenda. Such a contrast between words and acts, like all other distinctions (i.e., theory and practice, law and politics, etc.), is difficult to maintain in a posttheological world. Indeed, to treat talk and action as conceptually distinct is a hallmark of the kind of thinking that I have sought to discredit. The practical power of ideas or talk is not something to be underestimated. After all, without talk and ideas, it is difficult to imagine how it would be possible to identify the problems of contemporary jurisprudence and move beyond them. Moreover, in the broader context of social history, it is talk of ideas as much as acts of force that helps to hold oppressive regimes in place and that can contribute to their downfall: Both Vorster's and Mandela's career as well as Hitler's and Churchill's testify to that. What counts as a problem and what should be done about it implicates some theoretical assumption. Similarly, what tells one to act instead of only talk is itself a theoretical premise. Of course, what I mean by *theoretical* is not something to be set over, against, or above practice; it is part and parcel of the same enterprise. In a manner of speaking, talk is an act that, while it might not be as immediate or as obvious as Molotovs, is as necessary to what we do as anything else. In the same way that there are better and worse ways of acting, so there are better and worse ways of talking. Accordingly, there is no one way to challenge injustice; it takes many people doing many different things at many different times and in many different ways. Doing legal theory is one of those ways, no intrinsically better and no worse than any other ambition. But, as I have sought to argue, there are more useful and less useful ways of doing legal theory – my genuinely pragmatic perspective is more useful than either Dworkin's or Posner's jurisprudence. Theory is an act that makes possible other acts or, to put it more pragmatically, theory is itself a contextualized practice that is also one of the contexts within which acts take on shape and substance. Any theory's success at doing that will be a measure of its usefulness; such a measure will be situated and substantive, not abstract and conceptual. Pontificating from a Soapy pulpit or barking with a Bulldog accent are ways that stand to do as much harm as good.

---

[31] See A. Hutchinson, *Waiting for Coraf: A Critique of Law and Rights* 172–83 (1995).

It is not possible to tread a safe path into, through, and out of partisan politics. Not only will principled argument not be equal to the task, but it also might occasionally be a hindrance. Standing on principle is simply another way of sitting on some substantive ground and pretending that it is more solid and independent than it actually is. Indeed, being partisan is not the problem; it is what one is partisan about that is the only real issue worth caring or complaining about. Indeed, a large part of my critique is intended to encourage judges and jurists to be more politically candid and to drop the intellectual pretence that a principled stance has merit, regardless of the substantive content of that principle, and that it can lead to enlightenment or universal justice. There is no Big Plan and anyone offering one should be immediately suspect. There are only situation-specific and contingent commitments that continually change in substance and recommendation. However, it has been suggested that such a "critical pragmatism" is politically weak and falsely optimistic in that it lacks prescriptive bite: It offers no substantive guidelines for what counts as progressive change and, even when it does, these substantive positions amount to little more than personal and therefore unreliable commitments.[32] While I am not unsympathetic to such chagrin, this way of thinking is symptomatic of much jurisprudential thinking on both the Left and the Right. To suggest that there are no reliable or enduring substantive guidelines is not equivalent to conceding that politics is only a world of naked preferences in which might is the only source of right. This is part of the very monochromatic view of the world that I reject. A critical pragmatic approach is nether cynical nor naive. In recommending the virtues of engaged and situated exchange, it entirely rejects the worth of a right-is-might stance, whether it is enthusiastically embraced or resignedly conceded. The critical pragmatists offer reasons, but eschew Reason and pursue particular values but dismisse general -Isms. In its plea for more, not less, debate, it is a "put up or shut up" approach that is intended to flush out the pretentious and pusillanimous.

In the spirit of a critical and pragmatic perspective, I maintain that principle and substance go hand in hand in that each informs as it is informed by the other: "preferences *are* principles – not principles of the neutral kind but principles of the only kind there really are, strong moral intuitions as to how the world should go combined with a resolve to be faithful to them."[33] There is no neutral or principled method that will deliver a legal

---

[32] See, for example, R. Devlin, The Law and Politics of 'Might': An Internal Critique of Hutch's Hopeful Hunch, 38 *Osgoode Hall L. J.* 545 (2000).
[33] S. Fish, *The Trouble with Principle* 9 (1999).

truth independent of political exchange. That is why this pragmatic attack on principle is slightly more conducive to the Left than to the Right, at least insofar as the Left can be understood to consist of those who are more generally committed to challenging existing institutional values than revering them. Of course, I do not make these claims as a matter of principle. I simply claim that, while nothing *will* or *must* follow from this kind of critique, something *might* follow depending on the particular practical context in which the critique is made and political action is taken. Of course, under different conditions and in different ways, the Left might well be called to task when it cannot resist the temptation to enroll universal principle in defense of its political commitments – but that is more because the old-style Left too often fails to recognize that what is progressive is itself contextual and always open to revision. There is no right approach to particular problems outside of their historical and political milieu. And, because there is no Context of contexts, there is no easy, pat, uncontroversial, neutral, or exclusively principled way to decide what to do. Accordingly, moral or political improvement is simply about closing the gap between particular aspirations and contingent actuality so that the world can become a relatively better place. It is about taking a critical and pragmatic approach to the constant responsibility to do what is best in the circumstances.

In making this plea for a more useful jurisprudence, I ought not to be taken as part of the mainstream chorus for a shift in legal theory and scholarship. Although some maintain that the past twenty years have been a golden age for legal scholarship, others have argued strenuously that it has been a lamentable phase in which practical relevance has been sacrificed to theoretical indulgence. For instance, Justice Bastarache of the Supreme Court of Canada urges a move away from the kind of analytical legal theory that functions "in terms of abstract, logically coherent, formal conceptual systems" and "promotes stability and coherent changeability by affecting the substantive content of rights and by providing a rational basis for judicial decision-making." He laments such a preoccupation on three grounds. First, he maintains that such a jurisprudential perspective "presupposes a metaphysically untenable idea of objective moral truth." Second, he highlights the fact that such theorizing "is impractical in that it does not sufficiently attend to what works in real life." Third, he contends that legal theory "does not accurately describe what judges actually do when they reason through cases." By way of conclusion, he also points out that adjudication is pluralistic in that it concerns itself with more than legal theory and "is guided by a search for the correct balance of all relevant factors." While it ought to be more relevant and less sophisticated, the general aim is for legal academics to act as helpmates to the courts so that they can develop areas of the law in a technically sound and substantively fair way; "academic commentary that is *useful* to judges is that which assembles and rationalizes judicial decisions in a given field of law, draws out the general principles that these decisions imply, criticizes judicial decisions and suggests different approaches to particular areas of law."[34]

There is much to admire in Bastarache's dismissal of analytical jurisprudence with its precious emphasis on abstraction and its overweening respect for coherence. However, there is little reason to believe that Bastarache's alternative has more to recommend it. Indeed, his proffered alternative is more a variant on analytical jurisprudence than an alternative to it. Apart from drawing on the dubious virtue of principled consistency, Bastarache does much to tout the validity of traditional legal scholarship, suitably lifted a theoretical notch or two. Indeed, while there has been a significant increase in the amount of interdisciplinary work done by legal scholars, the fact is that a great deal of that work has been harnessed to the traditional academic task of performing so-called taxonomic scholarship (i.e., the classification and organization of legal rules). The performance of this traditional task has become much more sophisticated, but it remains devoted to the same set of jaded goals and ambitions.[35] The ability of mainstream scholarship to absorb and neutralize new insights and fresh perspectives on the study of law is truly staggering. Indeed, its intellectual agility in doing this is to be admired, although it is a great pity that such a prodigious talent cannot be put to more rewarding and less toadying effect. In short, there has been something of a shift from black-letter lawyering, but it has not gone much further than black-letter theorizing. Any significant transformation demands a switch in jurisprudential attention from the pursuit of metaphysical truth (even Bastarache's watered-down version) to the practice of political usefulness. A juristic account or proposal is mistaken not because it is philosophically wrong, but because it is not practically useful. Unfortunately, for Bastarache and his ilk, *useful* is exhausted in the same tired philosophical and apolitical sense.

---

[34] M. Bastarache, The Role of Academics and Legal Theory in Judicial Decision-Making, 37 *Alta L. Rev.* 739 at 740 (1999). See H. T. Edwards, The Growing Disjunction Between Legal Education and the Legal Profession, 91 *Mich. L. Rev.* 34 (1992). For a less jaundiced view, see J. Langbein, Scholarly and Professional Objectives in Legal Education: American Trends and English Comparisons, in *What Are Law Schools for?* 1 at 6 (P. Birks ed. 1996).

[35] See *Law and Learning: Report to the Social Sciences and Humanities Research Council of Canada* (1983).

When it comes to thinking about the adjudicative role, most jurists still exist in a semiconscious state in which the illusions of noble dreams and ignoble nightmares hold sway.[36] The overriding problem, though, is that it not entirely clear which is the dream and which is the nightmare. The choice between a vision in which judges admit to making law and one in which they claim to be simply applying it is itself dependent on two separate considerations – whether it is really possible to apply law without also making it and whether the law to be applied is substantively superior to what judges might decided for themselves. Indeed, it is my view that the courts cannot do one without also doing the other. Applying the law involves choice as much as that choice involves reference to existing law; it is a constant and organic interaction between choice and constraint, between amendment and application, and between direction and discretion. In a manner of speaking, judges will never get a good night's sleep (nor should they) as they are destined to struggle with the heavy responsibilities of doing justice. The best that they can hope for is that they will do enough good in their waking hours that they can get sufficient sleep to refresh themselves for the next day's travails. Judges who sleep without dreams or nightmares are either so smugly confident as to question their ability to do justice in a world in which what justice demands is always changing or so anxiously overwrought as to undermine their capacity to make difficult decisions in difficult circumstances. Doing 'justice through law', if that is not oxymoronic (and it is not under a pragmatic account), requires judges to concern themselves more with the bracing light of concrete day than the confusing shadows of abstract night. In this regard, Bastarache is correct – good judging is about much more than getting the theory right. However, he is wrong in thinking that good judging can be anything more than appreciating that the common law is a work-in-progress and that the judge's role is to make local and useful contributions to the resolution of the disputes that fall to be decided.

Bringing It Home

In advocating a useful jurisprudence, therefore, I ought not to be taken as championing some fixed or foundational idea of usefulness that is intended to inform and guide practice. On the contrary, I want to ensure that this definitional effort is an integral part of the very argumentative culture

---

[36] See H. Hart, American Jurisprudence Through English Eyes: The Nightmare and The Noble Dream, 11 Geo. L. Rev. 969 at 989 (1977).

that develops and allows transformations of what is and is not useful. Consequently, the emphasis on usefulness is not another disguised strategy of black-letter theorizing in which Usefulness replaces Integrity or Purity as the underlying standard of jurisprudential worth. In moving from truth to usefulness, a pragmatic jurisprudence does not set out to know things as they really are or to isolate a universal criterion of usefulness. Because usefulness is a continually contested and contextualized yardstick, it begs to be judged by its contribution to the ambitious project of challenging the present arrangements in order to improve the future. To do this, jurisprudence requires a different vocabulary more suited to its practical demands. There must be less formal talk of integrity, consistency, and harmony and more substantive talk of justice, well-being, and empowerment. Although, as I have been at pains to emphasize, pragmatism cannot answer the compelling question of *what to do next?* in any fixed or certain way, it can encourage the jurisprudential effort to ensure that valuable energies are not wasted on pseudodebates about truth and objectivity. In doing so, it will become possible to open a space in which people can engage directly about what is more and less useful in specific contexts at specific times.

In pursuing this useful agenda of jurisprudential study, mainstream theorists still have a possible role to play and a valued contribution to make. A demonstration that any theorists' ethical or political ideals do not flow inexorably from the extant law does not, of course, dispense entirely with their claim on our jurisprudential attention. While it robs these theories of their claimed authority as objective or natural truths, the practical recommendations that they entail must still be judged as one of a series of contingent proposals for making sense of the world and the possibilities for its remaking. Consequently, the work of Dworkin, Posner, and others still has value provided that its insights are treated as rhetorical interventions in a continuing democratic conversation, not as authoritative conversation stoppers regarding eternal verities. Once such jurists ditch their metaphysical baggage, not only might they get to their chosen destination quicker, but they also might accept that, as well as there being several paths to follow, the destination will change as events move on. Dworkin and Posner both should engage in a justificatory descent that will bring them down to earth so that they will talk more about unemployment, racism, poverty, and the like. If agreement can be reached on the problems to be addressed and their relative priorities, then more time can be spent on their practical resolution than on pseudodisputes about philosophical niceties. If there is disagreement on the problems or their relative priorities, it will not help much to take time out and argue about abstract notions of truth and objectivity. Even if there was agreement about such speculative matters, it has no necessary consequences for the more crucial and detailed efforts to improve the quality of people's lives. Instead, it is more productive to unpack and identify what is shared and to work to persuade each other how best to go forward as part of what should be a common commitment to improve society. 'Law is politics', and the more time that is spent on the politics than on resisting this conclusion, the better it will be.

Of course, the claim that law is always and inescapably political has profound implications for all lawyers and theorists. As well as undermining the mainstream jurisprudential project and its conceptions of law and lawyering, it obliges critical theorists to take seriously the legal process as a formative constituent of social life and as an important arena for political struggle. This does not mean a lemming-like rush into the courts nor an unconditional embrace of the Rule of Law: These alternatives are more suited to the born-again jurisprudential zealot than the progressive sceptic. A transformative view of law requires a critical understanding of the political nature of legal structures, their instrumental limitations, and their resistance to accommodate change. Mindful that there is no "outside" from which to work, there may be occasional strategic advantage in making "inside" resort to the courts in the struggle to advance social justice. Consequently, the key issues for those devoted to improving the lot of the oppressed and downtrodden are less systemic and more strategic – to determine what substantive changes will best achieve that objective, how those measures can best be implemented, and which institutions can best carry through on that agenda. In efforts to transform law and society, a sensitivity to the contingent possibilities of any particular moment in social history is important. This means that, while those devoted to change would be well advised to disabuse themselves of their habitual resort to the courts as the transformative forum of choice, the possibility of utilizing litigation in the struggle for social justice ought to be kept open. The attempt to make a silk purse of social justice out of the pig's ear of much common law can too easily become a fool's errand. Moreover, litigation is unlikely to do much good on its own because no initiative, legal or otherwise, will work by dint of its intellectual force alone. As celebrated efforts at legal reform such as *Brown* and *Roe* show, change is brought about by a concerted series of activist interventions on a broad number of different social fronts. The history of the common law reveals that legal transformations more often follow than lead political change.[37]

---

[37] See M. Minow, Law and Social Change, 62 *U. Mo. K. C. L. Rev.* 171 at 173 (1993) and A. Hutchinson, supra, note 31. Nevertheless, there remains considerable belief in the viability

Homelessness is one of the most pressing problems on the social and political agenda. So debilitating are its deprivations and so pervasive are its consequences that its eradication, or at least its amelioration, is paramount. However, before some possible strategies for change are suggested, it is important to be clear about the characteristics and contours of the problem itself. Too many efforts at reform take a typically grand and unidimensional approach to defining and addressing the problem. Both the traditional Right and Left seem to view homelessness from a global perspective, albeit entirely different ones. Whereas one understands it as a function of market failures and moral breakdowns, the other sees it as necessary consequence of structural and human deficiencies in capitalism. While each has something to say about the problem and its solution, neither has a monopoly on useful analysis and good sense. The fact is that any workable definition must be multidimensional. It is not so much that definitions of homelessness do not simply objectively describe people's access to dwellings. Rather, it is that definitions of homelessness reflect prior political values because any definition rests on particular and controversial goals of social policy. Consequently, homelessness is both a condition and a category; it has both quantitative and qualitative dimensions. In part, this explains why there is so little agreement on the extent of homelessness. Putting numbers to the homeless problem is as difficult as defining it because how it is defined – Is it about having a place to sleep or a place to call home? temporary relief or permanent remedies? any housing or reasonable housing? being on the street or at constant risk of being there? – affects who is counted as homeless. To make matters worse, the very condition of homelessness itself defies most efforts at counting.[38]

Moreover, the causes of homelessness are varied and, therefore, efforts at reform must be equally varied. Ironically, diversity has been most successful at penetrating the homeless ranks; there is ample representation from across the racial, gender, age, disabled, and socioeconomic spectrums. Accordingly, solutions that might benefit one group (e.g., battered women or persons with mental illnesses) will not necessarily help other groups (e.g., young people or visible minorities). Given the diverse character of the homeless population and the lack of consensus about the definition, causes, and extent of homelessness, it is hardly surprising that there is no agreement

of relying on a common law notion of experimentalism to inform public law. See C. F. Sabel and W. Simon, Destabilization Rights: How Public Law Litigation Succeeds, 117 *Harv. L. Rev.* 1015 (2004).

[38] For a subtle, accessible, and forceful contribution to the Canadian debate, see J. Layton, *Homelessness: The Making and Unmaking of a Crisis* (2000).

about the solution to the homeless problem. Accordingly, there has to be a combination of short- and long-term solutions as well as individualized and structural initiatives that run the gamut from emergency shelters and soup kitchens to guaranteed income policies and public housing projects. In short, because there is no one problem of homelessness, there will also be no one big solution: It will require varied, local, and tailored solutions. This is where the common law can come in. It can provide one possible forum for exploring local and pragmatic solutions to a complex and multi-faceted problem. It is tempting to propose a litigation strategy that strives to establish something like a legal right to private property or a constitutional entitlement to adequate housing. However, this seems to be exactly the wrong thing to do for many reasons. Not only does it smack of a Big Plan, but it also is so unlikely to happen that its advocacy is as much a sign of resignation as a portent of victory. Moreover, as with all such grand proposals, there is a danger that it will turn out to be of more use to the haves than the have-nots. Accordingly, a more local, modest, and immediately useful set of legal maneuvers – constructive trusts, proprietary estoppel, equitable licenses, affirmative tortious duties, unjust enrichment, and so on – seems more conducive to a critically pragmatic perspective and actual success.[39]

That having been said, it is important to be clear about what I am and am not asserting about the possible role of the common law in addressing homelessness. As part of the larger project of confirming that 'law is politics', it is enough to show that the available legal resources are sufficient to support a plausible argument that the common law could respond constructively, if not conclusively, to the plight of the homeless. Such a demonstration does not entail the claim that it is presently an accepted part of the established legal doctrine, that the historical momentum of the common law leads inexorably to such a conclusion, that the deep moral integrity of the common law recommends such initiatives, or even that it will occur. These are all part of the kind of theorizing, whether it is from a Soapy Sam quasi-theological stance or a Bulldog pseudoscientistic approach, that I resist. I defend the much more modest yet still radical idea that such an argument has an intellectual legitimacy and that its acceptance (or rejection) is less about its legal validity and more about its political usefulness. As part of the common

---

[39] There are many such proposals. See, for example, J. Waldron, *The Right to Private Property* (1988); J. Singer, The Reliance Interest in Property, 40 *Stan. L. Rev.* 611 (1988); Symposium on Law and The Homeless, 45 *U. Miami L. Rev.* 387 (1991); and Housing and Hope Symposium, 29 *Seton Hall L. Rev.* 1461 (1999). However, the response of the courts to such claims has been less than encouraging.

law's work-in-progress, a supportive response to the claims of homeless is always in the cards, even if it is not yet on the table. In the same way that Holmes insisted that "the Fourteenth Amendment does not enact Mr. Herbert Spencer's *Social Statics*," it can be reported that the common law in even its constitutional manifestation does not enact Marx's *Communist Manifesto*, Rawls' *A Theory of Justice*, or any other ideological program.[40]

Moreover, such a doctrinal engagement with the common law will reveal more fully what it means to be against grand theory. I am not so much against theorizing as I am insistent upon the need to resist the traditional tendency to offer the kind of integrated and comprehensive theory that claims universal and first-order significance in directing practical efforts at political improvement. For me, theory is both another form of practice and also, as such, never more than a contextual and contingent response to situated circumstances. In spite of the temptation to defend any particular initiatives as being necessitated by some universal or essential idea of what is progressive or useful, I believe that nothing is lost by refusing to go down that road and that much might be gained. While an argument that the common law must respond constructively to the plight of the homeless in the name of Justice would help to win an important battle, it might well lead to a larger defeat in the overall war of social justice. In short, the commitment to such a grand theory of justice is not only impossible to sustain as a theoretical matter, but it might do more practical harm than good in the long run. Too often, the most harmful and immediate suffering has been imposed on people in the cause of a greater yet particularized and historicized claim to Absolute Truth – fascism, communism, capitalism, colonialism, fundamentalism, and so on. In tackling homelessness, therefore, it is better to be more local and practical in both the scope and implementation of one's ambitions. The test of any positive intervention ought to be its actual success on the ground, not its theoretical consistency in the air. While there might be competing proposals as to *what to do next?*, the critical pragmatist approach will not let the best be the enemy of the good. Being critical, the pragmatist will approach most preferred solutions with scepticism and a certain pessimism. However, being pragmatic, the critic will not let ideological purity or institutional allegiance lead to cynicism or paralysis. Accordingly, I do not maintain that there is only one set of strategic legal proposals or that particular initiatives are more consistent with the kind of pragmatic perspective that I have taken; this would be a negation of the whole critical approach that I have

---

[40] *Lochner v. New York*, 198 US 45 at 75 per Holmes J, dissenting (1905). See generally P. Singer, *A Darwinian Left: Politics, Evolution, and Cooperation* (1999).

been trying to foster. I simply suggest that lawyers should make a situated assessment of what seems most likely to improve the lot of the homeless.

However, if the common law is thought be an appropriate forum for any remedial action, it is important to recognize that it is also part of the problem: The present conditions that give rise to homelessness are partly held in place and perhaps reinforced by the common law. Indeed, a recognition that the common law is part of the problem also indicates why the common law must be part of the solution. The resort to the common law is as much about doing away with existing doctrines as it is about implementing new doctrinal initiatives. Whatever the problem, the common law is involved; the only real question is, On whose side?. Indeed, the common law's apparent indifference to homelessness is a massive part of the problem.[41] By ignoring the problem, it contributes to the social sense that there is no real problem or that, insofar as there is a problem, its causes and cures are outside the common law's ambit of influence and responsibility. Of course, fresh legislative projects are likely more preferable to common law transformation; land-use planning, zoning laws, landlord–tenant statutes, and local taxation are obvious possibilities. Nevertheless, while a lack of legislative will is troubling in itself, it also suggests that common law change will also be difficult. Unless there are sufficient political forces in play, there will be little or no prospect of any improvement. After all, the fact that 'law is politics' means that the limits to law as well the likelihood of shifting them are matters of political moment and not merely legal strategy. The common law is largely hostage to its political context. Indeed, it would be surprising if the common law did not line up itself on the side of the haves; any other alignment would confound more general expectations about the connection between the common law and existing social interests. Accordingly, the critical task is twofold – to dismantle existing structures that help give rise to the problem of homelessness, and then develop initiatives to make law more constructively useful in overcoming homelessness. Of course, ever mindful that the common law is a work-in-progress, such interventions should be local, targeted, and pragmatic.

The Canadian aboriginal situation is indicative of both the deep roots of the homelessness problem and the possibility for focused and pragmatic intervention through the common law. Aboriginal people are severely

---

[41] The standard texts on real property have almost nothing to say on homelessness. Moreover, when there is any mention of restrictions on property owners' rights, it tends to be disparaging and begrudging. See Megarry & Wade's *The Law of Real Property* (C. Harpum 6th ed. 2000) and *Anger and Honsberger, Law of Real Property* (A. H. Oosterhoff and W. B. Rayner eds. 2nd ed. 1985).

overrepresented and experience more acutely both the personal and structural causes of homelessness. Indeed, the statistics are truly appalling – more than half of aboriginals reside in dwellings below general housing standards; many dwellings on reserves lack basic amenities; aboriginal homes are twice as likely to need major repairs as nonaboriginal houses and are ninety times more likely to be without a piped water supply; and aboriginal people are more likely to be tenants than house owners. When all this is combined with the fact that aboriginal household incomes are 25 percent lower than nonaboriginals, it is a very bleak picture.[42] Few would insist that aboriginal homelessness is simply a matter of poor housing policy; it is clearly part of a much larger understanding of the plight of aboriginal people generally. Without an adequate economic, social, and cultural base, the effort to resolve the homelessness problem will be merely stopgap at best and possibly self-defeating. Conversely, by ensuring that there is available and affordable housing, a good foundation will be laid for larger community well-being in the form of improvements in health circumstances, educational betterment, crime reduction, and the like. However, although I am not in any way suggesting that it is the only or best way to proceed, aboriginal people have had a some success in pursuing various land-related claims in common law courts. Largely closed out of the political arena, lawyers have been able to make arguments to judges that there is aboriginal title to customary lands that, while different in kind to traditional nonaboriginal proprietary rights, provides a similar level of common law protection; "aboriginal title is a legal right derived from the Indians' historic occupation and possession of their tribal lands."[43] The history of this struggle for recognition showcases the strengths and weaknesses of the common law as a work-in-progress that develops in fits and starts as it responds to changing social expectations and political forces.

Conclusion

As with much else, the relation between biology and human behavior, including theories about their relationship, is likely to be variable, complex, and indirect. In an important sense, this tension in law constitutes one more

---

[42] See *Canada, Report of the Royal Commission on Aboriginal Peoples: Gathering Strength* vol. 3, Housing chap. 4, The Intolerable Housing and Living Conditions of Many Aboriginal People subchap. 1, Aboriginal and Canadian Housing Conditions subchap. 1.1 (1996).

[43] *Guerin v. The Queen*, [1984] 2 SCR 335 at 376 per Dickson J. See also *Delgamuukw v. British Columbia*, [1997] 3 SCR 1010. See generally K. McNeil, *Common Law Aboriginal Title* (1989) and P. Macklem, *Indigenous Difference and the Constitution of Canada* 76–106 (2001).

corner of the action in the familiar battle between nature and nurture. It is hard to believe that this can be conceived of as an either–or choice. It is surely much more likely that it is a mix of both that occurs in a contingent and intricate way.[44] Accordingly, although it might be tempting to dismiss all law-and-biology positions as vulgarly reductionist or crassly essentialist, it would be mistaken. While law's development cannot be reduced to a simple evolutionary dynamic, this does not mean that there are no evolutionary forces at work. The role of evolutionary factors will be appropriately contingent and changeable. Evolution has no goal: There are directional trends of a lesser kind, but they are not overarching and they can end as abruptly as they began. Viewed in this way, both the Dworkins and Posners of the jurisprudential world can be understood as being both right and wrong. They are right because their accounts do offer large and useful insights into how the law is viewed, created, and changed; they each have something to tell us about the dynamics of legal change and judicial reasoning – the common law is both principled and pragmatic, ideal and instrumental, and thematic and discontinuous. They are wrong because they treat those helpful insights as universal sagacity about the nature of law and adjudication. Consequently, to the extent that law-and-economics and law-and-biology accounts avoid totalizing claims and steer clear of Hume's chasm, they might be useful projects that can divulge much about legal development and change. However, when so understood, they cease to be the kind of foundationalist theories that both Dworkin and Posner offer. Instead, they become the kind of critical projects that respect, even when they do not follow or produce, what my critically pragmatic perspective suggests.

In exploring the world of evolutionary theory and studying its applicability to the common law, I might be considered to have been long on theoretical critique and short on practical illustration. Indeed, for an approach that prides itself on the importance of elevating political insight over intellectual coherence, this might seem to be a serious and perhaps fatal error. At best, it seems to be a rather useless account in the critically pragmatic sense that I have been defending. Accordingly, in the next chapter (and other later ones), I redirect my efforts and concentrate on giving a more concrete and less abstruse account of how the common law might be viewed in line with the critique that I have elaborated up to this point. This is a heavy burden,

---

44 For a defense of the view that there is a complex interaction between social processes and scientific practice and that all is too fuzzy and complex to predict because any interaction with the environment is so context-specific, see R. Lewontin, S. Rose, and L. Kamin, *Not in Our Genes: Biology, Ideology and Human Nature* (1984) and H. Rose and S. Rose, *Alas, Poor Darwin: Arguments Against Evolutionary Psychology* (2000).

but the task is one that I believe can be satisfactorily achieved. The history of the common law is a rich and fertile source from which to mine the necessary raw materials to substantiate and reinforce the larger claims that I have made. Being a work-in-progress, the common law is revealed through its historical record, its present performance, and its future promise as the kind of institutional device that not only helps to hold in place the status quo but that might also offer possibilities to bring about substantial changes to it.

$$\text{CS} \quad 5 \quad \text{SO}$$

Tracking the Common Law:
The Routine and the Revolutionary

> Even when it is spoken by a handful of the harried remnants
> of destroyed communities, a language contains within itself the
> boundless potential of discovery, of re-composition of reality, of
> articulated dreams, which are known to us as myths, as poetry, as
> metaphysical conjecture and the discourse of law.[1]
>
> GEORGE STEINER

THERE IS NO BETTER SYMBOL OF THE COMMON LAW'S EVOLUTIONARY
quandary than the role of so-called great cases. These are cases –
Hadley, Donoghue, Hedley Byrne, and their ilk in English private law and *Brown,
Griswold, Miranda,* and their kind in American constitutional law – that are
regarded by almost all lawyers as landmarks of the common law tradition.
While their precise import and reach are continuously contested, any credible account of the common law has to be centered upon such decisions
and must be able to incorporate their authoritative intimations. However,
the very existence of such cases and particularly the circumstances of their
origin seem to confound the legitimacy of the process that they allegedly anchor and from which they purportedly arise. The sceptical observer might be
forgiven for thinking that great cases appear to be less a continuation of legal
tradition and more a break with existing traditions; they tend to exemplify
a deviation from existing commitments, not a derivation from them. Great
cases represent the impressive pragmatic strength of the common law in being able to adapt to fresh challenges and new conditions. However, they also
present jurists with their most pressing jurisprudential challenge of explaining the operation of the common law over time. Mainstream jurists must be
able to show that incremental adaptation is not simply a cover for radical

---

[1] G. Steiner, *After Babel: Aspects of Language and Translation* xiv (2nd ed. 1992).

realignment and, as importantly, that the balance between stability and change is neither ad hoc nor unpredictable. The balance struck must itself be explained by something other than ideological preference. Insofar as great cases are the heart and soul of the common law, therefore, it must be explained why that common law tradition is considered to extol all the virtues of restraint and caution that the creation and acceptance of great cases so gloriously flaunt. In other words, how is it possible for the common law to be constant and changeable?

It is my contention that mainstream efforts to provide an adequate account of great cases and therefore the common law have failed. Indeed, great cases seem to confirm that the common law is more of a political, unruly, and open-ended process than traditional scholars are prepared or able to admit. What is ironic is that, for a tradition-celebrating legal order, the common law's sense of its own tradition is attenuated and impoverished. There is little appreciation for the organic and evanescent character of tradition and its transformative possibilities. Accordingly, contrary to Holmes' opinion that "great cases, like hard cases, make bad law,"[2] I will place the incidence, importance, and influence of great cases at the heart of my jurisprudential project rather than treat them as anomalous occurrences that require special explanations. Once this is done, the tradition of the common law is seen to be less about stability and continuity and more about change and transformation. Beginning from the premise that a tradition is best considered and assessed by reference to its great moments rather than its routine practice, I offer an account of the common law tradition that is intended to be both descriptively accurate and prescriptively defensible. Moreover, when the common law is treated as an institutional commitment to the notion that anything might go, it becomes possible to integrate both the routine operation of the common law and the radical leaps that transform it into one consistent account. Although lawyers and jurists emphasize the routine, it will be the radical occasions of great cases that best capture its dynamic spirit. Indeed, contrary to conventional wisdom, it is the relentless critic who most closely grasps and continues the common law tradition, not the complacent apologist who insists on a timid acceptance of what has already been decided. To treat the law as static or to adopt an unquestioning posture toward it is to betray, not uphold, the common law tradition.

The chapter is divided into five parts. In the first part I explore the canonical nature and identity of great cases; my emphasis will be as much on the

---

[2] *Northern Securities Co v. US*, 193 US 197 at 400 per Holmes J (1904).

circumstances of their emergence as on the controlling influence of their elevated status. In the next two parts I look at the function and role of great cases in English tort law and American constitutional law; one underlying theme is to illuminate how the biological debate over gradual or punctuated evolution plays itself out in law. In the fourth part, I examine the traditional defense of the courts' reliance on stare decisis and criticize its inability to explain the legitimacy and significance of great cases' birth in the common law scheme of things. In the fifth part I pull together the various strands of my argument and deal with certain likely objections to my thesis that great cases confirm the relevance and accuracy of the claim that law is politics. Throughout the chapter, I contest familiar insights and persisting shibboleths about the ordered, incremental, and predictable evolution of the common law. In short, although Wasserstrom intended it in a slightly tongue-in-cheek manner, I want to make a more serious defense of the assessment that "precedents ought always to be followed except when they should not."[3] While great cases might well mark the end of an era and the beginning of another, they also represent the continuation of a tradition in which 'anything might go' and in which 'breaking with tradition' is as traditional as it gets. As great cases demonstrate, precedent is not the vital glue of the common law; it is its convenient shell.

Canons and Cases

Perhaps more than most academic specialities and professional practices, law is very much a canonical exercise. Certain texts and materials are given priority and centrality in legal debate; they are expected to impose discipline and bestow authority on various arguments and outcomes. The traditional basis for this authority is as much institutional as intellectual. Compared with their philosophical or literary counterparts, lawyers and judges do not consider themselves "free to go for the best . . . [because] they are constrained by history, by precedent, by the nature of legal and political institutions."[4] This reliance on canonical thinking is evident in the training of young lawyers, the work of practicing lawyers, and the craft of judges. The canon-based approach to legal education, law, and adjudication has two distinct parts – the selection and identification of canonical texts and, as importantly, the

---

3 R. Wasserstrom, *The Judicial Decision* 46 (1961). For the classic traditional account of how law develops incrementally, see E. Levi, *An Introduction to Legal Reasoning* 1–27 (1948).

4 M. Nussbaum, *The Use and Abuse of Philosophy in Legal Education*, 45 Stan. L. Rev. 1627 at 1642 (1993).

establishment of a reading method by which to elicit those texts' operative meaning. While the whole idea of canonical readings is absolutely central to the educational, legal, and jurisprudential enterprises, I will be concentrating more on the selection of canonical texts. Indeed, out of all the thousands upon thousands of cases that exist, it is revealing to examine those that take their place as great or leading cases in the common law canon – what they say, why they became prominent, and what they represent are some of the more interesting questions that can be asked of these landmark judicial decisions. Indeed, it is not going too far to suggest that the identity of great cases and the process adopted to confer such an elevated status upon them are some of the best indicators of lawyers' basic jurisprudential commitments.[5] In short, great cases offer a convenient and concise summary of the fundamental theoretical assumptions that underlie the common law.

In a very real and important sense, what counts as a great case is simply whatever people agree to designate as a great case. Of course, while some people, like appellate judges, exercise more clout than others in this process, court decisions do not attain greatness unless they can attract a critical mass of support among the legal community at large. There is nothing so self-evidently or intrinsically great about particular cases that it automatically guarantees their inclusion in any jurisprudential hall of fame. While this in itself is revealing, there is nothing about law that is different in this regard from literature or art; this status is as much a matter of communal acceptance as conformity with any universal metewand about the virtues of greatness. To put it another way, the quality of greatness is part of the communal debate rather than an external restraint upon it. In this way, the debate over what does and does not count as a great case is intimately tied to the informing debate over the nature and purpose of law and adjudication; what qualifies a case as great depends on the underlying view of law and adjudication being adopted. Consequently, it seems reasonable to utilize such cases as a convenient and compelling way to illuminate that debate and to evaluate contributions to that debate in terms of their capacity to explain the existence and evolution of great cases. Great cases – like *Donoghue*

---

5   See Symposium, Do We Have A Legal Canon?, 43 *J. Legal Educ.* 1 (1993); L. Levine, *The Opening of the American Mind: Canons, Cultural, and History* (1996); J. Balkin and S. Levinson, The Canons of Constitutional Law, 111 *Harv. L. Rev.* 964 at 1003 (1998); and D. E. Marion, The State of the Canon in Constitutional Law: Lessons from the Jurisprudence of John Marshall, 89 *Wm. & Mary Bill Rts. J.* 385 (2001). The issue of canon formation touches on raging debates that go to the heart of the intellectual enterprise. For a good summary of the debate, see *Canons* (R. Von Hallberg ed. 1994) and J. Mootz, Legal Classics: After Constructing the Legal Canon, 72 *N. Car. L. Rev.* 977 (1994).

and *Brown* – are simply those cases that the legal community continues to consider great. There is little that is intrinsically great about them outside of a particular context or agenda. At another time and in a different context, great cases might become simply run-of-the-mill affairs or, more usually and more revealingly, great mistakes and landmarks of what the law ought not to be.

The analogy between the legal and literary community in its adherence to the idea and importance of a canon of great cases and great books is strong and striking. In the same way that literary scholars seek to isolate a small group of texts that are claimed to represent the best of the prevailing tradition and that can ground readers in the core values of good literature, so the select library of great cases is offered as not only relevant in itself but also as the best that the law has to offer. In each case, the values and virtues that they embody are said to have withstood the test of time and distinguished themselves in the ruthless arena of literary or legal ideas. Taken collectively, the canon is treated as a treasured repository of a traditional wisdom that has been passed down through history and that transcends the particular circumstances of its making. By acting as its cultural stewards, lawyers and literary critics give humble recognition to the universality of the human predicament and their own precious but flawed contributions to its resolution. In addition, by attending to these totemic texts of law and literature, both lawyers and literary enthusiasts are supposed to be able to learn that modern society shares its fate and future with earlier generations. Offered as free-standing texts, great books and great cases reinforce the benefits of consistency and continuity: They recommend an unbroken and unchanging tradition of superior insights that is to be presently deviated from at considerable peril to society.[6] However, on closer inspection, these alleged universal verities are revealed to be ephemeral vanities. Whether packaged as scholarly commentary or professional exegesis, these values are often the interested views of privileged local commentators who simply happen to be invested with contingent authority. It is not the fact that the choices are political that is the problem. Rather, the problem is that this partisan politics is unfortunately occluded not only in the name of culture and sophistication, but also in the service of some imagined, overarching, and ostensibly neutral political program. Contrary to the traditional claim that great books and great cases achieve their rarified status by dint of their own intrinsic

---

[6] See A. Bloom, *The Closing of the American Mind* 22 (1987) and E. D. Hirsch, Jr., *Cultural Literacy: What Every American Needs to Know* 18 (1987). A startling example of this canonical tendency is R. Posner, *Law And Literature: A Misunderstood Relation* (1988).

merit and cogency, it is their continued compatibility and consonance with prevailing values and interests that gains them entry into the canon.

As regards great cases, there are a variety of ways that particular decisions and judgments can come to be considered important or of lasting significance – the immediate political background or social circumstances of the case might make the case memorable; the identity of the parties might be so significant as to warrant notoriety; the judge may have added an especially telling or imaginative twist to the law; the decision could be unexpected or perverse; or the social consequences of the decision might be far-reaching and substantial. While these are all possible bases for marking cases as worthy of celebration or noteworthiness, these are not my concern. I am interested in those cases that lawyers consider to be great: They might well possess some of these features, but they will not be determinative of their greatness. That said, it is not my intention to develop a definition of greatness and then proceed to harvest those cases that meet such criteria. On the contrary, my approach is more deconstructive in that I take what lawyers and judges consider to be great cases and utilize those cases to subvert the stability of the very process that they are said to showcase and ground. I give substance and weight to the nonfoundational insight that what is and is not treated as canonical will depend on the purposes of so-called canonisation. Because the focus and ambition of lawyers is legal as opposed to political or sociological, it ought not be surprising that what counts as canonical will relate to the operation of the law and be determined by its importance to the law's development as a relatively self-contained and coherent body of norms. Accordingly, those cases that are selected as great say more about the interests and purposes of those who select them than they do about the subjective matter of the cases themselves. Great cases are shorthand symbols for deeper and more elaborate theoretical commitments: Canonicity in law is said to be more about doctrinal integrity and authoritative designation than it is about social causes, political consequences, or aesthetic appeal.

That having been said, there does seem to be a general consensus among lawyers on the notion that great cases are those that have become sufficiently and widely accepted over time as being of central importance. Not only must any future development of the law be able to incorporate the holdings of great cases, but also such holdings are treated as capable of pointing in the direction or illuminating the path that such new development must take. This idea of great cases as "landmarks upon the trackless wilds of the law" or as "a fixed star(s) in the jurisprudential firmament" gives a sense of the belief in them as intellectual compasses for legal travelers who are uncertain where to turn or go.[7] However, there is a tendency to treat these great cases as more enduring and certain than they actually are; even stars explode or implode over time, and their fixity is always relative to location. In the traditional vocabulary, this definition of great cases suggests that there is something natural or given about their status and that their identification is more a process of discovery than creation. Again, this ought to come as no surprise. Mindful that canonization says more about those doing the canonizing than that being canonized, the depiction of great cases as found objects that orient and guide the humble lawyer reflects important underlying assumptions about the nature and development of the common law (i.e., it is more than a political and personal choice by judges to go their own way and follow their political intuitions). Great cases stand both as markers for wayward or lost lawyers and as monuments to the legal community's collective faith in the idea that the common law is, if less than godly, something more than the sum of its members' preferences.

In contrast to this jurisprudential staple of traditional thinking, I maintain that the recognition and fate of such great cases is very much about the willingness of the legal community to sustain faith in the importance of the case. A great case is only a great case as long as the lawyers and judges are prepared to treat it as one or as long as the broader community is not prepared to reject lawyers' animating values. Once the values that underpin a case no longer garner sufficient support or the informing context has changed substantially, a great case will fall by the wayside and be consigned to the ditch of errors, mistakes, and anomalies. For instance, the rise and fall of *Lochner*'s economic due process doctrine had little to do with the quality of its legal reasoning or its doctrinal structure. The case was good law while its values and consequences were considered desirable, and it became bad law when those values and consequences fell out of favor.[8] Accordingly, rather than view great cases as 'fixed stars' or 'landmarks', I think that it is more appropriate to think of them as temporary lighthouses, designed with a particular purpose in mind, constructed with available materials, and with a limited working life. As society moves, the need for such constructions fades,

---

[7] S. Warren, *A Popular and Practical Introduction to Law Studies* 434 (1835) and G. Gilmore, *The Death of Contract* 83 (1974). See also J. Stone, *Precedent and Law: Dynamics of Common Law Growth* 221 (1985); A. W. B. Simpson, *Leading Cases in the Common Law* (1995); and C. Sunstein, *Legal Reasoning and Political Conflict* 82 and 85 (1996).

[8] *Lochner v. New York*, 198 US 45 (1905) and *infra*, pp. 144–47. For a reluctant acknowledgment that canonicity is about substantive politics, not legal correctness, and that judgments are "redeemed for their holdings ... [and] other elements ... are secondary to the basic substance," see R. A. Primus, <u>Canon, Anti-Canon, and Judicial Dissent</u>, 48 *Duke L. J.* 243 at 279 (1998). While he laments this fact, I want to celebrate it.

and other, more useful devices are designed to take their place. For instance, although the House of Lords' decision in *Anns* on the two-step process for establishing a duty of care was considered by many to be a (potential) member of the select elite, its greatness was later denied and its importance rejected in *Murphy*.[9] As with celebrity, greatness in law is no less dependent on passing trends and shifting contexts. Depending on the audience, today's star is yesterday's wanna-be or tomorrow's has-been.

Moreover, simply because a particular decision has been accepted into the legal canon does not mean that the light it casts is clear or certain. Indeed, as with texts that have received canonical status in literature, the meaning and instruction of such judgments remain indeterminate and undecided. Precedents do not speak for themselves, and their interpretation is an occasion for interested and creative attempts at hermeneutical appropriation; they represent a site for the manufacture of meaning as much as an adequate grounding for a present case's resolution. For some, in law and literature, this richness and opacity are some of the qualities that recommend a text as great. In this sense, both Shakespeare's Hamlet and Lord Atkin's *Donoghue* are great not only because of their profundity, but also because of their profligacy; they lend themselves to diverse and contestable renderings. For instance, in *Donoghue*, the question for the court was whether a ginger beer manufacturer could be liable to someone who became ill after drinking some of its ginger beer, which had been bought for her and which contained a dead snail. It is entirely ridiculous to contend that the House of Lords' judgments (or even Lord Atkin's "neighbor" principle) give rise to any one overriding ratio or ruling. Depending on the context in which the inquiry is made, the leading judgment of Lord Atkin can be convincingly and legitimately analyzed to produce a vast array of rulings – what does it tell us about the responsibility of builders, accountants, parents, municipalities, and so on? What does it tell us about liability for omissions or failure to act? What does it tell us about recovery for loss of profits? The answer to each of these answers will emphasize a different facet of the judgment and suggest a slightly different shade of meaning. For instance, even in a most general way, Lord Atkin's judgment can be (and has been) not unreasonably interpreted to support a range of rulings that run from "(a) Scottish manufacturers in the late 1920s of opaque bottles of ginger beer are expected to check that

---

9   *Anns v. Merton Borough Council,* [1977] 2 All ER 492 (HL) and *Murphy v. Brentwood District Council,* [1990] 2 All ER 908 (HL). By way of emphasizing the common law's local character, it should be added that Canadian courts have not seen fit to abandon *Anns.* See *City of Kamloops v. Nielson,* [1984] 2 SCR 2.

dead snails are not left in them" through "(m) all persons who make goods or offer services to the public must ensure that they are fit for their intended purpose" to "(z) everyone should act with due care in their interactions with others."

Because the list of great cases is simply a matter of communal consensus, although it is a process in which some opinions carry more weight than others because the legal community is nothing if it is not hierarchical, the listing of great cases is very much an empirical question. As such, this process is largely uncontroversial: A cursory survey of leading textbooks and casebooks evidences a marked consistency in selection and emphasis. For instance, few tort scholars would doubt that *Rylands*, *Donoghue*, and *Hedley Byrne* were great cases, although many might disagree on their scope and meaning. Similarly, few constitutional scholars would disagree that *Brown*, *Griswold*, and *Miranda* were great cases. Indeed, once scholars do begin to disagree, the basis of a case's greatness is eroded and its celebrated status disturbed. Although some commentators would go so far as to say that "an approach to constitutional interpretation is unacceptable if it entails the incorrectness of *Brown*,"[10] it must be remembered that this assessment is only correct as long as the decision is accepted as correct. It is acceptability that sustains correctness, not correctness that determines acceptability. Nevertheless, the recognition of the greatness of these cases does little to explain why such cases have become celebrated as great cases. The definition is more about the *consequences* of being designated a great case rather than an *explanation* of why they became great cases in the first place.

One possible source of explanation is that such decisions and judgments are feted because of their exemplary stature as embodiments of the common law method through their expert use of legal reasoning and their superlative judicial craft. While such qualities are not irrelevant and are often touted by some jurists as the hallmark of great cases, such an explanation is unconvincing. If the formal qualities of judgments were determinative, there is little reason to believe that we would have the great cases that we have. Some presently included in the canon would be missing and others might be included. For instance, *Rylands* is hardly an exemplar of legal reasoning; there is little about Lord Cairns's judicial craft that makes his judgment stand out as exceptional or excellent. In the same way, Chief Justice

---

[10] C. Sunstein, In Defense of Liberal Education, 43 *J. Legal Educ.* 22 at 36 (1993). In a similar vein, Balkin and Levinson insist that "a constitutional theorist has to explain why *Dred Scott* or *Plessy* is bad constitutional law (and not just morally appalling) or she is out of the game"; supra, note 5 at 1019.

Warren's judgment for the Supreme Court in *Brown* is castigated by many as a very poor model of reasoned elaboration: It bears all the hallmarks of a political compromise intended both to get all members of the Supreme Court to sign on to a unanimous opinion and to cause as little political controversy as possible by limiting the decision and reasoning to school segregation and demographics. Furthermore, there are myriad examples of judgments that live up to the standard of *Donoghue*'s Lord Atkin or *Roe*'s Justice Blackmun. Indeed, the dissenting judgment of Lord Buckmaster in *Donoghue* or of Justices White and Rehnquist in *Roe* cannot be reasonably said to be inferior in terms of craft and professionalism. Consequently, while the stylistic or literary quality of a judgment helps, it is in no way decisive in itself. It is the rhetorical success and political acceptability of the decision that will carry the day.[11]

Form and Substance

The greatness of great cases is less about their formal attributes than it is about their substantive appeal. Although more removed from the glare of political scrutiny than constitutional decisions, the development of English tort law offers ample support for such a claim. As is so often the situation, what they do is more telling than what they say they do. While what judges say cannot be ignored, neither can it be taken as the final word. Judicial dicta are the beginning of inquiry, not its end. Decisions such as *Donoghue* and *Hedley Byrne* become defining moments in the shifting and developing doctrinal universe not because they are legally correct or analytically sound in that they follow precedent in predictable or prosaic fashion, but because they are considered politically valid and socially acceptable. Indeed, the very strength and singularity of such cases is that they break with the existing tradition of doctrine and carve out a new path for the law to follow. In this way, the genesis of great cases is to be found in strikingly creative and transformative acts of judicial bravado. The difference between *Donoghue* and *Hedley Byrne*, on the one hand, and other less celebrated cases has almost nothing to do with interpretive cogency or hermeneutical integrity in legal doctrine. It has everything to do with changing currents and concerns in the political context that frame and condition such germinal and disruptive judicial decisions. As Stanley Fish puts it, "the canon is a very historical, political and social product, something that is fashioned by men and women in the name

---

[11] See S. Levinson, The Rhetoric of Judicial Opinion, in *Law's Stories* 187 (P. Brooks and P. Gewirtz eds. 1996).

of certain interests, partisan concerns, and social and political agenda."[12] If this is true for literature, then it is doubly so for law. For instance, *Winterbottom v. Wright*, which restricted relief for defective products to contractual remedies, ceased to be a fixed point on the legal compass because it no longer enjoyed sufficient political confidence and support among the legal (and political) community. The perception that it had an analytically weak (or strong) status was virtually beside the historical point.[13] While the fact that a judgment is crafted in an analytically strong style will facilitate the acceptance of a novel or bold decision, it will not in itself carry the day. Rightness and, therefore, greatness is a matter of social policy and political persuasion, not legal doctrine and logical demonstration.

This point is well illustrated by the short career of a great case that never was, *Junior Books*. The case centered on the much-contested question of whether there could be recovery for pure economic loss resulting from a negligent act. In short, following *Anns*, it did away with the requirement of related damage to person or property and made the existence of defectively manufactured property sufficient to trigger tortious liability. As well as appearing to put recovery for economic loss on the same footing as other more physical losses, the House of Lords effectively placed Tort ahead of Contract in the doctrinal hierarchy of civil obligations. Under such a legal regimen, it would no longer be taken for granted that contract was the primary mode of imposing civil obligations or that, without the existence of a contract, people had no legal obligation to safeguard the economic interests of others. In reaching this decision, Lord Fraser maintained that "the present case seems to mean to fall well within limits already recognized in principle for this type of claim" and Lord Roskill believed that it represented "the next logical step forward in the development of this branch of the law."[14] In contrast, Lord Brandon's dissenting judgment took the view that, in its treatment of *Donoghue*, the majority had effected "a radical departure from long-established authority" and created "wholly undesirable extensions of the existing law all of delict."[15] Of course, the considerable irony of this is that *Donoghue* itself was "a radical departure from long-established authority"

---

[12] S. Fish, Canon Busting: The Basic Issues, *National Forum: Phi Cappa Phi J.* 13 (1989). See also D. Luban, Legal Traditionalism, in *Legal Modernism* 93–124 (1997).

[13] *Winterbottom v. Wright* [1842], 152 ER 402.

[14] *Junior Books Ltd. v. Veitchi Co.* [1983], 3 WLR 477 at 482 per Lord Fraser and 495 per Lord Roskill. One commentator heralded it as "a landmark decision in the law of torts, representing a development or advance comparable to that which occurred in *Donoghue*." See J. G. Starke, Comment, 56 *Aust. L. J.* 663 (1982).

[15] Id. at 499 and 500 per Lord Brandon.

and *Hedley Byrne* had been no more a radical departure from *Donoghue* than *Junior Books*. Lord Brandon's disagreement had more to do with the wisdom of introducing "a transmissible warranty of quality – a plaintiff in tort could be better off than a similar plaintiff with a relevant contract because warranties would run with the product: A subsequent purchaser could have a broader range of legal rights and remedies than the original purchaser."

As is now well known, this doctrinal transformation did not take place and *Junior Books* did not take its place among the ranks of great cases. The response to *Junior Books* was decidedly swift and negative. In a series of cases, the courts managed to undermine and cabin the decision without actually overruling it. Abandoning Atkin's search for some golden thread that would make general sense of the law's particulars, the judges opted for a less doctrinaire and more pragmatic approach to tort law. There is "no precedent for the application of strict logic in treading the path leading from the general principle established in *Donoghue* towards the Pandora's Box of unbridled damages at the end of the path of foreseeability."[16] Indeed, by the end of the decade, Lord Brandon had managed to persuade all his fellow judges to come over to his way of thinking. In *Murphy*, it was held that the contested loss was purely economic and was more appropriately dealt with under contract, not tort; liability based on a "transmissible warrant of quality" was to be strenuously resisted. The rare septet of law lords in *Murphy* overruled *Anns* (and, therefore, *Junior Books*) on the basis that it was not "capable of being reconciled with pre-existing principle" and, again ironically, that it was too big a jump from *Donoghue*.[17] However, any reasonable reading of the *Murphy* decision indicates that their rejection of *Anns* has more to do with policy concerns about such a doctrinal innovation than a somewhat belated condemnation of *Anns*' failing as a matter of legal analysis; the law lords were not prepared to allow Tort to eclipse Contract as the primary mode of civil obligation. Accordingly, *Junior Books*' fate offers substantial confirmation that a case's status as a great case has more to do with its substantive desirability than its legal unsoundness. If legal soundness (i.e., whether a decision was a reconcilable extension or modification of existing principle)

---

[16] *Greater Nottingham Co-operative v. Cementation*, [1988] 3 WLR 396 at 407 per Purchas J. See also *Muirhead v. Industrial Tank Specialities Ltd.*, [1985] 3 All ER 705 and *Caparo v. Dickman*, [1990] 2 WLR 358 at 362–65 per Lord Bridge, 374 per Lord Roskill, and 379–81 per Lord Oliver.

[17] *Murphy*, supra note 9 at 914 per Lord Keith and also 937 per Lord Oliver and 942 per Lord Jauncey. See also *The Aliakmon*, [1986] AC 785. On the (dubious) retrenchment from *Junior Books*, see D. Beyleveld and R. Brownsword, Privity, Transivity and Rationality, 54 Mod L. Rev. 48 (1991) and J. G. Logie, The Final Demise of Junior Books?, [1989] Jur. Rev. 5.

is the test, *Donoghue* itself, the epitome of a great case, would be rendered suspect.

Of course, to talk of legal soundness as though it were something entirely different from substantive desirability is an artifice. There are few judges, let alone jurists, who would be prepared to make such a formalistic pronouncement. While substantive desirability can act as a component of legal soundness, it cannot be reduced to it. The judicial effort to defend their work in terms of principled decision making is made for an eminently good and, at least in traditional terms, compelling reason. Judges are acutely aware that their primary role is supposed to be to develop and apply the law from existing principles, not to legislate with little regard to the past. A candid confession that great cases are less of a principled continuation of existing doctrine and more a radical departure from it puts the jurisprudential defense of the common law into serious jeopardy. For instance, in *Hedley Byrne*, Lord Reid was adamant that *Donoghue* "may encourage us to develop existing lines of authority, but it cannot entitle us to disregard them," and Lord Devlin emphasized that, "as always in English law, the first step in such an inquiry is to see how far the authorities have gone, for new categories in the law do not spring into existence overnight."[18] Nonetheless, while this effort is understandable, its convincing performance is fraught with difficulty. Indeed, attempts to explain the jurisprudential basis of great cases are caught between a rock and hard place. On the one hand, if great cases are seen to be a continuation of existing doctrine, it is a tradition that is so ample and generous that it can embrace almost any judicial act. The reality will be that 'anything might go' and that the limits of common law adjudication are nothing more (and nothing less) than the political limits of the judges. Judgments will stand or fall on the judges' rhetorical ability to persuade their colleagues of their political merit. Such a situation seems anathema to traditional opinion. On the other hand, if great cases are seen to be a break with existing doctrine, then their very legitimacy is questionable. Although law emphasizes the routine, it will be the revolutionary occasions of great cases that best capture its dynamic spirit. Either way, the judicial accounts of the common law's development as incremental and piecemeal concede too much (i.e., almost any case is seen to be a routine continuation of common law tradition) or too little (i.e., all great cases are seen to amount to a revolutionary change in the common law tradition) for their own jurisprudential good.

---

[18] *Hedley Byrne & Co. Ltd. v. Heller & Partners*, [1964] AC 467 at 482 per Lord Reid and 525 per Lord Devlin.

This dilemma can be easily and instructively demonstrated by reference to the competing judgments in *Donoghue* itself. Lords Buckmaster and Tomlin took the view that not only were the existing authorities against Mrs. Donoghue, but also that the common law did not evince any principles that would support her claim: "Although [the common law's] principles are capable of application to meet new conditions not contemplated when the law was laid down, yet themselves cannot be changed nor can additions be made to them because any particular meritorious case seems outside their ambit."[19] Of course, the minority did not rest their disagreement on legal analysis alone; they went on to take fundamental exception with the substantive wisdom of the majority's decision. In response, the majority pointed to the inconclusive state of the authorities and claimed that, although 'the neighbour principle' was not the only possible interpretation of the existing precedents, it was the best substantive outcome. However, both Lords Atkin and Macmillan were prepared to state that the law must keep pace with prevailing views of justice. Indeed, Lord Macmillan went so far as to approve of the view that "any proposition the result of which would be to show that the common law of England is wholly unreasonable and unjust cannot be part of the common law of England."[20] In short, while the effort to follow principle is to be preferred, such a formal responsibility will not stand in the way of substantive fairness: When push comes to shove, judges should favor justice over precedent. In this classic exchange between *Donoghue*'s minority and majority, the extent of the jurisprudential dilemma with which great cases confront the common law is revealed. In gallantly attempting to cover all the jurisprudential bases, the majority in *Donoghue* only manage to expose the fragile and, I will argue, illusory foundations of the common law.

While Lords Atkin and Macmillan can be applauded for their candor and their willingness to put substantive justice ahead of formal argument, they highlight the fact that the common law is not best understood as a limited, predictable, and peculiarly legal mode of decision making, but as an open, unpredictable, and distinctly political process in which 'anything might go'. Under even a minimalist traditional account of the common law, there is some obligation to maintain some critical distance between the two. Once

---

[19] *Donoghue v. Stevenson*, [1932] All ER 1 at 5 per Lord Buckmaster and at 20–21 per Lord Tomlin.

[20] Id. at 25 per Lord Macmillan, quoting *Emmens v. Poole*, 16 QBD 354 at 357–58 (1885) per Lord Esher. For an account of *Donoghue* as the culmination of "a course of development which had been taking place according to the traditional technique of the common law," see R. Pound, *Jurisprudence III*, 565 (1959).

substantive desirability is made the sole test of legal soundness, the common lawyer seems to have offered less an account of common law decision making than an account of decision making per se. However, if substantive desirability is the only test, then any pretense that the common law is about a formal adherence to existing rules and established principles is seen as a hollow and occasionally hypocritical stance. The common law is through and through a political project in which substance eclipses form. This is amply demonstrated by the role of great cases in constitutional law. Although there are obvious differences between the adjudicative performance in ordinary common law cases and constitutional cases, constitutional adjudication is simply a particular kind of common law adjudication; the basic components of the common law mind-set are adapted to the specialized demands of the constitutional context.[21]

Constitutional Challenges

In exercising their power of constitutional review, courts are as much or as little bound by the supposed doctrinal authority of great cases as they are by the controlling precedents of the common law. Thus, it is the canonical force of great cases as much as the explicit wording of the Constitution that is at the heart of constitutional adjudication. The balance between the two is contingent and contextual. Indeed, even a relatively passing familiarity with the history of American constitutional law confirms that judicial discourse is as much about squaring present decisions with past cases, albeit as privileged efforts to interpret the constitutional text, as it is about conformity to the actual words of the governing document. If anything, the American constitutional tradition offers a rich and potent demonstration that, while there is and likely will always be a canon of great cases that holds considerable doctrinal sway over the judicial and scholarly intellect, the number and identity of those cases as well as their meaning will change over time. Canonicity is about substantive effects, not formal attributes, and what gets treated as canonical will be a matter of continuing substantive acceptance rather than fixed formal recognition. The effort to rely on a fixed canonical tradition of constitutional great cases is as weak and unsuccessful as the judicial effort to utilize social tradition to ground constitutional interpretation.[22] Both traditions are so numerous, imprecise, and open that they

---

[21] For an extended account of constitutional law and these differences, see infra, chap. 7.

[22] See, for example, *Moore v. City of East Cleveland*, 431 US 494 at 513 (1977) and *Lawrence v. Texas*, 123 S. Ct. 2472 (2003).

can justify almost any reading. Indeed, this resort to tradition tends to more reinforce than resolve the problem because it is difficult to ascertain what would be the controlling tradition, constitutional or social, over and above a particular judge's honest conviction about what is was.

Brown is one of a handful of cases that almost everyone agrees has a special place in the American constitutional tradition. However, beyond that general fact, there is little agreement. Its judgment, the doctrinal basis of the decision, and its academic reception are all extremely problematic and hotly contested: The judgment in *Brown* represents a site for the manufacture of meaning as much as an adequate grounding for its actual resolution. In a rhetorically bland but politically explosive judgment, a unanimous Supreme Court held that the inconclusive nature of the 1868 Fourteenth Amendment's history obliged it to take notice of the contemporary state of public education and strike down *Plessy's* separate-but-equal doctrine. In reaching this decision, the Court delivered a judgment that was short on doctrinal argument and long on practical imperatives. Rather than cite text or precedent, the judges chose to rely on social statistics. Indeed, although the Court's brief judgment tried to sidestep the larger and more troubling questions of constitutional legitimacy, it only managed to emphasize their importance and the extent to which the *Brown* judgment itself was wanting as an exercise in constitutional adjudication. While couched in more conventional terms, academic commentators engaged in an almost unparalleled project of result-oriented rationalization. The rejoicing in the substantive result was only matched by the lamentation at its inadequate reasoning.[23] Indeed, the *Brown* decision points up the classic tension in constitutional adjudication. In general terms, it pits the originalists against the nonoriginalists in the challenge to avoid reducing adjudication to "the mere reflex of the popular opinion or passion of the day"[24] – if there is a move beyond framers' intent, even on the limited basis that it is impossible to isolate it in sufficient specificity, what is the source that judges can and ought to use to inform and limit their decisions? However, although the nonoriginalists face the more obvious and stiffer challenge of maintaining a distinction

---

[23] See, for example, A. Bickel, The Original Understanding and the Desegregation Decision, 69 *Harv. L. Rev.* 1 (1955); H. Wechsler, Toward Neutral Principles of Constitutional Law, 73 *Harv. L. Rev.* 1 (1959); *Learned Hand, The Bill of Rights* 42 (1958); J. Monaghan, Stare Decisis and Constitutional Adjudication, 88 *Colum. L. Rev.* 723 (1988); and R. Bork, *The Tempting of America* 74–83 (1990).

[24] See *Dred Scott v. Sanford*, 60 US 393 at 426 per Taney CJ (1857). The disagreement within these two approaches is almost as intense as that between them. See J. H. Ely, *Democracy and Distrust* (1980).

between law and politics, the originalists are no less implicated; the availability, applicability, and acceptability of original meaning are far from technical or nonpolitical inquiries.

Brown, therefore, points up the central dilemma in constitutional law – to demonstrate convincingly that *Brown* is not only politically appealing and that *Plessy* is politically deplorable, but that *Brown* is good constitutional law and *Plessy* is bad constitutional law. This is a more concrete way of expressing the more general challenge for common lawyers of refuting the critical claim that law is politics. While there is an obvious and necessary link between law and politics, even the most sophisticated of constitutional commentators and common law theorists insist that there is a definite and discernible difference between law as a public institution and political morality as a personal commitment: "telling it how it is means, *up to a point*, telling it how it should be."[25] Accordingly, constitutional judges and jurists must be able to explain why something is good constitutional law in terms other than simply because it is good politics. Once the difference between good law and good politics is no longer maintained, there is no reason to treat legal decisions as any more neutral, objective, or nonideological and, therefore, authoritative than political opinion. Efforts to delineate and sustain this distinction are ingenious and elaborate, but they either prove too little for their own political good or too much for their own legal good in responding to "the various crises of human affair."[26] The law fails to live up to political expectations, or political expectations call the legal tune. Although the task of reconciling constitutional law and partisan politics is difficult in a single case such as *Brown*, it become positively Sisyphean when one throws in all the other contested great or almost-great cases. How is it possible to demonstrate conclusively that some permutation of *Brown*, *Roe*, and *Lawrence* is or is not good constitutional law in a way that is somehow different from the general debate over what is and is not good politics? The answer is that it is not possible and that great cases are less landmarks to doctrinal integrity than monuments to its indeterminacy.

The fact that the constitution develops and changes is not so much the problem as the *how*, *when*, and *whether* constitutions develop and change. These crucial questions have to be answered largely by reference to the dynamics of constitutional law as a relatively separate and independent process from the volatility of changing political circumstances. Constitutional law

---

[25] R. Dworkin, *Freedom's Law: The Moral Reading of the American Constitution* 38 (1996) (emphasis added) and infra, pp. 152–55.

[26] *McCullough v. Maryland*, 17 US 316 at 415 per Marshall CJ (1819).

and politics cannot be one and the same thing, as there is no one politics and therefore no one constitution. The maintenance of such a law–politics distinction might be plausible in a society that shares a general consensus on politics. But, of course, that is not the case in American society, especially for (or perhaps because of) the constitutional cases that fall for judicial decision. The contested status of *Roe* is another example of the freighted dynamics of constitutional adjudication and the importance of substantive political values over formal legal arguments. Few cases have elicited such impassioned responses. This is not surprising in light of the divided social views on abortion. However, notwithstanding the best efforts of academic and professional opinion to present the debate differently, this is exactly what both sustains the legal antagonism and prevents the establishment of any settled constitutional stance. Although the contesting factions frame their arguments in the familiar vocabulary of legal legitimacy as much as political desirability, there is nothing to choose between them in terms of doctrinal correctness. While judges and jurists argue over whether the decision is routine (i.e., the incremental development of the privacy logic of *Griswold* and related cases) or revolutionary (i.e., the overstepping of accepted doctrinal boundaries of those cases), these are really nothing more than coded strategies for highly charged political initiatives.[27] Indeed, *Roe* and the committed efforts to retain or reduce its meaning represent as keenly as any other modern-day encounter the struggle over the soul of constitutional law. *Roe* will remain a valid and authoritative decision as long as its assailants are unable to persuade others of its substantive injustice and of the political wisdom of eroding still further the fragile legitimacy on which the Supreme Court so heavily relies for its continuing moral legitimacy when it is seen to act in such a transparently political way. The fate of *Roe* as a great or not-so-great case will, like all other cases, be determined by the contingent outcomes of political engagement. As politics goes, so goes the Constitution.

Of course, *Brown* was not entirely out of the blue; the Supreme Court had begun to chip away at the *Plessy* doctrine over the previous couple of

---

[27] *Griswold v. Connecticut*, 381 US 479 (1965). This is clear in the Roe judgments themselves. Whereas Blackmun J stated that "our task, of course, is to resolve the issue by constitutional measurement, free of emotion and of predilection," White J thought that the majority's judgment was "an improvident and extravagant exercise of the power of judicial review." See *Roe v. Wade*, 410 US 113 at 222 (1973) per White J. For the best example of this effort to couch political support and opposition in doctrinal terms, see *Casey v. Planned Parenthood*, 505 US 833 (1991).

decades.[28] However, as both the popular upheaval and professional fallout evince, the decision was far from a routine extension of existing precedent or a natural progression from established doctrine. Indeed, the brevity of the judgment, its unanimity, and its sparse argumentative basis all speak to the lengths that individual members of the Court were willing to go to present a consolidated front in the face of the controversial substance of the judgment, its likely implications, and the expected onslaught on the Court. Again, as I argued in regard to English tort law, if *Brown* is defended as a continuation of existing tradition, then the available resources of legal precedents are so capacious as to warrant almost any particular result or development. If that is the case, the level of generality and the placing of emphasis can be manipulated legitimately to favor or foreclose almost any line of doctrinal development. However, if *Brown* is treated as a deviation from existing traditions of constitutional doctrine, then the supposed discipline and regimen of constitutional adjudication is undermined. Transformation and change seem to be the traditional order of the constitutional day. Moreover, the thin doctrinal basis on which *Brown* was laid and the convoluted efforts of jurists to offer a more compelling legal rationale further support the critical claim that *Brown*'s general acceptance as a great case has much less to do with internal, doctrinal, and formal considerations and more to do with external, political, and substantive concerns. Although *Brown*'s tenure as a great case was up in the air for some time, it was not legal argument or academic rationalization that pushed it over the top. It is surely more convincing to concede that the genesis of *Brown* is to be found in both a strikingly creative and a relatively constrained performance of the judicial craft that breaks with existing legal traditions at the same time that it transforms those traditions. Great cases, like *Brown*, do not so much give the lie to the critical claim that 'law is politics', but provide the best evidence of its cogency and force: Law is thoroughly permeated with politics, and any attempt to distinguish one from the other is destined to be so trivial as to be of no theoretical significance or so convoluted as to be of no practical import.

Decisions like *Brown* become great cases in the shifting constitutional universe not because they are legally correct or analytically sound, but because

---

[28] See *Pearson v. Murray*, 182 A. 590 (Md. 1936); *Missouri, ex rel. Gaines v. Canada*, 305 US 337 (1938); *Sipuel v. Oklahoma*, 332 US 631 (1948); *Sweatt v. Painter*, 339 US 629 (1950); and *McLaurin v. Oklahoma State Regents*, 339 US 637 (1950). However, there was still considerable recent doctrinal support for *Plessy* at the time of *Brown*. See *Briggs v. Elliott*, 98 F. Supp. 529 (1951); *Boor v. Garrett*, 183 F. 2d (1950); and *Corbin v. County School Board*, 84 F. Supp. 253 (1949).

they are considered politically valid and socially acceptable. They remain in that exalted position only as long as their political base and social legitimacy can be sustained. The difference between *Plessy* and *Brown* has nothing to do with their interpretive cogency or hermeneutical integrity as a matter of constitutional doctrine. Indeed, there is little in *Brown* that makes it formally or stylistically superior as a legal decision to *Plessy*. It has everything to do with the changing currents and concerns in the shifting political context that frame and condition such germinal and disruptive judicial decisions. *Plessy* ceased to be a fixed point on the constitutional compass because it no longer enjoyed sufficient political confidence and public support; its perception as having an analytically weak or doctrinally suspect status was beside the historical or legal point. Its constitutional rightness was a matter of social policy and political persuasion, not legal authority or doctrinal cogency. When Justice Harlan predicted that the Plessy judgment "will, in time, prove to be quite as pernicious as the decision . . . in *Dred Scott*," he was talking about its substantive merits as a political event, not its formal qualities as a legal judgment.[29] Indeed, as the harrowed academic response to *Brown* again demonstrates, it was (and still would be) difficult for traditional common lawyers to recognize *Brown* as a sound or correct legal decision in the summer of 1954, without abandoning their cherished commitments to even a minimalist doctrine of stare decisis. Adding the fact that *Brown* is a constitutional decision only serves to compound the severity of the challenge. Consequently, although *Brown* is still revered as a great case whose intimations must be incorporated into any valid account of constitutional law, it actually throws judges and jurists on the painful horns of the perennial dilemma – either it is bad constitutional law, in which case it confirms the fear that constitution law is basically a reactionary practice, or it is good constitutional law, in which case constitution law is capable of sustaining all kind of diverse and often contradictory interpretations. In short, accept *Brown* and you accept almost all interpretations: Reject it and constitutional law is very problematic as a just source of democratic governance.

The relative fates of *Brown* and *Lochner* are very much on point. The Supreme Court's 1905 decision in *Lochner* has been pilloried and held up as an antigreat case; its canonical authority is found in its standing as exactly

---

[29] *Plessy v. Ferguson*, 163 US 537 at 559 (1896) per Harlan J. A century later, one commentator echoed this when he concluded that, from the viewpoint of gays and lesbians, "*Hardwick* and the military exclusion cases are no more legitimate than *Dred Scott* was for pre-Civil War slaves or *Korematsu* was for Japanese Americans. These decisions are not law because they deny us our citizenship and because they subject us to violence." See W. Eskridge, *Gaylegal Narratives*, 46 *Stan. L. Rev.* 607 at 639 (1994).

what the Constitution does not stand for and exactly what judges should not do if they want to act legitimately and appropriately. However, its genesis and trajectory are not dissimilar to *Brown*. Whether viewed as an extension of existing precedent or as a break from it, *Lochner*'s precise ambit left much open to interpretation. It neither followed inexorably from previous decisions nor represented an aberrational moment in constitutional discourse: Its doctrinal legitimacy was no more and no less assured than most other leading judgments.[30] Moreover, while its quality in terms of judicial craft is far from outstanding, it is clearly the match of *Brown*'s cursory product. Nevertheless, *Brown* was and is the case that has been acclaimed and treated as great. This can only be understood as a matter of substantive politics. In the same way that a literary work's greatness and authority is a function of historicized rather than universal standards of judgment, so the status of great cases is less a matter of formal accuracy than substantive appeal. Legal and literary texts are championed by people because their qualities speak to them in a powerful and stimulating ways – and they will remain of canonical stature for as long as people think that. However, their continuing preeminence is as much about what people think as it is about something intrinsic or transcendent in the texts themselves: Canonicity is what is bestowed on texts, not something that a text simply has. Great cases do have an authority and therefore a conversation-stopping quality in legal debate, but this is not because of some inherent or enduring force that they autonomously possess. Great cases have to earn their authority in the political squares of legal and popular opinion. Once that opinion begins to shift, the canonical force of such cases will be affected accordingly; talk of error or mistake is a rhetorical device to justify a particular substantive position or a change in the law.

Great cases are only as authoritative as the political values that they represent and by whose forbearance they are held in place. It is not so much that *Brown* got it right and *Lochner* got it wrong as a matter of textual exegesis or doctrinal development, but that the substantive values that *Brown* represents seem to remain more conducive to popular opinion than *Lochner*'s. However,

---

[30] *Lochner*, supra, note 8. Presaged by *Wynehammer v. People* and *Allgeyer v. Louisiana*, 165 US 578 (1897), *Lochner* was used extensively for twenty years, but not with any consistency in reasoning or result. The judges were divided over the reach and basis of the decision. Although *Lochner* was overruled implicitly in *Bunting v. Oregon*, 243 US 426 (1917), its waning influence continued and it only received its formal burial in *Lincoln Federal Labor Union v. Northwestern Iron and Metal Co.*, 335 US 525 at 535 (1949). Since *West Coast Hotel Co. v. Parrish*, 300 US 379 (1937), the Supreme Court has abandoned an explicit *Lochner*-style analysis and has not invalidated an economic regulation on substantive due process grounds.

I say "seem" because, although *Brown* is still loudly and regularly feted and *Lochner* is castigated with equal force, the reality may be different. On the one hand, *Brown*'s influence and, therefore, canonicity is waning as conservative forces reassert themselves; the metaphorical emphasis in equality doctrine on a color-blind constitution threatens to subvert the progressive tilt of a more situated and historically sensitive discrimination doctrine. On the other hand, *Lochner*'s influence is actually waxing as the ideological appeal of a substantive standard for protecting economic rights against state regulation becomes more attractive; the trend is to reject *Lochner* by name and reference but to resurrect it in style and substance.[31] These turn of events say much about the common law and the status of great cases in its development. As disturbing as they might be to some (and encouraging as they might be to others), they do little to sustain the idea that law and adjudication are driven by the law's intellectual discipline. On the contrary, politics is the motor force of the common law, and it is judges' attachment to particular and partisan substantive values that steers it in one direction or another.

When Balkin and Levinson ask "whether cases like *Miranda* and *Brown* are sacred cows that cannot be touched or whether they are revisable like everything else,"[32] the question is misconceived: Such cases are both 'sacred cows' and 'reversible like anything else'. As long as they are accepted as being part of the constitutional canon, they will have the authority and force that any canonical case has (which, of course, will be far from fixed or certain). However, because the contents of the canon are revisable, such cases are as reversible as any other. In a manner of speaking, constitutional law's sacred cows are only bovine and not divine; they serve someone's distinctly human purposes rather than validate those purposes as universal or enduring. There is no legal theory that will or can guarantee that *Brown* and *Roe* will remain or that *Plessy* and *Lochner* will never resurrect themselves. There are no doctrinal or jurisprudential formulas than can underwrite any particular course of constitutional development in dealing with "the various crises of human affair." Nor will judges who go in one direction rather than another

---

[31] *Plessy* has experienced something of a renaissance in the form of the rebellion against affirmative action: Any resort to race-based categories is treated as invalid. There are echoes of Brown J's dissent in *Plessy* in Thomas J's judgment in *Adarand Constructors Inc. v. Pena*, 512 US 200 (1995). See also G. Loury, *Individualism Before Multiculturalism* (1996). As regards *Lochner*, the decisions in *Nollan v. California Coastal Commission*, 483 US 825 (1987) and *Dolan v. City of Tigard*, 114 S. Ct. 2309 (1994) seem to embody a *Lochner*-style approach. See Note, Resurrecting Economic Rights: The Doctrine of Economic Due Process Reconsidered, 103 *Harv. L. Rev.* 1363 (1989) and J. E. Cohen, Lochner in Cyberspace: the New Economic Orthodoxy of "Rights Management," 97 *Mich. L. Rev.* 462 (1999).

[32] J. Balkin and S. Levinson, supra, note 5 at 997.

be able to claim that they are acting in a more constitutionally legitimate manner. This does not mean that there are no grounds for constitutional law in the sense of arguments or reasons; it simply means that there are none that are final or determinative by sheer weight of their normative force. As great cases show, judges can do much what they like, provided that they can persuade enough of their colleagues to support their view and that the ensuing decision will garner sufficient popular tolerance. Good constitutional law is whatever is accepted as good constitutional law: There is nothing else to it. Great cases are the proof of that critical claim, not its refutation.

Back to the Future

The occurrence and importance of great cases obviously has a marked effect on any claims about the nature and operation of the doctrine of stare decisis. While the circumstances of the birth of great cases challenge its whole conservative thrust, the tenacity and influence of great cases reinforces the centrality of precedential authority to the common law. Indeed, modern courts have begun to recognize that state of affairs. Instead of pretending that the common law's development is a seamless web of continuing substantive commitments, judges have sought to revise the doctrine of stare decisis so that it is better able to accommodate explicitly the apparently contradictory impulses to which great cases give rise. There must be some growth and flexibility in the common law, but there must also be some continuity and certainty. Contemporary judges frequently acknowledge that precedent has never been the refined practice that theory recommends. Indeed, the idea that the common law is or was a coherent body of organized rules that was applied consistently and conclusively is belied by the historical record. Nevertheless, this does not mean that stare decisis has no relevance or rigor. Judges have sought to develop a compromise position between an understanding that earlier decisions constitute an instructive baseline and have informational status and an understanding that such decisions are dispositive of present dispute. They have insisted that following precedent is not an all-or-nothing choice between blind adherence and total disregard. Some courts have been considered to have gone so far as to announce that "stare decisis is neither a doctrine ... nor a strict rule of law, but rather is a sub-doctrine of ostensibly wise judicial practice, procedure, and policy."[33] While I agree with such a stance, I do not think that it can be

---

[33] M. S. Paulsen, <u>Abrogating Stare Decisis by Statute: May Congress Remove the Precedential Effect of Roe and Casey?</u>, 109 *Yale L. J.* 1535 at 1538 and generally at 1551–66 (2000).

achieved or maintained as a matter of legal principle in some way distinct from substantive politics. On the contrary, I believe that such an effort at compromise by the judicial community is a concession and confirmation that law is thoroughly political and that 'anything might go'. As great cases confirm, both the cause and engine of the common law's development, as well as the constraints upon it, are substantive political commitments.

In utilizing the past to guide the future through stare decisis, the courts have paid special attention to the question of when is it appropriate to overrule an earlier decision or, to put it more informatively, when a court can hold that an earlier judgment that establishes a particular rule or principle has not only been erroneously decided but that it should be discarded and replaced by a different rule. It is trite learning, of course, that the mere fact that a later court considers an earlier decision to be wrongly decided is not enough in itself to warrant its abandonment or overruling. To maintain otherwise would be to rob stare decisis of any bite at all: It is ostensibly a formal doctrine that demands precedents be followed simply because of their historical pedigree, not only because of their substantive appeal. In short, overruling should only be permitted when there is some special or superjustification over and above the claim that the earlier decision is wrong. Although courts are understandably reluctant to break from a long-standing legal tradition or ruling, they are not only prepared to do so but place an obligation on themselves to do so at times.

For instance, in *Planned Parenthood v. Casey*, the Supreme Court divided over whether *Roe* should be overruled. Speaking jointly for the Court, the plurality of Justices Souter, O'Connor, and Kennedy stated that there are moments when the Court best fulfills its constitutional duty by repudiating earlier lines of cases: "In constitutional adjudication as elsewhere in life, changed circumstances may impose new obligations, and the thoughtful part of the Nation could accept each decision to overrule a prior case as a response to the Court's constitutional duty." According to the plurality, this should occur when the Court would have to pay a "terrible price" for a failure to act, as was the case in both *West Coast Hotel* and *Brown*. However, cautioning that "each generation must learn anew that the Constitution's written terms embody ideas and aspirations that must survive more ages than one," the judges maintained that *Roe* not only did not warrant overruling but that its repudiation "would seriously weaken the Court's capacity to exercise the judicial power and to function as the Supreme Court of a Nation dedicated to the rule of law." However, the plurality was careful to emphasize that its affirmation of *Roe* was based on a consideration of "the fundamental constitutional questions resolved by *Roe*, principles of institutional integrity" rather than exclusively on "the rule of *stare decisis*" alone: Documents and doctrines combined.[34]

In short, a plurality of the Supreme Court decided that, if the stakes are high enough, the fallout sufficiently severe, and the judges are so disposed, the breaking with established constitutional tradition will occur. This is exactly what the plurality endorsed. It was not that Justices Souter, O'Connor, and Kennedy thought that such a course of action was entirely illegitimate in the sense that the Court had no business overruling its own precedents. It was simply that *Casey* was not thought to be an appropriate occasion or time to act. It was an ideological call, not a legal one, about social circumstances and political climate. The plurality's judgment is not replete with extended parsing of established cases and principles, but is squarely framed in terms of a "series of pragmatic and prudential considerations."[35] Substantive fairness trumps legal soundness.

In pursuing the *Casey* approach to stare decisis, while I do not want to go far as to suggest that stare decisis is "a hoax designed to provide cover for a particular outcome, not a genuine, principled ground of decision," I do maintain that the doctrine of precedent does not prevent inventive judges from doing whatever they wish. They can still, as evidenced by Chief Justice Warren in *Brown* and Justice Blackmun in *Roe*, achieve the substantive result that they wish and claim to be following precedent.[36] Moreover, for the same reason, the invocation of stare decisis as a reason for not changing the law is no more convincing or principled; judges opt for inertia for political reasons as much as legal ones. There is no sharp distinction between a 'cover for

[34] *Casey*, supra, note 27 at 864, 865, and 901. See *West Coast Hotel Co. v. Parrish*, 300 US 379 (1937) (overruling the economic liberty doctrine) and *Brown v. Board of Education*, 347 US 483 (1954) (overruling the separate-but-equal doctrine). In a parallel development, the Supreme of Canada has recently insisted that, even if an earlier decision is generally assumed to be erroneous, a change in the common law should only occur if it is necessary "to keep the common law in step with the evolution of society, to clarify a legal principle, or to resolve an inconsistency." Moreover, it recommended that any change should be as incremental as possible and no change should be made unless "its consequences [are] capable of assessment" so as to avoid setting the law on an unknown and potentially disastrous course. See *Friedmann Equity Developments Inc. v. Final Note Ltd.* [2000], 1 SCR 842 at 871.

[35] Id. at 853.

[36] See M. S. Paulsen, Captain James T. Kirk and the Enterprise of Constitutional Interpretation: Some Modest Proposals from the Twenty-Third Century, 59 *Alb. L. Rev.* 671, 679–81 (1995). One recent study concludes that precedent "rarely" causes any members of the United States Supreme Court to embrace "a result they would not otherwise have reached." See H. J. Speath and J. A. Segal, *Majority Rule or Minority Will: Adherence to Precedent on the U.S. Supreme Court* 287 (1999). For an interesting philosophical analysis of stare decisis, see C. J. Peters, Foolish Consistency: On Equality, Integrity, and Justice in Stare Decisis, 105 *Yale L.J.* 2031 (1996).

a particular outcome' and 'genuine, principled ground of decision'. The only significant difference between principled and nonprincipled decision making (as distinct from corrupt or bad-faith decision making) is that, in the former, the general principles used and their particularized application win enough overall support to warrant their continued acceptance. Behind the rhetorical cover of principled argument is the genuine dispute over particular substantive political commitments. When the Supreme Court's catalogue of overruling criteria is taken seriously, there is no neutral or non-controversial way to determine what a series of pragmatic and prudential considerations demand, when changed circumstances are sufficient to warrant legal innovation, and how to ascertain when there are new obligations. These criteria are not so much solutions to a problem as restatements of the problems to be resolved; making law dependent on assessments of social change is the quintessence of a political undertaking.

In deciding any case according to the common law method, judges must perform two separate maneuvers – they must interpret what an earlier decision means and then determine what the doctrine of stare decisis requires to be done with that interpretation. These are sufficiently indeterminate and highly contested activities when understood independently, but, when they are joined together (as they must be), they become even less amenable to any precise and determinate instruction. In short, the different possible ways in which judges can legitimately perform their common law responsibilities are so many that they have an almost limitless range of choice: judges "know how to mouth the correct legal rules with ironic solemnity while avoiding those rules' logical consequences."[37] And, of course, the generation and pedigree of great cases is the best evidence of this. In short, there is no strictly legal method by which an earlier decision can be determined to be wrong, let alone that there is some other special justification for its overruling, that can be distinguished from a more open-ended ideological inquiry. Consequently, common law judges are always caught in a bind in which they must balance off competing considerations with neither weights nor scales to help them; it is an inevitable and inescapable political exercise.

Of course, any decision reached or judgment delivered can be criticized in terms of craft or political orientation, but it cannot be condemned as invalid or illegitimate simply because it was made with reference to particular and controversial political values. A decision is only wrong insofar as its

---

[37] *TXO Products Corp. v. Alliance Resources Corp.*, 113 S. Ct. 2711, 2742 (1993) (O'Connor J, dissenting).

antagonists would have reached another decision or constructed a different judgment. The continuing debate around *Brown* is the fabled example of this. Consequently, I do not so much deny the existence and force of stare decisis, as insist that the fact that judges tend to reach similar conclusions speaks more to their shared values than any disciplining legal protocol: Authority, casual or continuing, is something that judgments earn rather than possess. Any perceived legitimacy crisis in adjudication has less to do with the contemporary practice of adjudication itself than the greater diversity of society and its contested values. Judges do much the same as they have always done, only now that there is an increasing diversity in judicial ranks and a decreasing willingness on the public's part to accept judicial decisions at face value, the political quality of the judicial performance is less concealed. In acting legally, judges are also and always acting politically. Great cases are the most compelling evidence of this.

The failure of judges to provide a cogent defense of stare decisis' operation is matched by their juristic counterparts: Their analysis may be more sophisticated and sustained, but the result is the same. Although there is much disagreement among traditional scholars, there remains an important and unifying commitment to demonstrating that not only can the common law balance the competing demands of stability and change, but also that it can do so in a legitimate way that respects the important distinction between law and politics. It is clearly my view that such a commitment cannot be sustained and that, if the common law is a tradition, it is as much one of change and innovation as it is of stability and continuity. Great cases are an excellent pointer to the character and performance of the common law. They fit only partially, if at all, into traditional evolutionary accounts of the common law. Indeed, great cases are more of a refutation of the incremental hypothesis, not a demonstration of its validity. *Rylands, Donoghue,* and the like can hardly or reasonably be described as incremental adjustments to the common law body of rules and principles, let alone as affirmations of existing traditions. Again, judges and jurists are left with a stark choice – they can either recognize great cases as revolutionary moments in the common law's development and revise their accounts of the common law to accommodate them, with all the subversive consequences that entails, or they can deny that great cases are revolutionary moments and acknowledge that incremental change encompasses any and every change to the common law, with all its equally subversive consequences. In either case, the result will be both a realization (no matter how begrudging) that, when it comes to the common law, 'anything might go' and an abandonment (no matter how reluctantly) of the jurisprudential insistence that law and politics are separate.

Of course, contemporary jurists have sought to resist this result with all the theoretical means at their disposal. However, what begins its jurisprudential life as a reassuring promise of justifying incremental development runs the risk of quickly and easily turning into a subversive threat of permitting wholesale transformation. In searching for the fragile developmental equilibrium between stability and change, common law apologists tread a precariously thin line between a legitimate practice of unfolding reform and an illegitimate exercise in episodic revolution. This is a tall order for any legal theory and one that the demand to explain the emergence and existence of great cases turns into an almost impossible one. If great cases are the crowning glory of the common law tradition, they are equally the Achilles' heel of its jurisprudential apologists. Indeed, Posner has announced that judges and jurists should no longer be interested in such an endeavor. Even in constitutional matters, he maintains that their time would be better spent if they abandoned such theoretical indulgences and devoted their energies to examining the social contexts of constitutional issues, their causes, their costs, and their consequences. However, as I have sought to demonstrate, Posner's approach is more a strategic ploy than a genuine position. Although he unceremoniously throws moral and political theory out the front door of jurisprudence's mansion, he lets in its economic sibling sneakily through the back door. Thus, the Bulldog breed of jurist has not so much resolved the common law's dilemma of explaining great cases as ignored it.[38]

To his credit, it is again Dworkin who has sought to offer a comprehensive account that will encompass and explain the existence and force of great cases. However, his failure to succeed in this task is ominous for almost all traditional jurists who rely on a principled account of the common law's development as well as individual adjudicative performances. Dworkin advances an understanding of adjudication as a political practice that works the space between law's institutional past and its future possibilities. To him, any interpretation of the legal materials must be able to demonstrate some plausible connection to society's legal history and, in that important sense, be continuous with that past. While the better interpretation is not necessarily the one that accounts for the most decisions, the settled body of legal norms and justifications is claimed to be the motor force of principled adjudication: "Law's attitude . . . aims, in the interpretive spirit, to lay principle over practice to show the best route to a better future, keeping the right faith with the past." In short, Dworkin's interpretive ideal of judicial

---

[38] See infra chap. 4 and R. Posner, *The Problematics of Moral and Legal Theory* (1999).

integrity seeks to combine both backward-looking and forward-looking elements by insisting that judges view what they do as "an unfolding political narrative" that "begins in the present and pursues the past only so far as and in the way . . . that present practice can be organized by and justified in principles sufficiently attractive to provide an honourable future." Along with the idea of legal continuity, Dworkin maintains that the judges should treat the law as if it were a seamless web, providing complete and determinate guidance on all legal disputes; there is no need or justification to leave the law behind and engage in unconstrained choice. Accordingly, Hercules is most certainly no revolutionary figure and is trusted to uphold the wisdom of the past, albeit in imaginative and innovative ways:

> Convictions about fit will provide a rough threshold requirement that an interpretation of some part of the law must meet if it is to be eligible at all. . . . That threshold will eliminate interpretations that some judges would otherwise prefer, so the brute facts of legal history will in this way limit the role any judge's personal convictions of justice can play in his decisions. Different judges will set this threshold differently. But anyone who accepts law as integrity must accept that the actual political history of his community will sometimes check his other political convictions in his overall interpretive judgment. If he does not, . . . he is acting from bad faith or self-deception.[39]

Despite the ingenuity of his theory and its robust defense, Dworkin's efforts create more and larger problems for his general account of common law adjudication than they resolve. Dworkin wants it both ways. He wants to demonstrate that the common law is both open and closed: It is open in that the judges are able to develop the law in new and unexpected ways and, at the same time, it is closed in that judges cannot ignore "the brute facts of legal history" in favor of their own political convictions. The fact is that, within the traditional jurisprudential project, the price of having one is the cost of having the other, particularly so in regard to great cases. If his claims about fidelity to the legal past mean that any constructive account of the law must accommodate great cases, then his theory is on the mark as an account of adjudication as a partially closed as opposed to an entirely open practice. However, when such a constraining requirement is taken seriously, the birth and acknowledgment of future great cases – those that represent a radical departure from extant principles, not their incremental development – seems well-nigh impossible. On such an account, great cases negate

---

[39] R. Dworkin, *Law's Empire* 413, 227–28 and 255 (1996). See generally supra chap. 3.

rather than exemplify the quintessential character of valid adjudication; the common law is a complex of principles that justifies radically different and contradictory readings. As Dworkin himself concedes, how the dimensions of backward-pulling fit and forward-pushing substance relate to each other is "in the last analysis all responsive to [judges'] political judgment."[40] While this is an acceptable conclusion for someone, like me, who maintains that the common law is a work-in-progress and that 'anything might go', it is a curious and ultimately disappointing confession for any theorist devoted to refuting the critical claim that 'law is politics'.

Nevertheless, aware that his emphasis on fidelity with the past might back him into some politically unattractive corners, Dworkin tries to provide Hercules and lesser judicial mortals with a convenient escape route. Consequently, he argues that, in exceptional and unusual circumstances such as those in Nazi Germany and Apartheid South Africa, judges are entitled to forgo compliance with even the minimal demands of formal fit: "If a judge's own sense of justice condemned [the grounds of law] as deeply immoral . . . , he would have to consider whether he should actually enforce it . . . , or whether he should lie and say that this was not the law after all, or whether he should resign."[41] While this might seem to extricate Hercules from some tight spots, it actually has him jumping between the frying pan and the fire. On the one hand, if such a radical maneuver is only justified in grotesque societies such as Nazi Germany or Apartheid South Africa, it is difficult to envision how great cases meet that standard. Although *Donoghue* might have dealt with instances of consumer injustice that were by no means insignificant, it is a considerable stretch to place such injustice on the same level as what went on in those blighted societies. That being the case, Dworkin's "deeply immoral" exception will have problems incorporating and accounting for great cases. On the other hand, if the meaning of "deeply immoral" is to be determined by a judge's own sense of justice, then the opportunities to finesse the minimal backward-connecting demands of formal fit will be as broad or as narrow as the range of judges' political commitments. Accordingly, provided that judges do so on the basis of sincerely held beliefs, they are free to 'lie', 'resign', or 'refuse to enforce the law'. In short, judges need only keep faith with the past insofar as it accords with their own sense of justice. Or, as Lord Pearce put it rather more subtly (but no less revealingly) in *Hedley Byrne*, "how wide the sphere of the duty of care in negligence is to be laid depends ultimately upon the courts' assessment of the demands

[40] Id. at 255 and 257.
[41] Id. at 219.

of society for protection from the carelessness of others."[42] Indeed, the history of the common law is redolent with judicial pronouncements that the touchstone of good judging is the strength and sincerity of judges' political beliefs, not the moral force of the extant law or particular judges' fidelity to it. As Lord Macmillan concluded in *Donoghue*, "any proposition the result of which would be to show that the common law of England is wholly unreasonable and unjust cannot be part of the common law of England."[43] This is a powerful and appealing notion, but it undermines, not confirms, the Dworkinesque appeal to principled integrity as the heartbeat of the common law.

Routines and Riders

Throughout this chapter, I have made a series of critical claims that will likely ruffle the feathers of most, if not all, legal theorists. This, of course, is to be expected because the account of the common law that I have offered is intended to challenge existing ideas and to undermine traditional understandings. Rather than treat great cases as anomalous occurrences that require special explanations, I place the incidence, importance, and influence of great cases at the heart of the jurisprudential project. In this way, it becomes possible to appreciate that the price of the common law's ability to change and adapt is the cost of it being understood as a fundamentally political undertaking. If there is any unifying thread to the smorgasbord of modern jurisprudence, it is the theoretical conviction that law and politics are not one and the same, such that what judges believe to be good politics is also good law. I insist that such a fundamental distinction cannot be maintained. However, there is one likely response to my arguments that can be readily identified and warrants immediate rebuttal. Although it comes in various shapes and sizes, the basic riposte to the critical claim that 'law is politics' is that, while this might be a credible claim in some celebrated instances, the greater part of judicial activity is ordinarily formalized and politically detached. Specifically in regard to great cases, it is argued that, by their nature and status, they are more the exception than the rule and, as the proverbial wisdom has it, prove the rule – the common law is by and large a disciplined process that is exemplified by the routine and uncreative application of existing law. It is contended that to understand the common law only by reference to so-called great cases is to allow the political tail to

[42] *Hedley Byrne*, supra, note 18 at 536 per Lord Pearce.
[43] See supra, note 19.

wag the legal dog. Fortunately, time and attention have not been kind to this "routine" line of traditional argument. When it is understood properly, this familiar distinction between so-called routine and revolutionary cases adds fuel to the critical fire rather than extinguishes it.

While the claim is true insofar as much adjudication is mundane and prosaic, such a characterization cannot carry the jurisprudential day. To my way of thinking, all decisions are political in that even allegedly rigid deferences to tradition are more realistically characterized as normative approvals of the specific outcome suggested or of the tradition generally because it jibes with the present critical commitments of the judge. There is never a situation in which judges do not have the opportunity or responsibility to be creative; whether they choose to utilize that chance is a different matter. Once it is conceded, as it must be, that great cases are a valid feature and product of the common law process, the quotidian operation of the adjudicative function has to be viewed in a more expansive way. When judges appear to be following precedent and to be framing their judgments in terms of legal authority, it is more that they are approving of the substantive desirability of the outcome that arises from a reasonably traditional reliance on existing case law. In other words, it is the end result and not the reasoning means that is controlling. The specter of great cases – the possibility that judges cannot only reject traditional approaches, set off in new directions, and still be acting in an appropriately legitimate manner, but also be celebrated for so doing – suggests that, because there is always the strong discretion to do something else, judges must actually make a positive choice to opt for a precedent-directed decision. As it is the particular substantive values in play rather than the formal general logic of the law that govern, the judges in routine instances are choosing not to be radical or transformative. In any system that allows and provides for change, the decision to remain with the status quo cannot be politically neutral or apolitical. It really is as much a political decision to stand pat as it is to change. Indeed, when viewed in the critical light that I recommend, the jurisprudential problem becomes less about whether there are too many great cases but whether there are too few of them. As the late Roger Traynor wryly commented, "the real concern is not the remote possibility of too many creative opinions, but their continuing scarcity."[44]

For instance, a powerful constraint on judges is their felt need to protect the democratic legitimacy and integrity of the courts as they are thrust

---

[44] R. Traynor, Comment, in S. Paulsen, *Legal Institutions* 52 (1959).

into highly charged areas of public policy. There is a clear sense in judicial quarters that, unless it can be reasonably demonstrated that there is some certainty and predictability to law, public confidence in the Rule of Law and, therefore, the courts would be seriously jeopardized: "The doctrine [of stare decisis] permits society to presume that bedrock principles are founded in the law rather than in the proclivities of individuals."[45] Efforts to defuse this charge often manifest themselves in a heightened attachment to the doctrine of stare decisis or, at least, a rhetorical insistence on its constricting influence. However, this maneuver is less a turn away from politics and more a shifting of political ground. Stare decisis might be presented as a technical device, but it is a settled and indeterminate policy in that stability and continuity are value considerations that judges must weight and be weighed in their decision-making process. However, the way in which those values are calibrated must be done by reference to some other set of political convictions. It is the substantive justice of the result and the public reputation of the judicial process generally that has priority over the formal virtues of precedent adherence. It is surely the case that public confidence in the courts would be more seriously damaged if the court stuck to an established precedent when there was overwhelming support for a different substantive outcome. As the career of both *Brown* and *Roe* indicate, the connection between public support and judicial resolve is difficult to plot and is itself subject to varying political considerations. Although such traditional values are often passed off as peculiarly legal, formal, and neutral, they are as political, substantive, and contested as they come. By giving priority to institutional stability over individualized justice or wholesale reform, the courts are engaging in a very fundamental political exercise: Conservatism is no less ideological than progressivism. Moreover, a commitment to stare decisis is really no constraint at all.

Accordingly, the fact that great cases are few and far between does not support the claim that the judicial development of the common law is apolitically neutral or internally driven. Although it seems entirely reasonable and unexceptional for the common law to defend an approach in which what has happened previously will affect what will happen later, it is a huge step to advance the further claim that what has happened previously must necessarily constrain or bring about what will happen next.[46] When judges decide to

---

[45] *Vasquez v. Hillery*, 474 US 254 at 265 per Marshall J (1986). See generally D. Hellman, The Importance of Appearing Principled, 37 *Ariz. L. Rev.* 1107 (1995).
[46] O. A. Hathaway, Path Dependence in the Law: The Course and Pattern of Legal Change in a Common Law System, 86 *Iowa L. Rev.* 601 (2001).

follow existing doctrine rather than overturn it, they are not refraining from political assessment; they are choosing to make such evaluations in terms of either formal institutional values or substantive political commitments. The continuing battle over the importance and worth of *Roe* has as much to do with such institutional considerations as with substantive disagreements over abortion. Nevertheless, as great cases like *Griswold* powerfully attest, when the accumulating pressure of particular substantive values reaches a certain pitch, the conservatism of lawyers will succumb to the institutional wisdom of change and the democratic reputation of the court will depend on transformative innovation, not traditional steadfastness. The demands of judicial integrity are as political, contingent, and contested as any other values; what is required will depend on context and commitment.

There are, therefore, no routine cases if by that it is meant that they can be decided in a purely legal and objective manner (i.e., by the professional application of preexisting rules) without resort to political and contingent considerations. Because each case is a potentially great case, *all* cases have an actual and potential transformative element; it is less that they are of a different kind and more that they are of a different degree. On some smaller or larger scale, all cases transform doctrine or, at least, change it in the sense of advancing or refining it in regard to particular situations. While this insight is by no means novel, its implications for appreciating common law development and adjudication are largely ignored. For instance, in the 1930s, Justice Stone commented that the common law is "an evolutionary and variable product" and because "every new case has some new factors that require original consideration by the court, every new case is a case of first impression."[47] Accordingly, while the vast majority of cases might appear to be dealt with routinely, they are in fact low-level transformative occasions that do not shake the law's foundations and that confirm that the cut and line of existing doctrine satisfies the present political attachments of judges in that particular situation. For instance, in a consideration of whether *Donoghue* should be extended to auditors, reference writers, and so on, there might well be strong disagreement and dissent, but whatever happens is likely to be in the realm of the tolerable because it will not implicate larger social

---

[47] Stone, The Common Law of the United States, 47 *Yale L. J.* 1351 at 1352 (1938). See also K. Llewellyn, *The Bramble Bush* 156 (1930) ("constant movement, movement even in run-of-the-mill cases") and L. Fuller, *The Law in Quest of Itself* 40–41 (1940) ("the judge makes law even when he states that he is refusing to make it"). Even Dworkin does not recommend a different approach to hard and easy cases, although he maintains that judges' political involvement can be performed in a neutral and nonideological way. See R. Dworkin, supra, note 39 at 264–66.

values. This is clearly not the case with racism, abortion, or euthanasia. Of course, there actually are transformative cases, not merely the ever-present possibility of them. Great cases are those in which the transformative potential is acted upon and legal doctrine experiences a radical reorganization or realignment. In the same way that "any scientific change whatever will normally have both something 'normal' and something 'revolutionary' about it," so all legal cases are routine in that they require judges to engage in exactly the same process of reflection on and reaction to the political values that underpin particular doctrinal applications in the prevailing and particular social context.[48]

One jurist who has recognized that there are periodic revolutions in the common law's historical development and who has sought to incorporate them into a standard account of the common law's legitimate operation is Robert Lipkin. Although he confines his focus to American constitutional law, he offers "a theory of adjudication that attempts to capture the role of the Court in sustaining traditions of constitutional transformation" through "a deliberative method . . . that translates the revolutionary politics of the greater society into workable judicial paradigms." There is much in Lipkin's approach that is enlightening in its willingness to explain the common law process of adjudication through the incidence and importance of great cases. However, behind the pragmatic and critical gestures, it is simply another effort to hijack radical critique and domesticate it for traditional constitutional purposes; it puts a smooth gloss on the jagged workings of constitutional law and politics. Lipkin is very much in the tradition of Dworkinian jurisprudence with his insistence that "revolutionary judicial review is self-consciously concerned about politics in the sense of political theory, not partisan politics" and that, when taking society's ideological temperature, "[the judge's] focus is on the Constitution and political and moral culture, not on what she personally values and believes." Moreover, his differentiation between routine and revolutionary adjudication is exactly the kind of distinction that the common law's historical development and performance confounds. While there is a difference between routine and revolutionary occasions, it is a matter of degree, not kind; it is most certainly not one of method. All adjudication involves the resort to so-called external and contested political factors. It is simply that revolutionary cases tend to deal with those that are more heated, that demand greater change, and that

---

[48] See S. E. Toulmin, Does the Distinction Between Normal and Revolutionary Science Hold Water?, in *Criticism and the Growth of Knowledge* 39 at 115 (I. Lakatos and A. Musgrave eds. 1970) and infra, chap. 8.

prevent a more discrete approach than routine cases. It may be that "the best of law translates the best of politics into legal form," but what is 'best' in both politics and law is profoundly and irreducibly ideological.[49] For all Lipkin's talk of transformation, his is a very traditional rendition of legal theory. It is a pragmatic tempest in a formalist teapot.

Finally, when the emergence and existence of great cases are utilized to support the claim that common law adjudication is political in the sense that 'anything might go', three important riders have to be offered. The first is that my analysis and critique are jurisprudential; they are not intended as sociological claims about the practical impact of great cases. It is a central issue on the agenda of many social scientists to determine the instrumentality of court decisions on social struggle and conditions. For instance, a topic of considerable importance and debate remains the extent and quality of the effect that the decisions in *Brown* and *Roe* had on the practices of discrimination and the availability of reproductive health services in the United States.[50] This debate, both generally and specifically, is beyond the scope of my project. My limited brief has been to tackle the jurisprudential claims of mainstream theorists and to demonstrate that the nature of common law adjudication is more transformative and less traditional in terms of doctrinal development and judicial creativity than is commonly supposed. Any talk about transformation and change is to be treated as a matter of jurisprudential, not sociological, significance. Suffice it to say, however, that the precise impact of judicial decisions will be contingent and contextual: Sometimes it will be substantial and other times it will be superficial. Either way, it will not be possible to generate a general and abstract theory that will be able to predict consistently or accurately what will occur as a result of particular judicial decisions. The social utility of judicial decisions as a vehicle for political change or the political efficacy of courts as a strategic site for social transformation can only be determined episodically and cautiously.

The second rider is that, when the common law's development is explained as the interplay of the logical and the expedient, there should be no mistake that, when the logical push comes to the expedient shove, it is the political that will eclipse the doctrinal. As the great cases attest, the bottom line is that, as *Hedley Byrne*'s Lord Pearce put it, the force and reach of legal principle "depends ultimately upon the courts' assessment of the

---

[49] R. Lipkin, *Constitutional Revolutions: Pragmatism and the Role of Judicial Review in American Constitutionalism* 26, 120, 125, 219, and 228 (2000).

[50] For an excellent introduction to this debate, see W. Bogart, *Consequences* (2001). For my own perspective, see A. C. Hutchinson, *Waiting for Coraf: A Critique of Law and Rights* 172–83 (1995).

demands of society" and that, as *Donoghue*'s Lord Macmillan put it, "any proposition the result of which would be to show that the common law of England is wholly unreasonable and unjust cannot be part of the common law of England."[51] Of course, what passes as substantive justice will not be to everyone's liking, but this only serves to underline the contested and political nature of common law adjudication. Moreover, there is no better evidence for that conclusion than the career of great cases. The courts will follow doctrinal logic and formal authority only so far and for so long until political expediency and substantive justice win the day. That includes the fall as well as the rise of great cases. As the fates of *Lochner* and *Roe* show, a great case is only great as long as the historical circumstances and political currents support its continued prominence. Once the political winds change, the great case will lose its hallowed status and become one more precedent on the legal scrap heap. Although *Donoghue* and *Brown* seem unassailable in their greatness, the day could well come when they fall from political and, therefore, legal grace. In *Donoghue*'s case, the general consensus around carelessness as the ruling principle in tort might erode and another regime (i.e., a more progressive shift to "strict liability" or a more regressive move to "intentional harm") win the day. Or, in *Brown*'s case, the public commitment to maintain substantive equality might begin to crumble and a different approach, such as a formal and thinner conception of discrimination, may gain favor. Legal greatness is as eternal or as ephemeral as the political will that sustains it.

The third rider is that, because innovation and transformation are at the existential heart of the common law, it does not mean that such innovation and transformation will necessarily be progressive in doctrinal effect. Radical change is not an initiative that is exclusive to the political left or right, insofar as those designations still have any clear orientation. Apart from the considerable difficulty of determining what is progressive in any particular context, the recognition of the judiciary's inevitable role as agents of political activism opens up space in which the law's inevitable political possibilities can be exploited and in which claims that the law is fixed or given can no longer be used to evade responsibility for the actual decisions made. For instance, judges such as William Douglas and Alfred Denning were the most iconoclastic of judges and took a studiedly cavalier attitude to settled legal expectations. Indeed, their greatness was to be found in their innovative and ingenious dexterity with established doctrine. However, it would be silly to

---

[51] *Hedley Byrne*, supra, note 18 at 536 per Lord Pearce and *Donoghue*, supra, note 19 at 29 per Lord Macmillan. On the interplay of the logical and the expedient, see supra, chap. 4.

suggest that they were progressive in any consistent or committed way. As the history of the common law amply shows, there is no necessary or comfortable relationship between judicial boldness and political progressiveness.[52] Even though this acknowledgment shows that law's transformative character does not lead inexorably to social enlightenment and political emancipation, it does challenge the idea that things have to be the way that they are and, in so doing, opens up space for viable progressive action. No political strategy can eliminate the risk that it might have the perverse effect of legitimating the status quo or the unintended consequence of being regressive. However, society is much less stable and much more volatile than both conservatives (who extol its present justice) and progressives (who rail against its present injustice) allow. It is in a constant state of flux and contains the resources and possibilities for its own doctrinal transformation, albeit in both conservative and progressive ways.

Conclusion

In this chapter, I have sought to defend the claim that any account of the common law's development must put great cases at its explanatory heart. When this is done, it is hard to resist the conclusion that the common law tradition is more an open and creative one in which 'anything might go' than a bounded and cautious one. Moreover, the countless efforts by judges and jurists to resist this claim do as much to confirm the political and contested quality of law and adjudication as to deny it. Indeed, one of the few constants in law and adjudication is that change and stability are maintained through continuous acts of revision: Transformation is the lifeblood of the common law's vibrant tradition. Faced with this situation, academic commentators and judicial participants are given a Hobson's choice. On the one hand, they can recognize great cases as routine illustrations of how the common law develops incrementally and logically; this is a stance that most reject because, among other things, it would make it extremely difficult to explain why great cases were in any way great. On the other hand, they can concede that great cases are radical instances of how the law develops by breaking with its past; this is a stance that most reject because, among other things, it confounds the idea that the common law develops incrementally and logically. Accordingly, any acclamation of great cases is also a celebration of the critical insight that 'law is politics'. To be in praise of great cases is

---

[52] See infra, chap. 8.

a tribute to the force of the observation that "continuity with the past is only a necessity, not a duty."[53] In addition, judging from the history of its development through great cases, the common law has and continues to impose a duty on its personnel to respect the past best by revolutionizing it in regular acts of continuing transformation. As the next chapter shows, as a hermeneutical supplement to Darwin's evolutionary insights, the work of Hans-Georg Gadamer captures much of why that duty is imposed and how it can be satisfied.

[53] O. W. Holmes, *Collected Legal Papers* 270 (P. Smith ed. 1920).

◦❧ 6 ❧◦

Looking for Gadamer:
Traditions and Transformations

The conversation that we are in is one that never ends. No word is the last word, just as there is no first word. Every word is itself an answer and gives rise always to a new question.[1]

HANS-GEORG GADAMER

TO MANY, THE WORKS OF CHARLES DARWIN AND HANS-GEORG GADAMER will seem unrelated. Whereas one toiled in the fields of natural discovery, the other immersed himself in the libraries of textual exegesis. However, there is a deep and shared theme to their work – they both refused to accept that reliance on scientific method did or could lead the way to human understanding. For both, there is no fixed form, core function, or overarching goal to which social life is supposed to conform. Both embrace a thoroughly historicized and contingent view of human life as a perpetual struggle in which form, function, and goal are never given but shift and vary with context and over time. At bottom, neither Darwin nor Gadamer believes that science can offer much help in meeting political and moral challenges. In an important sense, what Darwin did for biological sciences, Gadamer has done for the human sciences. While reference to Gadamer's writings in legal theory are relatively few and far between, their influence is profound. The fact that the understanding of law as an interpretive exercise in which judges must grapple with fixed texts in a changing historical context has become a matter of trite learning is largely due to his influence. Gadamer turns around jurists' preoccupation with "taking the judge out of judging." Although he recognizes that judging is a human art as opposed to a scientific undertaking (as do almost all contemporary jurists), he also

[1] H.-G. Gadamer, Letter to Dallmayr, in *Dialogue and Deconstruction: The Gadamer–Derrida Encounter* 95 (D. Michelfelder and R. Palmer eds. 1989).

insists that not only can personal values not be subordinated to objective and neutral decision making, but also that such values are and should be at the heart of the adjudicative function. For Gadamer, legal interpretation is an inevitably political and thoroughly historicized undertaking. As he states in his magnum opus, *Truth and Method*, just as "there is undoubtedly no understanding that is free of all prejudices," so "the certainty achieved by using scientific methods does not suffice to guarantee truth."[2]

In continuing my critical account of the common law tradition of judging, I contend that Gadamer's hermeneutics can be utilized to offer a more radical and transformative reading of the common law tradition. By treating "truth" as the historicised experience of meaningfulness, he confirms that legal interpretation cannot be equated to abstract analysis or scientific method. It is only brought and rebrought to life in the active and persisting conversations between real people within, over, and across time. In this way, the common law becomes as much a historical location for these continuing interventions as a reliable resource of completed resolutions. Insofar as the common law is a tradition, it is a dynamic tradition of transformation. Indeed, Gadamer cautions that, while people exist and thrive within a tradition, "it is still in the nature of [people] to be able to break with tradition, to criticise and dissolve it" (p. xxxvii). Indeed, Gadamer concedes that his hermeneutic universalism in emphasizing and giving priority to the past and tradition does run the risk of having "a lack of ultimate radicality" (p. xxxvii). However, Gadamer insists that this may be the price that has to be paid in order to establish meaning in people's lives – "what [people] need is not just the persistent posing of ultimate questions, but the sense of what is feasible, what is possible, what is correct, here and now" (p. xxxviii). By my lights, this is both an unnecessary and unwise concession: The fear that radicality must be synonymous with "the nihilism that Nietzsche prophesied" (p. xxxviii) is unwarranted. On the contrary, it is both possible and desirable to run the risk of ultimate radicality. Rather than seek to confront "the ever intensifying criticism of what has gone before" with "something of the truth of remembrance: with what is still and ever again real" (p. xxxviii), it is better to abandon truth and remembrance entirely. So disencumbered, people might step forward into the real and the what is yet to come in the exciting hope of contributing to the work-in-progress of law, tradition, and politics.

---

[2] Hans-Georg Gadamer, *Truth and Method* 490–91 (J. Weinsheimer and D. Marshall trans. 2nd ed 1989); henceforth, all references to this primary text will be included in parentheses in the text.

Accordingly, I offer an account of what hermeneutical tradition and legal practice might look like and how it may be appreciated if the radicality of the hermeneutical insight was not cabined or contained. Although Gadamer tries to resist the charge that his work has "legitimated a prejudice in favour of existing relations" (p. 566), I maintain that Gadamer and his juristic followers, no matter how noble or progressive their intentions, have managed to curb rather than cultivate the "critical and emancipatory" instinct (p. 567). Accordingly, this chapter consists of five parts. In the first part I introduce the hermeneutical turn in jurisprudence; in the second, I estimate the basic thrust of Gadamer's intervention. In the third part, I canvass the different takes on Gadamer and offer my own particular cut on the Gadamerian insight. Next, I explore the central concept of *tradition* and critique its customary understanding in the common law. In the fifth part I develop the idea that 'law is politics' and that 'anything might go.' Throughout the chapter, my interpretation of Gadamer is controversial and not to everyone's taste. However, mindful of the concluding words to *Truth and Method* that "it would be a poor hermeneuticist who thought he could have, or had to have, the last word" (p. 579), I celebrate Gadamer in what I believe is the best and most respectful way. Challenging the textual letter of Gadamer's writings in the subversive spirit of Gadamer's hermeneutics, I treat Gadamer's answers as provoking, not precluding new questions and, perhaps, inviting and producing new answers. In this way, in contrast to most contemporary jurisprudential scholarship, I contend that Gadamer's hermeneutics can be utilized to explore what it means to treat law seriously as a living and transformative rhetorical tradition of evolution.

Truths and Methods

There is a growing lack of faith in the capacity of scholars to live up to the expectations that they have created – that reason is able to confront power and to deliver general truths that can ground specific efforts at human improvement. Although this critique has come from several quarters, a major source of this challenge has been the field of hermeneutics. Scholars have begun to take seriously the idea that truth is beholden to the discursive regimes through which it is apprehended and validated. Concepts such as truth, coherence, and objectivity, it is suggested, are best understood as internal to the historical debates over so-called theory and not as some external set of discursive categories available to validate particular theoretical conclusion to such debates. Thus, theorizing becomes not an attempted escape to some esteemed realm of pure thinking, but rather an engaged effort to understand the social entanglement and linguistic situation of thinking itself. In advocating a shift from epistemological truth to rhetorical knowledge, this hermeneutical critique of the traditional philosophical enterprise has been developed and expressed in many different ways. Nevertheless, a central division between these critics is the extent and force of the hermeneutical insight. Having set in motion a powerful antidote to traditional thinking, is it possible to contain it such that it does not impugn and invalidate the whole theoretical exercise? This is because, in its more extreme form, the charge is that, under the tutelage of a postmodern sensibility, philosophy has become a pasquinade of itself in which reason is reduced to customary ways of thinking, truth has become opinion, and objectivity is no more than consensus.[3] Deprived of a philosophical recourse to the reassuring epistemological terrain of objective truths, mainstream jurists have been obliged to reassess their whole intellectual strategy. Jurists must now question not only the truth of legal nature and its objective ascertainment, but also the nature of truth and objectivity themselves.

This combative encounter has taken place on the site of the common law. Jurists have locked theoretical horns over the nature of law in a system in which responsibility for its ascertainment and development, even in matters of constitutional doctrine, is entrusted to judicial officials. In a social world in which judges are increasingly asked to resolve some of its most morally contentious and politically fraught issues, it is considered as important as it has ever been that law be able to claim an institutional legitimacy and intellectual authority for itself that will be respected by the competing moral and political factions. There must be something objective and neutral about adjudication and law that sets it apart, however slightly, from the partisan conditions of moral and political debate. The central question for contemporary jurisprudence has become whether this traditional project of mainstream theorizing can withstand the corrosive implications of the hermeneutical insight. Of course, the response has been predictably varied. While some have imitated the ostrich and stuck their head deeper in the philosophical sand, others have redoubled their epistemological efforts to defend the philosophical establishment against the hermeneutical menace and still others have sought to utilize the hermeneutical insight as further grist for the nihilistic mill. Although each response deserves a full and sustained treatment,[4] I concentrate on the response that claims

---

3 See F. Fernandez-Armesto, *Truth: A History and a Guide for the Perplexed* (1997).
4 For an initial attempt to map and criticize these approaches, see A. C. Hutchinson, <u>Casaubon's Ghosts: The Haunting of Legal Scholarship</u>, 21 *Legal Studies* 65 (2001).

to take the hermeneutical insight seriously. Unfazed by the implications of the hermeneutical insight, these jurists embrace it as providing an exciting opportunity to place the adjudicative and jurisprudential enterprises on a much more secure and defensible footing. While there are obvious differences among these hermeneutical converts, they are united in their conviction that hermeneutics demonstrates that, rather than the common law's being an entity and adjudication's being a science, it is as much a process or practice as anything else. It is an argumentative tradition that cannot only balance the competing demands of stability and change but also do so in a way that respects the important distinction between law and politics. For these jurists, the hermeneutical insistence that rhetorical knowledge must replace epistemological truth as the touchstone of valid theorizing is the making, not the breaking, of the jurisprudential project.

Hermeneutics concerns itself with language and thought. It is an attempt to explore that space between words and thoughts in which confusion and misunderstanding can take hold. It is not only that there is an ineradicable gap between ideas and utterance, it is that each seems to inhabit the other so thoroughly that one does not stand prior to or independent from the other. Ideas and words are, if not entirely reducible to each other, so intertwined that any attempt to concentrate on one without the other is destined to result in less, not more, understanding. All of this would be difficult enough if such efforts took place in immediate, face-to-face encounters in a static world, but they become even more problematic when it is recalled that they occur in a world constantly on the move. This means that intentions, words, meanings, and ideas begin to slip and slide. As communication is a social practice, efforts to "say what you mean and mean what you say" are hostage to the social and political forces that are in play as history moves onward. In a manner of speaking, because history never sleeps, *you*, *say*, and *mean* are always works in progress such that attempts to treat them as finished or finishable are misguided and misleading. Moreover, while the difficulty of expressing oneself with clarity and certainty is a stiff enough challenge, talking about hermeneutics is a doubly difficult endeavor. As an area of study that might broadly be understood as being concerned with the principles of interpretation, once specifically biblical, now generally textual, there is the delicious and frustrating problem of interpreting the meaning of work that is itself about the task of interpreting meaning. Accordingly, in entering the field of hermeneutical scholarship, a certain willingness to put in play one's basic ideas about language and meaning seems to be a necessary price of admission. Unfortunately, too many see this less as an inexpensive opportunity for enlightenment and more as a costly toll on clear thinking.[5] To my mind, this begrudging and frankly insecure way of proceeding is especially evident in the jurisprudential reception given to the writings of Hans-George Gadamer. Rather than recognize the nontraditional and critical thrust of his work, jurists contrive to interpret and utilize him in the most traditional and uncritical fashion.

Nevertheless, whatever might be made of Gadamer's writings and ideas, it seems to be almost universally accepted that his work has a central place in the extant canon of hermeneutical writings. Writing in mid-century, he set himself the daunting task of confronting the imposing German tradition of hermeneutical scholarship and of wresting it from the suffocating grip of its metaphysical mind-set. Much of his argumentation is devoted to engaging with central ideas and thinkers in the German tradition, especially Wilhelm Dilthey, Immanuel Kant, G. W. F. Hegel, Edmund Husserl, Martin Heidegger, and, latterly, Jurgen Habermas. Gadamer's basic objective is to demonstrate that scientific method is neither the controlling nor even a helpful model for hermeneutical understanding. He does not offer a competing metric for hermeneutical understanding that can direct or control in the same way as the reputed scientific method, but he insists that "hermeneutics is an art and not a mechanical process" (p. 191). Instead of trying to construct a critical rationality that will do service in the humanities in the same way and to the same effect as in the sciences,[6] his work is presented as more a methodical corrective than a correct method in which "perhaps there is, properly speaking, no method, but rather a certain way of acting" (p. 26) Although his work is obscure in parts and highly philosophical in scope, Gadamer's ideas are (or, at least, should be) of particular interest to jurists and lawyers. Rather than treat the problems of legal interpretation

---

[5] The self-referential and subversive dimension of this challenge is too often ignored by jurists who interpret hermeneutical texts in the most simplistic ways. Scholarship that seeks to disturb traditional approaches to texts as repositories of the authors' meaning is read in the most traditional way. In arguing for greater openness and indeterminacy, such work assumes a closed and determinate meaning for itself; any fuzziness or imprecision is counted as a mark against it. Of course, this is not to suggest that there ought not to be a premium on accessible, understandable, and lucid scholarship. However, it is mistaken to expect that scholarship that argues for the instability and work-in-progress quality of language will itself not be subject to those very forces that it illuminates and emphasizes.

[6] Recent scholarship has contended that the methodological contrast between science and the humanities is less stark and more subtle than many traditional thinkers, including Gadamer, allow. See R. Rorty, *Philosophy and Social Hope* (1999); S. J. Gould, *The Hedgehog, the Fox and the Magister's Pox: Mending the Gap Between Science and the Humanities* (2003); and infra, chap. 8. Nevertheless, although this might undercut Gadamer's rhetorical contrast of his hermeneutical project with the supposed certainty and mechanicalness of the scientific method, it does not reduce the cogency of his general ideas.

as secondary or exceptional aspects of the hermeneutical enterprise, he places the interpretive problems of jurisprudence squarely at the heart of his own hermeneutical project: "Legal hermeneutics is no special case but is, on the contrary, capable of restoring the hermeneutical problem to its full breadth" (p. 328, emphasis omitted) and "the texts of law are the preferred objects of hermeneutics . . . [because they] present the problem of awakening a meaning petrified in letters from the letters themselves."[7] Accordingly, Gadamer's approach to law promises to be as stimulating and challenging as it is suggestive and disturbing.

Looking for Gadamer

For Gadamer, language is the key to a proper understanding of the human predicament and condition. Arguing that "language speaks us, rather than we speak it" (p. 463), he maintains that "language and thinking about things are so bound together" that it is impossible to conceive of one without the other or to imagine that language is a "pre-given system of possibilities of being for which the signifying subject selects corresponding signs" (p. 417). Although he commits himself to such a boldly discursive understanding of the human situation, he does not fall back into the stifling embrace of a metaphysical approach that views language as the fixed or stable grounding for human knowledge. Instead, he allies this basic insight to an equally important commitment to "the historical movement of things" (p. 285). For Gadamer, language is a socially situated practice that can never entirely escape the historical confines of its usage either as an originating act or an interpretive apprehension. When this attachment to both language as the fundamental medium of human existence and historical contingency as a compelling feature of human existence are grasped in their general force and detailed operation, it becomes clear that Gadamer's account of the hermeneutical process is very different from the traditional one. Emphasizing the dynamic quality of both text *and* interpretation, Gadamer adopts an approach that is both dialogic and dialectical – it is dialogic in that it involves an active engagement between text and reader and it is dialectical in that it demands a vigorous interplay between past and present. Hermeneutics is in the job of "bridging [the] personal or historical distance between minds" (p. PH95).

---

[7] Hans-Georg Gadamer, *Philosophical Hermeneutics* 90 (D. Linge ed. and trans. 1976); henceforth, all references to this text will be included in parentheses in the text, preceded by the prefix PH.

Thus, the effort to achieve hermeneutical understanding is not a passive reflection on a completed object; it is "an encounter with an unfinished event and is itself part of this event" (p. 99). Consequently, there is no completed object of interpretation that is waiting to be discovered or revealed in its wholeness, but only the invitation to engage and play with it in the hope that meaning will be forged in that encounter. Accordingly, "understanding is thought of less as a subjective act than as participating in an event of tradition, a process of transmission in which past and present are constantly mediated" (p. 290). Indeed, performance is not peripheral or secondary to the text, but it is "essential" (p. 134) to any genuine attempt to understand the text's meaning; "every performance is an event, but not one in any way separate from the work – the work itself is what takes place in the event of performance" (p. 147). In the same way that "reading music is [not] the same as listening to it" (p. 148), so reflecting on law is not the same as applying it. Moreover, when this dynamic is properly understood, it will be appreciated that the occasion and site for its performance will become highly unstable and political in that the values and commitments that frame the interpretive act – what Gadamer calls "prejudices" – can never be ignored or disregarded. The task of interpreters, as opposed to prophets or proselytizers, is to gain some critical distance from their own prejudices. This is not so that such prejudices can be left behind as "there is undoubtedly no understanding that is free of all prejudices" (p. 490), but so that they can be understood and recognized. However, consistent with his general hermeneutical schema, Gadamer emphasizes that there is no algorithm to "distinguish the true prejudices, by which we *understand*, from the *false* ones, by which we *misunderstand* . . . so that the text, as another's meaning, can be isolated and valued on its own" (298–99; emphasis in the original): The best that can be done is to "guard against over hastily assimilating the past to our own expectations of meaning" (305) and "arbitrary fancies" (p. 266). For Gadamer, therefore, it is a constant struggle to identify those "fore-conceptions" or prejudices so that interpretation does not become enslaved to "the tyranny of hidden prejudices that makes us deaf to what speaks to us in the tradition" (p. 270).

For Gadamer, therefore, this contextualized awareness will result in a shift in focus from technique and reflection to participation and engagement in which "from the hermeneutical standpoint, rightly understood, it is absolutely absurd to regard the concrete factors of work and politics as outside the scope of hermeneutics" (p. PH31). This hermeneutical performance functions as kind of play in the sense of a "to-and-fro movement that is not tied to any goal that would bring it to an end . . . ; rather, it renews itself in constant repetition"[8] (p. 103). When understood in terms of legal interpretation, in which application is front and center, this playful encounter ensures that "the gap [between the text and its application] can never be completely closed" (p. 384) and works to establish "a certain area of free-play" (p. 519) that "always and necessarily breaks off in an open indeterminacy" (p. 340). Indeed, for Gadamer, it is "thanks precisely to its open indeterminacy [that law] is able to produce constant new invention from within itself" (p. 498). In fulfilling their central task of deciding cases, judges must understand that there is not a two-step process of first understanding and then applying; the latter is part of the former because we cannot understand in the abstract or general but only in concrete and particular situations. Consequently, "judging the case involves not merely applying the universal principle according to which it is judged, but co-determining, supplementing, and correcting that principle" (p. 39) such that a text must be "understood at every moment, in every concrete situation, in new and different way" (p. 309). In this way, Gadamer drives home his fundamental hermeneutical point that "the law is always deficient, not because it is imperfect in itself but because human reality is necessarily imperfect in comparison to the ordered world of law, and hence allows of no simple application of the law" (p. 318). Law and adjudication are both made possible and problematized by the normative dimension of interpretation; the common law gains its constancy and growth from the same source of interpretive performance.

An important corollary of Gadamer's general theoretical position is that he has little truck with any metaphysical claims to the dominant authority of authorial intention in the hermeneutical engagement. It follows from his general orientation that "every age has to understand a transmitted text in its own way" (p. 198). A text's meaning does not depend only on the contingent situation of authors and their original audience, because those contingencies must themselves always be open to interpretation by the text's subsequent readers. Constituted in a dynamic context and reconstituted in an equally dynamic but different context, "the meaning of a text goes beyond its author ... [and] that is why understanding is not merely a reproductive but always a productive activity as well" (p. 296). For Gadamer, therefore, the passage of time or history is not so much the enemy of meaning but its enabling source: "The hermeneutic task consists in not covering up [the

---

[8] While the notion of play is a significant component in Gadamer's hermeneutics, I will not deal with it extensively here because I have already offered my own extended reflection on play. See A. C. Hutchinson, *It's All in the Game: A Nonfoundationalist Account of Law and Adjudication* (2000).

tension between the text and the present] by attempting a naive assimilation of the two but in consciously bringing it out" (p. 307). This being the
case, no text can be created so closed so that the space between saying and
meaning can be entirely effaced such that there will be no room for future
engagement. Nor can there be a fixed or canonized performance that demands no future reinterpretation. Accordingly, while every interpretation
strives to be correct, "in view of the finitude of our historical existence, there
is something absurd about the whole idea of a unique, correct interpretation" (p. 120). In Gadamer's hermeneutical universe, the work presents
and re-presents itself in its continuing performance such that its meaning
will present itself "so differently in the changing course of ages and circumstances" (120–21). When it comes to meaning, Gadamer is adamant that "in
truth, there is nothing that is simply 'there' ... [because] everything that is
said and is there in the text stands under anticipations" (p. PH121).

So far, my presentation of the general themes in Gadamer's work – the
importance of historical context and its contingency; the abandonment of
scientistic methodology in the humanities; and the performative dynamism
of hermeneutical activity – will, I would hope, go largely unchallenged. Perhaps naively in light of the topic, I have sought to provide an introduction
to Gadamer's ideas that is sufficiently general to garner broad approval.
However, from a jurisprudential point of view, the subversive effect of such
a basic approach to legal interpretation ought not to be underestimated.
Gadamer has traditional jurists squarely in his sights when he insists on the
entirely fluid, adamantly nonscientific, thoroughly contextual, and wholly
performative quality of legal hermeneutics. The claim that valid or worthy
legal work can be done in an exclusively mechanical or technical manner is
rendered hopelessly inadequate. Although technical skills have their role,
they can do little on their own. All interpretation has a social and political aspect that can only be hidden or ignored, not done away with. In this
sense, we are all interpretivists now – originalism, textualism, and literal-
ism are each different and unconvincing ways of denying the interpretivist
imperative. Whatever else he may be saying, Gadamer is telling lawyers that
interpretation is an inevitably active and therefore political process. Lawyers
cannot avoid working with and among the social forces that make interpretation both possible and problematic. It is not so much that the instability
of those social practices and forces renders communication impossible, but
that it ensures that the establishment of meaning will never be without
difficulty or uncertainty. The foundations of language and therefore law
will always be as contingent and shifting as the foundations of society and
history.

Nevertheless, any attempt to provide a more nuanced and less sweeping account of Gadamerian hermeneutics and its implications for jurisprudence soon finds itself in more contested critical waters. Beneath the relative calm of the surface, there is a seething mass of contending hermeneutical forces at work: This is where the courage and strength of different scholars' hermeneutical convictions are tested. When it comes to Gadamer's work, the central point of division is around how far it is possible or desirable to take his critical insights. Although there are a variety of possible interpretations, there are two general positions that can be taken. Is it that Gadamer has loosened the constraints on interpretation and, while forsaking the idea of a unique interpretation, remained within the gravitational pull of the metaphysical tradition that holds onto a traditional notion of hermeneutical truth, albeit more pluralistic and less hegemonic? Or is it that he has broken open the hermeneutical process to such an extent that any notions of truth are left in disarray and that, cut free from the metaphysical tradition, the interpretive process is not so much about truth and correctness as usefulness and persuasion? The pertinence of this division for jurisprudential debate is acute and obvious. On one side are those who believe that it is still practicable to talk about law and adjudication as separate from broader political debate: I call this the *conservative* approach. On the other side are those who, like myself, maintain that law and adjudication are one more site for political debate to take place: I will call this the *radical* approach. Again, this radical stance does not mean that 'anything goes'. Rather, it recognizes that there are bounds to the hermeneutical enterprise, but that those bounds are always in play as part of the larger political game of life.

A Jurisprudential Reading

The most well-known exponent of the conservative approach is Ronald Dworkin. Although his references to Gadamer are limited, it is apparent that his overall hermeneutical approach owes much to Gadamer's writings. Indeed, Dworkin gladly acknowledges as much when he notes that, in constructing his interpretive account of law and adjudication, "I appeal to Gadamer, whose account of interpretation as recognising, while struggling against, the constraints of history strikes the right note." While he has some reservations about whether Gadamer places the interpreter in too much of a subordinate position to the author and offers a too passive and unidirectional view of the hermeneutical encounter, many of the central motifs and ideas of Gadamer pervade Dworkin's own oeuvre. However, Dworkin relies on a very conservative reading of Gadamer. While Dworkin has done sterling work in demonstrating that adjudication is an inevitably creative and political undertaking, he still insists that judges can act in a way that is neither partisan nor unbounded; adjudication is (or ought to be) a principled affair in which intellectual coherence triumphs over ideological partiality. Dworkinian judges have considerable leeway in their work, but they are ultimately bound by the "brute facts of legal history" and, in placing the legal past in the best political light possible, they are to operate "on the assumption that [it was] created by a single author – the community personified."[9] In this way, Dworkin puts Gadamer to work in the central contemporary jurisprudential problem of establishing the democratic legitimacy of legal adjudication on the basis of its being both institutionally constrained and politically just. As such, Dworkin's theory is the flagship of liberal legalism; it claims to offer a stable method by which to keep the law up-to-date and by which to distinguish right from wrong answers.

A less celebrated but more explicit effort to utilize Gadamer's work in jurisprudence is that of Jay Mootz. In a series of learned and lengthy pieces, he has striven to present a sophisticated account of legal hermeneutics that plays out in more detail and rigor the implications of Gadamer's approach for law and adjudication. The great strength of Mootz's scholarship is that it has familiarized American theorists with Gadamer's work and has made a forcible case for its relevance to current problems of legal knowledge and judicial method; he makes Gadamer's work accessible and useful, but he retains its subtlety and richness. For Mootz, Gadamer's major contribution to jurisprudence is the insistence that law is a rhetorical practice and that any effort to appreciate adjudication must recognize the important role that rhetoric plays in fashioning and critiquing legal knowledge. Nonetheless, although his earlier work retained the possibility of a more radical reading of Gadamer, his most recent essays have taken a distinctly conservative turn. For all the good work that Mootz's efforts do, they are overshadowed by his willingness to put them in the service of an epistemological project that still clings to the possibility of reliable methods and dependable truths. According to Mootz, while Gadamer has decisively demolished any possibility for a science of correct interpretation and loosened the reins of hermeneutical authority, he has not abandoned the hope of developing a rigorous logic or art of rational interpretation that will be able to sanction some interpretations as clearly better than others by stint of its own rhetorical standards. In

---

[9] R. Dworkin, *Law's Empire* 62, 55, 225, 255, and 420 (1986) and *Freedom's Law* 1–39 (1996). For a critique, see C. Douzinas, S. McVeigh, and R. Warrington, Is Hermes Hercules' Twin? in *Reading Dworkin Critically* 124–25 (A. Hunt ed. 1992).

making a plea for greater attention to rhetoric in jurisprudential inquiry, Mootz contends that "rhetoric is defined not as a grudging resignation from the false hopes of a rigorous philosophy of truth, nor as a celebration of boundless and playful irrationalism, but instead as a disciplined encounter with the activity of rhetorical knowledge."[10]

In a particularly arresting and ambitious essay, Mootz seeks to stake out and colonize this middle ground between the barren conceptualism of legal positivism and the excesses of a postmodern critique. Drawing directly on the work of Gadamer as well as Chaim Perelman to substantiate the claim that "natural law philosophy and philosophical hermeneutics have significant points of convergence," he proceeds to propose a defense of legal hermeneutics that is committed to "reinvigorating (even if in dramatically new form) the natural law tradition." By this, Mootz intends to portray legal practice as a hermeneutical conversation that contains the conditions and resources for its own legitimate elaboration and critique. Thus, law is both a rationally bounded and politically responsive enterprise in which issues of legal validity and moral acceptability are blended rather than separated. Picking up where Lon Fuller left off and Lloyd Weinreb has recently taken up, Mootz leaves little doubt about the breadth or depth of his intellectual ambitions to construct a full-blown theory of law and justice from the generous quarry of Gadamer's hermeneutics:

> Gadamer's hermeneutical ontology implies a rhetorically based epistemology, a set of guiding principles by which legal practice can be assessed and criticised, even if without scientific precision and determinacy. Gadamer provides the theoretical backing for the practices that constitute law within flux; not in the sense of authorizing those practices from a privileged perch of reason, but in the sense of drawing general conclusions about the contours of those practices and describing how those practices may be fostered.[11]

---

[10] J. Mootz, Rhetorical Knowledge in Legal Practice and Theory 6 S. *Cal. Interdisciplinary L. J.* 491 at 497 (1998). In taking this line, Mootz draws heavily on the work of Gary Madison and Georgia Warnke. See G. Madison, *The Hermeneutics of Postmodernity: Figures and Themes* (1990). Also see G. Warnke, *Gadamer; Hermeneutics, Tradition and Reason* 79 (1987); G. Warnke, *Justice and Interpretation* (1992); and G. Warnke, Law, Hermeneutics and Public Debate, 9 *Yale J. L. & Human.* 395 (1997).

[11] J. Mootz, Law in Flux: Philosophical hermeneutics, Legal Argumentation, and the Natural Law Tradition, 11 *Yale J. L. & Human.* 311 at 313, 312, and 378 (1999). Other works of Mootz, include J. M. Mootz, Law and Philosophy, Philosophy and Law, 26 *U. Tol. L. Rev.* 127 (1994) and J. Mootz, Is the Rule of Law Possible in a Postmodern World?, 68 *Wash. L. Rev.* 249 (1995). See also L. Fuller, *The Morality of Law* (1969); L. Weinreb, *Natural Law and Justice* (1987); and L. Weinreb, The Moral Point of View in *Natural Law, Liberalism and Morality* 195 (R. George ed. 1996).

In an important sense, Mootz's "natural law" move should come as no surprise. After all, Dworkin has been profitably pursuing a similar line for the past two decades. However, apart from the candor and naiveté of Mootz's approach, it is the fact that he uses Gadamer as his primary grounding source that startles. There can be no doubt that there is ample textual support for this particular conservative reading of Gadamer: *Truth and Method* is replete with references and remarks that give support to such an interpretation. Notwithstanding the dynamic and dialogic quality of interpretation, Gadamer contends that there are occasions on which interpreters will be "pulled up short by the text" (p. 268): "The important thing is to be aware of one's own bias, so that the text can present itself in all its otherness and thus assert its own truth against one's own fore-meanings" (p. 269). Although perfect legal dogmatics is untenable, legal certainty and predictability can exist because "it is in principle possible to know what the exact situation is" (p. 329). This is because, according to Gadamer, the text has a certain "obligatoriness" that ensures that its interpretation cannot be "free and arbitrary" (p. 118), but is "subject to the supreme criterion of 'right' representation" (p. 118), which enables "the meaning of the text to assert itself" (p. 465). In this sense, Gadamer's own writings provide textual reassurance to the idea that interpretive creativity has its limits and they are to be found in the text itself; "neither the doctrinal authority of the pope nor the appeal to tradition can obviate the work of hermeneutics, which can safeguard the reasonable meaning of a text against all impositions" (p. 277). It is on these textual resources that Mootz anchors his conservative rendition of both Gadamer and the jurisprudential project. For all the touted experimental and inventive possibilities of interpretation, Mootz still presents legal hermeneutics as a conversational activity in which deferential interpreters await hermeneutical revelation from textual authorities: "the interpreter does not adopt a subjective attitude of dominance over the text, but rather suppresses her subjective aims and attends to 'the saying' of the historically effective texts as it is revealed in the particular circumstances."[12]

Nevertheless, there is much to applaud in Mootz's account. In concentrating on the vitality and motility of law as a professional practice and social phenomenon, he gives cogent voice to the rejection of "the scientific impulse to reduce law to a disciplined methodology of deductive application," the embrace of "the give-and-take experience of the interpreter within a given historical and social situation," and the emphasis on "the inter-penetration

---

[12] Mootz, Law in Flux, supra, note 11 at 318.

of the universal and the contextual." However, Mootz cannot or will not resist the almost overwhelming urge to shackle Gadamerian hermeneutics to
the conservative wagon of mainstream jurisprudence. Indeed, Mootz takes
for granted the central issue that divides conservative and radical jurists:
"lawyers know very well that argumentation is a bounded and rational enterprise that nevertheless cannot aspire to process of deduction from principles, even though the rhetorical conventions of legal practice and judicial opinion-writing ironically work to conceal this (supposedly dangerous)
fact." It is this very idea of boundedness and rationality that goes to the
crux of the jurisprudential debate. To varying degrees, mainstream jurists
(of whom Dworkin is the leading example) cling to the idea that the political debate that goes on within law is rendered bounded by the resources
of law and disciplined by the universal constraints of rationality. In hewing
such a rhetorical line, Mootz is a vast improvement on Dworkin as he is
much less attached to truth and method. Indeed, for all his hermeneutical
huff and puff, Dworkin is keen to develop an algorithm through which he
can approve of some readings over others. Mootz has challenged those assumptions and shown that, as a rhetorical practice, law generates its own
conventions of argumentation that establish the bounds of its own jurisdiction and the nature of its own rationality. As he puts it, "rhetorical knowledge
is a practical achievement that neither achieves apodictic certitude nor collapses into relativistic irrationalism; rhetorical knowledge therefore sustains
legal practice as a reasonable – even if not thoroughly rationalized – social
activity."[13]

Nevertheless, although Mootz has managed to break freer of the epistemological grip of traditional philosophizing, he refuses to take the necessary
steps to get beyond its cramping confines. In short, Mootz is still very much
in the conservative game of looking for theoretical backing and establishing
disciplined encounters: "Rhetorical knowledge is a constitutive feature of
legal practice that grounds any theoretical reconstruction and critique of
that practice." Like Dworkin, Mootz wants to make law safe for lawyers by
making legal practices understandable in their own right: "viewing law as intrinsically and irredeemably rhetorical reaffirms its integrity and legitimacy
as a practice of securing reasonable adherence."[14] Indeed, Mootz manages
to put Gadamer to work in exactly the kind of foundational tradition that
Gadamer purportedly criticizes and rejects. This turn to natural law, "even if
in dramatically new form," is exactly the wrong way to go. It emphasizes and

---

[13] Id. at 317, 315, 323–24, 327, and 377.
[14] J. Mootz, supra, note 10 at 566 and 568.

works with those conservative elements of Gadamer's texts that comprise part of his approach, but are by no means exclusive or exhaustive in their interpretation. At one point in his argument, Mootz asserts that Fuller and Weinreb's natural law approaches "are best viewed" as elaborating "the implications of philosophical hermeneutics in the context of legal theory" and as proceeding "in a manner that echoes Gadamer's postmodern philosophical claims."[15] This is wild stuff because either Fuller and Weinreb have become postmodernists (an unlikely possibility) or *postmodern* has become distinctly un-postmodern in Mootz's hands (a more likely possibility). Indeed, Mootz seems to want to have it both ways – to open up the hermeneutical process to more pluralistic and historically engaged possibilities and to limit that process so that interpretation is not open-ended. Moreover, Mootz runs with those ideas into far-off places. It is not that I am claiming that Mootz has got Gadamer wrong; this would be a very non-Gadamerian idea. Instead, I argue that it is not a helpful place to take Gadamer; Mootz tends to head toward the very locations of essentialism, rationalism, and foundationalism that much of Gadamer's work seems best interpreted to abandon. Mootz seems to want to foundationalize Gadamer and use his hermeneutical account as a ground from which to defend the legal enterprise against "the celebration of boundless and playful irrationalism."

When this issue is addressed, it is instructive to note Gadamer's own views on the subversive and nontraditional aspects of his own writings. Presumably, in light of Gadamer's own arguments, the authority of the text's author is severely diminished. Indeed, it is surely a staple of Gadamerian hermeneutics that the author has little authority in controlling or constraining the future interpretation given to the text and that the reader's own prejudices or foreconceptions are inevitably in play. He insists that "every age has to understand a transmitted text in its own way" (p. 198) such that its meaning does not depend on "the contingencies of the author and his original audience ... for it is always co-determined also by the historical situation of the interpreter" (p. 296). Accordingly, "not just occasionally, but always, the meaning of a text goes beyond its author" and "that is why understanding is not merely a reproductive but always a productive activity as well" (p. 296).

---

[15] J. Mootz, supra, note 11 at 312, 314, and 337. For a critique of Gadamer's lingering foundationalism, see H. Fairlamb, *Critical Conditions: Postmodernity and the Question of Foundations* (1994); D. Couzens Hoy and T. McCarthy, *Critical Theory* 188–200 (1994); and J. Caputo, Gadamer's Closet Essentialism: A Derridean Critique, in *Dialogue and Deconstruction: The Gadamer–Derrida Encounter* 258–64 (D. Michelfelder and R. Palmer eds. 1989). For a more rounded view, see *Gadamer's Century: Essays in Honor of Hans-Georg Gadamer* (J. Malpas ed. 2002).

This does not mean that Gadamer has no part to play in the unfolding debate over the meaning of Gadamer's hermeneutical texts, only that he must engage with the debate and his own texts as a future reader, not as their past author. Moreover, it seems odd that those scholars who claim to be disciples of Gadamer's hermeneutics should read Gadamer's text in such an un-Gadamer-like way. As Gadamer insists, the meanings of texts do not present themselves for inspection; they must be created in the encounter between the text and its interpreter: "the hermeneutic task consists in not covering up [the tension between the text and the present] by attempting a naive assimilation of the two but in consciously bringing it out" (p. 307). As I understand it, this is not to claim that the reader is sovereign and unconstrained, only that the reader has an inevitable and decisive part to play in the hermeneutical encounter. Neither the text nor its author can have the last word in what the text will come to mean. That insight must be as apposite for interpreting hermeneutical texts as it is for interpreting any other kind of text.

The problem is that, while Mootz and Gadamer (to a lesser extent) have historicized law and adjudication, they have only politicized it in the most superficial and sanitized way. If Gadamer and Mootz are right to chastise traditional philosophers and jurists for their failure to recognize the inevitable historicization of interpretation and dialogue, then I am right to chastise Gadamer and Mootz for *their* failure to politicize that inevitable historicization of interpretation and dialogue.[16] There is something missing from such jurisprudential accounts, and that something is the matrix of ideological forces that drive this historical process of rhetorical tradition. In a manner of speaking, Mootz has identified the Gadamerian vehicle and traced its hermeneutical route, but he has offered no explanation of how it moves and what determines that route; it is a road show without gas or drivers. While Gadamer and Mootz each incorporate values into their rhetorical accounts of law, they do so in such a way that the passion and commitment with which they are held and presented are filtered out and converted into rational entities to be weighed and balanced on the rhetorical scales. The world of Gadamerian politics is a sterile and barren world in which the material dirt of ideological politics and interests has been washed off so that judges and rhetoricians do not get their hands soiled with life as it is actually lived. However, this sanitization misrepresents the grubbiness and messiness

---

[16] For a general critique along similar but not the same lines, see T. Farrell, *Norms of Rhetorical Culture* (1993) and P. Goodrich, *Legal Discourse: Studies in Linguistics, Rhetoric and Legal Analysis* (1987).

of the real social world. In so doing, Mootz and other conservative jurists ensure that such a hermeneutical approach can only succeed by pretending that it is operating in a nonideological environment in which the reasonable has already been distinguished from the arbitrary, the disciplined from the anarchical, the stabilized from the fluxed, the authoritative from the irrational, and the playful from the serious. Mootz's Gadamer-inspired natural law program is abstract and arid; it is as much an escape from social life as the traditional philosophies that it claims to reject and replace.

At the root of this problem is the central notion of tradition. For Mootz, the confrontation between text and reader takes place within a tradition or conversation that obliges the interpreter to filter out the productive and approved prejudices from the unproductive and arbitrary ones. In this sense, the tradition has a tendency to engulf and swamp the interpreter to such an extent that he or she becomes part of it. As Gadamer puts it, the hermeneutical game has a spirit of its own that "masters" the players and holds them in its thrall (p. 106). Explaining that "the player experiences the game as a reality that surpasses him" (p. 109), he goes so far as to conclude that "the players no longer exist, only what they are playing" (p. 112). However, these Gadamerian claims have jurisprudential purchase or plausibility only if it is assumed that the rhetorical tradition of law is sufficiently coherent and homogenous to underwrite the evaluative claims that he makes for it. For instance, it is Mootz's assertion that, while legal practice is far from "a technique that delivers exact knowledge," it can and does generate "rhetorical principles to serve as aids in exercising good judgment when choosing between competing interpretations."[17] In order for this critical function to be fulfilled, these principles must be sufficiently ordered, expansive, and determinate to do the work that is asked of them. However, in modern society as well as in law and jurisprudence, there are simply too many traditions and none that receive the general approval or sanction that would enable Mootz's proposal to fly. While Mootz is right to advance the argument that "a just legal practice, like a life well lived, does not circle around a determinate truth," he is mistaken to conclude that such a practice "spirals forward from a shared tradition in the form of reasonable judgments about how to proceed."[18] When it comes to adjudication, difficulties tend to arise in those circumstances when there is no shared tradition and people are divided in

---

[17] J. Mootz, supra, note 11 at 378.

[18] J. Mootz, supra, note 10 at 583. For another critique of Gadamer that holds him to a monolithic and authority-imposing view of historical tradition, see T. Eagleton, *Literary Theory: An Introduction* 70–74 (1983).

their reasonable commitments. It seems a little hollow to recommend that such division should be mended or mediated through a resort to law's rhetorical traditions when the very existence of multiple or fractured traditions is what caused the problem in the first place. Consequently, tradition is not a grounding for anything if that means it can afford a solution rather simply provide a site for competing views. As I seek to demonstrate, there is another reading of Gadamer's work that plays down its foundational side and plays up its more radical possibilities.

Traditions and Transformations

There are two general notions of tradition that tend to dominate and organize debate. One is premised on the unstated notion that there is something normatively compelling or worthy about what has come before; the past is not followed simply because it precedes, but because it is superior to present understandings. Accepted by earlier generations and having withstood the test of time, tradition binds not simply because it has not been replaced or altered but because it has its own normative force. The past is not simply a store of information and materials but an obligatory source of value and guidance that is entitled to be given normative preference over present understandings and uninhibited ratiocination. The past is what fashions society into what is today, and the decision to respect it is what gives meaning to the lives of future generations. Viewing people as custodians rather than creators of tradition, this conservative Burkean approach talks in terms of "the great primeval contract of eternal society" in which "the partnership . . . between those who are living and those who are dead, and those who are to be born."[19]

The other approach maintains that, if there is to be genuine progress and emancipation, there must be a complete break from that past. This revolutionary stance is given expression in Marx's warning that "the tradition of all the dead generations weighs like a nightmare on the brains of the living" and that progressive activity "cannot draw its poetry from the past, [but] must let the dead bury their dead."[20] In this view, whatever is normatively compelling about the past is oppressive; to escape its baleful influence, people must become the undertakers, not the custodians, of the past. There

---

[19] E. Burke, *Reflections on the Revolution in France* 85 (J. Pocock ed. 1987). See also F. Hayek, *Law, Legislation and Liberty: The Political Order of Free People* 153–76 (1979); A. Watson, *The Evolution of Law* (1985); and A. Kronman, <u>Precedent and Tradition</u>, 99 *Yale L. J.* 1029 at 1037 (1990).

[20] K. Marx, *The Eighteenth Brumaire of Louis Bonaparte* 13 and 16 (C. Dutt ed. 1957).

must be a complete rescission of the contractual partnership between past and future generations.

Predictably, both of these polarized approaches are overstated and miss the mark. Burke's reverence for the past is as complacent as it is unrealistic, and Marx's condemnation of the past is as paralyzing as it is unrealizable. Both divert attention away from the available possibilities for change and transformation that always already exist within traditions and that cannot be expunged by even the most exhaustive or authoritative analysis. Marx's warning must be taken seriously in that the deadening force of tradition can cast a disabling pall over living efforts to improve the future, as must Burke's recommendation in that the past has much to offer that can be worthy of selective preservation. Although the Burkean appeal to tradition must be approached with scepticism and caution, Marx's plea is both impossible and unnecessary. It is impossible because there is no language or materials in the present from which to imagine a better future that are not passed on from the past; there is no way for people to step outside themselves to some elusive site or state of mind that is untouched by the past. Fortunately, it is unnecessary to attempt such a prodigious feat because the past is neither so dead nor so determined as to occlude its poetic revitalization in aid of future imaginings. There is no shortage of opportunities for transformative creativity. Therefore, there is no need to embrace either the Burkean traditionalist or the Marxian antitraditionalist stance: The celebration of tradition for its own sake or its condemnation for any other reason is a false dichotomy. This where Gadamer enters the picture. He offers an account of tradition – or, at least, the radical one that I intend to offer – that is much more nuanced and, therefore, much less dogmatic. In a more critical and suggestive account, tradition and transformation do not stand opposed – each feeds off and complements the other. In this way, as I am mindful that "tradition is the living faith of the dead, whereas traditionalism is the dead faith of the living,"[21] my approach is about tradition but is not traditionalist (i.e., in which continuity is valued over change), and it is about transformation but is not revolutionary (i.e., in which change is preferred to continuity). I call this 'work-in-progress'.

The fact that there is no choice other than to follow and therefore live, at least in part, in the past says nothing about what it is in the past that we must follow or respect. To uphold a tradition does not mean that it has to be done in an uncreative or uncritical way. There is choice, and, therefore,

[21] J. Pelikan, *The Vindication of Tradition* 65 (1984).

politics are always in play. As Jacques Derrida puts it, "that we are heirs does not mean that we have or that we receive this or that, some inheritance that enriches us one day with this or that, but that the being of what we are is first of all inheritance, whether we like it or know it or not."[22] Inheritance is an undertaking that those in the present are obliged to perform, but there is no one or only way to fulfill that definitive responsibility. What is given about any tradition is always open to appropriation and contestation, so resort to the past is therefore always and unavoidably political. There is no one monolithic and unified account of the past that stands in for history or that can claim to be the past's ineffable bruteness. Any attempt to justify a master narrative of the past (be it from a materialist right, a socialist left, a liberal center, or anywhere else) is destined to fail; it will be either so abstract as to ignore the contingent and nuanced facts or so detailed as to be little more than a literal recounting of those facts. Although the appeal to tradition is only meaningful if that tradition is sufficiently determinate and discrete, history shows that traditions are notoriously imprecise and that they are infuriatingly difficult to pin down. Like anything and everything else, traditions are not so much discovered as constructed in the act of following them. Moreover, because so much of the debate around tradition is less about its heterogeneity and more about the features that are seen to hold it together and that define its homogeneity, the ideas of tradition and transformation have come to be seen as antithetical. However, in most of life (and law), "breaking with tradition" is as traditional as it gets. Indeed, although he offers it more by way of caution than encouragement, Gadamer notes that, while people exist and thrive within a tradition, "it is still in the nature of [people] to be able to break with tradition, to criticise and dissolve it" (p. xxxvii). Whereas Gadamer worked to contain that instinct, I work to nourish it.

In the conventional understanding, tradition is held out as a dated accumulation of commitments, customs, and practices that are accepted with little room for critical examination or imaginative reformulation. In a more critical Gadamerian reading, tradition is not a dead thing of the past but a vital something of the present; people constantly participate in it and reconstruct it as they rely on it. Indeed, traditions survive by adaptation and change. If they do not change, they become ossified and die. In this way, traditions are alive, organic, and part of the present; they are not simply the flotsam and jetsam of the forward-moving ship of history as it steams into the

---

[22] J. Derrida, *Specters of Marx: The State of the Debt, the Work of Mourning, and the New International* 54 (P. Kamuf trans. 1994). See also E. Shils, *Tradition* 44 (1981).

future. Moreover, because traditions are understood as organic and social in that they are transmitted from one generation to another, change is at the dynamic heart of a genuine practice of tradition. As participants rely on the tradition, they are also contributing to and transforming that tradition:

> [The circle of understanding] is neither subjective nor objective, but describes understanding as the interplay of the movement of tradition and the movement of the interpreter. The anticipation of meaning that governs our understanding of a text is not an act of subjectivity, but proceeds from the commonality that binds us to the tradition. But this commonality is constantly being formed in our relation to tradition. Tradition is not simply a permanent pre-condition; rather, we produce it ourselves inasmuch as we understand, participate in the evolution of tradition, and hence further determine it ourselves. Thus the circle of understanding is not a methodological circle. (p. 293)

In this reading of Gadamer, "the circle of understanding" is historical and political. Traditions are neither fixed nor bounded and, in being passed on and assumed by individuals, they are constantly reworked and remade (as are the individuals who engage with them). The interpretation and application of a tradition is also an act of amending that tradition; "the thing which hermeneutics teaches us is to see through the dogmatism of asserting an opposition and separation between the ongoing, natural 'tradition' and the reflective appropriation of it" (p. PH28). This means that following a tradition is not simply a matter of identifying a fixed continuity between the past and present but also involves certain rearrangements, ruptures, and reversals. This act of reconstruction is both deconstructive and reconstructive. Although there is always the risk of confirming that which is being deconstructed, the most respectful reaffirmation of the past's traditions is realized in constantly placing them under critical scrutiny and transforming their substance as their spirit is observed. If a tradition is to remain alive and relevant, its institutional guardians must negotiate a paradoxical task that is the constant source of both their reassuring empowerment and unsettling usurpation. They must work with and against "the tension between memory, fidelity, the preservation of something that has been given to us, and, at the same time, heterogeneity, something absolutely new, and a break."[23] Like

---

[23] The Villanova Roundtable: A Conversation with Jacques Derrida, in J. Caputo, *Deconstruction in a Nutshell: A Conversation with Jacques Derrida* 6 (1997). For more on the Gadamer–Derrida connection in jurisprudence, see S. Feldman, *American Legal Thought from Pre-Modernism to Postmodernism: An Intellectual Voyage* 30–35 (2000).

the wicked, there is no rest or respite for these guardians. However, this is only a problem for those who mistakenly insist that change or newness is to be feared. Tradition and those assigned the task of interpreting it are works in progress whose character, if they have one, is to be always at work and always in progress.

Such an appreciation is at the heart of great moments in most arenas of human endeavor. It is not the person who diligently and expertly upholds conventional standards and expectations that will be recognized as great, but those who transform those standards and expectations as they exceed them. The hallmark of genius is not simply the ability to beat every one at their own game, but the capacity to envision and dictate a different game to be played. Pablo Picasso, James Joyce, and Albert Einstein had technical skills in abundance, but they also possessed a vision and capacity to reveal possibilities that others had not even seen or thought possible. While those rare moments of transformation reject certain traditions and conventional approaches, they operate within a broader tradition of creativity and originality that they reinforce and affirm in their revolutionary contributions. Indeed, such creative geniuses are exemplars of this idea that traditions are upheld by breaking them; it is not the substantive traditions themselves but the traditionality of change and innovation that they continue. Even the conservative T. S. Eliot, in his celebration of literary tradition, recognized that, when any individual's contribution is assessed, "novelty is better than repetition."[24] This credo of conservation and contestation of the past in a transformative tradition is adhered to by some of the great judicial innovators. Treading a thin and, at times, nonexistent line between heresy and heritage, they occupy a role that is part apostle and part apostate in which they recognize that another present way of understanding the past is to imagine a better future. They accept that the legal past is not a foundation on which to build but a resource site from which to draw. Past legal decisions combine to form a valuable institutional almanac of experimental strategies whose relevance and results are to be tested and retested in the service of making society a better place to live. Those judges – *Donoghue*'s Lord Atkin, *Hedley Byrne*'s Lord Reid, *Griswold*'s Justice Douglas, and *Lochner*'s Justice Holmes – who take most seriously the experimental imperative are those who flaunt conventional standards in the process of reformulating them; their judgments are the exceptions that prove the rule. Great judges of the common law

---

[24] T. S. Eliot, <u>Tradition and the Individual Talent</u> in *The Sacred Wood: Essays on Poetry and Criticism* (1920).

tradition are those who refuse to be hampered by customary habits of judicial mind.

The common law is a vast tradition of almost infinitely possible argumentative moves. What is actually done is never entirely justifiable by the principles or rules of the tradition alone of which it claims to be an application. A particular move cannot be detached from the overall tradition itself – each can only be fully appreciated in the context of the other. Indeed, the idea that there is complete freedom to decide makes no sense at all because it is only within a tradition of constraints, albeit thoroughly contingent and revisable in content and direction, that decision making can be comprehended. While this understanding of tradition is to be contrasted to the pedant's or formalist's timidity and dependence on rules, it is also to be set off against the anarchist's bravado in ignoring all rules. Freedom and its ultimate exercise in genius is less about divine detachment and more about the transformation of the existing traditions in novel and disruptive ways. Moreover, the choice is not, as Mootz and others suppose it to be, between "a disciplined encounter with the activity of rhetorical knowledge" and "a boundless and playful irrationalism"[25]: This is only to reinstall another false dichotomy between reason and nonreason. Consequently, legal reasoning is about the moves that are presently in play and which structure law's reasoning game in such a way as to enable choices between competing definitions of particular rules. However, while providing an argumentative context for reasoning and definition, these moves are themselves being contingently reworked. In this way, the rules of law's tradition do not so much constrain or cabin judges' room for maneuver as make it possible and operational: "to be situated within a tradition does not limit the freedom of knowledge but makes it possible" (p. 361). Viewed in this way, law is confirmed as a rhetorical activity and legal tradition is not simply a process that is to be known and thereby governed. It is part of an active engagement in which "tradition is a genuine partner in dialogue" (p. 358) with its judicial interlocutors and, in engaging in that dialogue, both the tradition and the interlocutor are "transformed into a communion in which [they] do not remain what [they] were" (p. 379).

When Gadamer states that, in a hermeneutical approach, "understanding is thought of less as a subjective act than as participating in an event of tradition, a process of transmission in which past and present are constantly

---

[25] J. Mootz, supra, note 10 at 497. See also F. J. Mootz, Nietzschean Critique and Philosophical Hermeneutics, 20 *Cardozo L. Rev.* 101 (2003).

mediated" (p. 290), I want to emphasize how the subjective act is not consumed by the tradition, but how the two interact. In the same way that the subjective act is not meaningfully comprehended or even possible outside the tradition, so the tradition does not stand independently of the subjective acts that create and re-create it. Furthermore, when Gadamer states that the hermeneutical challenge is that of "acquiring an appropriate historical horizon" (p. 303), I have no quarrels with this as long as long as *appropriate* is understood in a nonobjective, political, and contingent way. Accordingly, rather than talk about obligation in the sense of a fixed meaning or talk about freedom in the sense of no fixed meaning at all, I find it better to "think of the whole performance in a way that is both bound and free. In a certain sense interpretation probably is re-creation, but this is a re-creation not of the creative act but of the created work, which has to be brought to representation in accord with the meaning the interpreter finds in it" (p. 119). Although Gadamer is commenting on festivals, his remarks are apposite to the judicial encounter between law's tradition and the individual judge in reaching a discrete decision in a particular controversy:

> As a festival, it is not an identity like a historical event, but neither is it determined by its origin so that there was once the "real" festival – as distinct from the way in which it later came to be celebrated. From its inception – whether instituted in a single act or introduced gradually – the nature of a festival is to be celebrated regularly. Thus its own original essence is always to be something different (even when celebrated in exactly the same way). An entity that exists only by always being something different is temporal in a more radical sense than everything that belongs to history. It has its being only in becoming and return. (p. 123)

Under my portrayal of the common law tradition, not only is there no compelling justification why judges should rein in their own critical judgments in supposed deference to those implicit in law's substantive traditions, but there is also a cogent reason why they should give full and open expression to them. Judges respect the common law tradition best when they scrutinize, interrogate, challenge, and make it conform with justice. Of course, they do not do this from outside the tradition but work with and within the tradition. This idea is perfectly captured by Derrida when he states that, "for a decision to be just and responsible, it must, in its proper moment if there is one, be both regulated and without regulation: it must conserve the law and destroy it or suspend it enough to reinvent it in each case, rejustifying it, at least reinvent it in the reaffirmation and the new and free confirmation of it principles."[26] Accordingly, the style of judging that captures most faithfully the cherished traditions of the common law is one that involves both a constant reinterpretation of past decisions and a perpetual openness to future reinterpretation. And, of course, such a style of judging must equally question its own biases and implications. Nonetheless, if it is to be given its due, each new case is entitled to more than an unthinking reliance on existing doctrine or rules. It requires the judge to make a fresh judgment that actively reappraises as it reaffirms the traditions of legal doctrine. Indeed, contrary to conventional wisdom, it is the relentless critic who most closely grasps and continues the common law tradition, not those who insist on a timid acceptance of what has already been decided. To treat the law as static or to adopt an unquestioning posture toward it is to betray, not uphold, the common law tradition.

Some of the best evidence for this claim can be found in, dare I say again, the common law tradition of great cases. Contrary to more conventional views that emphasize stable continuity and incremental change, great cases showcase the transformative nature of the common law tradition. Despite the insistence of its most eminent practitioners and protagonists, the common law is neither firmly grounded, objectively given, incrementally developed, nor politically neutral. As evidenced by the emergence and existence of great cases, the common law is loosely assembled, creatively constructed, unpredictably changeable, and ideologically loaded. The progress of the common law is marked less by the evolutionary unfolding of an inherent logic and characterized more by its contingent responsiveness to historical circumstances. Thus, innovation, not preservation, is the quality that most represents the tradition of the common law. Indeed, great cases change the tradition not only by adding to it but also by changing common understandings about what the past was and how it can be seen in a new light. Moreover, great cases reinforce the insight that breaking with tradition is not only a part of the common law's tradition but a defining feature of it. They demonstrate that it is not only possible to continue tradition by adapting it, but that such a judicial attitude and approach is in the very best traditions of the common law. By emphasizing that the routine is revolutionary as much as the revolutionary is routine, adjudication is treated as an institutional responsibility of both derivation and deviation. By holding up the past to a better image of itself, judges can make future changes in the name and furtherance of that present image. Such inventiveness is more a reworking of law's substantive

---

[26] J. Derrida, Force of Law: The 'Mystical Foundation of Authority,' 11 *Cardozo L. Rev.* 919 at 962 (1990).

traditions under the tutelage of a more encompassing tradition of creativity and transformation than an abandonment of tradition completely.

Political Repercussions

If the common law and its adjudicative practice are anything to go by, there is, as Gadamer says, "something that hermeneutical reflection teaches us." However, it is not "that social community, with all its tensions and disruptions, ever and ever again leads back to a common area of social understanding through which it exists" (p. PH42). This is wishful thinking that does much more harm than good. It gives established and dominant values priority over marginalized and subversive ones simply because – and this is the crucial point – they are established and dominant. What hermeneutical reflection might teach us is that the extant traditions of discursive convention that make agreement possible are as much a result of force and power as of consensus and agreement. Commonality is not the same as sharedness; such an equivalence has to be actively demonstrated rather than passively assumed. There is a politics to all of this that Gadamer either ignores or downplays. It is not so much that values and reason are entirely collapsible into ideology and power; this is a nihilistic scenario that can withstand neither historical scrutiny nor critical analysis. It is that reason and power do not stand separate from or over the other. In a similar way that values and reason operate within the context of ideology and power, so are ideology and power affected by values and reason. Contrary to much jurisprudential thinking, the problem is not the intervention of power in the halls of reason, but the resilient belief that power can be somehow excluded and that there exists some noncultural and nonsocial standard of reasonableness. Disabused of this notion, the democratic ambition becomes not one of warranting that reason is detached from value or power, but of ensuring that the values and interests that help constitute reason represent and are conducive to a truly democratic society. Rhetorical knowledge, therefore, functions with, within, and upon political conditions. In legal terms, the connection between law as one kind of rhetorical activity and politics as another kind is one of interpenetration and fluidity, not independence and boundedness.

In putting forward the account that I have, I am not suggesting that adjudication is somehow an unmitigated sham or that judges are involved in a dark conspiracy to thwart democratic justice. I accept that judges largely do act in good faith in meeting their professional expectations. Nor am I suggesting that the inexorable consequence of accepting that law is politics is to unveil politics and, therefore, law as an exercise in arbitrary and unreasoned decision making. Such an account does justice neither to judges and mainstream jurists nor to me and most other critical scholars. My insistence that law is politics is no more (and no less) than a claim that it is not possible to engage in adjudication without also being drawn into and taking a stand on irreducibly contested political matters. Judges bring to their official duties what Holmes famously called "deep-seated preferences." These do run very deep and are often so seated that their holder has little conscious sense of them. However, I do not believe that they "can not be argued about" or that they do not change, even if they sometimes change through nonrational persuasion. I certainly do not believe that "when differences are sufficiently far reaching, we try to kill the other man rather than let him have his way" or that "his grounds are just as good as ours."[27] This implies that the only alternatives to an objective rationality is a desultory relativism in which anything goes or an apocalyptic nihilism in which arbitrariness is the only mark of political commitment. These possible alternatives say more about mainstream jurists and their own limited perspectives than anything else. For them, there is no practicable choice other than objectivity or subjectivity; anything that does not live up to the objective standards of truth is *mere* conviction, convention, ideology, opinion, and the like.[28] From my critical perspective, however, justification is a hermeneutical practice and what works or counts as good or reasons will depend on the social and therefore political context in which justification is sought and offered. This is the unrelenting message of a radical version of Gadamerian hermeneutics. Accordingly, while I believe that such deep-seated preferences are not rational in the sense of lending themselves to some objective validation or refutation, I do not believe that they are arbitrary or immoveable: Reasoned exchange and argument can occur as long as reason is understood as historically contingent, socially constructed, and politically charged.

Although my critical account of common law development runs counter to traditional depictions, it is nonetheless intended to be descriptively valid. It is my claim that common law adjudication is actually performed as a dynamic exercise in which 'anything might go.' However, my version is not entirely without precedent. The presentation of the common law as an abstract enterprise of principled elaboration is a relatively modern one: Vast

---

[27] O. W. Holmes, Jr., *Collected Legal Papers* 312 (P. Smith ed. 1921).
[28] See R. Dworkin, Objectivity and Truth: You'd Better Believe it, 25 *Phil. & Pub. Affs.* 87 (1996) and D. Farber and S. Sherry, *Beyond All Reason: The Radical Assault on Truth in American Law* 7, 22, 73, 119, and 133 (1997).

efforts were made by common lawyers over many centuries to resist the deductive methods of Roman law. Indeed, the effort by many contemporary jurists to treat law and adjudication as a largely philosophical pursuit is itself something of a transformative maneuver. Nevertheless, by asking judges and lawyers to become grand theorists, they neglect the pragmatic roots and strengths of the common law, which are much more casuistic and customary than principled and formalized. It is this jurisprudential effort to re-present law and adjudication as hermeneutical practices of rhetorical persuasion that is a considerable advance. However, as I have sought to demonstrate, it is important that any attempt to understand the common law as a profoundly historical endeavor must take the extra step and recognize that the historicization of the common law must also entail its politicization. It is at this point that Darwin's evolutionary sagacity can be blended effectively with Gadamer's hermeneutical insights – the common law is part of the overall human struggle to cope with the contingent and dynamic demands of the historical environment. There is no one path that people can follow and no one method on which people can rely to make a success of life. Thus, the history of the common law is not the clean and tidy process that many jurists describe or desire it to be; it is only comprehensible as a rather dirty and messy context for all that happens within its unavoidable context. In short, in seeking to take what is basically "a body of practices observed and ideas received over time by a caste of lawyers" and turn it into an elaborate exercise in aseptic ratiocination,[29] mainstream jurists manage to elide the political dimensions of common law adjudication. In so doing, they misrepresent the whole quality and character of common law adjudication. Again, quite simply, there can be no historicization without politicization.

In times past, the legitimacy of the common law and therefore the authority of judges was taken as residing in the fact that the common law was an artifact of the community whose values the judges were entrusted to articulate and institutionalize. While judges had considerable discretion in performing this task, they were not completely left to their own devices. The common law comprises a process whereby its rules can be updated and refreshed in accordance with changing social norms. As long as those customary values were fairly homogeneous and broadly based, the pragmatic

---

[29] B. Simpson, The Common Law and Legal Theory in *Legal Theory and Common Law* 20 (W. Twining ed. 1986). See also M. Hale, *The History of the Common Law* (2nd ed. 1716); J. G. A. Pocock, *The Ancient Constitution and the Feudal Law* (1957); and M. Horwitz, *The Transformation of American Law, 1780–1850* (1977).

judicial effort to combine formal law and customary values appears to be relatively apolitical and neutral. However, once that fact or pretense is relaxed, the cogency of such a claim soon begins to unravel. It is true that, until quite late in the common law's development, judges looked for guidance not from philosophical principles but from particular customs of the communities over which they presided. This meant that, in its formative Anglo-Saxon years, there was nothing common to the law as England consisted of only a fragmented, decentralized, and local series of fiefdoms. It was only in later centuries, as part of a broader centralization of governmental power, that the common law really came into existence through "the "blending of the diverse local customs of the different parts of England into one custom common to the whole country, by a process of judicial fusing and interpretation."[30] However, it was never the case that the common law was simply the formalization of traditional customs; judges always had the power to vet and veto competing customs by shaping them into a common and approved body of norms, even if those rules turned out to be unprecedented and novel. In this sense, the judges exercised a strong political discretion in favoring one set of values over another. Indeed, it is more accurate to say that the common law was less custom based and more "the common erudition of the legal profession" passed off as custom.[31] Again, it was less that judges acted as conduits for received wisdom and more that they passed off as wise those parts of customary values that they thought should be received: Law was anchored in the community, but only selectively and conditionally so.

One theorist who has made some headway in this pragmatic direction is Melvin Eisenberg. Unfortunately, it is a case of two steps forward and three back. He offers a "generative" concept of the common law in which a combination of doctrinal principles and social propositions is effected and governed by a series of institutional rules that bind judges in the performance of their adjudicative responsibilities. These institutional principles are intended to ensure legitimacy in a democratic society – *objectivity* (i.e., impartial judges applying universal rules); *support* (i.e., these universal applied rules are supported by general standards of society); *replicability* (i.e., they are generated by a consistent methodology that allows reliance and predictability); and *responsiveness* (i.e., which methodology attends to professional corrective discourse about the law and its shortcomings). Viewing

---

[30] E. Jenks, *English Law: Sources and Judicial Organization* 25 (1931). See also A. Hogue, *Origins of the Common Law* (1966); T. Plucknett, *A Concise History of the Common Law* (1981); and S. Milsom, *Historical Foundations of the Common Law* (1969).

[31] J. W. Tubbs, *The Common Law Mind: Medieval and Early Conceptions* 194 (2000). See also H. P. Glenn, *Legal Traditions of the World* 207 (2000).

the common law as an activity as much as a body of rules, Eisenberg claims to explain how the common law achieves both certainty through the existence of overriding doctrinal principles and flexibility through the incorporation of social propositions. The institutional principles are claimed to be able to reconcile the tensions that arise out of law's need to utilize the past to resolve disputes and to contribute to the future by enriching the supply of legal rules. In the language of science, there is gradual as opposed to "punctuated evolution." In identifying such social proposition, he concedes that this resort to social morality will not be an empirical or value-free exercise; judges are to draw upon those norms that they believe would likely obtain social support and favor by all. Within such a scheme, "the landmark cases of the common law do not involve an attempt by the courts to change existing social standards, but a decision by the courts to bring legal rules into congruence with existing social standards."[32] In this way, Eisenberg offers an account of common law development that ties what the law is to what it should be, but in a way that is intended to be sufficiently disciplined and controlled to satisfy the formalist demands of mainstream jurisprudence.

Expressed in such general terms, Eisenberg's dynamic account has much to recommend it; its attempt to integrate legal rules and social values is ingenious. However, once his ideas are pushed a little further, their soundness becomes very suspect. At bottom, Eisenberg tends to refute rather than confirm his traditional hypothesis that law is not political in any deep or partisan way. At a crucial juncture, he notes that "using the norms of the general community in fashioning common law rules [only works] so long as the community is not exceptionally pluralistic and the norms claim to be rooted in aspirations for the community as a whole." However, in conflicted and class-ridden societies such as the United States and the United Kingdom, this means that Eisenberg has nothing to contribute by way of explanatory justification. His theory runs out at the very point where it is most needed in the resolution of most disputed matters. He has little legal advice to offer judges in disputed matters of law. As if this were not enough, Eisenberg compounds the problem by stating that, in monitoring the interplay between social and doctrinal propositions, judges must balance social congruence, systemic consistency, and doctrinal stability. However, this does not so much resolve the traditional problem of setting off substantive justice against formal reliance as restate it. He concludes that precedents should be followed if there is substantial social congruence, "even though another

---

[32] M. Eisenberg, *The Nature of the Common Law* 126 and 19 (1988).

rule would be marginally better."[33] This is tantamount to admitting that what drives the common law is political evaluation rather than legal analysis. To put it another way, this reduces legal analysis to nothing more than political debate. This, of course, is exactly what Eisenberg and other traditional defenders of the common law are supposed to be flatly against. To state, as Eisenberg does, that judges should do what they think is politically reasonable whether it involves applying, extending, distinguishing, exceptionalizing, reformulating, or overruling existing rules is to give the whole jurisprudential game away. Consequently, although Eisenberg's account is promoted as a centrist view, it plays out as an account of the common law in which anything might go. The limits of adjudication are nothing more and nothing less than the honest personal views of individual judges about what is and is not socially acceptable or reasonable. This seems much less a formula for legal restraint than an overt invitation to political choice.

In presenting adjudication in this critical light, I believe it should become clear that I am not suggesting that there is no resort to political values, only that the shared nature of those values gives the appearance that the judicial performance is objective. If there is conflict over the values to be incorporated in the law, the political nature of adjudication is simply revealed rather than hidden. It is not that politics somehow begins to intrude in what is otherwise an apolitical process. The choice to uphold the status quo or traditional values is no less and no more political than the decision to rupture or reinterpret the those values in the name of an emancipatory impulse. As Gadamer is at pains to emphasize, "preservation is as much a freely chosen action as are revolution and renewal" (pp. 281–82). *Any* engagement with and within tradition is political in that it involves choice between competing ways of presently making the past the best future that it can be. As such, it is traditionalism that is to be deplored, not tradition itself. The allegedly uncritical preservation of static commitments is bogus because, when understood in the more radical way that I recommend, the tradition itself is so capacious, nuanced, multitextured, motile, diffuse, and irrepressible that there is no one simple given tradition whose name it is possible to be claiming to act in. Accordingly, when the common law is politicized as well as historicized, it becomes clearer that, rather than celebrate tradition as a source of authority and meaning, it is authority that is

[33] Id. at 21 and 75. For equally fatal concessions, see R. Posner, *The Problematics of Moral and Legal Theory* 262 (1999) ("provided there is a fair degree of value consensus among the judges, as I think there is, [a pragmatic account of adjudication] can help the judges seek the best results unhampered by philosophical doubts") and R. Dworkin, supra, note 9 at 108–09 ("legal argument takes place on a plateau of rough consensus").

the source of tradition's meaning. Tradition can no more ground authority or meaning than anything else. Authority and meaning, like tradition, are to be *earned* in the rhetorical give and take of hermeneutical exchange. Such a historical exchange is only properly appreciated when its political context is grasped, admittedly in an inevitably partial, incomplete, and contingent way. In this way, the common law is more usefully understood as a radical work-in-progress.

Consequently, the emancipatory task of a radical hermeneutics is not exhausted in the important effort of unmasking tradition-following initiatives as inevitable interventions in and of politics. Although the critical significance of this demonstration is not to be underestimated, it also important to point out the inner contradictions, negations, elisions, and tensions within the tradition so that they can be appropriated, reformulated, and worked to progressive effect. Because adjudicative decision making is context dependent and it is not possible to delineate the relevant context with sufficient completeness, certainty, or detail, the exercise of judicial discretion will always have be an indispensable dimension of judgment or choice. The judges' moral values and political commitments will confound any attempt to turn legal adjudication into a largely technical and objective reckoning rather than a contestable commitment to particular values and interests. Moreover, even if it were, it is surely the case that "being just is not a matter of calculation" and "a democracy or politics that we simply calculate . . . would be a terrible thing."[34] Rather than view the critical claim that law is politics as an indictment of adjudication or as a betrayal of democracy, it surely better to treat such an assessment as opening up the possibility for law and adjudication to meet its democratic obligations and satisfy the expectations that it places on itself to dispense justice. Judges do this best when, instead of pretending that law is bounded and objective, they neither mask their political commitments nor grind a favored political axe: They must put those values in curial play so as to interrogate and rework them better. Aware that tradition is never statically given but is always organically open to dynamic reinterpretation, judges will go on doing what they have always done, albeit more candidly and less cowardly. They will seek to make a critical accommodation with and within legal tradition by "combining heresy and heritage into fruitful tension."[35] However, what is fruitful will itself be contingent and contested so that there is no fully settled or adequate combination that can claim to be authoritative by dint of its balance or fruitfulness. To be in a

---

[34] J. Derrida, supra, note 22 at 17 and 19.
[35] P. Freund, *On Law and Justice* 23 (1968).

state of tension is not aberrational or anomalous; it is the usual experience of life and tradition.

Conclusion

In this chapter, I have sought to offer a reading of Gadamer, tradition, and the common law as works in progress. In particular, I have put forward my Gadamer, not some objective or essential Gadamer who stands over and supervises the meaning of his own text. To think that were possible would be to miss some of the most dominant themes in his work, namely the author's lack of authority, the contingency of the interpretive act, and the applicative indeterminacy of the text. My goal, therefore, has not been to argue over the correct interpretation of Gadamer's text. As he concludes in his masterly work, "it would be a poor hermeneuticist who thought he could have, or had to have, the last word" (p. 570). However, some jurists have not been able to resist that temptation and to put Gadamer's authority to work in supporting the adjudicative tradition of the common law. That effort has tended to blunt any political edge that a legal hermeneutics might have. When choice and contingency are thrown into the mix, the result is a unstable concoction that challenges all that is taken for granted or assumed. But it is not to be feared – on the contrary, it provides an opportunity for transformation and renewal. In contrast to its conservative sibling, a radical jurisprudence does not hedge on the subversive implications of the hermeneutical insight: It makes no artificial distinction between what is and is not up for grabs. Because everything has been constructed, everything can be deconstructed and reconstructed. By failing to politicize the historical imperative of hermeneutics, conservatives apprehend more benign and accidental forces at work in social life than is the case; they mistake commonality for sharedness and acquiescence for acceptance. In law, this means that legal reasoning must be treated as being as much about political power as it is about ethical consensus; the common law is thoroughly and relentlessly a work-in-progress.

Like Darwin, Gadamer is at least partially to blame for the reception given to his work. There is a fatalistic as well as a quietistic aspect to Gadamer: He comes close to insisting that things are simply the way they are and that there is little that can be done other than to accept it. I have tried to argue that not only can Gadamer be read in a more radical style, but also that social, legal, and hermeneutical traditions are much more transformative and less determinate than Gadamer or his jurisprudential disciples allow: "The willingness of many social and legal theorists to suppress such dynamism in favour of a 'stable' status quo is itself but a rhetorical device."[36] Contrary to the fearful scholarship of Gadamer and his conservative interpreters, this acknowledgment is not a precursor to chaos or anarchy. It is an invitation to challenge the status quo, to change the world for the better, and to argue constantly about what *better* is and demands. Most importantly, my effort to advocate a radical hermeneutics is most definitely not intended to demonstrate how meaning and understanding are impossible. On the contrary, it is devoted to showing how meaning and understanding are possible at all by elucidating the historical processes, social practices, and material interests within which meaning and understanding arise. The critical dimension is on tracing the political consequences of meaning's endless instability, not the frankly ludicrous project of demonstrating meaning's impossibility. As the next chapter evidences, constitutional law is one of the locations at which it is possible to demonstrate the extent to which both the substantive rules and the judicial mentality that creates and applies them are works-in-progress.

---

[36] S. Burton, Critique And Comment: Determinacy, Indeterminacy and Rhetoric in a Pluralist World, 21 *Melb. U. L. Rev.* 544 at 582 (1997).

⌒ 7 ⌒

Reading Between the Lines:
Courts and Constitutions

> Nobody would claim that their own thinking was ideologi-
> cal just as nobody would habitually refer to themselves as
> Fatso.... Ideology like halitosis is in this sense what the other
> person has.[1]

TERRY EAGLETON

ONSTITUTIONS ARE CONSIDERED THE FOUNDATION ON WHICH LAW
and politics are built. Whether made up of formal documents or formalized customs, they are supposed to contain the terms and conditions on
which political power is to be obtained, allocated, exercised, and controlled
in a legal manner: They are meant to be an institutional and constant matrix
within which the ebb and flow of political action occurs. Indeed, great stock
is set by the extent to which states subscribe to such constitutional promise
and strive to achieve such constitutional practice. Those that function in
line with such an aspiration are respected as being largely democratic and
just; those that do not are dismissed as despotic and inequitable. Accordingly, the claim that constitutions can operate as an institutional constant
has very important implications for both the theory and practice of democratic law and politics. If the claim can be defended and validated, much
progress will have been made in promoting the virtue of such constitutional
democracies; those countries that subscribe to constitutional government
will be vindicated as being both politically legitimate and legally sound. If
not, then the validity of such regimes will be suspect. Those same states may
then be seen as no more legitimate or lawful than those tyrannical regimes
that openly flaunt such ambitions. In short, without some defensible notion
of a stable and predictable constitution, constitutional democracies will be

---

[1]   T. Eagleton, *Ideology: An Introduction* 3 (1991).

obliged to defend their democratic legitimacy as much by reference to their substantive fairness as to the formal accoutrements of constitutionalism. This is no bad thing – good governance ought to be as much about the *what* is decided as *how* it is decided. However, the idea and practice of government based on a stable and constant constitution proves more illusory than real: The belief that constitutions can ground anything is a dangerous conceit.

Instead, in line with the critical approach that I have been developing, I insist that constitutional law operates in much the same way as the common law generally. There are two principal differences. First, the stakes are usually higher in constitutional law in that, unlike with common law decisions, the courts are striking down legislation and their decisions cannot be easily countermanded by the legislature. Second, when dealing with constitutional matters, courts have to respect in some way the formal and written documents that form the basis for both their striking-down power and the circumstances in which such power can be exercised. However, while these differences ought not to be trivialized, it is reasonable to assume that their effects do not unduly affect the character of adjudication. In the same way that common law judges are not entirely free to do whatever they choose (i.e., they recognize a felt obligation to situate their decisions within the body of existing legal doctrine), so constitutional judges are not entirely restricted in their ability to act in a way that best effects justice (i.e., they note that formal written texts do not give the kind of specific guidance that can mechanically resolves concrete disputes). In this way, judges work the considerable space between choice and constraint and, in the process, are both free and restricted in their fulfillment of their institutional responsibility. Indeed, it would be odd if the difference between the style of constitutional and common law adjudication was substantial or striking as it is exactly the same judges who engage in both. The difference is more a matter of emphasis and degree than difference and kind. Judges bring to each task a shared sense of both the similar challenge – acting in a way that does not entirely collapse the distinction between constrained legal analysis and open-ended ideological decision making – and the appropriate method for meeting it – utilizing the past to resolve present problems in a way that helps to clarify the future. Constitutional adjudication, therefore, is simply a particular kind of common law adjudication. The basic components of the common law mind-set are adapted to the specialized demands of the constitutional context.

In this chapter, therefore, I contend that constitutional law is an organic work-in-progress whose lifeblood is the continuity of change; any distinction between its formal and informal revision or between its fixed and fluid dimensions is mistaken. There is a constitutional tradition of political trans-formation in which there is development and growth, but not always in grad-ual ways or progressive directions.[2] In the first part of the chapter, I look at the grand historical sweep of Canadian constitutional law and explain how its contours have often been shaped in unexpected ways, with unpredictable results, and by powerful political forces. In the next three sections, I grapple with the jurisprudential debate on legal hermeneutics that has been played out through the recent American Supreme Court physician-assisted suicide decision in *Glucksberg*. Concentrating on the pivotal judgment of Justice Souter, I first situate the case and its judgments in their jurisprudential con-text, then unpack some of the hermeneutical claims of Souter's judgement, and lastly explore the political implications of this style of judicial decision making. In the final section, I return to the Canadian scene and offer a reading of the Supreme Court of Canada's decision in *Re Quebec Reference* that illustrates the kind of legal reasoning that my critical approach recom-mends. Throughout the chapter, I advance the critical theme that what can and does distinguish one political system from another is the political sub-stance of their governmental practices, not the formal legitimacy of their legal procedures. This, of course, is simply another way of driving home the critical message that 'law is politics' – there is no escape from politics and, as importantly, nothing for the democrat to fear from that realization.

The Not-So-Frozen North

In the heated world of constitutional hermeneutics, the existing debate in jurisprudential theories is between those (let us call them *documentarians*) who prioritize the words and texts of the constitution and place all other sources of constitutional meaning in a distinctly and at best secondary cat-egory and those (let us call them *doctrinalists*) who tend to play down the precise wording of these documents and look to the courts' precedential

---

[2] I am acutely aware that I have not dealt with the hugely important topic of statutory inter-pretation. This is not an intellectual oversight but a logistical consideration. Any convincing claims that I can make about the common law approach to constitutional interpretation are doubly valid in their application to statutory interpretation. As a leading scholar observed, statutory provisions evolve in much the same way as a common law rule. See F. Bennion, *Statutory Interpretation* 618 (2nd ed. 1992). Of course, this begs the central question, In what way does the common law evolve? In answering that crucial question, I reject the traditional contrast between the natural beauty of the common law and the unsightly accommodations of statute. For a provocative discussion of this volatile relationship, see J. Beatson, The Role of Statute in the Development of Common Law Doctrine, 117 *L. Q. R.* 247 (2001).

efforts at interpretation. In the same way that few argue that the doctrine is irrelevant to the interpretation of the documents, few also contend that the documents are immaterial to the development of the doctrine. Nevertheless, while generally overlooked or assumed in constitutional debate, the prior question ought to be, What is this constitution to be interpreted and where is it to be found? The idea that the constitution stands available and ready for interpretation is a very limited and limiting understanding of a much broader and richer concept. Indeed, such a static idea of a constitution is as misleading as it is mistaken. At least as evidenced by the Canadian context, a constitution is an organic process through which states determine the kind of society and citizens that they are and can become. While there is an acknowledgment that change occurs, it is perceived to be gradual and progressive. Constitutional law's natural development occurs by way of slow growth, not abrupt transformations of the constitutional landscape. While the formal documents and conventions of nationhood represent a privileged resolution of constitutional debate, each attempt to interpret and reinterpret that compromise gives fresh meaning and effect to it. The formal documents of legal statehood no more contain a nation's constitution than an electrocardiogram's chart captures the life of the patient under its observation. Locating the constitution and interpreting it are flip sides of the same coin. In the Canadian context, where the courts locate it and how they interpret it is continually surprising and largely as unpredictable as tossing coins.

Reflecting its British roots, the formal documents of the Canadian constitution are not intended to be complete or definitive. The constitution comprises both formal and informal sources. Indeed, the critical tension between constitutional documents and legal doctrine is at the heart of Canadian constitutional law. Up to its patriation in 1982, the formal constitution was a minimalist document that simply laid the basic framework for confederation: Civil liberties were not covered. This did not preclude the courts from using the common law to bridle arbitrary government acts and locate an implied bill of rights within the interstices of the British North America Act. These efforts were sporadic and half-hearted, but they spoke to the vibrant possibilities of the common law.[3] Since 1982, of course, the Charter has also placed certain limits on the kind of action that any particular

---

[3] See *Entick v. Carrington* (1765), 95 ER 807 and *Roncarelli v. Duplessis*, [1959] SCR 121. On the implied Bill of Rights, see *Alberta Press*, [1938] SCR 100, *Switzman v. Elbling*, [1957] SCR 285, and *Co-operative Committee on Japanese-Canadians v. A-G for Canada*, [1947] AC 87.

government or legislature can take. For instance, Canadians have a constitutionally guaranteed freedom of communication and the right to life, liberty, and security of the person that government cannot infringe. In this way, contemporary constitutional law is as much about the substantive content of government action as it is about its formal source in the federal system. However, the one thing that constitutional patriation did not do was consolidate or completely codify Canada's constitution. Unlike in the United States, there is no one founding document that claims to occupy the whole constitutional field. For instance, although Section 52 of the Constitution Act of 1982 contains a definition of "The Constitution of Canada," it is not exhaustive and is merely exemplary. Indeed, in the *New Brunswick Broadcasting* case,[4] the Supreme Court of Canada expressly confirmed that the constitution comprised a variety of written and unwritten sources that were far from finite or fixed in definition and number. Parliamentary privilege is part of the constitution, even though it is contained in no formal document or text. In short, the constitution is dealt with in the familiar way of the common law; it is a process as much as a product and it is a site for development as much as a completed structure. In an early Charter decision, Chief Justice Dickson left little doubt that the constitutional interpretation is as much about substantive values as it is about formal documents:

> A constitution . . . is drafted with an eye to the future. Its function is to provide a continuing framework for the legitimate exercise of governmental power and, when joined by a Bill or a Charter of Rights, for the unremitting protection of individual rights and liberties. Once enacted, its provisions cannot easily be repealed or amended. It must, therefore, be capable of growth and development over time to meet new social, political and historical realities often unimagined by its framers. The judiciary is the guardian of the constitution and must, in interpreting its provisions, bear these considerations in mind. . . . The Court must be guided by the values and principles essential to a free and democratic society which I believe embody, to name but a few, respect for the inherent dignity of the human person, commitment to social justice and equality, accommodation of a wide variety of beliefs, respect for cultural and group identity, and faith in social and political institutions which enhance the participation of individuals and groups in society.[5]

4 *New Brunswick Broadcasting v. Nova Scotia*, [1993] 1 SCR 319.
5 *Hunter v. Southam Newspapers*, [1984] 2 SCR 145 at 155. This, of course, builds on Lord Sankey's famous dictum that "the constitution is a living tree capable of growth and expansion within its natural limits." For an extended discussion of this arboreal metaphor in terms of the common law, see infra chap. 9.

As the history of constitutional law and decision making evidences, this process of growth and development is much more open-ended and unstructured than the courts and commentators would have us believe. While the law changes to meet new and different political conditions, it does so in a way that confounds any retrospective claims that such historical evolution is gradual and incremental. Canada's constitution is a place where the nation works through its competing anxieties and shifting aspirations, often in the most abrupt way and with the most unexpected results. For instance, while most of the wording of the Constitution Act of 1867 has not changed in more than 125 years, the meaning and effect of its provisions on the division of provincial and federal powers have gone through a process of continual redefinition. The bulk of constitutional law comprises the many judicial cases that have sought to interpret and apply constitutional arguments to changing social and political circumstances. Indeed, the different substantive effects of the formal acts of amending the constitution and the informal acts of interpreting it are difficult to pin down. In an important sense, the constitution is amended every time it is judicially reinterpreted. However, like Canada itself, the terrain is too vast and too variable to do more than sample some of the more striking examples of how the constitution has changed over the years and how its development has not been the measured and principled growth that its common law defenders insist. Accordingly, what follow are some thematic suggestions about the ways in which constitutional doctrine has shifted and changed over the years.

Things that are in the written parts of the constitution can move in and out of the constitution over time – Under Sections 55, 56, and 57 of the Constitution Act of 1857, the British government retained the right to "reserve and disallow" Canadian statutes. However, this power has not been exercised since 1878 in the case of reservation and since 1873 in the case of disallowance. Moreover, under Section 90 of the Constitution Act of 1867, the federal government has the powers of reservation and disallowance over provincial laws. But this has not been exercised since 1943. It is the received wisdom that any attempt to utilize these powers would not only be politically objectionable but legally inoperative. Indeed, in 1981, the Supreme Court of Canada stated that "reservation and disallowance of provincial legislation, although in law still open, have, to all intents and purposes, fallen into disuse."[6] Nevertheless, efforts to amend the constitution have sought to include provisions that

---

[6] *Re Resolution To Amend The Constitution*, [1981] 1 SCR 753 at 802. See also *The Queen v. Beauregard*, [1986] 2 SCR 56.

would explicitly delete such powers from the constitution. This is an instance where the writing has remained but the meaning has been lost.

Another example of this is the overall division of legislative powers between the federal government and the provinces. Whereas Section 91 of the Constitution Act stipulates the federal powers, Section 92 lays out the provincial powers. While each section states that the powers are granted "exclusively" to each branch of government, the traditional practice is to allow each level of government to legislate on the same issue if the subject matter validly falls under both heads of authority. For instance, traffic laws can fall within both the provinces' "property and civil rights" power and the federal government's "criminal law" power. However, if a valid federal and provincial law conflict, the federal law has paramountcy. The courts have interpreted *conflict* in a very narrow manner and decided that statutes only conflict where "compliance with one law involves breach of the other."[7]

Things that are not in written parts of the constitution can move in and out of the constitution over time – A good example of the power of judicial interpretation is the case of *Sparrow* in which the courts had to interpret the meaning and effect of Section 35 of the Constitution Act of 1982, which reads that "existing aboriginal rights . . . are hereby recognised and affirmed."[8] This section is outside the Charter of Rights and Freedoms and so is not governed by the limiting force of Section 1 of the Charter, which states that all the rights and freedoms in the Charter are "subject only to such reasonable limits prescribed by law as can be demonstrably justified in a free and democratic society." Nevertheless, the Supreme Court held that, although the text of Section 35 has no mention of reasonable limits, the federal government has the continuing general power to impose reasonable restrictions on the exercise of any aboriginal rights protected under Section 35. If this is valid interpretation, it is difficult to imagine in what substantive, as opposed to formal, ways an amendment of the constitution would differ from it.

Things that are written in the constitution can be limited and controlled by things that are not written in the constitution – The Canadian constitution is rife with examples of conventional and customary rules (i.e., restricted powers of the Governor-General and terms of exercise of royal assent). While such conventions are seen to be the product of accretion over a period of observant practice, there are instances in which conventions seem to have sprung full-grown into constitutional life. A (in)famous illustration of this is the so-called

---

[7] *Smith v. The Queen*, [1960] SCR 776 at 800. This is the case even if the statutes duplicate each other; see *Multiple Access v. McCutcheon*, [1982] 2 SCR 161.

[8] *R. v. Sparrow*, [1990] 1 SCR 1075.

Patriation Reference.[9] The Supreme Court was asked to determine if there were legal or conventional requirements that the consent of the provinces be obtained before the federal government could seek amendments to the constitution (i.e., a Charter of Rights) that would affect provincial powers. The court held that there was no legal requirement, but that constitutional convention demanded that there be a "substantial degree" or "substantial measure" of provincial consent. In this instance, convention had as much (and more) political bite than legal rule.

Things that are written in the constitution can take on different and occasionally contradictory meanings over time – The history of the interpretation of the "peace, order, and good government power" granted to the federal government is an object lesson in how words remain but meanings change. Apart from the continuing debate over whether the so-called POGG power is a residuary power or whether it includes the whole of the federal power, the extent and scope of this power has taken on different guises as circumstances demand. For instance, it has been used to transfer powers to the federal government over matters of national concern and where there is an emergency, even if such matters would otherwise fall under provincial jurisdiction.[10] The fact that these two doctrines do not sit easily together has not escaped the attention of commentators. Moreover, these doctrines seems to have been fashioned from whole cloth: Another illustration of this phenomenon is the historical tension between the federal government's "trade and commerce" power under Section 91(2) of the Constitution Act and the provinces' "civil rights and property" power under Section 92(13). While the courts have mapped out different spheres of authority in terms of interprovincial and intraprovincial trade,[11] there is still much vagueness and confusion around the details of the doctrine.

Things that are written in the constitution can be circumvented by things that are not written in the constitution – The problem of delegation exemplifies this well. The key issue is whether the federal and provincial governments can agree to swap powers (i.e., can the federal government give the provinces' power to levy indirect taxes, a strictly federal power, in return for the provinces' giving the federal government power to establish a pension scheme, a strictly provincial power?). The Supreme Court of Canada has said that, as there is no express authority in the constitution, it was not allowed because it would

---

[9] *Re Resolution to Amend the Constitution*, supra, note 6. See also Quebec Veto Reference, [1982] 2 SCR 793.

[10] See *R. v. Crown Zellerbach*, [1988] 1 SCR 401; *Anti-Inflation Reference*, [1976] 2 SCR 373; and *R. v. v. Hauser*, [1979] 1 SCR 984.

[11] See *General Motors v. City National Leasing*, [1989] 1 SCR 641.

amount to de facto constitutional amendment. However, the courts did allow the federal government and provinces to delegate powers to administrative bodies established under the authority of the other.[12] In effect, what could not be done by legislative delegation could be achieved by administrative delegation; what could not be done directly was done indirectly. The upshot of allowing delegation is that the federal and provincial governments can agree to circumvent the constitution's written division of powers.

Another example of how the written constitution can be easily end run is the exercise of the federal spending power – are there restraints on how the federal government can distribute its considerable tax revenues? For instance, while the administration of hospitals comes within provincial competence, the federal government has exercised great influence over health care policy by the conditional deployment of federal funds. The debate is whether the federal government can spend only within its designated fields of federal competence or whether it can also fund projects that fall within provincial competence. The prevailing view is that the federal government can indeed fund in provincial areas as it is a choice for any province to accept such funding under the conditions it is granted or not. The Supreme Court of Canada has given tacit approval to such practices.[13]

This list could go on almost indefinitely, but these given samples are sufficient to make my crucial point – that the law often changes in the most abrupt way and with the most unexpected results. Constitutional law is a baffling mishmash of texts, customs, conventions, ideals, and cases that are only given a semblance of order and continuity after the fact. It is more instructive and more convincing to view constitutional law as a historical and political tour de force of the episodic and unpredictable occasions on which judges and jurists contribute to the efforts of Canadians to come to terms with who they are and who they want to be. There is no resolution or finality to that process and there certainly is no gradual getting-better-all-the-time progress. Despite the self-understandings of its judicial and juristic practitioners, constitutional interpretation is a volatile tradition of transformative politics. Indeed, David Strauss captures this phenomenon well when he states that "the forces that bring about constitutional change work their will almost irrespective of whether and how the text of the Constitution is changed" and the "constitutional order would look little different if a

---

[12] See *Nova Scotia Inter-Delegation Case*, [1951] SCR 31 and *PEI Potato Marketing Board v. Willis*, [1952] 2 SCR 392. See also *Brant Dairy v. Milk Commission*, [1973] SCR 131 and *R. v. Furtney*, [1991] 3 SCR 89.

[13] *Re Canada Assistance Plan*, [1991] 2 SCR 525.

formal amendment process did not exist." He ascribes the appreciation that the heart of a constitution is in its almost unhindered judicial interpretation to the finding that "constitutional law is best seen as the result of a complex, evolutionary process, rather than of discrete, self-consciously political acts by a sovereign People."[14] I both agree and disagree wholeheartedly with this assessment. I agree in that it is not so much that the political arena in itself does not matter, but rather that the same ideological forces play themselves out through the courts. However, I disagree in that, if Strauss means that the constitutional law's complex, evolutionary process is gradual and contained, the common law does not change in an incremental and principled way. Common law adjudication is itself a political process, albeit one that is different than the legislative branches of government. It is a work-in-progress affected by and responsive to its social, historical, and political environment. It is to a constitutional example of how that occurs that I now turn; this time I use an American example.

The *Glucksberg* Opening

Faced with a challenge to Washington's legislative prohibition of assisted suicide, the Supreme Court of the United States had to grapple with the due process clause of the Fourteenth Amendment, which declares that states may not "deprive any person of life, liberty or property, without due process of law." The Court decided that the right to die was not presently so fundamental a liberty that it was protected by the due process clause and, therefore, its infringement by government was permissible. Although the Supreme Court was unanimous in its decision, it was divided over the appropriate reasoning for this decision.[15] The case has predictably engendered much debate and disagreement. However, apart from the popular and strictly ethical discussion about the propriety of right-to-die statutes, the *Glucksberg* decision has become the focus of considerable jurisprudential engagement. Although there were six separate judgments, the more expansive judgments of Chief Justice Rehnquist and Justice Souter have commanded the most

---

[14] D. A. Strauss, The Irrelevance of Constitutional Amendments, 114 *Harv. L. Rev.* 1457 at 1458–59, 1505, and 1457 (2001).
[15] *Washington v. Glucksberg*, 521 US 702 (1997). Rehnquist CJ delivered the opinion of the court, in which O'Connor, Scalia, Kennedy, and Thomas JJ joined. O'Connor J filed a concurring opinion, in which Ginsburg and Breyer JJ joined in part. Stevens, Souter, Ginsburg, and Breyer JJ filed concurring opinions. For a good conceptual mapping of the debate, see P. Lewis, Rights Discourse and Assisted Suicide, 27 *Am. J. L. And Med.* 45 (2001).

attention. Each represents a very different approach to due process analysis and, thereby, to the freighted and contested judicial task of charting the connection between legal analysis and ethical or political values in constitutional and common law decision making generally. In short, jurists have critically examined the jurisprudential basis on which the competing judges approach that task and the overall style of adjudicative reasoning.

In speaking for a majority of the Supreme Court in *Glucksberg*, Chief Justice Rehnquist relied on a fairly predicable approach to substantive due process doctrine. While he accepts that the Fourteenth Amendment's protection of liberty is broader than a mere absence of physical restraint, he insists that the limits of such fundamental values must be studiously noted and observed. In order to ensure that there is a requisite degree of objectivity to the recognition of such values, Rehnquist demands that only those values that are deeply rooted in the nation's history and traditions can be accorded constitutional sanction. Accordingly, he holds that, because "for over 700 years, the Anglo-American common-law tradition has punished or otherwise disapproved of both suicide and assisting suicide," there is no legitimate ground on which to recognize a protected right to assisted suicide. Indeed, Rehnquist is so opposed to a balancing of competing interests that he is prepared to concede that there might not be any "principled basis" for defining the actual reach and extent of the fundamental rights that are protected. For him, the vaunted objectivity of the traditional process outweighs any perceived gains to be made by a more nuanced yet less neutral approach to substantive due process. In going out of his way to defend the traditional analysis, the Chief Justice clearly and expressly has the alternative method of Justice Souter in his jurisprudential sights.[16] In contrast, Justice Souter's approach to the substantive due process doctrine is much less historicist and more critical than Rehnquist's. He is not prepared to treat what is historically rooted as being constitutionally decisive. While the embeddedness and longevity of a particular social practice is an important factor in determining its constitutional protection, it is not the exclusive or necessarily decisive one.

Justice Souter offers a plausible telling of the doctrine in which the absolutism of *Dred Scott* and *Lochner* has given way to a more restrained approach that favors legislative intervention and curbs only arbitrary and egregious exercises of that power. For Souter, this entails "the scrutiny of a legislative resolution (perhaps unconscious) of clashing principles, each quite

---

[16] *Glucksberg*, <u>supra</u>, note 15 at 711 and footnote 17, 721 per Rehnquist CJ.

possibly worthy in and of itself, but each to be weighed within the history of our values as a people." Rather than a logical deduction from some textual first premise, Souter treats the doctrine as demanding "a comparison of the relative strengths of opposing claims," which empowers the courts not to "substitute one reasonable resolution of the contending positions for another, but . . . to supplant the balance already struck between the contenders only when it falls outside the realm of the reasonable." The judicial challenge is to avoid "the absolutist failing of many older cases without embracing the opposite pole of equating reasonableness with past practice described at a very specific level." To achieve this, Souter draws on the idea of ordered liberty, which comprises a continuum of rights to be free from "arbitrary impositions and purposeless restraints." As the source for the legitimacy of this balancing approach to substantive due process analysis, Souter points to the celebrated dissent of Justice Harlan in *Poe v. Ullman*, where he states the following:

> Due Process has not been reduced to any formula; its content cannot be determined by reference to any code. The best that can be said is that through the course of this Court's decisions it has represented the balance which our Nation, built upon postulates of respect for the liberty of the individual, has struck between that liberty and the demands of organized society. If the supplying of content to this Constitutional concept has of necessity been a rational process, it certainly has not been one where judges have felt free to roam where unguided speculation might take them. The balance of which I speak is the balance struck by this country, having regard to what history teaches are the traditions from which it developed as well as the traditions from which it broke. That tradition is a living thing. A decision of this Court which radically departs from it could not long survive, while a decision which builds on what has survived is likely to be sound. No formula could serve as a substitute, in this area, for judgment and restraint.[17]

There are many motifs in these famous dicta – no formulaic solutions, the balancing of interests, a rational process, the caution against roaming judges, the lessons of history, the force of tradition, the organic quality of tradition, and restrained judgment – that Souter seeks to draw together into an integrated and dynamic account of what substantive due process analysis demands and has become. However, Souter is much more ambitious in the

---

[17] Id. at 764–65, quoting *Poe v. Ullman*, 367 US 497 at 542 per Harlan J (1961). For an earlier rendition of his "reasoned judgment" line, see *Planned Parenthood v. Casey*, 505 US 833 (1992).

claims that he makes for this style of judicial practice. In stressing that "this approach calls for a court to assess the relative 'weights' or dignities of the contending interests," he underlines the fact that "[this] judicial method is familiar to the common law." This, of course, is not surprising. Indeed, it would be odd if the difference between the style of constitutional and common law adjudication was substantial or striking, as it is exactly the same judges that engage in both. Nevertheless, Souter is quick to point out that there are two important constraints in constitutional matters, particularly when one is undertaking substantive due process review. First, there must be some objective basis to the values protected that goes beyond the "merely personal and private notions" of justice of any particular judge. Second, having identified the existence of fundamental values, one must determine whether "the legislation's justifying principle, critically valued, is so far from being commensurate with the individual interest as to be arbitrarily or pointlessly applied that the statute must give way." In other words, it is not enough to simply locate "a reasonable resolution of contending values that differs from the terms of the legislation under review."[18] Notwithstanding these riders, Souter is clear and open in his belief that substantive due process analysis is simply a particular kind of common law adjudication; the basic components of the common law mind-set are adapted to the specialized demands of the constitutional context.

In undertaking this general adjudicative task, Souter urges an "explicit attention to detail that is no less essential to the intellectual discipline of substantive due process review than an understanding of the basic need to account for the two sides in the controversy and to respect legislation within the zone of reasonableness." Again, drawing on Harlan's dissenting judgment, Souter observes the following:

> Just as results in substantive due process cases are tied to the selections of statements of the competing interests, the acceptability of the results is a function of the good reasons for the selections made. It is here that the value of common-law method becomes apparent, for the usual thinking of the common law is suspicious of the all-or-nothing analysis that tends to produce legal petrification instead of an evolving boundary between the domains of old principles. Common-law method tends to pay respect instead to detail, seeking to understand old principles afresh by new examples and new counterexamples. The "tradition is a living thing," albeit one that moves by moderate steps carefully taken. "The decision of an apparently novel claim must depend on

---

[18] Id. at 767, 767 (quoting Harlan at 544) and 768.

grounds which follow closely on well-accepted principles and criteria. The new decision must take its place in relation to what went before and further [cut] a channel for what is to come." Exact analysis and characterization of any due process claim is critical to the method and to the result.[19]

Having laid out what he believes to be the best and most appropriate approach to substantive due process analysis in particular and common law adjudication in general, Souter turns to the resolution of the concrete dispute before the Supreme Court. In line with his defended approach, he asks whether, as part of the traditionally recognized claims to autonomy in deciding how their bodies and minds should be treated, patients' requests to obtain the services of a physician in committing suicide "is said to enjoy a tradition so strong and so devoid of specifically countervailing state concern that denial of a physician's help in these circumstances is arbitrary when physicians are generally free to advise and aid those who exercise other rights to bodily autonomy." After engaging in a close and contextual survey of the law, practices, and arguments in play, Souter concludes that, although the importance of the individual interests are substantial, "whether that interest might in some circumstances, or at some time, be seen as 'fundamental' to the degree entitled to prevail is not, however, a conclusion that I need draw here, for I am satisfied that the State's interests ... are sufficiently serious to defeat the present claim that its law is arbitrary or purposeless." In reaching this conclusion, Souter accepts the practical difficulties in controlling or limiting the exercise of the alleged right. Indeed, he is very committed to ensuring that the courts do not step on the toes of legislatures who have a much greater claim to the open floor of political dancing and are authorized to take the choreographic lead in deciding the style and direction of political movement. When it comes to recognizing the existence and scope of the unenumerated rights of the due process clause, it will not be arbitrary for the legislature to act when "the facts necessary to resolve the controversy are not readily ascertainable through the judicial process; but they are more readily subject to discovery through legislative fact-finding and experimentation." To answer otherwise "would simply create a constitutional regime too uncertain to bring with it the expectation of finality that is one of this Court's central obligations in making constitutional decisions." Nevertheless, in line with the contextually nuanced imperative of Harlan's

---

[19] Id. at 765, 769–70, and 772. In reaching this decision, Souter seems to follow, but without direct reference, the advice offered by Sunstein on how to decide the issue. C. Sunstein, The Right to Die, 106 *Yale L. J.* 1123 (1997).

favored methodology, Souter concludes that "I do not decide for all time that respondents' claim should not be recognized; I acknowledge the legislative institutional competence as the better one to deal with that claim at this time."[20]

In the rush to jurisprudential judgment, Soapy Sam Dworkin and Bulldog Posner have, as expected, played the leading roles. Predictably, Dworkin chastised the court for its failure to fully understand the philosophical dimension of adjudication and the ethical responsibilities of judges in interpreting the Constitution. Having joined with other leading liberal philosophers in submitting an amicus brief in support of the respondents, Dworkin condemned the decision not simply because it found resoundingly against his particular moral views on assisted suicide, but because the judges did not properly appreciate their sophisticated task as constitutional interpreters. Dworkin has little good to say about Rehnquist, Scalia, and Thomas, whose historicist approach (i.e., insisting that what has been accepted as politically fundamental is what is legally fundamental) ignores the philosophical element of constitutional adjudication, thereby reducing it to a conservative enterprise in empirical inquiry. In contrast, although Souter's judgment is "reasonable in principle,"[21] Dworkin remains unconvinced that the facts are so sufficiently in dispute as to warrant a hands-off approach by the courts. Taking the *Glucksberg* bait, Posner chastises Dworkin for his mistaken views on both how the right-to-die claims should be resolved and what valid constitutional adjudication should comprise. He is adamant that the Supreme Court is correct to stay out of the moral debate around the right-to-die issue and to prefer the solid earth of policy analysis to the soggy turf of moral philosophy. In his view, there was no obviously shared or objective moral resolution available; democracy is at work and seemingly proceeding

[20] Id. at 774, 782, 786–87, 788–89, and 789. Although Souter took a similar pragmatic approach to substantive due process analysis in his majority opinion in *County of Sacramento v. Lewis*, 523 US 833 (1998), it was chastised by Scalia J for being overly subjective and having been rejected by the Court in *Glucksberg*. See *Lewis*, 523 US at 860–61 (1998) per Scalia J.

[21] See R. Dworkin, Assisted Suicide: What the Court Really Said, 44 *N.Y. Rev Books* 42 (Sept. 25, 1997) and R. Dworkin, Darwin's New Bulldog, 111 Harv. L. Rev. 1718 (1998). For the amicus brief, see R. Dworkin, The Philosophers' Brief, *N.Y. Rev. of Books* 41–47 (March 27, 1997) and R. Dworkin et al., The Fifth Annual Fritz B. Burns Lecture: Euthanasia, Morality, and the Law, 30 *Loy. L. A. L. Rev.* 1465 (1997). With characteristic ingenuity, Dworkin refused to accept that all was lost. Arguing that five of the six justices who wrote opinions did not reject his ethical stance out of hand, he hoped that the Court might later come to its constitutional senses and validate a constitutional right to die. See R. Dworkin, Reply, 29 *Ariz. St. L. J.* 431 (1997) and Assisted Suicide and Euthanasia: An Exchange Between Yale Kamisar and Ronald Dworkin, 44 *N.Y. Rev Books* 68–70 (Nov. 6, 1997).

satisfactorily without judicial interference. Further, he notes that the issue demands very complex rules of implementation that courts are ill-equipped to draft. For Posner, therefore, *Glucksberg* is a prime example of the benefits and legitimacy of construing constitutional adjudication as a practical task of institutional instrumentalities, which most judges can do, as opposed to an abstruse exercise in philosophical reflection, which most judges cannot.[22]

While the spat between Dworkin and Posner goes to the contemporary heart of much jurisprudential debate, there is another take on the *Glucksberg* decision that is worthy of serious consideration. It is Mootz's suggestion that Justice Souter's judgment ought to be celebrated as a paradigm example of what it means to take a sophisticated and Gadamerian-inspired approach to the judicial task: "Souter's opinion persuasively describes the adjudication of fundamental rights as a hermeneutical–rhetorical project in terms that Gadamer . . . would endorse, even though Souter articulates his reasoning in the idiom of contemporary constitutional discourse." Moreover, Mootz maintains that Souter's legal pragmatics taps into the natural law tradition, albeit in a nontraditional and new form. At the heart of Souter's approach is alleged to be not only the outright denial of adjudication as a technical and pseudoscientific exercise in textual exegesis, but an enthusiastic embrace of the hermeneutical idea. Mootz rephrases Souter such that he is seen to assert that adjudication involves immersion in an organic tradition of reasoned judgment and principled argumentation in which a balanced mediation of past commitments and present concerns is negotiated. Inspired by the work of Lon Fuller and Lloyd Weinreb, Mootz puts together a plausible case for his informed assessment that "Souter's practice affirms that rhetorical knowledge is possible and that human understanding is dialogical" and that "this mode of conversational understanding acknowledges the natural law groundings of legal practice while simultaneously rendering the law current by means of application and judgment."[23] Accordingly, Justice Souter's opinion warrants a close and critical reappraisal in light of these ambitious claims.

---

[22] R. Posner, *The Problematics of Moral and Legal Theory* 133 and 227 (1999). For challenge to Posner's account of *Glucksberg*, see J. Mikhail, Law, Science, and Morality: A Review of Richard Posner's *The Problematics of Moral and Legal Theory*, 54 *Stan. L. Rev.* 1057 at 1118–26 (2002). See generally Symposium on Physician-Assisted Suicide, 109 *Ethics* 497 (1999).

[23] J. Mootz, Law in Flux: Philosophical Hermeneutics, Legal Argumentation and the Natural Law Tradition, 11 *Yale J. of Law & Human.* 311 at 326, 377, and 381 (1999). For a further development of this theme and response to my critical approach, see J. Mootz, Nietzschean Critique and Philosophical Hermeneutics, 20 *Cardozo L. Rev.* 101 (2003).

Nevertheless, although Souter's judgment and its thoughtful reflection on adjudicative legitimacy are a vast improvement on the other American judicial approaches on offer, I do not believe that it can bear the jurisprudential weight that hermeneutical jurists like Mootz wish to place on it. As with my treatment of Gadamer and legal hermeneutics generally, I intend to take the basic claims that Souter makes and, rather than hedge on their radical import as Gadamer, Mootz, and Souter do, push through on them in an uncompromising manner. When this is done, they each appear to be quite conservative in that they are unwilling to take seriously the radical implications of their own views. However, my quarrel with Souter and Mootz is less with how they depict the operation of the common law than with the claims that they make for this account. Indeed, while I agree in large part with their description of the common law method, I disagree that this hermeneutical method can live up to the traditional expectations that are placed upon it. Rather, it fails to deliver on the formalist promise that common law adjudication is a bounded and objective process that can give rise to relatively determinate and predictable resolutions of disputed controversies. In short, it cannot distinguish legal decision making from overtly political or ideological disputation. Consequently, rather than offer a compelling illustration of Gadamerian-inspired legal argumentation, Souter's judgment actually gives credence to the alternative hermeneutical account of the common law that I am proposing: There is no method that can absolve people from the responsibility and challenge of constantly arguing and rearguing what should and should not be done in particular contexts at particular times, and there is no escaping politics to a technical or sanitized conversation in which the basic struggle over whose interests count and what they count for can be sidestepped. Of course, such a debate will itself be ungrounded and political; there is no way to talk about politics that is not itself political. Politics, like the law in which it plays itself out, is a work-in-progress.

The Souter Move

In many ways, Souter's judgment is a jurisprudential tour de force; it takes the opportunity presented by the particular dispute to offer a reflective and expansive general justification of adjudicative responsibilities in a constitutional democracy. In this way, Souter attempts to provide little less than a comprehensive theory of common law decision making that, in its emphasis on attention to detail, historical erudition, conceptual flexibility, and critical insight, is as ambitious as it is sophisticated. Although Justice Souter might never have heard of, let alone read, Gadamer, his opinion in *Glucksberg* is seen to be not only the best example of such a pragmatic approach to law and adjudication but also a passable defense of the propriety of so proceeding. Like Moliere's Monsieur Jourdain, he might be forgiven for exclaiming, "Par ma foi! Il y a plus quarante ans que je dis de Gadamer sans que j'en susse rien."[24] As his judgment is not for the jurisprudentially timid at heart, it is not surprising that it should have received such critical attention and lively debate. While there is much to comment on in Souter's judgment and its general jurisprudential reception, I restrict my response to the effort to treat it as an exemplary illustration of philosophical practice in the mode of Gadamerian hermeneutics. That having been said, such a response will touch on a wide range of theoretical issues and practical controversies. Accordingly, as part of that critique, I utilize Souter's sophisticated opinion as a convenient route into three of the central problems that define and dog contemporary jurisprudence – first, that there is some objective basis to the protected values and the methods used to ascertain them that goes beyond the "merely personal and private notions" of justice of any particular judge; second, that it is possible for judges to identify "arbitrary impositions and purposeless restraints" by legislative bodies in a strictly legal as opposed to openly political way; and, third, that there exist recognizable traditions in law that allow judges to engage with contested matters of social, legal, and judicial practices in a determinate and defensible way. Or, to put it more bluntly, that there is a practicable way of resisting the critical claim that 'law is politics'.

My quarrel with Souter, Mootz, and, to a lesser extent, Gadamer is not so much with how they depict the prosaic operation of the common law but more with the extravagant claims that they make for their account. Indeed, while I agree in large part with their pragmatic description of common law adjudication, I disagree that this hermeneutical method can live up to the traditional expectations that are placed on it; it fails to deliver on the formalist promise that common law adjudication is a bounded and objective process. It cannot give rise to relatively determinate and predictable resolutions of disputed controversies in a way that distinguishes legal decision making from overtly political or ideological disputation. Accordingly, having offered an alternative and critical hermeneutical account of the common law, it is incumbent on me to make good on my claim that 'law is politics'. I need to show that, far from being a check on or remove from

---

[24] Moliere, *Le Bourgeois Gentilhomme* II, iv (1670).

political debate, constitutional adjudication is another site, albeit stylized and technical, for political confrontation in which 'anything might go'. In short, I must demonstrate that Justice Souter's judgment implodes from the hermeneutical force of his own arguments. Whatever the claims that he or his jurisprudential apologists make for it, his judgment actually confirms rather than refutes that there is no method that can absolve judges or anyone else from the responsibility and challenge of constantly arguing and rearguing what should and should not be done in particular contexts at particular times. As Souter himself said in an earlier judgment, "even when jurists reason from shared premises, some disagreement is inevitable . . . [but] that is to be expected in the application of any legal standard which must accommodate life's complexity."[25] Moreover, Souter's *Glucksberg* judgment corroborates rather than confutes that there is no escaping from politics, especially through a resort to reasoned judgment and tradition, to a technical or sanitized conversation in which the basic struggle over whose interests count and what they count for can be sidestepped. Read with a critical eye, the judgment and its ensuing juristic reception make the critical case that 'law is politics' in that adjudication is only bounded and objective insofar as its bounds and values are themselves thoroughly political and revisable.

It will be remembered that, in determining the existence and scope of any constitutionally protected right to die, Souter considered that his judicial task is not to substitute the court's view of what is or is not the most reasonable balance of competing interests, but to check whether the legislative view "falls outside the realm of the reasonable" and imposes "arbitrary impositions and purposeless restraints." To do this, judges must be engage in "reasoned judgment" that will ensure that they do not indulge the "merely personal and private notions" of justice of any particular judge. This reasoned judgment will eschew all-or-nothing analysis in terms of either textual or extratextual absolutes. Instead, operating at "the proper level of generality" and "paying respect . . . to detail," judges must restrict those values deserving

---

[25] *Casey*, supra, note 17 at 878. It is no part of my critique whether Souter got it right or wrong on the particular facts. Any resolution of *Glucksberg* and the physician-assisted right to die is a political and contested matter, not a neutral or objective one: The debate is morally contested and so can be temporarily clarified but never conclusively settled. However, for the record, I should state that my *present* position is that the recognition of such a right, suitably narrowed and regulated, is warranted. While I recognize that there is a pertinent difference between killing and failing to save, I agree with Oscar Wilde – "Yet each man kills the thing he loves/ By each let this be heard,/ Some do it with a bitter look,/ Some with a flattering word./ The coward does it with a kiss,/ The brave man with a sword!" *The Ballad of Reading Goal I*, vii (1898).

constitutional protection only to "those exemplified by 'the traditions from which [the Nation] developed,' or revealed by contrast with 'the traditions from which it broke.'" Consequently, after such an "exact analysis," Justice Souter reached the conclusion that, while "the importance of the individual interest here . . . cannot be gainsaid [and] . . . whether that interest might in some circumstances, or at some time, be seen as 'fundamental' . . . , I am satisfied that the State's interests . . . are sufficiently serious to defeat the present claim that its law is arbitrary or purposeless." Although Souter accepted that there is a tradition of extending patients' rights to bodily integrity and to medical care, he maintained that the state's slippery slope concern "is fairly made out here . . . because there is a plausible case that the right claimed would not be readily containable by reference to facts about the mind that are matters of difficult judgment, or by gatekeepers who are subject to temptation, noble or not."[26]

There is no doubt that Souter's judgment is sophisticated and plausible. It offers a reasoned and reasonable intervention in a controversial debate. Indeed, there is much in Souter's excursus on common law method that emphasizes the Gadamerian themes of historical context, performative dynamism, and organic tradition; "just as results in substantive due process cases are tied to the selections of statements of the competing interests, the acceptability of the results is a function of the good reasons for the selections made." Indeed, there are three particular traditions – social, legal, and judicial – that are in play in *Glucksberg* and that Souter maintains are receptive to the hermeneutical kind of reasoned judgment that he recommends. However, there are several argumentative maneuvers or rhetorical ruses that rob the judgment of the hermeneutical cogency that it claims and craves. In the Gadamerianesque prose adopted by Souter, "if the acceptability of the result is a function of the good reasons given," then the result is not acceptable because the supporting reasons are wanting and not persuasive. Despite the Gadamerian trappings, there is still the underlying commitment to the idea that adjudication is a largely technical endeavor that demands rigorous discipline, that lends itself to exact analysis, that is amenable to close criticism, and that repays attention to detail, all of which can be achieved in a politically neutral manner. Contrary to Souter's (and Mootz's, Gadamer's, and most other traditional jurists') fervent hope, it simply is not possible to perform this judicial task in a way that makes the legal outcome completely independent of the "merely personal and private

---

[26] *Glucksberg*, supra, note 15 at 782 and 785 (quoting *Poe*, supra, note 15 at 542 per Harlan J).
See generally L. Tribe and M. Dorf, *On Reading the Constitution* 65–120 (1991).

notions"[27] of justice of any particular judge. Such notions can be concealed or overlooked, but they cannot be excluded or eliminated. A closer reading and parsing of Souter's arguments make such a critical evaluation both clearer and more convincing.

The first traditions that Justice Souter looks to are those social practices that surround and inform the particular right claimed. He examines the constitutional, legal, and social history of suicide and physician assistance to the dying. However, as Souter recognizes, there is not only no one tradition but the several existing traditions are indeterminate in scope and often compete with each other. This will mean that it is crucial to identify a device by which to determine "the proper level of generality" at which these competing traditions are to be characterized so as to ascertain which is entitled to constitutional protection. This, of course, is where reasoned judgment enters the doctrinal picture: "selecting among such competing characterizations demands reasoned judgment about which broader principle, as exemplified in the concrete privileges and prohibitions embodied in our legal tradition, best fits the particular claim asserted in a particular case." To do this with "exactitude," Souter recommends a number of requirements, such "as applying concepts of normal critical reasoning, as pointing to the need to attend to the levels of generality at which countervailing interests are stated, or as examining the concrete application of principles for fitness with their own ostensible justifications." Mindful that all of this has to be done in an objective and neutral manner without illicit reliance on the merely personal and private notions of justice of any particular judge, Souter has sent judges on a sleeveless errand. There is no way that they can complete such an analysis as a purely technical or strictly legal matter. Once it is accepted that reliance on dominant traditions without more is unjustified, Souter is into the dangerous political game of deciding which traditions, to paraphrase Justice Harlan, are those "from which the country should develop" and those "from which the country should break." Because "tradition is a living thing," it is the self-assumed responsibility of judges to decide which parts of the tradition should die in order for the tradition to thrive.[28] This is a profoundly political task. It becomes more so and not less so, when it is allegedly done by deference to existing traditions.

[27] Id. at 770 and 767. I am not suggesting that the only choice is between "merely personal and private notions" of justice and robustly objective and public notions. See supra, chaps. 3 and 4. My purpose is to demonstrate that there is no objective method available to judges by which they can finesse the intrusion of political prejudices. It is not the measuring itself but the meter used with which I take issue.

[28] Id. at 772, 771 footnote 11, 773, 765, 767.

Although the appeal to tradition is only meaningful if that tradition is sufficiently determinate and discrete, history shows that traditions are notoriously imprecise and that they are infuriatingly difficult to pin down. Like anything and everything else, traditions are not so much discovered as constructed in the act of following them. Even when pitched at a classificatory level of great specificity, tradition does not speak for itself and cannot excuse judges from making critical and contestable choices. This seems to suggest that tradition is one factor in the doctrinal decision of whether to recognize certain liberties as sufficiently fundamental, but it is not the only, and certainly not the decisive, criterion. Indeed, although the right claimed in *Glucksberg* is quite discrete as it involves a limited group (i.e., doctors) in limited circumstances (i.e., dying and suffering patients), it is next to impossible to identify a physician-assisted right-to-die tradition in Anglo-American law and society. Rehnquist surely has the best of this argument in *Glucksberg*. While there are incipient signs that such a tradition might be taking shape (e.g., there has been a general decriminalization of suicide), the claim that such a tradition has moved beyond some initial threshold of viability would mean that almost any practice could claim to be a tradition. This would result in almost anything claiming to be worthy of at least being taken seriously in constitutional discourse, even if not ultimately accepted as a fundamental value. Moreover, if tradition is the decisive test of whether something is a fundamental interest or not, many of the leading cases in the substantive due process tradition would not cut the constitutional mustard. The most spectacular example of this is *Roe*. There was no obvious tradition in Anglo-American legal tradition of such a right being recognized. If anything, the denial of such a right was more an integral part of any extant tradition.[29]

Souter's efforts to steer clear of this political terrain are based on the possibility that judges can restrict themselves to policing the boundaries of reasonableness. Rather than argue over whether one approach is more or less reasonable than another, judges can confine their analysis to whether the legislative intervention "falls outside the realm of the reasonable" and whether its "justifying principle, critically valued, is so far from being commensurate with the individual interest as to be arbitrarily or pointlessly applied."[30] However, this assumes that what is and is not arbitrary and

---

[29] See *Roe v. Wade*, 410 US 113 at 130–41 (1973). Other examples include a right to contraceptives outside of marriage, see *Carey v. Population Servs. Int'l*, 431 US 678 (1977) and *Eisenstadt v. Baird*, 405 US 438 (1972), and any general right to marry, see *Loving v. Virginia*, 388 US 1 (1967) and *Zablocki v. Redhail*, 434 US 374 (1978). See generally C. Sunstein, Against Tradition, 13 *Soc. Phil. & Policy* 207 (1996).

[30] *Glucksberg*, supra, note 15 at 764 and 768.

purposeless is seen to reside outside the historical flow of social tradition and, therefore, outside politics. This smacks of the most ahistorical and inorganic approach to tradition. The maneuver only works if the arbitrary and the purposeless are simply givens that can be discovered, not chosen – yet the history of America's social traditions suggests that such assumptions are invalid. There is nothing arbitrary about, for example, bigotry. While racist or sexist prejudice might be unreasonable, it is not arbitrary or purposeless; bigots have as many reasons for their beliefs and actions as liberals. The identity of the arbitrary and purposeless has to be argued for, as it is inside and not outside the political forces that it is meant to regulate and evaluate. The fact that there might be almost complete agreement on whether certain values or activities are outside the pale of reasonableness does not make such a conclusion any less political. It is not about whether there are reasons; there always are. It is about whether those reasons are considered good or bad ones. After all, racism and sexism of the most rampant kind were once, as Souter would agree, so broadly accepted and deeply rooted that they brooked little challenge, at least among those with political power and franchise. In the world of the past, it would have been the antiracist or the feminist who would have been arbitrary and purposeless.

Furthermore, if a reliance on social tradition, albeit in a modified and sensitive manner, is used to identify constitutional rights, it will be those minorities who most need protection against majority views that will be denied constitutional protection. Unless tradition is expanded to include whatever people have done whether in support or opposition to traditional values, constitutional protection will only extend to those whose values and activities conform with the tradition and who are less likely to require such protection. Once tradition is interpreted so broadly and indiscriminately, its legal use becomes entirely vacuous because there is no legal test, which is not itself political, to organize social practices into acceptable and objectionable traditions. Mindful that the level of generality is so vague and so variable, it is possible to use tradition to support all kinds of competing positions.[31] After all, it was not so long ago that the use of racial discrimination was 'deeply rooted' in America's constitutional and demographic history. More recently, the Supreme Court has accepted that homophobia, while again 'deeply rooted' in the nation's constitutional and demographic history, is a tradition from which the courts should break rather than on which they

---

[31] For a general critique of using tradition as any kind of foundation, see J. H. Ely, *Democracy and Distrust: A Theory of Judicial Review* 60–63 (1980) and R. Cover, Nomos and Narrative – Supreme Court Foreword, 97 *Harv. L. Rev.* 4 (1983).

should build. Mindful that it depends on the level of generality at which such so-called tradition analysis is plausibly made, it is not exactly a stretch to treat private homosexual relations as falling within the established intimacy and privacy concepts of constitutional liberty.[32] What determines the proper level of generality remains as elusive and as crucial as it has always been. There is no proper level of generality without some initial attachment to a preexisting commitment to what liberty might entail. Such a question goes to the very heart of politics, not law – or, as I have sought to emphasize, 'law is politics' because the heart and soul of law *is* politics.

A Traditional Stance

Moving on from social tradition, one can apply a similar kind of critique to reliance on legal tradition. Indeed, the effort to rely on a fixed or determinate tradition of substantive legal doctrine is as weak and unsuccessful as the judicial effort to utilize social tradition to ground constitutional interpretation.[33] Both traditions are so numerous and imprecise that they can justify almost any reading. Indeed, this resort to tradition tends more to reinforce than resolve the problem because it is difficult to ascertain what the controlling tradition would be, constitutional or social, over and above a particular judge's honest and evaluative conviction about what it should be. Souter only grounds his decision by building a foundation for it and, once history moves, that ground will itself be rendered unstable and disclosed as only the function of Souter's contingent and personal commitments, not its grounding. He fails to grasp that legal tradition is not simply a process that is to be known and thereby governed. It is part of an active engagement in which "tradition is a genuine partner in dialogue" with its judicial interlocutors and, in engaging in that dialogue, both the tradition and the interlocutor are "transformed into a communion in which [they] do not remain what [they] were."[34] I want to add that that "communion" is itself temporary, provisional, and contingent. It is a work-in-progress that stands inside, not outside, the matrix of ideological forces that drive the historical

---

[32] See *Lawrence v. Texas* 123 S. Ct. 2472 (2003) and infra, chap. 9. The writing was already on the doctrinal wall for *Bowers v. Hardwick*, 478 US 186 (1986) in *Romer v. Evans*, 517 US 620 (1996). On racial discrimination, see *Regents of the University of California v. Bakke*, 438 US 265 at 291 per Powell J. (1978).

[33] See, for example, *Moore v. City of East Cleveland*, 431 US 494 at 513 (1977) and *Michael H. v. Gerald D.*, 491 US 11 (1989).

[34] H.-G. Gadamer, *Truth and Method* 358 and 379 (J. Weinsheimer and D. Marshall trans. 2nd ed. 1989).

process of rhetorical tradition. As Gadamer reminds us (even if he often forgets it himself), "from the hermeneutical standpoint, rightly understood, it is absolutely absurd to regard the concrete factors of work and politics as outside the scope of hermeneutics."[35]

When it comes to legal traditions, it has to be remembered that, as well as being multiple and fractured, they are capable of being abandoned when circumstances demand. Although courts are understandably reluctant to break from a long-standing legal tradition, they are not only prepared to do so but place an obligation on themselves to so act at times. For instance, in *Planned Parenthood v. Casey*, the Supreme Court divided over whether *Roe* should be overruled. Speaking jointly for the Court, with Justices O'Connor and Kennedy, Justice Souter stated that there are moments when the Court best fulfills its constitutional duty by repudiating earlier lines of cases: "in constitutional adjudication as elsewhere in life, changed circumstances may impose new obligations, and the thoughtful part of the Nation could accept each decision to overrule a prior case as a response to the Court's constitutional duty." According to Souter, this should occur when the Court would have to pay a "terrible price" for failure to act, as was the case in both *West Coast Hotel* and *Brown*. However, cautioning that "each generation must learn anew that the Constitution's written terms embody ideas and aspirations that must survive more ages than one," he maintained that *Roe* not only did not warrant overruling, but that its repudiation "would seriously weaken the Court's capacity to exercise the judicial power and to function as the Supreme Court of a Nation dedicated to the rule of law."[36] In short, if the stakes are high enough, the fallout sufficiently severe, and the judges are so disposed, the breaking with established constitutional tradition will occur. This is exactly what the minority proposed to do. It was not that Justice Souter and his colleagues thought that such a course of action was entirely illegitimate, simply that *Casey* was not the appropriate occasion. It was a ideological call, not a legal one, about social circumstances and political climate.

If this general critique is pertinent for social and legal traditions, it is doubly applicable for the other judicial tradition that is in play. Beginning with the decision in *Glucksberg* itself, a cursory familiarity with substantive due process doctrine and constitutional law in general easily confirms that

---

[35] H.-G. Gadamer, *Philosophical Hermeneutics* 90 (D. Linge ed. and trans. 1976).

[36] *Casey*, supra, note 17 at 864, 865, and 901. See *West Coast Hotel Co. v. Parrish*, 300 US 379 (1937) (overruling the economic liberty doctrine) and *Brown v. Board of Education*, 347 US 483 (1954) (overruling the separate-but-equal doctrine).

there is no one tradition of judicial justification. Whatever the topic on which they join issue, the judgments of the Supreme Court (and all other inferior courts) are always engaged in a concerted effort to legitimate their decisions by virtue of the method adopted. In Souter's terms, they realize that "the acceptability of the results is a function of the good reasons given." Nevertheless, what amounts to reasons, let alone good ones, is as divided as almost any other item on the constitutional agenda. Sometimes, the disagreement remains muffled and marginal; at other times, it becomes voluble and central. Indeed, much of the disagreement between Souter and Rehnquist is framed in terms of their respective approaches to the problem of determining whose interests are to receive constitutional protection. Nevertheless, although the general formal methodology adopted will lean toward a particular substantive preference, it will not be decisive. To believe otherwise would be to disregard entirely Gadamer's primary insight that there is no necessary connection between truths and methods; whether one is an originalist, a textualist, an interpretivist, or any other stripe of constitutional jurist will not of itself determine the result reached. While the adoption of a specific interpretive approach on a specific occasion will make certain outcomes more likely and more justifiable than others, it is the substantive political prejudices or, as Souter has it, the merely personal and private notions of justice of any particular judge, that begins and ends the process.

At the end of the day, it seems apparent that Souter was not sufficiently enamored of the claimed physician-assisted right to die as to warrant its recognition. However, this was not because it failed the tradition test but because it was not fundamental in Souter's scheme of justice. If he had wanted to recognize such a right, there were ample rhetorical resources for him to draw on in fashioning a hermeneutically adequate argument. However, as with the decision he actually made, the "acceptability of the result will be a function of the good reasons given" and, without some account of the particular prejudices that motivate and constitute him, those reasons are lacking. As Gadamer himself noted, "there is undoubtedly no understanding that is free of all prejudices." Gadamer insisted that a large part of the hermeneutical performance entailed a sustained effort to "distinguish the true prejudices, by which we understand, from the false ones, by which we misunderstand," even if this cannot be done outside the very historical (and, therefore, political) process at which efforts are being made to understand. Souter seems not to take seriously the fact that any method, including his proffered reasoned judgment, will retain some element of prejudice. For Souter, it is the merely personal and private notions of justice of any particular judge or what I call simply political commitments. As Gadamer warned, unless there is a constant struggle to identify rather than to ignore those prejudices, interpretation will become enslaved to "the tyranny of hidden prejudices that makes us deaf to what speaks to us in the tradition."[37] It is the act of hiding those prejudices that is the problem, not the acknowledgment of their existence: Interpretation is part of, not apart from, political commitments. The refusal to recognize the importance of those political commitments mean that tradition loses its vital quality as "a living thing" or, as I put it, a work-in-progress. While Souter, Mootz, and others are content to leave the sources and direction of its development to some almost mystical historical *volkgeist*, I prefer to see it for what it is – a heuristic device that does the bidding, no matter how tentative and provisional, of its social artisans and judicial arbiters.

Viewed in this light, Justice Souter's judgement in *Glucksberg* is not the masterful piece of hermeneutical artistry that he wants it to be or his jurisprudential admirers wish it to be; the reasons given for the result are not good enough to warrant its acceptability. If Mootz's suggestion that "Souter's opinion persuasively describes the adjudication of fundamental rights as a hermeneutical–rhetorical project in terms that Gadamer . . . would endorse"[38] is right, then Gadamer's hermeneutical–rhetorical project is seriously deficient and in need of substantial reformulation. That is exactly what I have recommended. It is only on a more critical and radical reading of Gadamer that it is possible to provide a compelling account of common law adjudication. While there is some objective basis to the protected values and the rhetorical methods used to develop doctrine and to decide cases, there is none that stands entirely apart from the 'merely personal and private notions' of justice of any particular judge. There is a constant toing and froing between the objective and the personal and between the public and the private that defines and energizes legal and judicial traditions. Understood in this way as works-in-progress, there do not exist recognizable traditions in law that allow judges to engage with contested matters of social practices in an objectively determinate and neutrally defensible way because those traditions are too much part of the very politics that they are claimed to bypass or obviate.

To rework Justice Souter's chosen Gadamerianesque line that 'the acceptability of the results is a function of the good reasons given', it is that the goodness of the reasons (i.e., their rhetorical effectiveness) and the

---

[37] H.-G. Gadamer, supra, note 34 at 490, 270, and 298–99 (emphasis in original).

[38] J. Mootz, supra, note 23 at 326.

acceptability of the results (i.e., their political resonance) interact and function together. What counts as good reasons is not separate from the political context in which they arise and into which they intervene. In the particular debate at hand in *Glucksberg*, the quality and ferocity of the political forces at work is much more muted, although not absent, than in other contested areas of constitutional controversy, such as abortion and homosexuality. Like all the related questions of death and dying, assisted suicide provokes an endless debate. It is not unreasonable to assert that, while medical technology has done much to improve health and combat suffering, it has also created entirely new situations that have so affected humankind that it has changed the world. In such a society, the power to define and control this continuing social revolution is inevitably political. In the same way that philosophy has a history and, therefore, a politics, so moral philosophizing about life and death is embedded within certain historical protocols of professional and technological power. Medical practice and the health industry begin to construct and validate the rationality by which its problems and their solutions are resolved. As the pace of medical innovation ever quickens, anxiety has become so pervasive and profound that there has come to exist "a state of epistemological turbulence . . . [in which] rather than studying social phenomena as if they were natural phenomena, scientists now study natural phenomena as if they were social phenomena."[39] Against this chilling backdrop, it is naive at best for Souter to maintain that the constitutional dimension of these matters can be settled in an exclusively technical and legal manner that obviates or sidesteps reference to these deeper and more tumultuous debates. Although Justice Souter is not short of company in this conceit, he is no less culpable for his presumption. Reason is as disciplined as disciplining in its interaction with the sociopolitics of bioethics and health care.

A French Connection

Perhaps more than most, Canada is a country that has a continuing debate about its constitutional arrangements. This debate covers not only the legal structure of such arrangements but also the process by which such a structure

---

[39] B. De Sousa Santos, *Toward a New Common Sense: Law, Science and Politics in the Paradigmatic Transition* 34 (1995). For a broader assessment of this trend, see U. Beck, *The Risk Society: Toward a New Modernity* 204 (1992) and I. Illich, *Limits to Medicine: Medical Nemesis: The Expropriation of Health* (1976). For reflection on the consequences of *Glucksberg* for medical practitioners, see P. King, Washington v. Glucksberg: Influence of the Court in Care of the Terminally Ill and Physician Assisted Suicide, 15 *J. L. & Health* 271 (2001).

can connect to the political debate for its alteration. Although this leads to more than its fair share of national angst, Canada has at least been obliged to attend to the legitimacy and substance of the basic building blocks in its constitutional toolkit. Of course, at the heart of this contemporary debate is the persistent problem of French-speaking Quebec's continued relationship with the rest of Canada. This takes many different shapes and forms, but the pressing issue is under what conditions, if any, can Quebec determine its own constitutional and political fate. This brings to the fore a whole host of difficult and enduring concepts and practices – democracy, sovereignty, self-determination, federalism, and, of course, the Rule of Law. Few constitutional challenges call so acutely into question the whole issue of what constitutions are, where they are to be found, and how they are to be given meaning. A few years ago, the Supreme Court of Canada was pushed reluctantly into the breach and required to provide its legal judgment on whether and under what circumstances Quebec might be able to secede unilaterally from Canada. The decision of the Supreme Court is an object lesson in the dilemmas that confront any theoretical efforts to give meaningful and legitimate practical content to constitutional law in a modern democracy. The fact is that the Supreme Court offered a more sophisticated account of the problem and its possible solutions than much of the then-existing jurisprudential reflection.

The main question to be answered was, under the Constitution of Canada, can the National Assembly, legislature, or government of Quebec effect the secession of Quebec from Canada unilaterally? The Supreme Court decided that it could not. Any political decision to secede is constrained by and must be implemented in accordance with existing constitutional commitments. However, in a subtle analysis of the relation between democracy and the Rule of Law, it also held that, if there was a clear democratic vote in favor of secession, the rest of Canada would be obliged to negotiate with Quebec over the terms of its withdrawal from the Canadian confederation. Balancing constitutional rights and obligations as well as legal structures and political initiatives, the Supreme Court sought to clarify the delicate interplay between law and politics in a democracy and its own role in that dynamic confrontation. For instance, it decided that, whereas the legal order of the constitution prevented unilateral acts and required collective action, what constitutes a clear democratic vote and legitimate negotiations was a political matter that fell outside the legal mandate of the courts. As a unanimous Supreme Court concluded, "the task of the Court has been to clarify the legal framework within which political decisions are to be taken 'under the Constitution' and not to usurp the prerogatives of the political forces that operate within that framework."[40] In reaching its specific decision and justifying it generally, the Supreme Court's judgment resonates strongly with the themes of my critical perspective. In examining the importance and limits of democratic process, the nature and status of the Rule of Law, and the relationship and balance between the two, the Supreme Court adopted a jurisprudential modus operandi that reflected, even if it did not explicitly embrace, the kind of 'work-in-progress' dynamic approach to common law adjudication that I have been describing.

Recognizing that the written constitutional rules must be interpreted in light of the underlying unwritten principles that have been developed over time, the Supreme Court took the view that any particular ruling must incorporate both the documentarian and doctrinalist sources of constitutional law. The enacted text is to be understood against the foundational principles of democracy, federalism, the Rule of Law, and respect for minority rights. Constitutional texts are primary, but they do not exhaust the constitution and there is "an historical lineage" whose underlying principles "inform and sustain the constitutional text." One of the essential interpretive considerations is the principle of democracy. However, the Supreme Court realizes that the meaning and demands of that principle are far from self-evident or universally accepted. While Anglo-Canadian constitutional history has tended to equate this with majority rule, democracy consists of much more. It is not simply concerned with the process of government: There is a substantive dimension that cannot be overlooked. According to the Supreme Court, these substantive goals include "to name but a few, respect for the inherent dignity of the human person, commitment to social justice and equality, accommodation of a wide variety of beliefs, respect for cultural and group identity, and faith in social and political institutions which enhance the participation of individuals and groups in society." However, and of vital importance to a critic like me, the Supreme Court concedes that what those values are, how they can be defined, and how they interact is itself never fixed but is part of the continuing debate over what democratic commitment entails: "a democratic system of government is committed to considering dissenting voices and seeking to acknowledge and address those voices in the laws by which all in the community must live."[41]

In adopting such an approach, the Supreme Court seems to have made a giant leap beyond many of its juristic counterparts. Its judges recognize that constitutional law is fluid and evanescent, not fixed and unmoving.

[40] *Re Quebec Secession Reference*, [1998] 2 SCR 217 at 294.
[41] Id. at 257.

This broader and more nuanced understanding of democracy leads to an obvious difficulty. The two fundamental principles to which constitutional democracy is committed (i.e., majoritarian process and substantive justice) are, at worst, incompatible and, at best, in the most severe tension. According to one principle, the will of the citizens as expressed through the available political procedures should govern and any limits on this exercise of popular power are unjustifiable. However, this principle competes with another equally important principle. This holds that the majority cannot do whatever it likes in the name of democracy; there are certain outcomes that cannot be tolerated in a society that claims to be just, no matter how democratic the procedures that gave rise to them.[42] For societies to be worthy of the label *democratic*, there must be a balance between procedural and substantive dimensions, which, being contingent and contextual, will change and vary over time.

In order to operationalize this view of democracy as demanding more than majority rule, the Supreme Court recognized that popular sovereignty has to be supplemented and constrained by other constitutional principles. After acknowledging that it is "a highly textured expression" that lends itself to diverse interpretations, the Supreme Court confirms that the Rule of Law, along with federalism, is a basic requirement of any stable, predictable, and ordered society. Staying at the relative safety of high abstraction, the Supreme Court identified three major components to the Rule of Law – the existence of one constitution and set of rules for both government and private persons; the creation and maintenance of an actual order of positive laws that embodies the more general principle of normative order; and the insistence that the exercise of all public power, including that by the courts, must find its ultimate source in a legal rule. Accordingly, explicitly adopting a minimalist version of this constitutional axiom, it maintained that "the Rule of Law principle requires that all governmental action must comply with the law, including the Constitution." For the Supreme Court, therefore, majority rule combines with other constitutional principles, such as the Rule of Law, to ensure that democracy is implemented and respected in a procedural as well as substantive way:

> The consent of the governed is a value that is basic to our understanding of a free and democratic society. Yet democracy in any real sense of the word cannot exist without the Rule of Law. It is the law that creates the framework within which the "sovereign will" is to be

[42] S. Holmes, Precommitment and the Paradox of Democracy in *Constitutionalism and Democracy* 196–97 (J. Elster and R. Slagstad eds. 1988).

ascertained and implemented. To be accorded legitimacy, democratic institutions must rest, ultimately, on a legal foundation. That is, they must allow for the participation of, and accountability to, the people, through public institutions created under the Constitution. Equally, however, a system of government cannot survive through adherence to the law alone. A political system must also possess legitimacy, and in our political culture, that requires an interaction between the Rule of Law and the democratic principle. The system must be capable of reflecting the aspirations of the people....

Constitutional government is necessarily predicated on the idea that the political representatives of the people of a province have the capacity and the power to commit the province to be bound into the future by the constitutional rules being adopted. These rules are "binding" not in the sense of frustrating the will of a majority of a province, but as defining the majority which must be consulted in order to alter the fundamental balances of political power (including the spheres of autonomy guaranteed by the principle of federalism), individual rights, and minority rights in our society. Of course, those constitutional rules are themselves amenable to amendment, but only through a process of negotiation which ensures that there is an opportunity for the constitutionally defined rights of all the parties to be respected and reconciled. In this way, our belief in democracy may be harmonized with our belief in constitutionalism. Constitutional amendment often requires some form of substantial consensus precisely because the content of the underlying principles of our Constitution demand it. By requiring broad support in the form of an "enhanced majority" to achieve constitutional change, the Constitution ensures that minority interests must be addressed before proposed changes which would affect them may be enacted. It might be objected, then, that constitutionalism is therefore incompatible with democratic government. This would be an erroneous view. Constitutionalism facilitates – indeed, makes possible – a democratic political system by creating an orderly framework within which people may make political decisions. Viewed correctly, constitutionalism and the Rule of Law are not in conflict with democracy; rather, they are essential to it. Without that relationship, the political will upon which democratic decisions are taken would itself be undermined.[43]

So expressed, the Supreme Court is adamant that majority rule is not tantamount to democracy and does not take precedence over all other values and principles in the Canadian constitutional order. Any other argument profoundly misunderstands the meaning of popular sovereignty and the nature

[43] Supra, note 40 at 256 and 260–61.

of a constitutional democracy. In reaching this understanding, the Supreme Court clearly assumes that such ideals are attainable in the sense that "rules rule"; its approach is premised on the claim that rules can be stated and applied in a relatively determinate and uncontroversial way in the vast number of circumstances. This continued preoccupation with the need to ground an objective practice of judicial interpretation that obviates judicial value-choice and that does not tread on the democratic toes of legislative decision making is doomed to failure. The history of twentieth-century jurisprudential and constitutional theory has been dominated by almost countless attempts to provide an account of the courts' role that is consistent with the democratic priority of majoritarianism. As judicial review involves unelected judges' invalidating the actions of elected legislators, all judicial review is antimajoritarian and, therefore, presumptively undemocratic; no theory can reconcile judicial review with majority rule. What is perhaps more important is that this continued search for the jurisprudential grail is unnecessary. Having abandoned the crude Bickelian countermajoritarian challenge to the courts' democratic legitimacy,[44] the Supreme Court should follow through on the political logic of its own analysis; it must have the institutional courage of its own jurisprudential convictions.

Once liberated from the confining strictures of traditional thinking, the question of how and whether courts act with democratic legitimacy is of a very different order and character. The Bickelian difficulty has little to say about what values are important to democracy other than an unthinking regard for majoritarian processes. Once the principle of democracy is accepted to have a substantive as well as formal dimension, the justification for judicial action must also be viewed in substantive as well as formal terms. The work of courts need not be judged by their capacity to be objective and impartial nor by their willingness to be consistent with and not interfere with majority politics. Instead, they can be evaluated in terms of the value choices that they make and the contribution that their decisions make to the promotion of democracy in the here and now. If the traditional assumptions – that legislatures are unprincipled and political and that courts are principled and reasoned – are dropped, it is possible to arrive at a very different understanding and account of the relation between courts and legislatures. For instance, the conclusion is possible that legislatures and

---

44 See A. Bickel, *The Least Dangerous Branch: The Supreme Court at the Bar of Politics* 14–18 (2nd ed. 1986). For a more sophisticated approach, see E. Chemerinsky, *Interpreting the Constitution* 11–12 (1988) and E. Chemerinsky, Foreword: The Vanishing Constitution, 103 *Harv. L. Rev.* 43 (1989).

courts are both principled and unprincipled to greater and lesser extents at different times and that each can further (as well as inhibit) the cause of democratic justice on a particular issue as well as the other. The more pressing conundrum, therefore, is this: If democratic procedures do not guarantee democratic outcomes and democratic outcomes need not result from democratic procedures, how can we best organize constitutional arrangements so that democracy as a whole is more (rather than less) likely to prevail? Accordingly, the appropriate inquiry in a constitutional democracy is not to ask whether the courts have acted politically and, therefore, improperly, but whether the political choices that they have made serve democracy. Moreover, in a democracy, what counts as being democratic is contingent and contextual. Because this is substantive and rhetorical, not formal and analytical, it will always be a contested and contestable issue. Law is politics.

Nevertheless, what counts as a democratic decision is not entirely reducible to a political and, therefore, open-ended debate about what is most appropriately democratic at the time and under the circumstances. The formal dimension of democracy insists that some account is taken of the general institutional location and position of relative governmental agencies. The fact that legislators are elected and judges are unelected has some political salience. However, that allocational decision will itself be political. As the Supreme Court said, it was "the Court's own assessment of its proper role in the constitutional framework of our democratic form of government." Like the general mix between the Rule of Law and its other constitutional components, the democratic demands of the Rule of Law will be context specific: "These defining principles function in symbiosis; no single principle can be defined in isolation from the others, nor does any one principle trump or exclude the operation of any other."[45] Sometimes, it will play a minor role and sometimes it will play a much larger one. Of course, there is no metaprinciple that is not itself political and controversial that can fix that role and balance; it is part of the continuing debate about democracy itself. For example, in societies such as Eastern Europe and Latin America that are in transition from repressive regimes to democratic governance, what is considered just and appropriate will depend on the contingent extent and intransigence of prior injustice. The Rule of Law may have a valuable role in facilitating that shift and, "rather than grounding legal order, it serves to mediate the normative shift in justice that characterises those extraordinary

---

[45] Supra, note 40 at 248.

periods."[46] Indeed, in certain circumstances of crisis and upheaval, the courts might be temporarily better placed to effect large or important changes in an effective manner. The task of determining what courts should and should not do is a work-in-progress of the most enduring and political kind.

Conclusion

While it is understandable why most judges and jurists wish to present adjudication as a bounded and objective enterprise in which reasoned judgment can dissolve and resolve problems that have proved inhospitable to legislative resolution, it is a misplaced ambition. Because there is no way to bring such a project to a satisfactory conclusion, continuing attempts to do so merely exacerbate the problem of democratic legitimacy and erode the very confidence that the legal establishment is trying to maintain. A better response would be to acknowledge that adjudication in a society of diverse and conflicting politics is an inevitably ideological undertaking. Once this acknowledgment is made, courts will not necessarily become otiose or surplus to democratic requirements. Instead, it might be accepted that both courts and legislatures are involved in the same game, namely delivering substantive answers to concrete problems. Furthermore, in doing that, neither courts nor legislatures have a lock on political judgment about what it is best to do. For example, although Souter in *Glucksberg* states that legislatures are the place to engage in "fact-finding and experimentation," which "should be out of the question in constitutional adjudication," he does concede that "sometimes a court may be bound to act regardless of the institutional preferability of the political branches as forums for addressing constitutional claims." On the issue in hand in *Glucksberg*, Souter actually concluded that "I do not decide for all time that respondents' claim should not be recognized; I acknowledge the legislative institutional competence as the better one to deal with that claim at this time."[47] This seems right. The respective responsibilities of judges and legislators cannot be defined outside the never-ending debate about what democracy demands and by what is best served at any particular time. In both judicial and legislative decision making, it is mistaken to allow theoretical principle to be the enemy of pragmatic good or to allow general institutional competence to be the

---

[46] R. Teitel, Transitional Jurisprudence: The Role of Law in Political Transformation, 106 *Yale L. J.* 2009 at 2116 (1997).

[47] *Glucksberg*, supra, note 15 at 788–89 and 789.

enemy of specific substantive good. What courts and legislatures do, as well as how that work is divided, is a highly political matter whose resolution will inevitably be contingent, contextual, and contested.

In what appeared to be a typically astute comment, the late Stanley de Smith stated that "legal theorists have no option but to accommodate their concepts to the facts of political life."[48] Even a rudimentary survey of mainstream constitutional theorists suggests that de Smith was engaging in wishful thinking. Judged by their persistent refusal to ensure that conceptual analysis retains some connection with political reality, contemporary legal theorists have managed to keep their options wide open. Using Canada as my example, I have tried to demonstrate that constitutional law is a site for political conflict, not a structure for it, and that constitutionalism is an endlessly fluid process in which change is the only constant. In this regard, the wrangle between documentarians and doctrinalists is a faux debate; each assumes that there is some solid and apolitical plane on which to stand when, in fact, there are only more or less slushy surfaces to navigate. Of course, this realization is only a problem for those who insist that the need for stable and dry ground is necessary for there to be a legitimate and functioning constitutional democracy. I am not one of those. Instead, I maintain that such an understanding is not fatal to the important project of constitutional democracy, but it demands that lawyers learn and hone a different set of skills and attitudes. When there is water all around, the best thing to do is to start swimming. Contrary to what the Soapy Sams might believe and what the Bulldogs might hope, trying to walk on water is a feat best left to others.

[48] S. De Smith, *Constitutional and Administrative Law* 68 (6th ed. 1989).

∽ 8 ∾

Making Changes: Progress and Politics

Evolution is change, nothing more or less.[1]

CARL ZIMMER

IT IS A TRITE OBSERVATION THAT TIME AND TIDE WAIT FOR NO ONE. Canute learned this much to his chagrin – and every other would-be commander or commentator is well advised to remember this mundane wisdom. Indeed, change is one of the few indisputable facts of life. In truly paradoxical fashion, it can safely be reported that change is a constant feature of the world. Whether considered locally or over vast eons of time, change is what makes the world what it is. The central challenge, therefore, for any one who wishes to understand or affect the world is to come to terms with change and incorporate its dynamics into any account of how the world or its constituent parts work. Consequently, any account of legal and biological life that does offer an important role for the fact and effects of change will soon itself become a victim of historical change. Nevertheless, human attitudes to change are no less complex or perplexing than the phenomenon of change itself. Being part of the changing world, human views on the hows and whys of change are themselves constantly changing. At the heart of this intellectual challenge is the persistent effort to fathom the relation, if any, between change and progress. While there is a wide, if often begrudging, acceptance that change is inevitable and inexorable, there is also considerable disagreement over not only the pace and dynamics of such movement but also its direction and putative destination. This debate and controversy is as heated in law as it is in any other field of study. In a world in which law has a relatively privileged place in addressing and channeling political power, the issue of whether the common law is merely changing or making

---

[1] C. Zimmer, *Evolution: The Triumph of an Idea* 135 (2001).

progress is of considerable moment. As (I would hope) is obvious by now, my own take on what counts as progress is that it is itself as much a matter of change as anything else. As a work-in-progress, progress itself is a question of changing sensibilities.

The basic thrust of the jurisprudential as well as the biological challenge is to explain the tension between stability and change. Whereas even the most reactionary theorist admits to some need for change, the most radical critic concedes that a degree of stability is desirable. However, despite the often robust disputes over the appropriate balance of these forces, there seems to be a shared commitment to the underlying idea that there is some elusive but enduring method or measure by which to locate a workable proportion between stability and change or between tradition and transformation. Moreover, this algorithm must not only achieve such an equilibrium but also ensure that any changes or transformations are always in the direction of normative improvement. In short, jurists and judges must be assured that, in spite of the occasional setback or wrong turning, things are getting better and better by dint of the common law's own social discipline and historical development. This is a ludicrously tall order. The search for fixed foundations or constant equations to guarantee the common law's progress is as mistaken as it is unrealizable. The best that can be hoped for is that, like nature itself, the common law remains supple, experimental, and pragmatic. While judges and jurists must forego the quest for a formal method to direct and sanction universal change, they must not abandon the pursuit of substantive solutions that might contribute to local justice. Indeed, in finding ways to improve the quality of the common law, critics and commentators might do well to heed Darwin's apparent conclusion about nature at large that "it is not the strongest of the species that survive, nor the most intelligent, but the one most responsive to change."[2] Nevertheless, in being alive to the possibilities of change, it is important for lawyers to resist the temptation to essentialize or deify change. There is no lasting or greater normative appeal to perpetual change as opposed to perennial stasis: The balance between the two will be local, variable, and tentative. As the history of the common law amply demonstrates, it is often possible for there to be change without improvement, but it is rarely possible for there to be improvement without change – *change might be constant, but progress is contingent*.

In this chapter, therefore, I explore the political terrain on which the different accounts about when, what, and how some changes might be counted as being more progressive than others take place. Indeed, the very notion of

---

[2] This quotation is almost universally attributed to Darwin, but I have been unable to locate a precise source or citation in Darwin's own writings.

progress is as problematic as it is central to the biological and jurisprudential community. In the first section, I canvass the debate in biology and law over how change might be interpreted as being progressive and suggest the difficulties with such a debate. In the second section I continue this inquiry by focusing on the methodological disputes in science over whether ideas of progress can be attributed to claims about knowledge. Drawing on these epistemological encounters, in the third section I demonstrate how a particular Darwinesque explanation of evolution jibes well with the common law's historical development. In the fourth section, I explore the implications of genetic engineering and biotechnology generally for the validity and worth of efforts to understand evolution in biology and law through the kind of Darwinian lens that I have proposed. In the fifth section I look at the common law's potential for effecting good and bad changes as a measure of its moral and political valence. Throughout the chapter, my overall ambition is to problematize the whole notion of progress and demonstrate that what passes as progressive is as local and historical as any other idea. As Robbie Burns put it, "Look abroad through nature's range./ Nature's mighty law is change."[3] Like life and law, progress itself turns out to be a work-in-progress.

A Better Fit

One of the central issues that has dogged both scientific and jurisprudential debate has been the perennially controversial question of progress. It behooves any scientist or jurist who is serious about his or her discipline to take some stand on the freighted relation between the notions of change and progress. To frame this debate in terms most appropriate to the project of this book, the enduring line of division is fairly predictable. Is change in nature or law simply a shift from one state of affairs to another over time? This is what I call the *chronological thesis*. Or does that shift occur in the direction of a better from a worse state of affairs? This is what I call the *normative thesis*. There is obviously an intimate connection between this controversy and the question of whether nature or law is unfolding in line with some design or is moving closer to a more perfect approximation of its essential self: The capacious shadow of a Creationist approach falls over most of the entanglements in both scientific and jurisprudential study. Notwithstanding this, many scientists and even more common lawyers subscribe to an evolutionary account that eschews a Creationist commitment but still

---

[3] R. Burns, <u>Let Not Woman E'er Complain</u>, in *Poetical Works of Robert Burns* 435 (W. Wallace ed. 1902).

insists that there is a positive and progressive movement to nature or law's development. However, it ought to come as no surprise to learn that I do not subscribe to such a position. I maintain that nature and law are simply moving on largely in response to the demands and opportunities of their changing environmental situation. Neither always getting better (or worse) nor advancing in any particular direction, they are simply changing. While no one should be taken only at their word, I tend to agree with Darwin's own assessment that, "after long reflection, I cannot avoid the conviction that no innate tendency to progressive evolution exists."[4]

The debate in biology over whether nature progresses is persistent. Since before Darwin's time and now after, scientists have locked horns over whether there is any normative direction to nature's chronological development: Is there advancement or only alteration? Is there an evolutionary scale or order that measures the relative pace and development of particular organisms? Is the bear higher on the evolutionary scale than the beetle or birch? And has the bear progressed in evolutionary terms more than the beetle or birch? Despite the few explicit attempts to argue that there is evolutionary progress and the many implicit acceptances of such evolutionary progress, there are almost no cogent accounts of what the concept of evolutionary progress might mean and what valid inferences might be drawn from such a concept. Moreover, I would argue that there can be no explanation of evolutionary progress that does not smuggle specific prescriptive preferences into universal descriptive terms. The distinction between facts and values and between objective and subjective is by no means as clear as many scientists and lawyers would argue or assume. The line is deceptively blurred and itself shifting between (a) accounts of progress in terms of the phenomena to be described or evaluated and (b) accounts of progress in terms of the methods or explanations that are used to describe or evaluate those phenomena.[5] On the account of Darwinian evolution that I have elaborated and defended so far in this book, there is no reason to assume that evolution would move in a straight line at all. Indeed, there are many reasons to suggest that evolution would not move in a straight line. Even if it did move in a straight line, there is no reason to assume that it is constantly moving from good to better.

---

[4] Letter from Darwin to Alpheus Hyatt, December 4A, 1872 in *More Letters of Charles Darwin* 344 (F. Darwin and A. C. Seward eds. 1903). For contrary reading of Darwin's view on evolutionary progress, see R. Richards, *The Meaning of Evolution* (1992).

[5] For good introductions to this debate in biology, see *Evolutionary Progress* (M. Nitecki ed. 1988) and R. Dawkins, Progress, in *Keywords in Evolutionary Biology* (E. Keller and E. Lloyd eds. 1992).

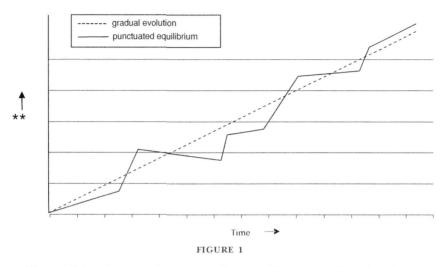

gradual evolution
punctuated equilibrium

**

Time →

FIGURE 1

The traditional normative approach generally assumes that there is some upward movement to evolution; see Figure 1. Whether evolution is thought of in gradualist terms (i.e., through a relatively stable and incremental flow over time) or in punctuational terms (i.e., by large saltations sandwiched between periods of stasis), it is claimed that there is, over the long haul, a sure and steady progress. However, the key challenge for proponents of this approach is to identify and define the elusive quality [**] that evolution is supposedly embodying more and more over time. Although it was not always the case, there are few scientists who would insist that there was an overt ethical cast to this quality [**]; the belief that evolution possesses an ethical quality is confined to the hard-line Creationists. The two main candidates for the task of fleshing out the quality [**] are complexity and fitness, yet their similar and related claims do not hold up to critical scrutiny. For instance, the connection between greater complexity and progress is far from clear. First of all, complexity is not an all-or-nothing quality; it can be a balance between more and less complex. The relative complexity of an organism is usually accountable more by reference to its rate of evolution than any definite assessment of its overall structure. While some organisms change more quickly than others, this is hardly tantamount to their being more advanced or better. Moreover, it is unclear whether this measure of complexity is to apply to nature at large or to particular organisms. While the overall system might be becoming more complex,[6] this not at all the

---

[6] I am assuming that in the "back-and-forth dance between complexity and simplicity, compli-cation usually gains a net edge over time." See W. B. Arthur, On the Evolution of Complexity in *Complexity: Metaphors, Models and Reality* 71 (G. Cowan et al. eds. 1994).

same as claiming that all organisms are becoming more complex or that an increase in complexity is the same as progress in the sense of getting better.

Furthermore, there is little necessary correlation between becoming more complex and becoming more fit; the relatively less complex earthworm is no less fit than the relatively more complex emu in the sense of its environmental or reproductive success. In general, there are three general adaptive levels of organisms – the well adapted, the ill adapted, and the adaptively neutral. While their particular balance will likely shift and change, it is likely that they will all be present at anytime. However, the adaptiveness of any organism is not absolute and intrinsic to the organism; it will itself vary relative to its local environmental context. To take any other position is to essentialize *adaptiveness*, which is a long way from the evolutionary ideas of Darwin. The tendency to local (i.e., in specific historical and environmental circumstances) adaptation in individual organisms cannot be equated with any systemic tendency to universal progress. The animal that changes from being darker furred to fairer furred in response to changing environmental conditions is not by virtue of that fact becoming more fit in any universal sense. Indeed, the creature might well be relatively less adapted than its earlier darker-furred ancestor. Today's well-adapted organism can become tomorrow's ill-adapted organism if there is a significant enough change in environmental conditions. Consequently, while complexity might increase at certain times and in certain ways, it is neither an inevitable nor inexorable phenomenon. Progress is not about greater complexity. It is only about organisms changing in ways that are a better adaptive fit to the present circumstances of their lives. Of course, this can occur by an organism becoming more simple than complex: The average survivor is better adapted than the average nonsurvivor.[7] However, this only applies if the environment remains relatively stable. If there is a significant change, then previously well-adapted organisms will become less adapted or even maladapted.

Against the so-called normative accounts of natural selection, therefore, one can argue that evolution does not progress or result in perfect or optimal results; it is an entirely context-specific and relative process that picks the best of what may be a bad lot. Indeed, mindful that about 99 percent of all species that have ever existed are now extinct, one can state with confidence that the failure to adapt is more the rule than the exception. *Fitness* is not equivalent to *better*, but simply a shorthand conclusion for the fact that an organism or one of its evolved features works well in the sense of being

---

[7] For the earlier example of the furry animal, see supra chap. 2. See generally E. Mayr, *What Evolution Is* 278 (2001).

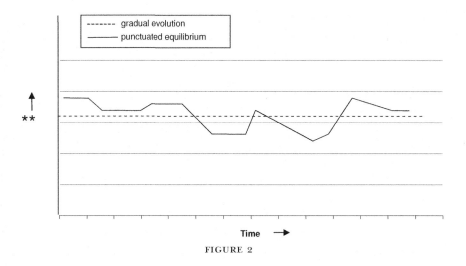

FIGURE 2

adaptively successful in particular circumstances. Indeed, it is highly unlikely that a process such as natural selection, when properly understood, would move in a straight line, whether morally enhancing or not. By and large, evolution will be asymmetrical in that organisms adapt to the environment, not vice versa; see Figure 2. Moreover, while some organisms will have an impact on their local and immediate environment, which in turn will affect the evolution of the fittest organisms, there is no evidence to suggest or suppose that the environment itself changes in accordance with any set plan or predictable logic. By assuming that adaptation has some Whiggish tendency, Darwin's central ideas are ignored or shamelessly bastardized. In this regard, Bulldog Huxley and his pack are much closer to Soapy Sam's flock than either would care to contemplate.

In light of these particular cautions about talk of evolutionary progress in the natural world, it is possible to offer some general observations about progress in the common law's development. The conclusions are far from encouraging to those committed to any kind of ordered or progressive movement: The chronological thesis seems to have a considerable edge over the normative thesis. There is little basis for jurists' tendency to maintain that evolution is weeding out the ethically bad from the ethically good. It is, of course, entirely sensible to talk about law in terms of its substance and merit; this is the standard fare of much jurisprudential work. However, if it is difficult to give a fixed and objective meaning to the quality [**] in biological study, it is doubly so in the world of law. If it is intended to signify some moral standard, the debate over the criteria for substantive or ethical worth is as contested as any debate could be. Even if one could agree on such criteria, it is hard to imagine that the common law's development would be moving in one advancing direction, whether by smooth gradations or by jerky steps, as suggested by Figure 1. Even the most traditional scholar is prepared to concede that there are spurts and stalls in the law's development. Moreover, it is also unlikely that the movement of the common law would be historically flat lined, as the gradualist approach urges in Figure 2. No traditional jurists would seriously advance the claim that the law is always in exactly the same state of moral worth (whether it be high, low, or middling). It is much more likely that, insofar as law could be measured by reference to one particular set of moral lights, it would rise and fall in its success, as recommended by punctuated equilibrium approach in Figure 2. Accordingly, if we are looking to locate some regimen or rule to describe and forecast the future development of either the common law or its social environment, then we can do no better than the subscribe to "the law of higgledy-piggledy."[8] As tantalizing as it is, both the common law and the social environment only offer up the secrets of their development after the event. Jurisprudential wisdom, like most varieties, is always better in hindsight.

In both law and nature, ideas of progress quickly become confused with directionality; it is difficult to posit progress in any moral sense without positing a destination toward which such change is getting closer and closer. However, such a possibility remains attractive to the common lawyer as it holds out the promise of both predictability (i.e., knowing where we have been and where we are headed will tell us what comes next) as well as an authority (i.e., the basis for prediction is scientific as much as speculative) to the common law's historical development. However, if there is no progress and there is no historical directionality, the acceptance of historical accident and contingency will perhaps persuade people to abandon claims to authority and predictability. Furthermore, people might also come clean on their own normative preferences and recognize that law does not give meaning to life, but that life gives meaning to law. In short, accepting that life is as much accidental as planned, one might grasp that the ambition of total command is illusory. While it is true that law might "evolve in the direction of greater fit with its environment,"[9] there will always be a productive

---

[8] J. Herschel, as quoted in Darwin, Letter to Charles Lyell, December 10, 1859 in *Charles Darwin's Letters: A Selection 1825–1859* 208 (F. Burkhardt ed. 1996). Even *Brown* has received opposition and *Lochner* has garnered support. See supra chap. 5.

[9] E. D. Elliott, Law and Biology: The New Synthesis?, 41 *St. Louis U. L. J.* 595 at 600 (1997). See Ruhl, Complexity Theory as a Paradigm for the Dynamical Law-and-Society System: A Wake-Up Call for Legal Reductionism and the Modern Administrative State, 45 *Duke L. J.* 849 (1996).

tension between the law's notion of fit and the changing social, political, and cultural makeup of that environment. Like nature, the common law is a pragmatic and piecemeal response to changing social conditions over time. It is a historical and, therefore, political endeavor in which anything might go. That anything rarely does go is an indicator not of certain natural qualities to law but of persistently constructed constraints that require examination for relevance and validity. Again, it is the common law's tendency to stability rather than transformation that baffles. The fact that law changes is a given; the fact that it does so selectively and slowly is what should engage jurists' attention and analysis.

Making Progress?

As the debate over whether there is progress in nature discloses, the possibility of offering a factual and value-free account of biological development is itself a matter of considerable controversy. The most recent and most important contretemps over the matter of 'scientific progress' involved the titanic clash between Karl Popper and Thomas Kuhn. Although they each stake out apparently incompatible positions, there is much that is shared in their epistemological conclusions; this exaggerated sense of opposition is as true for them as it is for Wilberforce and Huxley and, also, Dworkin and Posner. Both Kuhn and Popper recognized the necessary prerequisites of commensurability and testability. More importantly, in contrasting the prevailing views of these scientific philosophers, they both agreed on the essentially cumulative nature of science in that it was the facts that a theory revealed rather than the theories themselves that were accumulated. However, they disagreed over the role of values in scientific methodology and the measure of scientific progress. In a striking parallel with similar jurisprudential exchanges, while they share an acceptance that history must be given a more prominent and inclusive role to play in the tradition of scientific explanation, they are at odds over the nature of that role. Although Popper is clear that "the history of science is, by and large, a history of progress,"[10] he casts history as a rather clean and tidy process; it is a source of order rather than disruption. In contrast, Kuhn recognizes the unsettling quality of history and adopts a more warts-and-all approach. While both Popper and Kuhn rely on a Darwinian model, they profoundly disagree over the force and consequences of such an alignment. In short, like their

---

[10] K. Popper, The Rationality of Scientific Revolutions in *Scientific Revolutions* 94 (I. Hacking ed. 1981).

jurisprudential counterparts, they part company over which idea of progress is implicated in an evolutionary approach: Is it possible to historicize without also politicizing? Is political development about improvement or simply change?

Popper explicitly contends that change in science can be modeled on that of Darwinian evolutionary biology. As with birches and bears, he claims that there are continuing cycles of variation, selection, and transmission in the realm of knowledge and ideas. He suggests that there is an analogue between genetic mutation and the proliferation of new ideas and theories. In the same way that nature selects among the proliferation of mutations, so the scientific community tests and chooses between the competing theories on the basis of scientific falsifiability. For Popper, the empirical method does not test for the truth of theories but seeks to corroborate them through failed efforts to prove them false. The ambition is "not to save the lives of untenable systems, but, on the contrary, to select the one which is by comparison the fittest, by exposing them all to the fiercest struggle for survival."[11] Accordingly, in the world of science as in the realm of nature, while truth is more protean than transcendental and knowledge is more contingent than constant, there is nonetheless a direction to knowledge that is progressive and orderly; there is a move forward in knowledge in both quantitative and qualitative terms. Importantly, however, Popper does acknowledge that, while a theory (or, at least, the set of facts that it adduces) becomes more corroborated and reliable, it will never become complete and true in any eternal sense. Moreover, not content to make such assertions in the world of scientific research, Popper makes the trademark Bulldog move and draws political conclusions from his epistemological claims. He maintains that the best institutional structure and political arrangements to establish and ensure such evolutionary progress through a conflict of ideas is to be found in the liberal tradition of democratic governance; such an open society is recommended not only as an ideological preference but as a scientific necessity.

From what has already been argued in this book, it ought to be clear that Popper's conception of Darwinian evolution is extremely controversial and frankly unpersuasive. Rather than resolve the debate over whether progress occurs in a Darwinian account, Popper simply argues by assertion and assumption. The role of history and environmental conditions is reduced to a neutral and contained backdrop to the dynamic and almost exclusively

[11] K. Popper, *The Logic of Scientific Discovery* 42 (1934).

internal operations of the scientific community. Indeed, there are so many problems with Popper's claimed Darwinian approach – the static relation between process and environment, the vague mechanism of variation, the mysterious criteria of selection, and unexplained method of transmission – that is difficult to take it seriously as anything more than an unwarranted and unwise attempt at homological comparison: It is more the Darwinian imprimatur that is sought than any imitation of its theoretical integrity.[12] Nevertheless, that having been said, it is not surprising that there is much tacit sympathy for such a Popperian perspective in jurisprudential circles. When applied to law, such a gradual and inevitable process holds much appeal as it showcases the virtues of ordered development, substantive betterment, and principled continuity. Like birches and bears, the law is considered to move forward by adapting its past to present conditions and by ensuring that this adaptation carries forward the past into the future: The common law advances by evolution, not revolution. Moreover, it is not only a *naturalized* process but also a sanitized one in which the true and good will always triumph over the false and bad. Serving the political ends of many liberal jurists, it validates the claim that law is not politics by insisting that adjudication is somehow a neutral and insulated process, uncorrupted by the ideological forces of power and self-interest. Standing in almost direct contrast to Darwin's proposal in the biological world (where organisms' historical development is largely a series of localized responses to changing environmental conditions), this Popperian account has legal and scientific ideas advancing almost solely by dint of their own essential rational logic and their own internal epistemological force.

In the same way that this view has not gone unchallenged in the jurisprudential world, Popper's account of scientific inquiry has not persuaded all scientific commentators. The most decisive and debilitating response to Popper has come from Thomas Kuhn. Whereas Popper maintained that scientific knowledge accumulates through a so-called falsification process akin to natural selection, Kuhn expanded on this by showing how science was an inescapably social undertaking and that it was, therefore, "difficult to see scientific development as a process of accretion." Science occurs and was made possible by the existence of disciplinary matrices or "paradigms," which are situated within history's political currents, not apart from them. According to Kuhn, paradigms are essential to scientific inquiry because "no natural history can be interpreted in the absence of at least some implicit

---

[12] See supra, chap. 2.

body of intertwined theoretical and methodological belief that permits selection, evaluation, and criticism."[13] The typical developmental pattern of a
mature science is not through a steady and cumulative acquisition of knowledge, but through the successive transition from one paradigm to another
through a revolutionary phase. Moreover, in that paradigm shift, there is a
degree of so-called incommensurability between past and present. Within
an established paradigm, progress is obvious and largely uncontested in that
a set of shared problems are answered in a mutually agreed fashion so that
there is an increase in articulation and specialization: Scientists work only
for an audience of colleagues that shares values, beliefs, and standards that
can be taken for granted. However, this ought not to be treated as comparable with an inexorable closing-in on some ultimate truths. More solutions to
more problems might be achieved, but this is not the same as an ever-closer
approximation to a final and complete account of nature. Because there is
a movement away from something does not mean that science is making an
irresistible advance toward some fixed, objective, and supreme destination.

Not surprisingly, Kuhn too likened his approach to that of Darwin. He
concluded that the analogy between the evolution of organisms and the
evolution of scientific ideas "is nearly perfect." Like Darwin on biological
evolution, Kuhn did the same for the evolution of scientific knowledge in
that he refused to accept the existence of any teleological or goal-directed
account of evolution. At best, what occurs is that "successive stages in that
developmental process are marked by an increase in articulation and spe-
cialisation." Eschewing any internal or directional logic to evolution, Kuhn
insisted that, in the same way that the interaction between organisms and
changing environmental conditions determines the course of natural evolution, the resolution of scientific crises is effected by the conflict within the
scientific community over the fittest way to practice future science. In short,
for Kuhn, scientific progress is as much about professional values and institutional commitments as it is about neutral methodologies and objective
knowledge:

> [There has been] a process of evolution *from* primitive beginnings – a
> process whose successive stages are characterised by an increasingly de-
> tailed and refined understanding of nature. But nothing has been or
> will be said that makes it a process of evolution *toward* anything. . . . If we

---

[13] T. Kuhn, *The Structure of Scientific Revolutions* 3 and 16–17 (3rd ed. 1996). For interesting
takes on the Kuhn–Popper debate, see P. D. Hutcheon, Popper and Kuhn on the Evolution
of Science, 4 *Brock Rev.* 28 (1995) and S. Fuller, *Kuhn vs. Popper: The Struggle for the Soul of
Science* (2003).

can learn to substitute evolution-from-what-we-do-know for evolution-toward-what-we-wish-to-know, a number of vexing problems may vanish in the process.[14]

As a result, for Kuhn, scientific inquiry follows a messy and meandering path rather than develops in an orderly and linear progress: "it is only the list of explicable phenomena that grows; there is no similar cumulative process for the explanations themselves."[15] These theoretical paradigms stand or fall not only on strictly scientific criteria of verification and predictability, but also on the sociological basis of their ability to provide emotional satisfaction and thus to inspire commitment in specific social, political, and historical conditions. Indeed, the reception of Darwin's evolutionary theories are a good example of Kuhn's idea of scientific revolution. There is a continuing and repetitive history of resistance, controversy, change, and acceptance that rolls on over time. The shift between biological paradigms is about persuasion as well as proof and about how to look at facts as much as the facts themselves. While Kuhn's conclusions are not equivalent to stating that "in the sciences might make right,"[16] they oblige an acknowledgment that the line between science and politics is as murky and shifting as any other historically situated demarcation. Whereas Popper insisted on the political necessity and logical possibility of a clear boundary between the ideological and scientific approaches to reality, Kuhn contended that all that existed or could exist was an observable cultural and sociological distinction. In this way, Kuhn saw scientific knowledge as neither relative nor absolute, but rather as the efficacious product of an irreversible and nondirectional historical process. Whereas Popper saw a smooth and progressive curve to that history, Kuhn recognized that history was much more jagged and less serene, with science moving not only in fits and starts, but also in many directions at once. For Kuhn, what turns out to be the fittest way to practice science is a historical function of the prevailing consensus within the scientific establishment, not simply the result of a chronological progression in line with a logical criterion of validity. Science is distinctly of the messy world that it seeks to explain and understand, even if it too often pretends that it is not.

[14] Id. at 172, 172 and 170–71.

[15] T. Kuhn, *The Copernican Revolution: Planetary Astronomy in the Development of Western Thought* 264–65 (1957). See also N. Hanson, *Patterns of Discovery* (1958).

[16] T. Kuhn, supra, note 13 at 167. For an interesting intervention into this debate, see J. A. Harrington, 'Red in Tooth and Claw': The Idea of Progress in Medicine and The Common Law, 11 *Soc. & Legal Stud.* 211 (2002). For obvious comparisons between Kuhn's and Gould's ideas, see S. J. Gould, *The Structure of Evolutionary Theory* 966–72 (2002).

Shift Happens

The historical record suggests that Kuhn's ideas and interpretation of Darwinian evolution have a definite salience for explaining the common law's development. In the same way that there is progress in 'normal science' (i.e., within an accepted and established paradigm in which there are a wide series of group commitments) in that puzzles are solved and facts accumulated, there will also be progress in law: Rules will be refined and principles will be honed. This can be illustrated by numerous common law or constitutional doctrines in which the court makes a breakthrough decision and then sculpts out the more detailed contours of the new rule over an extended period. For instance, having established the general concept of privacy in *Griswold*, the courts have worked to interpret and carve out the precise contours and limits that substantive due process possesses in particular circumstances. Again, having abandoned the separate-but-equal interpretation of the Fourteenth Amendment's guarantee of equal protection in *Brown*, the courts have busied themselves with identifying the shape and substance of a more encompassing mode of constitutional equality. In both situations, however, it should be clear that, while the development of such doctrinal details may appear to be technical and uncontroversial, their elaboration is as political as the initial decision that made the original breakthrough, albeit often it is of a more modest and focused nature. Moreover, in the same way that the breakthrough decision often occurred as a relatively revolutionary decision, so there will arise a subsequent doctrinal crisis, as in *Roe* and *Lawrence*, in which what was once thought settled no longer meets contemporary demands or expectations.[17] It is not so much that the developed doctrine will have run into internal difficulties in the sense of being found to possess latent illogicality or incoherence (although it well might). Rather, the doctrine will be seen to have outlived its substantive usefulness and the courts will be tempted to discard it for a more immediately well-adapted set of rules and principles. It is as much that it has lost its political salience from an external perspective as it is that it has been found professionally wanting from an internal standpoint. In short, law and its particular doctrines are seen to be thoroughly political in their rise, elaboration, and demise; legal tradition demands political transformation.

However, while it is reasonable to talk about progress within a particular doctrine, it seems wrongheaded to talk about overall progress in

---

[17] See *Griswold v. Connecticut*, 381 US 479 (1965); *Brown v. Board of Education*, 347 US 483 (1954); *Roe v. Wade*, 410 US 113 (1973); and *Lawrence v. Texas*, 123 S. Ct. 2472 (2003).

constitutional law or the common law generally in the sense that a particular doctrine reaches a level of sophistication, complexity, or fitness that makes it somehow perfect or even simply better for all time. Like the biological organism, the common law is only as good or bad as its informing environmental context. No legal rule is intrinsically good or bad in some global, eternal, and abstract sense: The lessons of 9/11 confirm that what is and what is not settled or desirable law is always open to revision and alteration. Lawyers too often mistakenly label a highly adapted doctrine as a universal legal good that can be relied on in all circumstances, in all places, and at all times. However, the history of the common law suggests that all such judgments about doctrinal merit must be contingent and conditional. As the furry animal cannot be said to have the perfectly colored coat outside of a particular environmental milieu (i.e., brown for temperate conditions and white for polar conditions), so a legal rule or principle cannot be said to be legally ideal outside of its environmental setting. Moreover, because there is a movement away from some particular legal doctrine toward a different one, it does not mean that the common law is becoming more pure or more close to its immanent supreme form. Any particular doctrine must be assessed in local as opposed to universal terms. The fact that the doctrine of substantive due process was once thought to be inapplicable to the privacy claims of gays and lesbians or that it is later thought to be applicable is evidence of prevailing views of political substance, not enduring attributes of legal form. As one commentator has astutely observed, the common law can only be understood if it is seen for what it is:

> [It is] not a romantic ideal or a divine gift or the acme of judicial genius or even the legal aspect, naturally superior, of the most politically wise and refined race, but an interesting human construct, the creature of times and places, of economic forces and class interests, of battles for power between political factions and trials of wits between lawyers of great skill and inventiveness.[18]

Whatever else it is, the common law is a work-in-progress that is always on the move and that is moved along by historical, social, political, and moral forces, themselves beyond any simple or fixed elucidation.

The history of the common law is as much one of discontinuity and contingency as anything else: Lawyers struggle to deal with the sociopolitical forces that impinge on their lives and to which they contribute to their activities. Progress is an entirely practical and temporal matter as opposed to

---

[18] D. Roebuck, *The Background of the Common Law* 10 (1988).

some abstruse and metaphysical measure; it is simply about solving problems by closing the gap between present aspirations and existing actuality so that the world can become a locally better place.[19] Not only will those problems change over time, but those aspirations will also change. Indeed, there is no epistemology that operates as something above rhetoric and there is no metaphysics that is something above rhetoric. Like debates about substance, there is nothing beyond persuasion among real people in real situations. The demand for integrity or consistency falls down because, at a suitable level of analysis, sometimes high and sometimes low, most things can be made to look more or less coherent. Indeed, despite its hubristic arguments and ambitions, modern jurisprudence manages to confirm the modest Kuhnian-style claim that the practices of law and philosophy, like science, are no more (and no less) than a human pursuit – situated, fragmentary, and flawed. Like all histories, the development of the common law is best understood as a way of coping that is more or less successful in direct proportion to its capacity to achieve substantive justice in the contextual circumstances. Judges who make so-called bad decisions do so largely because of their substantive political leanings, not because of the weak or incorrect judicial method that they deploy. The decisions in *Roe* or *Lawrence* are not right or wrong because of the formal merit of their judicial techniques, but because of the lasting appeal of their substantive politics. Settled or fixed principles are simply those that have acquired and still manage to retain sufficient support in the political scheme of things; basic principles do not so much obviate the need for politics as provide a marker for them.[20] Contrary to what mainstream jurists believe, formal methods cannot save the law and judges from themselves. Judgment is a substantive instinct that can never be applied in any easy, sweeping, or uncontroversial way.

For example, in a recent historical foray into the common law, D. J. Ibbetson provides an informative and detailed tour of the law of obligations' history. It is a fascinating and traditional trip; it is almost entirely descriptive and accepts most things at face value. There is no real effort to capture the dynamics of the common law or its sociohistorical setting; it is a formalistic and internalist account of law. Instead, Ibbetson relies on an implicit and immanent logic in the common law that seems to thread together the eclectic efforts of multitudinous judges across vast time and varied contexts. There is a strong Popperian flavor to this process. For Ibbetson, the

---

[19] R. Rorty, *Achieving Our Country: Leftist Thought in Twentieth Century America* 28 (1998). See also supra chaps. 2 and 3.

[20] See S. Fish, *The Trouble With Principle* (1999).

common law proceeds by way of an internal, mysterious, and fixed logic that balances the pull of tradition and the push of transformation. In an admittedly untidy and apparently chaotic process, the common law manages to twist and turn itself through tried-and-tested maneuvers (i.e., inventive gap filing, extensive exceptionalism, subtle distinction drawing, etc.) to meet fresh demands as it remains true to its controlling and enduring ideas; the price of flexibility is the cost of complexity. Informed by such an account, Ibbetson argues that there is a "structural continuity" that runs through the law of obligations from the twelfth century to the twenty-first. After a sweeping series of extravagant claims, he concludes that the virtues of ordered development, substantive betterment, and principled continuity are present:

> Whatever changes have occurred on the surface of the law, and whatever accretions have been incorporated into its fabric, at a deep level the structure of the common law has remained remarkably slow-moving. . . . Like an ancient building in continual use for centuries but readapted to satisfy the needs of each generation, the medieval ground plan of the Common Law of obligations remains visible through all the reordering of its internal features and change of use of its component rooms.[21]

There is so much that is wrong with Ibbetson's analogy. It suggests that change has been reluctant, that there is a steady decline in the common law, that the common law is a relatively inorganic process, that the sources of change are mysterious, and that there is a "structural continuity" that transcends or underpins any changes effected by time. Most importantly, this architectural analogy entirely elides the fact that the development of the common law is not simply a neutral alteration by the ravages of time. Insofar as there is any continuity over time, it is the combined work of particular actors and social forces. Historical patterns and doctrinal trends are little more than medium-term effects of local efforts at the best thing to do. What counts as the best thing to do will change as the political circumstances and social contexts shift. As Kuhn asserts, "part of the answer to the problem of progress lies simply in the eye of the beholder." I take this to mean that perspective is important and that what counts as progress will not be a given fact but a matter of commitment to particular paradigms, because "there is . . . no theory-independent way to reconstruct phrases like 'really

[21] D. J. Ibbetson, *A Historical Introduction to the Law of Obligations* 294–95 and 299 (1999). See also D. J. Ibbetson, Natural Law and Common Law, *Edinburgh L. Rev.* 4 (2001).

there.'"[22] Of course, there can be a workable level of prediction at a very local level and in specific contexts, but the larger and more general questions will never be resolvable in any final or persuasive manner. The sheer complexity and richness of contingent social life ensure that confidence or certainty in fixed solutions will remain elusive. This is no bad thing. As Popper ironically noted, "there can be no explanation which is not in need of a further explanation."[23] If this is relevant to scientific enquiries, it is doubly pertinent to studies of law and society: There simply is no fact of the matter when it comes to understanding the historical development of the common law in particular societies.

Another way of expressing this idea that is more salient to this book is that law and legal theory are never an answer that can speak for themselves. It all depends on the political context, which, of course, always speaks out of both sides of its mouth and in a garbled accent. Kuhn identifies the existence of such a state of affairs in science, even if he does not chart them in any sustained or detailed fashion. He showed how science was much like any other discipline in that it required sources of cognitive authority and intellectual control in order to protect the communal culture from rebels and renegades; these sources might include pedagogical techniques of professionalization and knowledge management, hermeneutical devices for delineating the range of accepted meanings, and institutionalized procedures for legitimating transformative initiatives. If such conditions are in play in science, they are doubly evident in law. There is no need to go as far as Kennedy's claims that law school is an education site for the reproduction of hierarchy in order to demonstrate that initiation into the common law tradition is as much about acquiring certain habits of mind and internalizing certain values as it is about learning vast bodies of legal rules and honing various research strategies.[24] The law school experience and early years in legal practice combine to offer the common lawyer not simply the facts of law but a particular way of looking at those facts. Indeed, it is the considered view of many jurists, both of a Soapy Sam and Bulldog strain, that law school can only do its job satisfactorily if it supplies prospective lawyers with a so-called suitable (i.e., one that reflects the particular advocate's professional and political commitments) orientation about law's role in society. As with science, what turns out to be the fittest way to *practice* law is a historical function of

---

[22] T. Kuhn, supra, note 13 at 163 and 206. For a different and organic analogy of common law growth, see infra chap. 9.

[23] K. Popper, *Objective Knowledge: An Evolutionary Approach* 195 (rev. ed. 1979).

[24] D. Kennedy, Legal Education as Training for Hierarchy in *The Politics of Law: A Progressive Critique* 40 (D. Kairys ed. 1982).

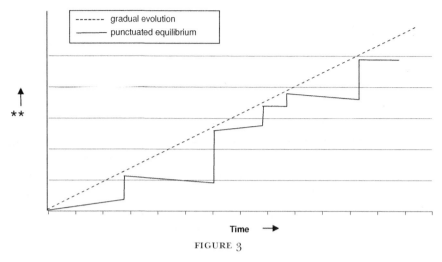

FIGURE 3

the prevailing political consensus within the legal establishment; it is not simply the accumulated outcome of an objective and logical process. Law is most distinctly of the messy, contested, and value-saturated world that it seeks to understand and regulate, even if it too often pretends that it is not.

The only injunction that the common law seems to offer to its judicial and juristic operatives is 'go slowly'. The claim is made that the common law is not only a formal process of argumentive growth, but that it is also a substantive framework that places real constraints on the content and direction of common law development. However, the history of the common law recommends, contrary to what Ibbetson and his jurisprudential clan propose, that 'anything might go' provided that one can persuade others that such a doctrinal change is substantively desirable. Of course, if it is possible to persuade an already institutionally predisposed audience of lawyers that such a change is more a continuation of a doctrinal tradition that a radical break with it, then so much the better. However, as the incidence and importance of great cases illustrates, even a doctrinal and abrupt revolution will be accepted and the "go slowly" injunction ignored, if the proposed change is sufficiently palatable to the substantive political appetites of the legal and, on occasion, public establishment. As Figure 3 shows, the legitimacy of the common law is more dependent on the rate and style of doctrinal development than its substantive content and direction.[25] Legal feathers are much more ruffled by sudden switches in direction than slow accretions

[25] See supra chap. 5. In Figure 3, I leave aside the central problem of whether the common law can ever be said to be constantly improving over time in its moral or political worth. See Figures 1 and 2, supra, pp. 239, 241 .

over time; the snail is the chosen biological symbol of the common law, not the hare. Nevertheless, such a traditional "go slowly" account of the common law (even when its injunctions are actually being heeded) has nothing to say about what is the best thing to do, where to go slowly, or whether there are any substantive limits on change – it is all about the pace, not the direction, of movement. Again, the common law is a work-in-progress whose progress is not channeled by law's own logic, structure, or extant values. On the contrary, the common law simply works itself in line with mediated pressures of its informing social, historical, and political situation. Like so much else, to repeat Kuhn's view of scientific work, "part of the answer to the problem of progress lies simply in the eye of the beholder."[26]

In a post-Kuhnian world, it has been said that "to experience discomfort at the discovery of the uncertainties inherent in science is a mark of nostalgia for a secure and simple world that will never return."[27] I might add, that this is 'a secure and simple world' that never existed in the first place: It only appeared to be secure because admission to the scientific ranks was usually granted to the elite few, and it only appeared to be simple because there was a reasonably wide consensus on the values to be promoted. A similar situation holds in law, where nostalgic sentiments for a simpler and more stable world are regularly and wistfully expressed. This is a political *cri de coeur* if ever there was one. The claim that uncertainty is a modern phenomenon is entirely belied by even the most rudimentary grasp of the common law's past – the Victorian Age, as illustrated in Dickens' *Bleak House*, is hardly the fabled stuff of clarity and simplicity. The yearning for certainty is a thinly veiled plea for more homogeneity and uniformity in the legal profession; the trend toward a more diverse demographic in terms of gender, race, class, and sexuality is to be halted (or at least to be limited to altered appearances than changed values). Even more so than science, law is a site where the facts are intimately connected to the approved way of looking at them; what counts as a valid contract is hardly conceivable outside a particular legal ideology. However, rather than view recent changes in personnel and values as harmful and discomforting, common lawyers would do better to recognize that such developments are not at all inimical to the proper understanding of the common law as a work-in-progress. If the common law is a professional and political tradition, it is one of change and transformation – *shift happens.* This ought to be a cause for reassurance, not regret.

---

[26] T. Kuhn, supra, note 13 at 163.

[27] S. O. Funtowicz and J. R. Ravetz, Three Types of Risk Assessment and the Emergence of Post-Normal Science in *Social Theories of Risk* 254 (S. Krimsky and D. Golding eds. 1992).

Off Lamarck

While there are a number of similarities between movement and development in law and in biology, the operation of the common law has been different in that law is not as ultimately restricted in the short term as natural organisms or patterns of behavior. In biology, what presently exists limits the extent of the changes that can be made over the immediately ensuing generations; the structure of existing organisms precludes certain changes and mutations. After all, bugs cannot become bears overnight, even if they might do so given enough time and with the appropriate range of environmental prods. The evolutionary trip from the primal soup to gourmet bouillabaisse is a very long one of over 4 billion years. In law, the transformative possibilities are more immediate; the trip is much shorter. Although the precedential traditions of law might well act as a kind of institutional check on doctrinal metamorphosis, its structural constraints are not as embedded and unavoidable as those necessitated by the mechanisms of Darwinian descent by modification in the natural world. Nevertheless, in the world of common law adjudication, it is quite possible for such dramatic transmogrifications to occur – common lawyers can create and select any solution they wish. Indeed, not only are there ample real-world examples of such revolutionary interventions, but these so-called great cases are often celebrated as defining moments in the life and process of the common law: "the point about the common law is not that everything is always in the melting pot, but that you never quite know what will go in next."[28] Consequently, as history reveals, the rate and control of change in the biological and legal worlds was very different. However, whatever has been the case is now no longer as obvious or as uncontested. The relatively recent advent of biotechnology, especially genetic engineering, has put a change to all that – change might be as immediate and as controlled in biology as it has been in law.

Genetic engineering is not a new phenomenon. The ability to manipulate or modify organisms through controlled breeding and experimental matings has existed for centuries. What is new is the sophisticated advance of genetic engineering. Only a couple of decades ago, the innovative frontier was located around efforts to perfect artificial selection and reproductive intervention through a variety of biomedical techniques (e.g., in vitro fertilization). This is now relatively old hat in that all the present commotion is about

---

[28] A. W. B. Simpson, The Common Law and Legal Theory in *Oxford Essays in Jurisprudence* 91 (A. W. B. Simpson ed. 1973). See supra, chap. 5. For more on so-called gradual and punctuated equilibrium, see supra, chap. 2.

biochemical efforts to manipulate directly the genes themselves through re-combinant DNA technology (e.g., cloning). Scientists have developed the capacity not only to create new species, but also to interfere deliberately in the cellular constitution of existing organisms so that specific changes will persist as a particular cell multiplies. While there are many limits to the application of these techniques, it is likely that these will become fewer as scientific research continues: Logic, physics, imagination, and moral sensibilities will become the only restraints. Moreover, once it is appreciated that these techniques cannot only be used to breed desirable traits in plants and livestock but also be utilized in reengineering human chromosomes, the broader implications (i.e., political, social, moral, etc.) become readily apparent. In this way, genetic engineering, as well as other biotechnological innovations (e.g., cognitive neuroscience and neuropharmacology), holds out immense promise as well as enormous peril for its future development and use – *human control over life's processes.* There now exists the opportunity and responsibility to tamper with the very fundamental terms of existence. It is a challenge of Promethean proportions because now "a species is not merely a hard-bound volume of the library of nature,... [but] it is also a loose-leaf book, whose individual pages, the genes, might be available for selective transfer and modification."[29]

For all the improvements in medical treatment and agricultural production, there are likely to be dubious possibilities for human well-being from genetic engineering as well as unintended and malign consequences; the spectre of eugenics (a term originally coined by Darwin's cousin, Francis Galton, for the study of human biological improvement) hovers over biotechnology. There are as many Jeremiahs on the biotechnology scene as there are Polyannas; *genetically transformed* is not exactly a universally favored moniker, whether applied to pomegranates or people. While we seem to have cracked the code of life, it does not follow that we know what it means or what should be done with it. Like all other languages, the genetic code will not speak for itself. Indeed, the biotechnology revolution not only changes what we can do but threatens who we think we are; it challenges our moral and ontological sense of ourselves as much as our medical and social appreciation of ourselves. However, there is no reason to assume that this colossal power will be exercised for the human good or that there will be developed concurrently a better critical faculty for discerning what that human good is. Ironically, it was Bulldog Huxley's grandson, Julian, who foretold some of

---

[29] T. Eisner, <u>Chemical Ecology and Genetic Engineering</u> in *Symposium on Tropical Biology and Agriculture* 47 (1985).

the philosophical implications of the trend toward greater control over the future development of life. He said that humans are no longer satisfied to understand the creative mysteries of life because they are fated to become the creators of those mysterious lives. As such, people become not merely the products of the evolutionary process but also "the business managers for the cosmic process of evolution."[30] It is an exciting as well as frightening prospect.

In an important sense, the biotechnology revolution has introduced a Lamarckian-like dimension to evolutionary biology. It will be remembered that Jean Baptiste de Lamarck (1744–1829) laid the foundations for much of modern evolutionary biology. He convincingly explained the contested move across time from simple molecules to complex organisms. However, he made the unfortunate blunder of claiming that such development was brought about through the heritable effects of learned habit modifying the various parts to fit and adapt to changing environmental conditions. This notion of evolution through the inheritance of acquired characteristics is in direct contrast to Darwinian's thesis of modification by descent. If one keeps in mind the fact that Lamarck was working even further before the discovery of Mendelian genetics than Darwin, then his failure to understand the principles of mutation and transmission is hardly surprising. Nevertheless, not only has the Lamarckian implication that there is only an indirect effect of changed environmental conditions as the organism experiences new needs and adopts new habits been decisively rejected, but the related claim that variation and evolution was, therefore, more directed than random has also been abandoned. The presumed connection between growth and inheritance is no longer a part of accepted wisdom in that genetic research has demonstrated that inheritable DNA is not affected by the growth of the parental organism. Instead, it is now accepted that mutations occur independently of and are transmitted without recourse to the development process. While Darwin had conceded that habit, after sifting and repetition, might become instinctual over time and be duly inherited, he did not accept that such adaptations occurred through a conscious act of will by the organism.[31] Consequently, while organisms have an inherent capacity to vary, a Darwinian account of evolution stands against the Lamarckian idea that there is an innate tendency to progressive perfection because

---

[30] J. Huxley, *Evolution in Action* 31 (1953). For more contemporary analyses, see J. Rifkin, *The Biotech Century: Harnessing the Gene and Remaking the World* (1998) and F. Fukuyama, *Our Posthuman Future: Consequences of the Biotechnology Revolution* 17 (2002).

[31] See P. Bowler, *The Mendelian Revolution: The Emergence of Hereditarian Concepts in Modern Science and Society* (1989).

such a concession would import an unsustainable teleological element into biology.

By suggesting that the biotechnology revolution has introduced a Lamarckian-like dimension to evolutionary biology, I do not mean that Darwinian ideas must be reconsidered or that Lamarckian insights are valid again. On the contrary, I simply mean that it is now possible for one species to obtain a degree of willed control over the evolutionary process not only of themselves but the biological world in general. There is now the realistic possibility of the "nurture of nature." Consequently, by *Lamarckian*, I simply make shorthand reference to the idea that some willed intervention in the Darwinian process of evolution is possible. However, I most certainly should not be taken to concede that an organism can will its own physiological and mental transformation such that they can become heritable through genetic transmission or in a genelike memetic way as some commentators, like Dawkins and Dennett, recommend.[32] In the same way that snakes did not lose their legs through prolonged lack of use and giraffes did not develop long necks by stretching them and passing on the "stretched neck trait" to their offspring (as Lamarckians suggest), so a brown-furred creature cannot become a white-furred one by only a concerted exercise of its will, no matter how sustained and necessary such a change is to its continued existence. However, what genetic engineering does allow is for such feats to be performed quickly and clinically by the human species. Consequently, while the biotechnology revolution introduces a Lamarckian element to the evolutionary process, it does not replace the Darwinian dynamic. Genetic engineering must act within and in accordance with the accepted Darwinian framework. Humans can transform the snake and the giraffe, but the snake and giraffe still cannot transform themselves.

The modern capacity to reengineer natural development, especially the ability of humans to transform other humans, has important and wide-reaching implications for any effort to understand law in light of evolutionary principles. In particular, the whole notion of design must be revisited in light of the biotechnology revolution. In both science and law, it can be reported that people make plans and act on them. After all, law has always been a rational activity in that people reflect on what is best to do and how that might be achieved; it is not a game of chance or a blatant exercise of arbitrary action. However, even though science has now developed the tools to ensure that biology is not only a random (i.e., change is dependent on unplanned and unpredictable genetic mutations) and necessitated

---

[32] See *supra* chap. 2.

(i.e., the surviving mutations are those that benefit the organisms' adaptive fit) response to environmental situations, it still remains largely beholden to its environmental context. Even after the biotechnology revolution, currently well-adapted organisms (e.g., humans) can be devastated by substantial change in environmental conditions (e.g., global warming or galactic disturbance). Even on a smaller scale, in both biology and law, individual initiatives are often overwhelmed by a more general unplanned and aggregating dynamic that is response to external conditions. The whole does not discipline the parts in the way that jurists tend to believe; instead it tends to direct the parts in a way that is externally explicable, even if not internally rational. There is no invisible hand that is working to coordinate the scattered efforts of judicial generations, except perhaps the erstwhile after-the-fact efforts of traditional jurists. Indeed, in contrast to legislation, the common law's traditional appeal is found in its relatively uncoordinated and organic character. Contrary to the Soapy Sams of the jurisprudential world, the common law's whole is no greater than the sum of the parts, at least not on some consistent or moral basis. Over time, the quality of the common law will occasionally move between being less and more than the sum of its parts, but it will usually be the total of its disparate parts. The common law is chaotic and coherent in relatively equal and contingently shifting measures.

Nevertheless, even though in both biology and law, design is a genuine possibility, it does not mean that either scientists or common lawyers are free to do or achieve whatever they wish. Technology has loosened the constraints on design, but it has not done away with them entirely. There are two specific constraints that warrant consideration – the so-called environmental and Frankenstein factors. The first flows from the general fact that any organism's individual development is as heavily influenced by its environmental conditions as it is by its genetic composition. This is particularly the case with human development, which is plastic but not indefinitely so. The connection between genetic engineering and social behavior remains indistinct and tenuous. How a particular individual develops is historically contingent and will itself depend on environmental conditions and adaptation. Even clones will not be exactly alike, as the identical genetic makeup will be differently expressed in varying environmental circumstances. Indeed, the possibility of isolating the molecular pathways between particular genes and particular behavior is remote because of the complex interaction between genes and the environment: The genotype (i.e., the DNA) does not exclusively determine the phenotype (i.e., the actual organism), because this development is influenced by a host of different and interacting environmental factors and facts. It is a complex meld of nature and nurture in which "the genes lay down the ground rules, but in the end our upbringing and experience makes us what we are."[33] Accordingly, while genetic engineering increases the opportunities for human design, it does not dispense entirely with any limits to how biotechnological tools are utilized.

Indeed, common lawyers have always known this – the power to reshape the world in line with some desired vision, utopian or dystopian, is still conditional upon environmental factors. The pragmatic bent of the common law has made lawyers and judges understandably sceptical about such grand undertakings; the tentative probe is preferred to the systemic overhaul. This is largely because there is a recognition that whether a particular solution is viable or valuable will depend on the prevailing social and political milieu, which is susceptible to unexpected change. Consequently, while it might be thought that the destiny of life and law is very much what we make it, what we make it will be a combination of what we wish to make it and what we manage to achieve in line with those wishes. What is most important is that the changing environment (political, historical, social, moral, etc.) will have an impact on both processes – what we wish to do and what we are able to do. Insofar as many will maintain that what we wish for will be somehow tied to a particular notion of human nature, it must be remembered that there is no nature that somehow stands outside history or its environment that can helps us decide what values are and are not worth defending; human nature is to have no nature or, the same thing, many natures.[34] Humans (including common lawyers) are not free to do whatever they want to do, because what they want to do is affected by the *wheres* and *whens* of doing it. Lawyers are as much a product of the social environment as everyone else, albeit with a privilege and position to affect to some extent how that social environment changes; lawyers are what they are because of the society in which they live and to which they contribute. However, while humans have increased control, they are also not in control. Moreover, it is dangerous and misleading to leave the impression that humanity as a collective is in charge. The fact is that most people are not in control and never will be. Unless there are some massive changes to the extant political systems, it is the fate of many to be the playthings of the few. As recent history painfully reveals, the cloning daydreams of some can so easily become the chimerical nightmares of others.

---

[33] I. Wilmut, K. Campbell, and C. Tudge, *The Second Creation: The Age of Biological Control by the Scientists Who Cloned* 303 (2002). Also see R. Lewontin, *Inside and Outside: Gene, Environment and Organism* (1994).

[34] See P. Ehrlich, *Human Natures: Genes, Cultures and the Human Prospect* (2000).

As with scientists' deciding what to do about biotechnology (i.e., should there be human cloning?), lawyers cannot claim to resolve the future of the common law as though it were a technical matter; they are both matters of philosophy, politics, and even theology. There is a technical component, but it is much more limited and much less contained than lawyers or scientists would have us believe – and even technical matters are much less technical than lawyers or scientists claim.[35] In both science and law, the central issue becomes a political one. Having the power to impact and manipulate the broader physical environment and social landscape, the agenda of study and research must explicitly include questions such as, What do we want to accomplish? and What are we willing to do or give up to achieve that goal? In addressing those questions, be it in law or science, viewpoint will matter – Who are we asking? How do we decide who to ask? What criteria are they to use? How do we decide between equally legitimate but competing visions? No matter how scientists and lawyers seek to finesse these questions, they will underlie all the technical work that they do. Moreover, there are no easy or final answers to be discovered. As both Gadamer and Darwin insist, it will be a matter of historical timing as much as anything else because we are, at the most profound level, historical creatures whose faculties and fate are beholden to changing historical contexts. There is no method, scientific or hermeneutical, that will rescue humanity from these heavy responsibilities. Effectively, life is a dare whose only resolution is to be found in the injunction to 'keep on daring'. Although this will give cold comfort to most people, the real monster is the idea that, having cloned themselves, humans will believe that what they produce is deserving of admiration for that fact alone. In this sense, it is as much the specter of hubris as that of eugenics that haunts present efforts at transforming the future in both science and law.

The second constraint on depicting nature and law as now amenable to direct and designing interventions is the Frankenstein factor. As with any mode of legal revision, genetic engineering will have unintended consequences and those consequences are, in the longer term, as likely to be bad as good. The ecological interaction between nature and the environment is complex and sensitive. There is no entirely reliable way to predict the future consequences of present changes. Even small quantitative changes can wreak considerable qualitative havoc; the flutter of a butterfly's wing

---

[35] See D. Kennedy, The Political Stakes in 'Merely Technical' Issues of Contract Law, 19 Eur. Rev. of Priv. Law 7 (2001).

can begin a chain of events than can have massive consequences. This is evident in law: The effects of a decomposing mollusk in a Glaswegian's birthday tipple and of an overflowing Mancunian millpond are still being analyzed and assessed today across the common law globe.[36] Because law is always on the move, fixing one problem will often produce problems elsewhere (e.g., extending the circumstances in which tort recovery for pure economic loss is available undermined the limiting effects of contractual privity), and what was once a good or adaptive solution might soon become a bad or maladaptive one (e.g., the fixed notion of property developed for a largely land-based economy is unsuited to the requirements of an e-commerce world). Similarly, there are many unanticipated or exaptive features of legal rules that can be put to better use than the purposes for which they were originally contrived (e.g., the revival of trespass to chattels to prevent incursions into commercial Web sites). Again, as a work-in-progress, the common law is seen to have no inherent essence or tendency to progressive improvement: It is a constantly changing and contingent response to the constantly changing and contingent demands of its environment.

By understanding the common law as an organic process as much as a collection of fixed rules, it becomes possible to appreciate that good judging is about local usefulness as much as global coherence. Being a work-in-progress, the judicial job is never done and must console itself by accepting that this is for the best, not the worst. Moreover, Mary Shelley's cautionary tale of the scientist-made monster who sets off a series of terrible occurrences is worth heeding. Although the chilling force of her original novel has been lost in the slew of derivative shlock horror movies, her message seems to be that it is not so much that people should do nothing for fear of disaster, but that people should be careful that, in doing something, they do not set off a train of events that they will not only regret but be unable to halt.[37] Nevertheless, as a work-in-progress, the common law dares its judicial participants to run that risk. After all, as both the best of life and law have shown, progress is what people make it. When it comes to the common law, what lawyers make it will be both their responsibility and their legacy. Accordingly, in the last section here, I explore the common law's general potential for effecting both good and bad changes. In the process, I again confirm the force and extent of the critical claim that law is politics.

---

[36] See *Donoghue v. Stevenson*, [1932] AC 562 and *Rylands v. Fletcher* (1868), LR 3 HL 330.
[37] See M. Shelley, *Frankenstein* (1831).

For Better and Worse

While there is a grain of wisdom to the insight that "genes are Darwinian, but civilization is Lamarckian," it is exaggerated and misleading.[38] If it is meant that people adapt to environmental conditions as much by choice as by randomly (or, at least, as instinctive reactions to changing social conditions), it has some salience. To deny such modest claims would be silly. However, if it is meant that genetic makeup or the interaction between genetic material and environmental conditions has no relevance for civilized activities, like law, it is wrong. While people have considerable control over the development of civilization (and, increasingly, the development of nature because biotechnology can achieve what previously took eons of environmental agitation), it is folly to suggest that such control is determinative or self-sustaining. The possibility of social engineering remains as much a conceit as it has ever been. Not only is there no guarantee that the best-laid legal plans of mice and men will not come to naught, but there are no historical grounds for confidence that such interventions will not do more harm than good. As with genetic engineering and legal efforts to regulate it, there is a tendency for lawyers to be asked to shut the institutional barn door after the scientifically modified horse has bolted. The most and the least that can be expected of lawyers and judges is that they *do what is best*, mindful that this can never be done in anything more than a conditional, contextual, and modest way. Indeed, there is no better example of the common law's concurrent strength and weakness in tackling contemporary moral and political challenges than its halting and tentative efforts to confront the ethical challenges of the biotechnology revolution.[39] Nevertheless, the injunction for lawyers and judges to do what is best will seem at best platitudinous and at worst perilous. It will be protested that they need more specific and substantive advice. For better and worse, none can be offered.

The key difficulty is that *evolution* is largely accepted in the biological sciences as being simply a synonym for change. Unlike in the social sciences generally and in the common law especially, there is no common supposition of improvement or advancement in any universally appealing sense. In short, evolution is an empirical phenomenon of alteration that has no necessary link to normative claims of value. Adaptation to changing conditions is the only standard of success, and this metewand is itself only temporary and local in character. Once conditions change, an adapted feature can become maladapted to its circumstances.

[38] M. Roe, Chaos and Evolution in Law and Economics, 109 *Harv. L. Rev.* 641 at 665 (1996).
[39] See M. Somerville, *The Ethical Canary: Science, Society and the Human Spirit* (2000).

Because contingency is the order of the day, it has to be grasped that the quirky as much as the quotidian is the measure of development and change; yesterday's peculiar is today's prosaic and tomorrow's passé. In a manner of speaking, 'we are all mutations now' – who we are and what we do are functions of the vibrant dynamic between the constantly active environment and the constantly varying gene pool. In such a world, the common law's fabled injunction of *stare decisis et non quieta movere* (i.e., let the decision stand and do not disturb things that have been settled) seems to be entirely the wrong sentiment or mandate. By relying too heavily on the past to resolve present disputes, common lawyers are likely destined to get the future wrong. It is necessary to cultivate an attitude that holds the push of tradition and the pull of transformation in some sort of balance. However, that balance will not be found in nature because it has no moral quality. Nature is amoral and simply *is*: Any attribution of moral worth to nature is an entirely human projection. As such, any questions about the moral status of any particular natural state of affairs can only be asked and answered in moral terms. Furthermore, this stricture applies to the "nature" of the common law because it has none independent of its particular content and shape at any specific historical moment. Any balance between stability and change or between tradition and transformation will have to be constantly achieved and reachieved in the maelstrom of history's changes.

Accordingly, it is the main force of Darwinian evolutionary theory that biological creatures have no common or essential properties, particularly those that might be grouped together under the rubric of human nature. If they did possess such an ahistorical or noncontingent quality, it would undermine much of evolutionary theory because the microdynamics of natural selection feed on constant change. Variation, whether it is by genetic mutation, sexual couplings, hereditary drift, or the like, is the sine qua non of evolution; species develop and originate from this fundamental process. Moreover, confronted by changing environmental conditions, these mutating organisms do the best they can to make the best of their situation. Indeed, those organisms that do best are the approximate fitness maximizers. In environmental conditions that can change relatively quickly and often, it is better for one to be jack-of-all-trades because one is better able to adapt to new conditions than if one were master of one trade.[40] In a biological way of speaking, organisms that survive and thrive tend not to put all their varied eggs in the same adaptive basket. As for the common law, it is those

---

[40] A. Rosenberg, The Biological Justification of Ethics: A Best-Case Scenario in *Darwinism in Philosophy, Social Science and Policy* 125 (2000).

doctrines and principles that are best able to adapt to changing social conditions that are more likely to persist and hold their own in the pressure cooker of dispute adjudication.

For instance, the fault standard in Anglo-Canadian negligence law has had such a relatively long and successful life because, at least in part, it has been malleable enough to adapt itself to a host of changing demands and expectations. While its political appeal has been crucial, its capacity to adjust its focus (i.e., from injurious acts to misleading statements), its reach (i.e., from physical damage to economic losses), and its standards (i.e., from novices to experts) has enabled it to be vital as well as reliable and to be directive as well as flexible. Of course, this is not to suggest that its adaptability is the perfect or pure manifestation of the common law's enduring essence.[41] It is simply to conclude that, for much of the twentieth century, *Donoghue* has been able to remain sufficiently well adapted to the social and economic milieu such that its claims to allegiance are relatively better than its immediate doctrinal competitors. If conditions change or more fit competitors appear, there might well be a change of doctrine.

Some have gone so far as to argue that the common law works best when it pays scant attention to changing social circumstances. For instance, Richard Epstein offers a self-consciously static conception of the common law. He contends that the substantive principles of the common law not only can be evaluated as normatively good or bad in themselves without regard to extant social conditions, but also that they should be judged in such an ahistorical way: "in no way do [social changes] require, or permit, parallel changes in the legal order."[42] To put it mildly, this seems a huge overstatement of the common law's operation as an enduring body of transcendent principles. It offers a formalist account that outdoes even the most devoted and fundamentalist of Soapy Sam's disciples. By making an outright rejection of the common law as any kind of work-in-progress, Epstein seems to elevate the virtue of stability to almost absurd heights and confound the opinions and commitments of almost all judicial artisans of the common law as to what they are and should be doing. Nevertheless, if such a static conception of the common law has any merit (and this is a big *if*), it is to act as a timely corrective to those who are minded to conclude that the role of the common law is and ought to be exhausted in the effort to simply track and reflect prevailing and changing social circumstances. In other words, in recognizing the common law as a work-in-progress, it is important to guard against

---

[41] See, for example, E. Weinrib, *The Idea of Private Law* (1995).

[42] R. Epstein, <u>The Static Conception of the Common Law</u>, 9 *J. Legal Studies* 253 at 256 (1980).

the tendency to convert the need to be adaptive to change into a moral imperative in itself. Apart from the obvious fact that it would be a particularly foolish method by which to attempt a crossing of Hume's chasm, there is little redeeming by way of moral appeal to such an injunction. There is more to life and law than a "context-breaking brio" in which the ideal lawyer becomes Bruce Springsteen's rebel forever "born to run."[43] Such freedom is illusory in that rebellion is not a way of life in itself, but a possible prelude to a different and better life. In social and political terms, there is a difference between the cure and the cured condition.

Mindful that change is not always for the better, it will occasionally be the case that doing nothing will be the best way to *do what is best.* However, it is entirely another thing to suggest that doing nothing will always (or more likely than not) be the best way to *do what is best.* For instance, after asserting that evolutionary change in the realm of ideas is not necessarily for the better, Judge Easterbrook concluded a judgment by stating that "most mutations in biology and law alike are inferior."[44] By any lights, this is a colossal bastardization of Darwinian thought. Mutations are neither good nor bad in themselves; a particular mutation will only be good or bad in relation to its immediate environmental context. In the same way that the utility of a darker- or lighter-furred mutation will depend on the organism's natural and immediate environment, so the worth of a doctrinal mutation will also depend on the particular social and historical context within which the mutated rule is supposed to operate. For instance, it is mistaken to assume that long periods of evolutionary stasis are reflective of evolutionary excellence. Such stable periods of development usually reflect practical equilibrium rather than theoretical perfection. It simply indicates that organisms have achieved a suitable balance with and within the environment, not that the organism has somehow developed to such an extent that it is the pure realization of its own immanent essence. What exists or what amounts to the so-called natural order has no necessary claim on people's conscience or moral faculty. While it is accurate to state that "the smallpox virus was part of the natural order until it was forced into extinction by human intervention,"[45] it would be surprising to hear people argue that such a

---

[43] R. Unger, *Politics: False Necessity* 583 (1989). See generally supra chap. 4.

[44] *Jansen v. Packaging Corporation of America,* 123 F. 3d 490, 556 (7th Cir. 1997) per Easterbrook J. Of course, any literal application of biological evolutionary processes to law is extremely problematic. See supra chap. 2.

[45] L. Silver, *Remaking Eden: Cloning and Beyond in a Brave New World* 257 (1998). Darwin himself was equivocal in his assessment of the natural world. While he sometimes often looked disapprovingly on "the clumsy, wasteful, blundering, low, and horridly cruel works of nature,"

forced extinction was unnatural and, therefore, immoral. Whether it is the smallpox virus or contractual privity, its moral status is an independent assessment rather than a related calculation of whether it is part of the natural order. As a work-in-progress, the merits of the status quo must be defended, not merely assumed.

However, in jurisprudence, it is contended that a bias in favor of the status quo is a natural feature of the common law: Judges are required to give added weight to existing precedents and institutional allegiance in their decisions about how to *do what is best*. In this sense, common lawyers, much like their scientific counterparts, are not divine designers because they rarely give themselves permission to start from scratch. In both nature and even the laboratory, biological evolution has to work from the available genetic material. The same is generally true in the common law. Lawyers and judges do not (or are not supposed to) design doctrinal renovations off the top of their heads; they engage in a mode of bricolage or cobbling together over time of whatever is at hand to make the best contrivance that is possible. In this way, it is about situational optimalization, not absolute perfection.[46] Moreover, even if they do wipe the doctrinal slate clean and treat it as if it were a legal tabula rosa (which is a task that most courts claim to shun in favour of legislative intervention), it must still be conceded that judges operate within a particular historical context that not only frames the problem to be addressed, provides the 'fittest way to practice law, and recommends the utility of any proposed solutions, but also helps to shape the values and commitments that they bring to those adjudicative chores. Accordingly, understanding the common law as a work-in-progress leads to the appreciation that adjudication is a subtle combination of freedom (i.e., judges can cobble together the broad range of available doctrinal materials into the artifacts of their choosing) and constraint (i.e., judges are historical creatures whose imagination and craft are bounded by their communal affiliations and personal abilities). In this way, anything might go. As their incidence and career suggest, great cases are where a Lamarckian biotechnological dimension and a Darwinian evolutionary dynamic come together. A new doctrinal species can evolve not only by developing existing threads of legal argument, but also by engaging in the judicial equivalent of genetic engineering.

he also spoke glowingly of the "grandeur" of nature, which "from so simple a beginning endless forms most beautiful and most wonderful have been, and are being evolved." Darwin to J. D. Hooker, July 13, 1856 in *The Correspondence of Charles Darwin* 178 (F. Burkhardt et al. eds 1990) and C. Darwin, *The Origin of Species*, 429 (6th ed. 1872).

[46] R. Lewin, *Complexity: Life at the Edge of Chaos* 164 (2nd ed. 1999).

John Donne's celebration of change as "the nursery of music, joy, life and Eternity" captures the kind of attitude that common lawyers should take (and the very best among them have) to their judicial duties.[47] Rather than resist or resent change, they should recognize that the main attraction and strength of the common law are its invigorating willingness to keep itself open to change and to adapt as and when the circumstances require. Of course, when it is best to change and in what direction change should occur will be a matter of normative judgment, because 'law is politics'. Because the common law is a work-in-progress through and through, there is no manual or guidebook to follow in determining when to change or whether such change will be progressive. However, contrary to the reservations of many judges and jurists, the common law has shown that its capacity to adapt to changing circumstances is a vital feature of its historical struggle for both survival and success. Indeed, the common law seems to have been energized by recognizing the force of the old adage that "when you are finished changing, you are finished." It is a compliment to the political wit and institutional savvy of common law judges that, whatever they or their theoretical apologists might say, they have largely taken a pragmatic approach to their adjudicative responsibilities; they tend not to let abstract considerations get in the way of practical solutions. This is not to suggest that the solutions they choose or the changes they make are always the best or even the better ones; this is a matter for social evaluation and political contestation Accordingly, while they might mouth certain traditional platitudes about the need for predictability and stability in the common law, the judges tend to act on a quite different basis. As the iconoclastic William Douglas put it, "the search for static security, in the law and elsewhere, is misguided . . . [because] the fact is security can only be achieved through constant change, through the wise discarding of old ideas that have outlived their usefulness, and through the adapting of others to current facts."[48] Indeed, the success of the common law has been this ability to be flexible, open, experimental, and adaptable. The knack is to intervene in such a way so as not to establish rigidities and ossification, but to maintain the capacity for change and alteration in the immediate interventions made. To the extent that it can do this, the common law will have gone some way toward redeeming its performance and potential as a work-in-progress.

[47] J. Donne, The Nursery of Music, Joy Life and Eternity: Elegie III ll.35–36, in *The Complete Poetry and Selected Prose of John Donne* 59 (C. Coffin ed. 2001).

[48] W. Douglas, Stare Decisis, 49 *Colum. L. Rev.* 735 (1949).

Conclusion

Thus, it can be reported that the Kuhnian lessons of Darwinian evolution are that everything is always on the march, that changing one thing will likely affect everything else, and that progress is a temporary and contextual achievement. In terms of law, therefore, it is important to grasp that, whatever else it might or might not offer (and it might well have no application to law), an evolutionary perspective is not about generating a universal agenda for change or providing a justification for law's particular development. Instead, it is about developing an attitude or approach to law that recommends, among other things, cultivating a healthy scepticism about formulaic recipes for legal success, about simplistic notions of legal progress, about the predictive power of rational planning, about the widespread tendency toward reductionist explanations, and about the sense that jurists are or can ever be entirely on top of things. Lawyers and judges need to nurture situation sense and practical savvy as much as philosophical sophistication and abstract theorizing. If there is still to be talk about evolution, then it must be in a throughly descriptive and morally neutral manner. Moreover, insofar as evolution talks in terms of natural selection as being about solving problems, it must not be forgotten that it has nothing to tell us about the problems that will require solutions – this is a crucial insight for common lawyers as well as evolutionists of all persuasions. In a jurisprudential manner of speaking, common law judges offer up what they believe to be the best answer to a pressing problem out of a varying series of possible good answers. However, there is no one right answer or perfect solution; the complexity and contingency of the social environment make that possibility fantastical and far-fetched. In a Gadamerian way of speaking, there is no one 'Context of contexts' and, therefore, no set or self-evident problem to be answered, let alone one right answer to be sought or given; the task of interpretation permeates the whole problem-answering process.

Whether particular innovations work over time will be as much a matter of serendipitous accident as deliberate design. Because the environment *will* change (and the only question is how it will change), law will also have to change in order to adapt to those changes. However, in fulfilling their roles and responsibilities as participants in a work-in-progress, judges and jurists of the common law will be well-advised to look beyond the habits and ideals of the Soapy Sams and Bulldogs of the contemporary jurisprudential world. Instead of trying to pin down the essence of the common law or grope toward formulaic solutions, it is surely better to admire the complexity and dynamism of the common law and to appreciate its essential unessential-ness. By holding on to the desire for constancy and coherence, the search for a better understanding of life and the common law will be seriously compromised. In this regard, Wittgenstein's typically gnomic criticism of many traditional theoreticians for maintaining that "the solution to the problem of life is seen in the vanishing of this problem" is to the pragmatic point.[49] There are no permanent solutions to life's problems because life is problematic, and any effort to resist that conclusion is itself a problem. Progress in law will only be made when judges and jurists stop thinking in terms of eternal problems and universal solutions. Instead, true to the common law's most useful image of itself, they must embrace the fact that the common law is a tradition of transformation in which both existing law and its possible changes are works-in-progress.

[49] L. Wittgenstein, *Tractatus Logico-Philosophicus* 6.521 (1922).

∽♥ 9 ♥∾

Among the Trees: A Conclusion

Prediction is extremely difficult, especially about the future.

YOGI BERRA

DESPITE THE REVOLUTIONARY QUALITY OF HIS IDEAS, CHARLES Darwin lived a very traditional and settled existence at Down House in the Kent village of the same name. As a privileged member of the landed class, he assumed his pastoral responsibilities toward its 500 or so inhabitants with characteristic goodwill. He was appointed a Justice of the Peace in 1857 and fulfilled his parochial duties until his death. Across the lobby from his comfortable study where he wrote *The Origin of Species*, he would sit in the dining room behind a large table with a high-backed chair and mete out amiable justice to local miscreants. His magisterial agenda ran the limited gamut from prosecuting poachers through discouraging animal cruelty to issuing pig licenses.[1] The contrasting images of Darwin as a morning naturalist and an afternoon judge are so suggestive of the main themes that I have sought to identify and develop throughout the book. Indeed, Darwin's daily routines capture the nexus, both literal and figurative, between large scientific themes and focused legal applications: The complete Darwin is equal parts theorist and equal parts practitioner. Similarly, while biology and jurisprudence seem to be entirely separate disciplines, the fact is that they share a vital dependence on close and contextualized study that is as much accountable to parochial circumstances as it is to generalized principles. In particular, Darwin's life and work emphasize the always intimate, but often ignored, connection between the reflective and the active, between the universal and the local, between the enduring and the contingent,

---

[1] C. Moore, Darwin of Down: The Evolutionist as Squarson-Naturalist in *The Darwinian Heritage* 132 (D. Kohn ed. 1985).

271

between the chaotic and the ordered, and, as has most concerned this book, between the fixed and the fluid. Not only must theory explain practice, but theory lives in the same house and across the corridor from practice.

In the course of this book, I have sought to suggest an account of 'evolution' that stands in stark contrast to the musings of traditional common law scholars. In so doing, my task has not been to offer a Darwinian critique of the common law and, still less, to propose that there is a Darwinian dynamic at the heart of the common law. It has been the more modest and sceptical one of taking seriously the common law's attachment to an evolutionary dynamic and holding it up to critical scrutiny. I have invoked Darwin because his work is the definitive account of evolution and one that jurists trade on in their claims about the common law. Of course, Darwin did not write about law or other human artifacts. At best, his evolutionary ideas offer a useful way to think about them, but not in any specific or detailed way. This is where Gadamer comes in. In the human sciences, his ideas are complementary to Darwin's, even if they are not at all a perfect analogue to them. As well as eschewing the value of scientific method in understanding human affairs, Gadamer develops a hermeneutical approach that recognizes both the enabling and disabling force of historical contingency. It enables because, as in Darwin's evolutionary account, the constantly changing social and environmental conditions are what give meaning and shape to human efforts at understanding and progress. It disables in that, also like Darwin's evolutionary account, these same changing conditions undermine any attempt to fix or freeze the true essence of a human artifact. Whether one is talking about animals or texts, meaning and value percolate up from below; they are always produced from and vulnerable to history. In this way, whether one is interpreting organisms or texts, knowledge is interpretive and therefore provisional. There is no ultimate method by which to control or predict conclusively what will happen next. This is a message that Darwin, Gadamer, and other sceptics have labored to deliver. I have suggested that common lawyers would do well to heed such advice and take such insights seriously.

Making Sense

So is evolution at work in the common law? While most scientists concur with Theodosius Dobzhansky's assessment that "nothing makes sense in biology except in the light of evolution," can the same be said for jurists and jurisprudence?[2] As with most legal answers, the best that can be said is that 'it depends'. The answer is a resounding "no" if it is meant that the common law develops slowly and incrementally by an internal methodology that mandates the cautious extension of established principles in the direction of refined justice. As in nature, there is no inherent logic or overarching purpose to the common law such that it progresses by dint of a self-improving ethic that allows it to approximate more closely its own purified essence. This is the stuff of fantasy and says more about the hubristic aspirations of its juristic apologists than the actual operation of the common law itself. However, the answer is a guarded "yes" if it is meant that the common law is a messy, episodic, and experimental effort to respond and adapt to the contingent demands that the political and social milieu places upon it. If there is a method to the common law's madness, it is to be found in its participants' diverse and unorchestrated attempts to adapt to changing conditions and shifting demands. Nature and the common law, like all efforts to explain and understand them (including this one), are works in progress: They are the revisable result of manifold compromises between variability and stability in which present utility is always a give and take between past promise and future potential. In this way, biological and legal evolution are both a strange mix of universal predictability (i.e., change will occur as organisms and behavior adapt to changing circumstances) and local unpredictability (i.e., the specific outcomes of that general process in any given circumstances will be uncertain). In other words, life and law are works in progress that thrive on the productive tension between tradition and transformation so that they are better able to make the best of their environmental lot. What is "best" will itself, of course, be susceptible to such processes and forces.

The courts are wont to proclaim that "judges can and should alter the common law to reflect [social, moral, and economic] needs as they change over time."[3] That judges *should* strive to do this is neither surprising nor controversial; any other position would be eccentric and unreasonable. However, it is the *can* that has proved more controversial. Obviously, judges can do whatever they want; they can augment, amend, abandon, or ignore legal doctrines as they see fit. However, in seeking to alter the common law to reflect needs as they change over time, judges are caught in a debilitating double bind. First, they require some politically neutral device by which to

[2] T. Dobzhansky, Nothing Makes Sense in Biology Except in the Light of Evolution, 35 *Am. Biol. Teacher* 125 (1973). See also T. Dobzhansky, *Genetics and the Origins of Species* (1937).
[3] *RWDSU, Local 558 v. Pepsi-Cola Canada Beverages (West) Ltd.*, [2002] 2 SCR 8.

calculate and calibrate the changing needs of society; this seems to be an unavoidably political and contested task. Second, having elucidated such needs, the judges must alter the common law to reflect such needs. Apart from the difficulty of ascertaining what rules best satisfy certain needs, they must alter the law in a way that best respects the common law's own evolutionary expectations about itself – the legitimacy of adjudication is seen to reside in the fact that judges keep in check their partisan political preferences by resort to the formal discipline of principled argumentation. As I have sought to demonstrate, it is simply not accurate or convincing to claim that judges can or do perform such a formal and disciplined mode of alteration. It is not that judges ignore the extant rules or that they follow the rules in a mechanical manner. It is that, in applying the rules, they are engaging in a profoundly political and value-laden act because what the rules are and what it means to apply them inescapably and inevitably implicates the very ideological commitments that they are supposed to avoid.

Contrary to what traditional scholars insist, the common law is awash in the roiling and mucky waters of political power. While judges and lawyers claim to keep relatively clean and dry by wearing their institutional wet suits of abstract neutrality and disinterested fairness, they are up to their necks in ideological muck. This is no bad thing. Because it is only when judges come clean, as it were, and admit that they have political dirt on their hands that they will appreciate that the common law is an organic and messy process that has a similarly organic and messy connection to those social needs that it claims both to reflect and shape. So enlightened, they might begin to accept that they are involved in a political enterprise whose success and legitimacy are best evaluated not by its formal dexterity and technical competence, but by its substantive contribution to the local advancement of social justice. Abandoning the persistent attachment to a false distinction between a relatively unsoiled practice of principled adjudication and a contaminated involvement in crude politics would be an excellent place to begin such a commitment. On the one hand, as long as its practitioners present the common law as an insulated and insular process, the common law will run the considerable risk of being unresponsive and unreflective of the needs it is supposed to address. On the other hand, if judges and jurists are more willing to concede that the worlds of law and politics are intimately related, it might become possible to give society's needs the kind of direct and substantive attention that they merit. It is difficult enough for judges (and anyone else) to *do what is best* without having them pretend at the same time that they are engaged in an entirely different enterprise. Efforts at local substantive justice are not enhanced by a mistaken belief that universal formal coherence is at stake. Legitimacy is best attained by candor and frankness, not by denial and dissemblance.

It has become almost cliché to admonish people that, if they ignore the past, they will be destined to repeat it. However, when it comes to the common law, judges and jurist work from the converse premise – that, by ignoring the past, lawyers will run the present risk of not repeating history and thereby compromise society in its future pursuit of justice. The common law professes the maxim that the past is the repository of wisdom and that it is ignored at society's (and lawyers') peril. However, this backward-looking stance does a disservice to the past as well as the present. This turn to history makes the same mistake that Vico, Comte, Hegel, Marx, and even Fukuyama do when they insist that there is a predictable and lawlike explanation to the workings and direction of history. To some extent, the official credo of the common law reflects elements of this historical and pseudoscientific method of thinking – the reliance on formal methods and argumentative techniques that somehow operate independently of the substantive values and commitments on which they are premised and to which they arrive. The traditional emphasis is more on the method than on the history; it is about history with a capital H. However, as Holmes emphasized in his seminal statement that "the life of the law has not been logic: it has been experience,"[4] it is not so much the past that animates the common law, but a selective account of it. Even in its more formalist guises, the common law distills history into experience and uses it to validate particular practices and positions. However, it is not history that is doing the work here, but the specific values and commitments that inform the process of distillation; substance is not so much hidden in the formal techniques of legal reasoning as secreted in the putatively neutral category of experience. While the resort to the wisdom and guidance of experience is not good or bad in itself, there is nothing impartial or detached about that maneuver. The invocation of experience is less an escape from politics and more a reliance on it by more indirect means.

Nevertheless, contrary to the theoretical pronouncements of judges and jurists, common lawyers have been wise enough in practice to realize that those who only remember the past are destined to miss out on the future. The common law has retained its present vitality and future relevance by playing fast and loose with the past; its practitioners have taken an anything might go approach to its operation and development. While its past has

---

[4] O. W. Holmes, Jr., *The Common Law* 1 (1881).

operated as a presumptive baseline for action and adjudication, the common law has never allowed the past to hinder its present practice or to determine its future. It is the willingness of the common law to adopt a cavalier and experimental attitude to its own formal techniques and substantive commitments that is at the dynamic heart of its organic development. Consequently, an important lesson to be drawn from my account of the common law's evolution is neither that the past has no merit nor that the past cannot or should not be utilized to resolve present disputes. It is that resort to the past is no more legitimating than any other legal maneuver because there is no one past to be identified, no one way of applying that past to the present, and no way of knowing whether the present utilization of the past will be relevant to the problems of the future. The common law is more tentative than teleological, more inventive than orchestrated, and more pragmatic than perfected. It is not that no sense can be made of the common law, but that any such effort to make sense of it must itself be contextualized and tentative. As a work-in-progress, the common law does not possess some enduring or essential core that transcends its historical elaboration; there is nothing more (or less) to the common law than the on-the-move and seat-of-the-pants workings of its own development.

Insofar as reported cases comprise the residual depository of common law wisdom, the system amounts to little more than "chaos with an index."[5] However, I maintain that it is possible to offer a sensible account that suggests that there is little global coherence to law even if there are local and contingent patches of sense. While the law takes shape by virtue of a series of creative and purposeful local interventions, the sheer number of these interventions and the bewildering complexity of the changing circumstances in which they are made render them unpredictable. Of course, it is merely sloppy scholarship to announce without more that law is chaotic, undisciplined, and unpredictable. Any account that suggests that law is beyond rational and compelling organization bears a heavy burden of demonstration. However, it is not simply a cop-out to urge that law is indeed chaotic and undisciplined, provided that this conclusion is reached after extensive study and scrutiny. It is my belief (and, I hope, not conceit alone) that such a claim can be made about law. As always, the challenge is to offer sensible accounts of why local phenomena may have a sensible explanation, but,

---

[5] Sir Thomas Holland, cited by Norman Marsh, Book Review, 30 Int. & Comp. Law Q. 486 at 488 (1981). See also Harold J. Spaeth and Jeffrey A. Segal, Majority Rule or Minority Will: Adherence to Precedent on the U.S. Supreme Court 287 (1999). For a more satirical account, see J. Swift, Gulliver's Travels iv, chap. 5, 296 (1967).

when aggregated, these phenomena have no sense as a systemic set. While the common law is always moving, it is not progressing in any planned or concerted fashion. In this way, the common law perpetually inhabits that narrow and precarious present between the old and dying and the new and about to be born. No legal doctrine is or can be ideal and pure. As one commentator has aptly described it, "laws are not static, forever preserved in their original state like flies in amber; they are living things, which evolve over time and adapt to new needs and circumstances."[6] However, like flies, these laws evolve in no particular direction and according to no particular methodology: They are works-in-progress whose development is a matter of local adaptiveness, not universal design.

When it comes to the common law, the best that can be hoped for is that doctrines might develop that are useful in the sense that they serve particular purposes, that they adapt to local conditions, and that they have a certain flexibility to remain relevant in a changed environment. The success or persistence of any particular innovation is a context-sensitive assessment; there is nothing inherently superior about one type of legal principle over another. Accordingly, any Darwinian or Gadamerian talk about contingency is not to be taken as denoting only random occurrences or blind chance. The law takes shape by virtue of a series of creative and purposive local interventions: "for evolution, the archaic features of life merely reveal its tortuous history, like the archaic features of human language or common law."[7] Whereas chance operates in such a way as to prevent any explanation of particular events, contingency precludes the possibility of ex ante prediction, but allows for the possibility of sensible ex post explanations. As in so much else, jurisprudential insight is always wiser in retrospect. The problem is that most judges and jurists blur the ex ante and the ex post such that the common law is presented as more coherent and less contingent than it is and as more the progressed work than the work-in-progress that it is. Any cogent account of the common law must be thoroughly pluralistic and multifaceted if it is to respect and reflect the complexity and contingency of the common law's workings. Consequently, not only is the common law best thought of as an organic work-in-progress, but so are the jurisprudential efforts to explain its operation and development. In the next section, I put some doctrinal muscle on these skeletal generalizations to demonstrate this organic quality of the common law.

---

[6] B. Slattery, The Organic Constitution: Aboriginal Peoples and the Evolution of Canada, 34 Osgoode Hall L. J. 101 at 110 (1996).

[7] M. Rose, Darwin's Spectre: Evolutionary Biology in the Modern World 81 (1998).

Toward a Jurisprudence of Doubt

In recent years, one of the most oft-cited American constitutional dicta is that "liberty finds no refuge in a jurisprudence of doubt."[8] The immediate thrust is clear and uncompromising – that people can only be secure in their constitutionally protected liberty when courts hold fast to settled interpretations and do not change the law as social and political sentiments change. However, there is also a broader message to be heard in the Supreme Court's admonition – that, mindful of constitutional adjudication's precarious legitimacy in a republican democracy, courts would do well to respect the dictates of stare decisis, even where substantial resistance is building to the wisdom or soundness of disputed precedents, and to harbor no doubts about the validity of the declared law: An earlier decision is only to be tampered with in the most extenuating circumstances. If courts changed constitutional tack with shifts in the political wind, both the constitution's and the courts' integrity would be seriously undermined. Certainty and fidelity to precedent are considered the underwriters of constitutional and judicial legitimacy: Constitutional truths are for the ages, not for each generation, and still less like "a restricted railroad ticket, good for this day and train only."[9] However, in this book, I have taken the position that, contrary to much received wisdom, the common law in a constitutional democracy finds its most secure and compelling refuge in 'a jurisprudence of doubt'. It is the hubristic pretense to absolute and timeless truths that subverts the democratic project. Moreover, I also want to suggest that the mode of constitutional adjudication that best institutionalizes a jurisprudence of doubt is that based on a common law methodology with its pragmatic reliance on the connection between legal development and social values. While there is nothing about the common law that recommends it as peculiarly suited to a constitutional democracy, there is also nothing about it that forecloses possible reliance upon it.

Although *Lawrence* is still in its precedential infancy, it has already ruffled many feathers in both the legal and public body.[10] Apart from its highly controversial subject matter of so-called gay rights, it is likely to gain expedited entry into the canon of great cases. A majority of the Supreme Court came to an explicit and unequivocal decision to overrule its own decision of barely

[8] *Planned Parenthood of Southeastern Pennsylvania v. Casey*, 505 US 833 at 844 (1991) (O'Connor, Kennedy, and Souter JJ, plurality opinion).

[9] *Smith v. Allwright*, 321 US 649, 669 (1944) (Roberts J, dissenting).

[10] *Lawrence v. Texas*, 123 S. Ct. 2472 (2003).

seventeen years ago. This is no regular occurrence. Nevertheless, whether *Lawrence* becomes a great case (as seems likely) or simply flares and fizzles in the constitutional heavens (as seems unlikely) will depend on its longer-term acceptability to the legal and broader community. Either way, the decision is presently important not only because it resolves a matter of significant moral controversy, but also because it is amplifies further and puts in practice the Supreme Court's understanding of the role of stare decisis in constitutional law. While it cannot be presently grouped in the exalted company of *Brown* and *Roe*, *Lawrence* has all the potential, for political good and bad, to be a watershed in the development of constitutional law. Moreover, through an examination of *Lawrence*, I will further defend my central claim that constitutional law is an organic work-in-progress whose lifeblood is the continuity of change; any distinction between its formal and informal revision or between its fixed and fluid dimensions is mistaken. There is a constitutional tradition of political transformation in which there is development and growth, but not always in gradual ways or progressive directions: Common law adjudication is less a significantly bounded and largely neutral tradition of argument and more a site for episodic encounters, albeit stylized and staged, between contesting ideological forces.

In 1986 in *Bowers*, the Supreme Court upheld, in a 5–4 decision, the constitutionality of a Georgia law that made it an offense to engage in sodomy. It decided that homosexuals had no fundamental right under the substantive due process doctrine to engage in sodomy.[11] Although there has since been a barrage of criticism aimed at *Bowers* and the Supreme Court itself has frowned on its constitutional propriety, *Bowers* remained very much a part of the constitutional canon. However, in *Lawrence*, a majority of the Supreme Court determined that this was an occasion on which, "in constitutional adjudication as elsewhere in life, changed circumstances may impose new obligations, and the thoughtful part of the Nation could accept each decision to overrule a prior case as a response to the Court's constitutional duty."[12] Accordingly, in a 6–3 decision, the Supreme Court struck down as unconstitutional a Texas statute making it a crime for two persons of the same sex to engage in certain intimate sexual conduct. The major burden of the majority's judgment was to justify, in light of their refusal to overrule *Roe* in *Casey*, that overruling *Bowers* was not only a desirable political option but also a required legal duty.

[11] 478 US 186 (1986).
[12] *Casey*, supra, note 8 at 864.

The judgment of the Court was given by Justice Kennedy. In reaching his bold decision, he had to explain why it was appropriate to overrule a decision made only seventeen years before. This was particularly important because three of the majority in *Lawrence* had been members of the Court's decision in *Casey*, which had trenchantly reaffirmed the essential values of stare decisis in constitutional adjudication. In resisting the growing pressure to overrule *Roe*, it had been declared that, in matters of "intensely divisive controversy", "to overrule under fire in the absence of the most compelling reason ... would subvert the Court's legitimacy beyond any serious question."[13] Mindful that gay sex was no less an 'intensely divisive controversy' than abortion, Justice Kennedy insisted that the doctrine of stare decisis was not "an inexorable command."[14] While paying lip service to the Court's aversion to a jurisprudence of doubt, he considered that the reasons and criticisms of *Bowers* were so "compelling" as to warrant overruling. This was an instance in which the demands of democratic governance and constitutional duty combined to make doubt the better part of constitutional valor.

In overruling *Bowers*, the Court determined that not only was the constitutional question too narrowly framed in *Bowers* (i.e., it was about liberty more generally expressed and not simply the right to engage in particular sexual conduct), but also that the historical basis of the *Bowers* Court's decision was questionable (i.e., animosity toward homosexual conduct was not as long-standing or as settled an American tradition as previously assumed). Moreover, the animating principle in *Bowers* had been subject to considerable dissension: It had been the butt of considerable academic criticism, its holdings had been rejected by many international courts, and its authority had been eroded by the subsequent holdings in both *Romer* and *Casey* itself.[15] Accordingly, as the political opinion on gay rights had become much more positive since 1986, the majority held that the "intimate choices" dissenting opinion of Justice Stevens in *Bowers* should have been controlling and that "*Bowers* was not correct when it was decided, ... it is not correct today, ... [and] should be and now is overruled." Further, because there was insufficient detrimental reliance as in *Roe*, he concluded that any other course would simply exacerbate the fact that "*Bowers* itself causes uncertainty, for the precedents before and after its issuance contradict its central

---

[13] Id. at 866.

[14] *Lawrence*, supra note 10 at 2483. See *Payne v. Tennessee*, 501 US 808, 828 (1991) – "*Stare decisis* is not an inexorable command; rather, it 'is a principle of policy and not a mechanical formula of adherence to the latest decision'" (quoting *Helvering v. Hallock*, 309 US 106, 119 (1940).

[15] See *Casey*, supra, note 8 at 833 and *Romer v. Evans*, 517 US 620 (1996).

holding."[16] As such, Justice Kennedy held that *Bowers* was no longer valid in terms of its legal status as well as its political credibility.

In a blistering dissent, Justice Scalia raged against Kennedy's judgment as being doctrinally irresponsible and disingenuous. In a veritable tour de force, he condemned the majority for having "taken sides in the culture war, departing from its role of assuring, as neutral observer, that the democratic rules of engagement are observed." Acting illegitimately as "a governing caste that knows best," the Court's majority is taken to task for "having laid waste the foundations of our rational-basis jurisprudence." With uncompromising vigor, he offers a telling critique of how the majority's stance rides roughshod over widespread understandings about what is and is not a fundamental right, what does and does not amount to a legitimate state interest, and what can and cannot be treated as meriting equal protection. In particular, he refuses to place any reliance on the fact that other nations have decriminalized homosexual conduct because it would be dangerous for American courts to "impose foreign moods, fads, or fashions on Americans." Moreover, Justice Scalia insists that, in adopting such a cavalier approach to established constitutional doctrines and distinctions, the Court has sown the seeds of an institutional whirlwind that has the indiscriminate force to effect "a massive disruption of the social order." Indeed, in Justice Scalia's view, the majority's judgment "effectively decrees the end of all morals legislation," including and especially the state's ability to make "a distinction . . . between heterosexual and homosexual unions, insofar as marriage is concerned. Like Justice Thomas, Scalia claims to "have nothing against homosexuals," but he urges that the states' hands "should not be stayed through the invention of a brand-new 'constitutional right' by a Court that is impatient of democratic change."[17]

---

[16] *Lawrence,* supra note 10 at 2484 and 2483. In her concurring opinion, O'Connor J did not believe it was necessary to overrule *Bowers.* Instead, she eschewed a dispositive analysis in terms of substantive due process. Maintaining that moral disapproval of homosexuality was insufficient to satisfy rational review as a legitimate state interest, she concluded that the Texas law was in breach of the Constitution's equal protection doctrine and, therefore, invalid. While Kennedy J was sensitive to this argument, he refrained from pursuing an equal protection analysis as this would not deal with *Bowers* directly and still might leave open the possibility that a differently drawn prohibition might satisfy constitutional muster and opted to invalidate the Texas law by way of the equal protection doctrine. Id. at 2482.

[17] Id. at 2497, 2495 – quoting *Foster v. Florida,* 537 US 990 at 990 (2002) (Thomas J, concurring in denial of *certiorari*), 2491, 2495, and 2497. In a separate dissent, Thomas J accepted Scalia J's arguments but went on to contend that, while he would as a Texas legislator vote against such "silly" laws, he was unable to find anything in the Constitution that grounded a general right to privacy. He, therefore, declined to invalidate the Texas law or to overrule *Bowers.* Id. at 2498.

However, despite the force of his doctrinal onslaught, Justice Scalia reserves his most dismissive comments for the Court's stance toward the doctrine of stare decisis. The basic thrust of his objections is that the Court only respect the dictates of precedential constraints when it suits particular judges' political agendas. Indeed, he maintains that the *Lawrence* decision reveals for all to see "the result-oriented expedient" that the Court seeks to pass off as a principled and impartial approach to constitutional adjudication. While Scalia asserts that he does not "believe in rigid adherence to *stare decisis* in constitutional cases," he nevertheless maintains that its invocation should be "consistent rather than manipulative."[18] Indeed, the not so hidden subtext of his opinion is the claim that, if the reasons to overrule *Bowers* are so compelling, then the Court is equally obliged to overrule *Roe*, which a majority in *Casey* doggedly refused to do. At the very least, Justice Scalia contends that, if the Court is not prepared to revisit the 'intensely divisive controversy' of *Roe* and abortion, it should not reopen the equally 'intensely divisive controversy' of *Bowers* and homosexuality.

In drawing comparisons between the situations in *Casey*, where the Court refused to overrule *Roe*, and in *Lawrence*, where the Court overruled *Bowers*, Justice Scalia disagrees with each of the three grounds on which the majority "distinguish the rock-solid, unamenable disposition of *Roe* from the readily overrulable *Bowers*." First, while Justice Scalia concedes that *Romer* did indeed eat into *Bowers'* rational-basis holding, he notes that the breadth of *Roe's* holding was narrowed by *Casey* and that the doctrinal substantive due process foundations of *Casey* were themselves eroded further by *Washington v. Glucksberg*.[19] Second, while also recognizing that *Bowers* has been subject to fierce criticism, he is adamant that Roe has received an equal share of unrelenting criticism. Third, Scalia points out there has been substantial social reliance on *Bowers* by courts and legislatures in their continuing efforts to regulate sexual morality in matters of bigamy, bestiality, obscenity, and the like: Overruling *Roe* would not make abortion unlawful, but it would leave each state to determine its legality. When these reasons about stare decisis are combined with Scalia's profound reservations about the doctrinal flaws of Kennedy's opinion, Scalia is able to make an entirely plausible case for

---

[18] Id. at 2491 and 2488. Scalia is, of course, an implacable critic of a dynamic approach to constitutional interpretation. He has dismissively rejected the notion that "the ascendant school of constitutional interpretation affirms the existence of what is called The Living Constitution – a body of law that . . . grows and changes from age to age, in order to meet the needs of a changing society." A. Scalia, *A Matter of Interpretation: Federal Courts and the Law* 38 (1997).

[19] Id. at 2490. See *Washington v. Glucksberg*, 521 US 702 at 721 (1997).

why what is precedential sauce for the *Roe* goose should also be sauce for the *Bowers* gander. Accordingly, as regards the force and importance of stare decisis, Justice Scalia has thrown down a gauntlet that merits a more spirited and convincing response than that offered by Justice Kennedy and his concurring colleagues.

As Scalia puts it, "the problem is that *Roe* itself – which today's majority surely has no disposition to overrule – satisfies [those conditions which the majority stipulate must be met before it is acceptable to overrule an erroneously decided and intensely divisive decision] to at least the same degree as *Bowers*." However, it is this very claim that backs Scalia into a rhetorical corner of his own making and opens him to a more convincing refutation. For him, the doctrine of stare decisis is no more (and no less) a "result-oriented expedient" than it is for Justice Kennedy. Each is willing to utilize the formal doctrine when and how best to achieve those substantive results that they each deem to be politically defensible. Although Justice Scalia strives to travel the constitutional high ground of principle, he is revealed to be crafting his own route to what he believes is the desirable substantive route. If the arguments in favor of overruling *Roe* are indeed as strong as those in *Lawrence* for overruling *Bowers*, then Scalia presumably is saying either that both *Roe* and *Bowers* are to be overruled or that neither is to be overruled. However, it is absolutely clear that he believes that *Roe* should be overruled but that *Bowers* should not. Scalia is playing exactly the same formal shell game as Kennedy, but they are each driven by a different substantive agenda. Indeed, no less than Kennedy, Scalia is hoist by his own petard because he is equally guilty of having "taken sides in the culture war, departing from [his judicial] role of assuring, as neutral observer, that the democratic rules of engagement are observed."[20]

What distinguishes the arguments of Kennedy and Scalia is not their differing respect for the dictates of stare decisis, but the different sides that they take in the so-called culture war. Whereas Kennedy aligns himself with the liberal sector of the political spectrum with its defense of abortion and gay rights, Scalia squarely sides with the more conservative sections of the political community that has little time for gay rights or abortion rights. Of course, this is no great revelation in regard to Kennedy or Scalia,[21] but what

---

[20] Id. at 2497.

[21] It might be observed that Scalia is not quite so predictable or conservative as suggested. After all, he does claim to "have nothing against homosexuals" (2497). However, the latter part of his opinion is a jeremiad against the threat of same-sex marriages and the inhibition that *Lawrence* will place on states on regulating deviant sexual behavior. It also must be remembered that he dissented strongly in *Romer* – see 517 US 620, 636

is surprising is that anyone would imagine that it could be any other way for them or any other judges. It is the substantive commitments of judges on controversial issues that ultimately tend to drive their opinions, not their rhetorical attachments to the formal legal doctrines of stare decisis. The common law is as much about substantive results, especially when it concerns the Constitution, as it is about formal integrity. This is not say that either Kennedy or Scalia simply indulge their political or moral preferences (which, on occasion, they might or might not do), but only that their judicial bottom line is based on their assessment of what is and is not an acceptable political and substantive rendering of the decision. Indeed, the fate of *Lawrence* as a great case will not ultimately depend on the cogency of Kennedy's doctrinal arguments about the correctness of *Bowers*; these are not irrelevant, but they are not decisive. What will determine the future role of *Lawrence*, like *Brown* and *Roe*, is the extent to which the constitutional protection of gay rights is able to muster general political support and resist a homophobic backlash. As with all great cases, whether notorious or renowned, their lifespan and influence is a function of their political viability, not their legal soundness.

In *Lawrence*, therefore, the Supreme Court did not reject a jurisprudence of doubt. Instead, whatever its judgments appear to say, it endorsed a jurisprudence of doubt not only as a standard for its own extant judicial practices but also as an appropriate method and justification for the legitimate exercise of constitutional adjudication in a republican democracy. By embracing a doctrine of stare decisis that attempted to balance stability and change, the Court gave the lie to any claims that there is a constitutional truth or fact of the matter when it comes to adjudicating on controversial political and moral issues of the day. The tension between the judges was less about whether so-called doubt has a valid role to play in constitutional adjudication, but more about when and how doubt should be allowed to inform the decisions of the Supreme Court. Of course, whether Kennedy or Scalia in *Lawrence* were somehow right as a matter of legal soundness is beside the point. Behind the rhetoric and the reasoning, both judges accepted that the pull of stability and the push of change could not be balanced by resort to a neutral or formal algorithm, but by taking a particular and substantive stand on the substantive issues under contention. Consequently, insofar as it can

---

(1996) (Scalia J, dissenting opinion: "the Court has mistaken a *Kulturkampf* for a fit of spite"). In this regard, Michaelson was extremely prescient. See J Michaelson, On Listening to the Kulturkampf, Or, How America Overruled Bowers v. Hardwick, Even Though Romer v. Evans Didn't, 49 *Duke L. J.* 1559 at 1612 (2000) ("the Supreme Court must listen to the *kulturkampf* in determining the meaning of critical constitutional terms").

be already designated as a great case, *Lawrence* offers further support for the claim that the courts will follow doctrinal logic and formal authority only so far and for so long as political expediency and substantive justice allow. As the fates of *Lochner* and *Roe* show, a great case is only great as long as the historical circumstances and political currents support its continued prominence. Once the political winds change, the great case will lose its hallowed status and become one more precedent on the legal scrap heap. Although, for instance, *Brown* seem unassailable in its greatness, the day could well come when the public commitment to maintain substantive equality might begin to crumble and a different approach, such as a formal and thinner conception of discrimination, may gain favor. Legal greatness is as eternal or as ephemeral as the political will that sustains it.

Because law is not religion, it asks its participants to be doubting Thomases rather than faith-based absolutists. Ironically, in the journey and judgments from *Bowers* to *Lawrence*, the judges gave expression to that doubt and ultimately changed the present course of constitutional law on gay rights. Indeed, although they claimed to reject a jurisprudence of doubt, the plurality in *Casey* and the majority in *Lawrence* offer a rare glimpse at the doubt that the Court's members experienced about the best thing to do. Sadly, judges too often tend to keep their crisis of doubt in their chambers and present a certitude to the public that is neither authentic nor persuasive, yet their anxieties and actions were not an irresponsible dereliction of their constitutional duty, but a proud performance of it. Because society *will* change (and the only question is how it will change), law will also have to change in order to adapt to those changes. As a jurisprudence of doubt recommends, there are no permanent solutions to life's problems because life is problematic and any effort to resist that conclusion is itself a problem. *Casey*'s plurality was correct in noting that there was "a point beyond which frequent overruling would overtax the country's belief in the Court's good faith." However, they were mistaken to equate such doubt and, in some cases, overruling with "vacillation."[22] Doubt is not vacillation, and it is only a lingering belief in absolute truth and enduring values that encourages such chastisement. A jurisprudence of doubt is a necessary part of democratic liberty in that citizens and its officials must always be prepared to question themselves and resist

---

[22] *Casey*, supra, note 8 at 866. It should be clear that I do not share the view of Paulsen that *Casey* was the worst constitutional decision of all time because it involved serious misinterpretation and serious harmful consequences. See M. S. Paulsen, The Worst Constitutional Decision of All Time, 78 *Notre Dame L. Rev.* 995 (2003). On the contrary, I maintain that *Casey*, at least when viewed in the way that I recommend, is an important and entirely defensible decision.

the temptation to hubris. Whether it goes under the name of fundamental values, tradition, reason, consensus, or progress, constitutional adjudication will involve judges making a better or worse fist of ascertaining what social justice requires in the particular circumstances of a given case. Accordingly, for as long as courts remain at the center of constitutional politics,[23] there simply is no other way to do constitutional interpretation than for judges to do what they think is the right thing to do as a matter of substantive values. In this way, a jurisprudence of doubt is the best complement to a vigorous democracy.

In the Woods

It will be remembered that Darwin spent much of his life demonstrating why William Paley's claims – "every manifestation of design, which existed in the watch, exists in the works of nature, of being greater and more"[24] – were false. Emphasizing that even the most complex of biological creatures required no designing hand or orchestrating intent, Darwin insisted that the wonder of nature was in the very fact that flora and fauna were as sophisticated and as adapted to their environment as they were – the historical, opportunistic, and unguided process of evolution had done the work all by itself. However, despite Darwin's best efforts, the most complete refutation of Paley did not come until 1986, when Richard Dawkins took direct aim at Paley. Using Paley's own examples, he showed how it was even more wondrous and awe-inspiring that nature's intricate complexity should be the result of gradual and insistent evolution over time than the draftsmanship of a designing deity. Emphasizing the unplanned, unconscious, and automatic processes of nature, Dawkins concluded that "natural selection . . . has no purpose in mind, . . . has no mind and no mind's eye, . . . does not plan for the future, . . . has no vision, no foresight, no sight at all . . . [and,] if it can be said to play the role of watchmaker in nature, it is the blind watchmaker."[25] It was a devastating refutation of the design thesis.

---

[23] Of course, there is no reason why that should remain the case. For instance, Mark Tushnet has been developing a rich and provocative body of work on how best to develop non-judicial forums for constitutional decision making. See, for example, M. Tushnet, *Taking the Constitution Away from the Courts* (1999) and M. Tushnet, Non-Judicial Review, 40 *Harv. J. On Legis.* 453 (2003).

[24] W. Paley, *Natural Theology* 473 (1970), which is a reprint of W. Paley, *Natural Theology: Or, Evidences of the Existence and Attributes of the Deity, Collected From the Appearances of Nature* (1802). See supra, chap. 3.

[25] R. Dawkins, *The Blind Watchmaker* 5 (1986). For more on Dawkins' ultra-Darwinism, see supra chap. 2.

Nevertheless, while there are some advantages to thinking about nature through this mechanistic watchmaker metaphor, there are definite limitations. It tends to suggest a too inorganic and planned dimension to nature. Indeed, Darwin himself preferred to talk about the process of natural selection in more organic terms. His most favored and most celebrated simile was the great Tree of Life:

> The affinities of all the beings of the same class have sometimes been represented by a great tree. I believe this simile largely speaks the truth. The green and budding twigs may represent existing species. . . . At each period of growth all the growing twigs have tried to branch out on all sides. . . . The limbs divided into great branches, and these into lesser and lesser branches, were themselves once, when the tree was small, budding twigs. . . . From the first growth of the tree, many a limb and branch has decayed and dropped off; and these lost branches of various sizes may represent those whole orders, families, and genera which have now no living representatives, and which are known to us only from having been found in a fossil state. . . . As buds give rise by growth to fresh buds, . . . so by generation I believe it has been with the great Tree of Life, which fills with its dead and broken branches the crust of the earth, and covers the surface with its ever branching and beautiful ramifications.[26]

There is much here that one can profitably use to understand the growth and development of the common law – the budding of new ideas, the branching out from old ideas, the decay of some rules, the varied ramifications of different rules, and so on. While it can be easily observed that common law is not Paley's rock, jurists have still not learned this lesson entirely. As sceptical and as pragmatic as some claim to be, jurists still seem to believe that they might one day stumble across the reputed philosopher's stone that will allow them to turn the prosaic materials of the common law into a burnished example of Essential Law. Indeed, at different times and in different ways, the Soapy Sams and the Bulldogs of the jurisprudential world rely on such a forlorn hope and forget that the common law is as much an activity as a thing. Nevertheless, even if law is understood as a way of acting, the common law is not the horological enterprise that Dawkins suggests. While law is more like a watch than it is a rock, it is certainly less like a

---

[26] C. Darwin, *The Origin of Species by Natural Selection* 104–05 (6th ed. 1872). Some still persist in seeing a designing hand at work in the tree's growth. See M. Denton, *Nature's Destiny: How the Laws of Biology Reveal Purpose in the Universe* 320 (1998) ("the evolutionary tree of life on earth was generated by direction from a unique program embedded in the order of nature").

watch than many common law jurists would like to believe. Although law is a human creation, it is not a device that has no life of its own or that is unaffected by the rich environmental milieu in which it functions and that it strives to regulate. While law can occasionally seem like a rock in its brute thereness and seem like a watch in its created sophistication, it is better understood as a more organic and less precise entity than a rock or a watch: "The common law perpetually is in flux, always in a process of further becoming, developing, and transforming, . . . with a suppleness that resides in its inseparability from each discrete, concrete set of facts, the facts of the lived experiences which formed the basis of the litigation that led to the prior relevant court adjudications."[27] Of course, as I have been at pains to emphasize, there is a distinction between the growth of biological organisms that are randomly mutating and those of the common law species that are at least trying to adapt with some degree of designing intent to the changing historical circumstances. However, it remains productive to think about the common law as an organic work-in-progress and to draw on the imagery of the evolutionary Tree of Life in explicating its hermeneutical existence.

Mindful that it is more an activity than a thing, one can understand the common law as the cultivation of a stand of trees by a devoted band of professional arborists who work together but not in concert. Indeed, one of the most popular metaphors in Canadian constitutional law is the idea of the constitution as a living tree. Originally coined by Lord Sankey to justify a large and liberal interpretation of the British North America Act of 1867 (Canada's founding constitutional document), which "planted a living tree capable of growth and expansion within its natural limits," it can be used to powerful metaphorical effect when understood in a slightly different way.[28] It is important that law is to be found neither in the trees themselves nor in the arborists' efforts, but is best understood in terms of the interaction between them: Law is most definitely not a stone and it has no inherent tendency to shape itself into any particular form. The specific configuration that law takes at any specific time will be a result of the ceaseless interaction between the growth of the trees, the environmental context, and the efforts

---

[27] V. G. Curran, Romantic Common Law, Enlightened Civil Law: Legal Uniformity and the Homogenization of the European Union, 7 *Colum. J. Eur. L.* 63 at 74 (2001).

[28] See *Edwards v. Attorney General for Canada* [1930], AC 124 at 136. Resort to this metaphorical understanding of law remains commonplace in Canadian courts. See, for example, *Reference Re Provincial Electoral Boundaries (Sask.)* [1991], 2 SCR 158 at 180 per McLachlin J and *Gosselin v. Quebec (Attorney General)* [2002], 4 SCR 429 at 491–92 per McLachlin CJ and 603 per Arbour J. For a different and more traditional defence, see A. Kavanagh, The Idea of a Living Constitution, 16 *Can. J. L. & Juris.* 55 (2003).

of the arborists. Law can be grasped both as a site, with all the practical possibilities and parameters that this suggests, and as an exercise, with all the imaginative openings and occlusions that this implies. Within such an understanding, it is more likely for people to recognize that law is neither a perfectly operating restraint on human actions nor a completely realizable occasion for human fulfillment; law is to be found in the organic engagement between restraint and realization, limit and possibility, and design and accident. Like nature, law is always an active and adaptive work-in-progress.

By thinking of legal and judicial practice as the tending and training of social trees, there is an opportunity to capture the created and creative aspect of law in which human ingenuity, organic development, and environmental context interact; it suggests both agency and determination, choice and constraint, and chance and necessity. Moreover, by presenting evolution as not being about a ladderlike climb to some designated spot, but about the growing tips of a tree, Sankey's metaphor wonderfully illustrates as it contradicts the main thrust of Darwinian evolution when applied to the common law: Natural limits are distinctly the stuff of political and therefore decidedly nonnatural contestation. In addition, when these natural limits are set against growth and expansion, the dynamic tension is caught between a kind of spontaneous evolutionary growth in response to changing environmental conditions and a more reflective form of human husbandry in law's development. The common law is a combination of the tree's organic capabilities in adjusting to its environment and also the deliberative intervention of gardeners and topiarists in order to facilitate its growth and configuration. The limits to growth and expansion are a site for the constant negotiation between human initiatives and biological opportunities; climate, soil conditions, and other environmental factors present both an obstacle and an opportunity for social development. The idea of the so-called natural is a contested and contingent limit to change that is part of the very process of development that it is considered to contain. Accordingly, in law, it is not so much that there is a blind watchmaker at work, but that there is a coterie of fully sighted arborists who take charge of the trees' cultivation and who, despite their frequent claims to the contrary, are unable to foresee or control fully the trees' future development. The illusion of total command is maintained by a willingness to accept that the environment will have to be respected. While it is true that law might "evolve in the direction of greater fit with its environment,"[29] there will always be a productive tension between

---

[29] E. D. Elliott, Law and Biology: The New Synthesis?, 41 *St. Louis U. L. J.* 595 at 600. See J. B. Ruhl, Complexity Theory as a Paradigm for the Dynamical Law-and-Society System: A

the law's notion of fit and the changing social, political, and cultural makeup of that environment; law and environment will interact in organic ways that will defy simple, consistent, or coherent explanation. In short, law will always be a relatively open-ended and stylized form of politics in which 'anything might go'.

In evoking this arboreal metaphor and throughout the book generally, I have not sought to assert that evolution is applicable to legal development, let alone that there is a Darwinian dynamic at work. My claim is only that it is a useful metaphor to think about law and legal change. Moreover, mindful of Gadamer's strictures, I state that while law is a self-reflective process of decision making, it is far from being reducible to an activity that is governed by a strict philosophical discipline or that is exclusively explainable in its own internal terms. All the talk about grand purposes or guiding minds is pitched at such a high level of generality that what they might or might not recommend in any particular situation is almost impossible to predict. Or, to turn that around, the solution to any particular problem can be interpreted in accordance with a variety of very different, often competing, and occasionally contradictory ideals that can each claim a plausible threshold purchase on the extant legal materials. Consequently, while law is undeniably a teleological enterprise in that judges act with a purpose, the system as a whole cannot be said to have a directing mind such that it moves forward in one direction as if pulled along or pushed toward a given goal. In law, there are many theoretical possibilities, but the actual decision made is as much about external circumstances as anything else: Principles prosper or perish not only by dint of their intellectual merit but also by their capacity to adapt to material conditions. Holmes' warning has been ignored, especially by those evolutionary jurists who claim to follow in his intellectual footsteps: "We have evolution in this sphere of conscious thought and action no less than in lower organic stages, but an evolution which must be studied in its own field."[30]

Consequently, in contrast to the dewy-eyed accounts of traditional jurisprudence, I have taken seriously Lon Fuller's assessment that the common law "mirrors the variety of human experience; it offers an honest reflection of the complexities and perplexities of life itself."[31] Like life, law is an organic process (i.e., events are the products of functional and localized

---

Wake-Up Call for Legal Reductionism and the Modern Administrative State, 45 *Duke L. J.* 849 (1996).

[30] O. W. Holmes, The Path of the Law, 10 *Harv. L. Rev* 457 at 447 (1897).

[31] L. L. Fuller, *Anatomy of the Law* 106 (1968).

causes) rather than miraculous one (i.e., events are the result of some divine plan or supernatural intervention). How honest that process is at any particular time, in the sense of being a complete and authentic reflection of life's manifold forces, may be debatable, but there is little doubt that the common law is a progeny of life's rich and controversial activity. In short, the common law is a work-in-progress – evanescent, dynamic, messy, productive, tantalizing, and bottom up. The common law is always moving, but never arriving; is always on the road to somewhere, but never getting anywhere in particular; and is rarely more than the sum of its parts and often much less. Such a work-in-progress account of the common law is intended to be utterly nontheological in origin and ambition. In line with Darwin's suggestions, it strongly implies that humanity is not the be-all and end-all of nature's grand design, but simply one more development in a continuing and endless process; humans are part of the Tree of Life. When this is supplemented with a Gadamer-style approach, the hermeneutical limb of law is seen to be a significant as well as equally unruly part of that continuing and endless process. Indeed, after Darwin and Gadamer, it has now become possible to admit that human progress is a distinctly human project that cannot be validated or advanced by reference to some putative nonhuman lights.

However, abandoning the dubious solace of divine procreation, I find no cause for despair or resignation. Instead, people generally and lawyers particularly might grasp that "moral inquiry is our struggle, not nature's display."[32] Insofar as law is one of the main institutional sites and practices through which contemporary society takes part in that struggle, lawyers and judges might accept that their participation is as modest artisans of social justice, not as false conduits for philosophical truth. As a political product and process, the common law's evolution is a responsibility, not a necessity. Accordingly, commentators and critics of all stripes, including and especially progressive ones, can and should make their own political evaluations about how and when they might engage in that struggle. Neither the Soapy Sams or the Bulldogs of the jurisprudential world come close to exhausting the legion possibilities for nurturing law's development and substantive orientation. Both of them are needed – one as a hopeful reminder that we must strive to rise above the limitations of our own predicament and the other as a sober caution that we are as much beasts as gods. And we need much else besides.

---

[32] S. J. Gould, *Eight Little Piggies: Reflections in Natural History* 152 (1993). See also R. Rorty, *Philosophy and Social Hope* 266 (1999) and S. J. Gould, *Leonardo's Mountain of Clams and the Diet of Worms* 282 (1998).

Conclusion

In his magisterial *The Origin of Species*, Darwin began by explaining that his aim was "to throw some light on the origin of species – that mystery of mysteries, as it has been called by one of our greatest philosophers."[33] His brilliant efforts have not only illuminated that particular puzzle but have also managed to shed light on much else besides. Whether Darwin's insights can enlighten jurisprudential efforts to understand the common law remains as contested and controversial as the full meaning of Darwin's own ideas themselves. However, if Darwin began by posing the compelling question for biological studies, then Gadamer continued that task for hermeneutical studies. In reflecting on human understanding, his own answer to the 'mystery of mysteries' can be found in his commitment to the idea that "all responsible philosophizing...takes the habits of thoughts and language built up in the individual in his communication with his environment and places them before the forum of the historical tradition to which we all belong."[34] For both Darwin and Gadamer, everything is understandable by historical reference to the contingent interaction between individual and environment. An awareness of that insight does not so much dissolve the mystery of either biology or hermeneutics as allow an appreciation of the mysterious in the familiar and the familiar in the mysterious. When it comes to the common law, its familiar mystery can best be grasped and handled by treating law and jurisprudence as works-in-progress.

---

[33] C. Darwin supra, note 26 at 1. The phrase "mystery of mysteries" was first coined by John Herschel in 1836. See M. Ruse, *Mystery of Mysteries: Is Evolution a Social Construction?* (1999).
[34] H.-G. Gadamer, *Truth and Method* xxv (J. Weinsheimer and D. Marshall trans. 2nd ed 1989).

Index

Printed in Great Britain
by Amazon

47118004R00175